volume

1

KASUMI
かすみ

Story by
Surt Lim

Art by
Hirofumi Sugimoto

Lettered by
Monkey Square

DEL REY

BALLANTINE BOOKS . **NEW YORK**

A Del Rey Manga Trade Paperback Original

Kasumi volume 1 copyright © 2008 by Monkey Square, LLC

Published in the United States by Del Rey Books, an imprint of The Random House Publishing Group, a division of Random House, Inc., New York.

DEL REY is a registered trademark and the Del Rey colophon is a trademark of Random House, Inc.

ISBN 978-0-345-50354-1

Printed in the United States of America

www.delreymanga.com

9 8 7

Art Director—Stanley Adrianus
Translation—Harumi Ueno
Lettering—Monkey Square

CONTENTS

Special Thanks

My dream of creating *Kasumi* has finally come true!
I share this dream with these very important people.

I wish to dedicate *Kasumi* to Stanley, whose unwavering
support and faith in me and Sugimoto-san, made the
Kasumi manga possible. You are our toughest critic who's
always willing to tell it as it is. Thank you for pushing us to go
beyond our abilities and for helping us when we're in need.

I also wish to thank Sugimoto-san for always believing in
the world of *Kasumi* and for telling my stories through
his beautiful, expressive characters and scenes. Without you,
Kasumi would only live as words on a page. I also would like to
thank Komamiya-san and Natuki for their assistance. Harumi,
thank you for your detailed translations and contributions.
Your love and dedication to *Kasumi* shines through in how smoothly
you connect our thoughts and words. And lastly, our heartfelt thanks
to Tricia, our editor, and Del Rey Manga, whose trust and support
gave us the wings to fly. ^_^

Honorifics Explained

Throughout the Del Rey Manga books, you will find Japanese honorifics left intact in the translations. For those not familiar with how the Japanese use honorifics and, more important, how they differ from American honorifics, we present this brief overview.

Politeness has always been a critical facet of Japanese culture. Ever since the feudal era, when Japan was a highly stratified society, use of honorifics—which can be defined as polite speech that indicates relationship or status—has played an essential role in the Japanese language. When you address someone in Japanese, an honorific usually takes the form of a suffix attached to one's name (example: "Asuna-san"), is used as a title at the end of one's name, or appears in place of the name itself (example: "Negi-sensei," or simply "Sensei!").

Honorifics can be expressions of respect or endearment. In the context of manga and anime, honorifics give insight into the nature of the relationship between characters. Many English translations leave out these important honorifics and therefore distort the feel of the original Japanese. Because Japanese honorifics contain nuances that English honorifics lack, it is our policy at Del Rey not to translate them. Here, instead, is a guide to some of the honorifics you may encounter in Del Rey Manga.

-san: This is the most common honorific and is equivalent to Mr., Miss, Ms., or Mrs. It is the all-purpose honorific and can be used in any situation where politeness is required.

-sama: This is one level higher than "-san" and is used to confer great respect.

-dono: This comes from the word "tono," which means "lord." It is an even higher level than "-sama" and confers utmost respect.

-kun: This suffix is used at the end of boys' names to express familiarity or endearment. It is also sometimes used by men among friends, or when addressing someone younger or of a lower station.

-chan: This is used to express endearment, mostly toward girls. It is also used for little boys, pets, and even among lovers. It gives a sense of childish cuteness.

Bozu: This is an informal way to refer to a boy, similar to the English terms "kid" and "squirt."

Sempai/Senpai: This title suggests that the addressee is one's senior in a group or organization. It is most often used in a school setting, where underclassmen refer to their upperclassmen as "sempai." It can also be used in the workplace, such as when a newer employee addresses an employee who has seniority in the company.

Kohai: This is the opposite of "sempai" and is used toward underclassmen in school or newcomers in the workplace. It connotes that the addressee is of a lower station.

Sensei: Literally meaning "one who has come before," this title is used for teachers, doctors, or masters of any profession or art.

-[blank]: This is usually forgotten in these lists, but it is perhaps the most significant difference between Japanese and English. The lack of honorific, known as *yobisute*, means that the speaker has permission to address the person in a very intimate way. Usually, only family, spouses, or very close friends have this kind of permission. It can be gratifying when someone who has earned the intimacy starts to call one by one's name without an honorific. But when that intimacy hasn't been earned, it can be very insulting.

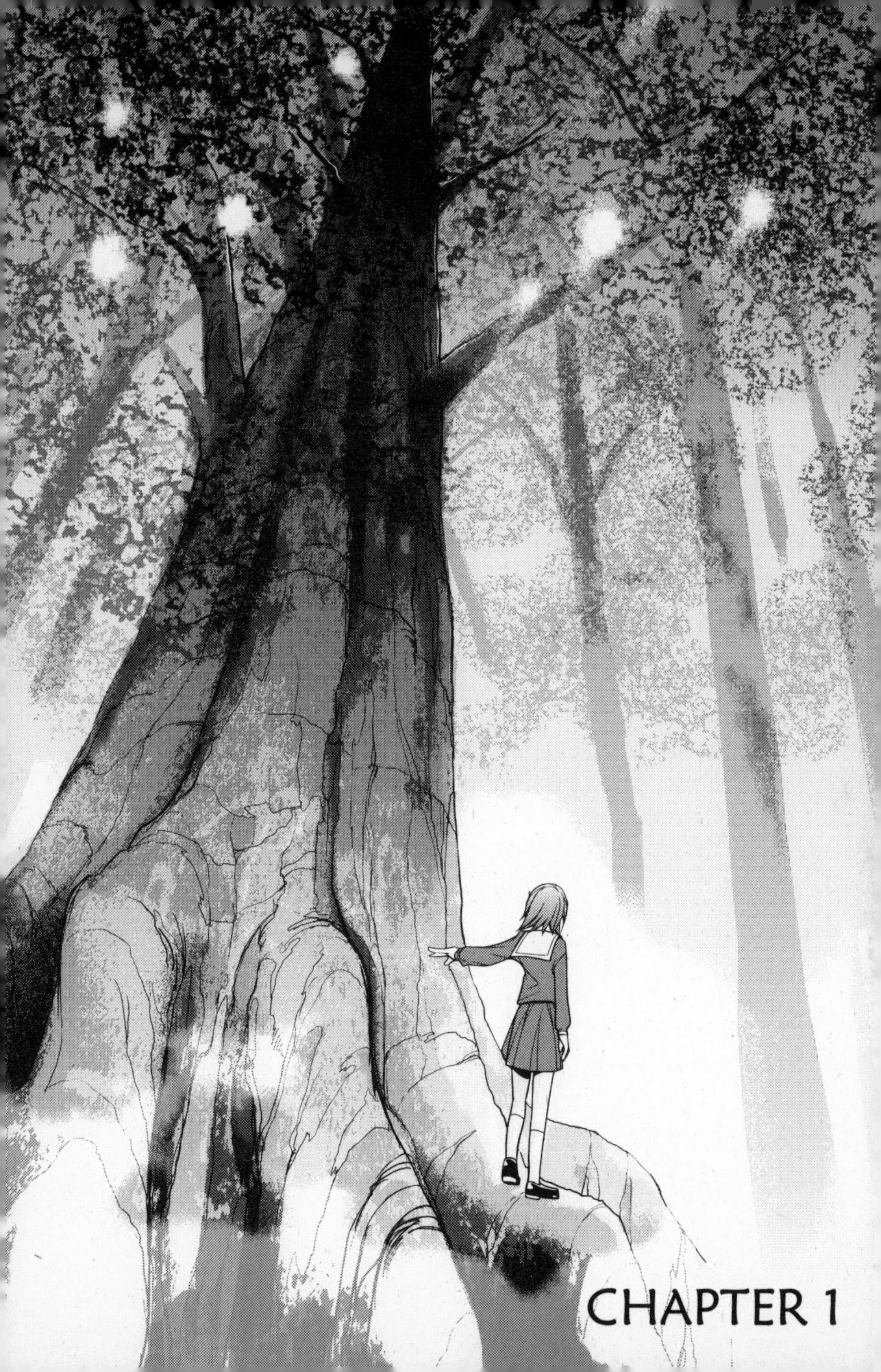

CHAPTER 1

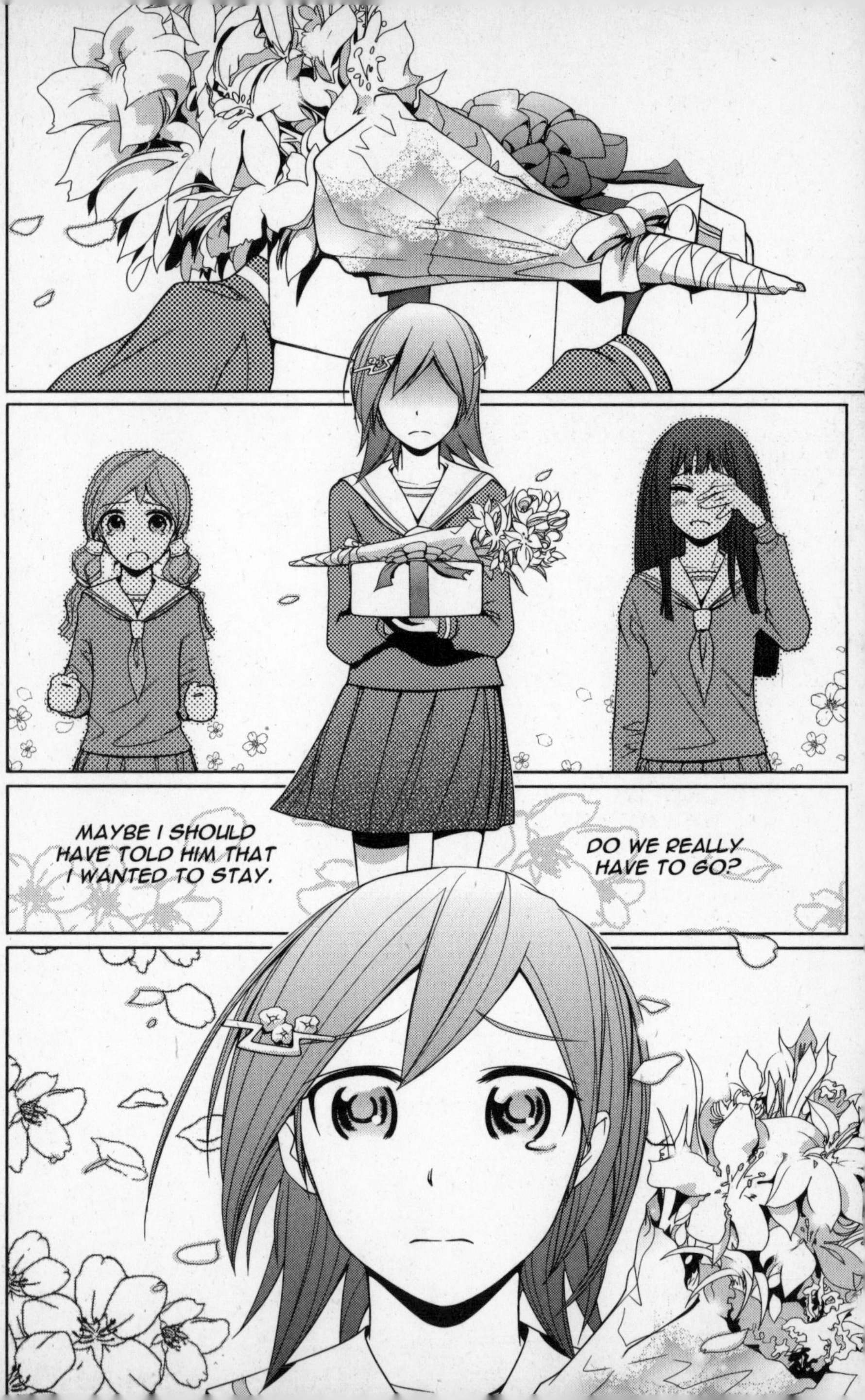
DO WE REALLY HAVE TO GO?
MAYBE I SHOULD HAVE TOLD HIM THAT I WANTED TO STAY.

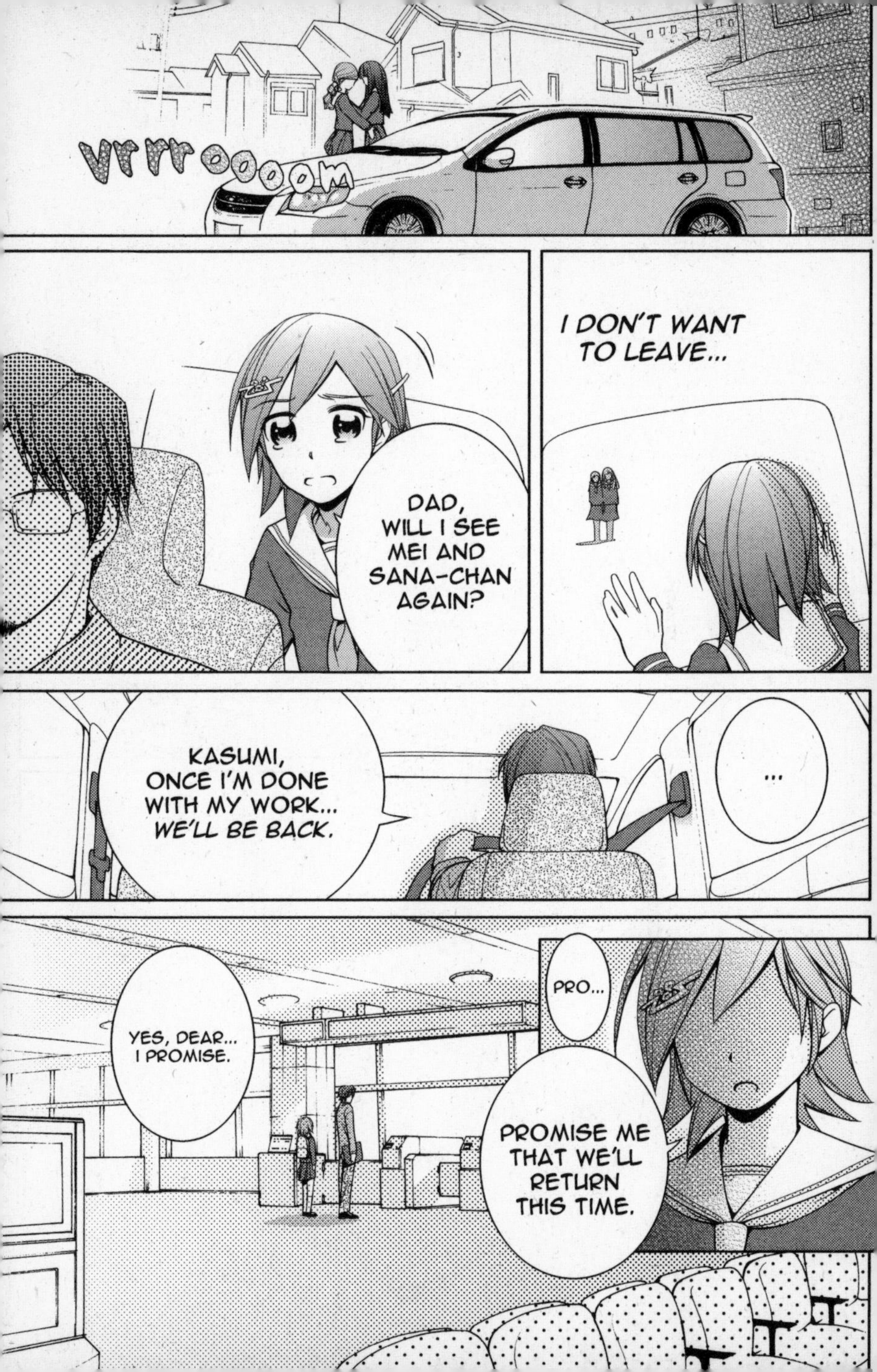
vrrroooom
I DON'T WANT TO LEAVE...
DAD, WILL I SEE MEI AND SANA-CHAN AGAIN?
...
KASUMI, ONCE I'M DONE WITH MY WORK... WE'LL BE BACK.
PRO...
PROMISE ME THAT WE'LL RETURN THIS TIME.
YES, DEAR... I PROMISE.

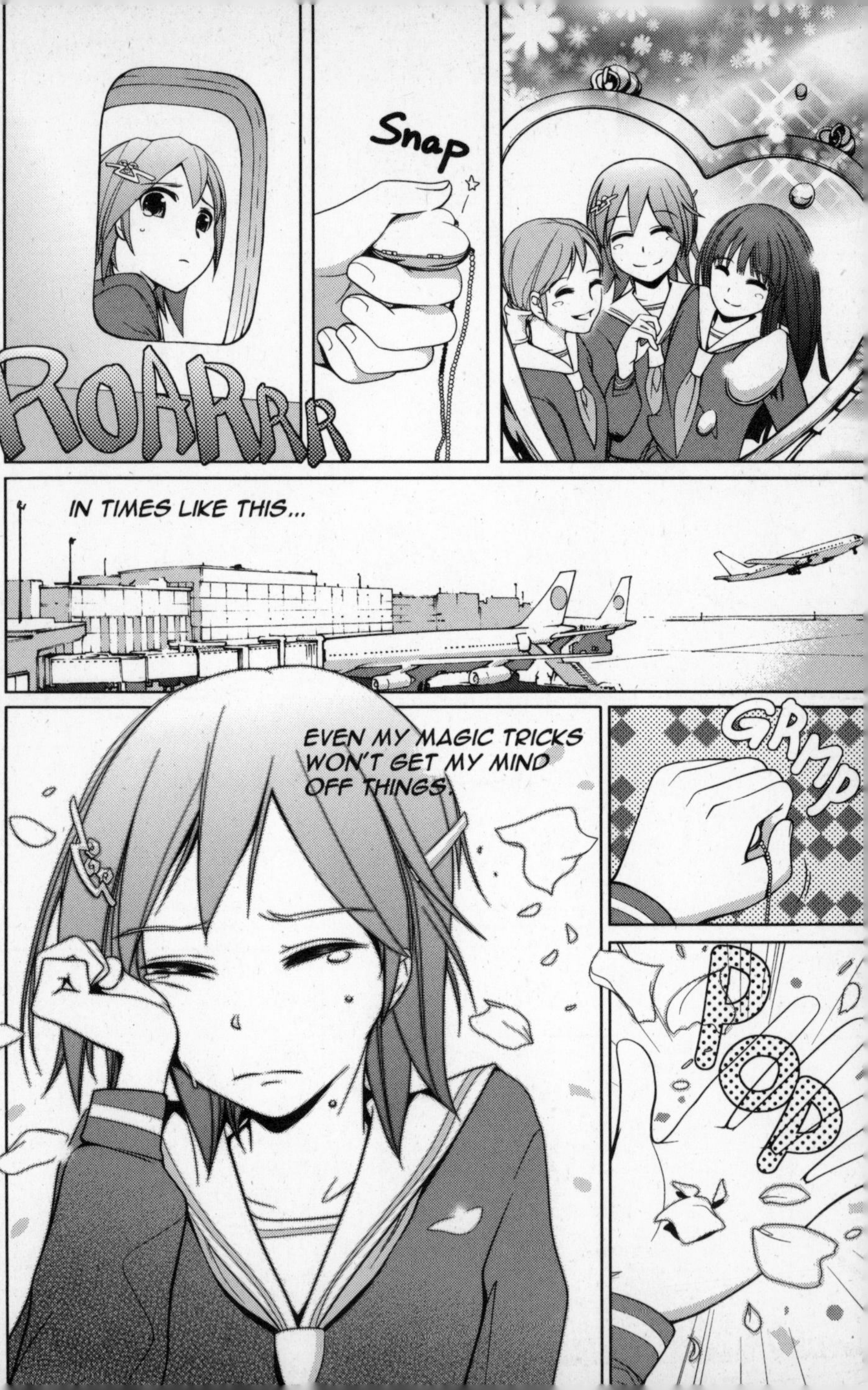
Snap
ROARRR
IN TIMES LIKE THIS...
GRMP
POP
EVEN MY MAGIC TRICKS WON'T GET MY MIND OFF THINGS.

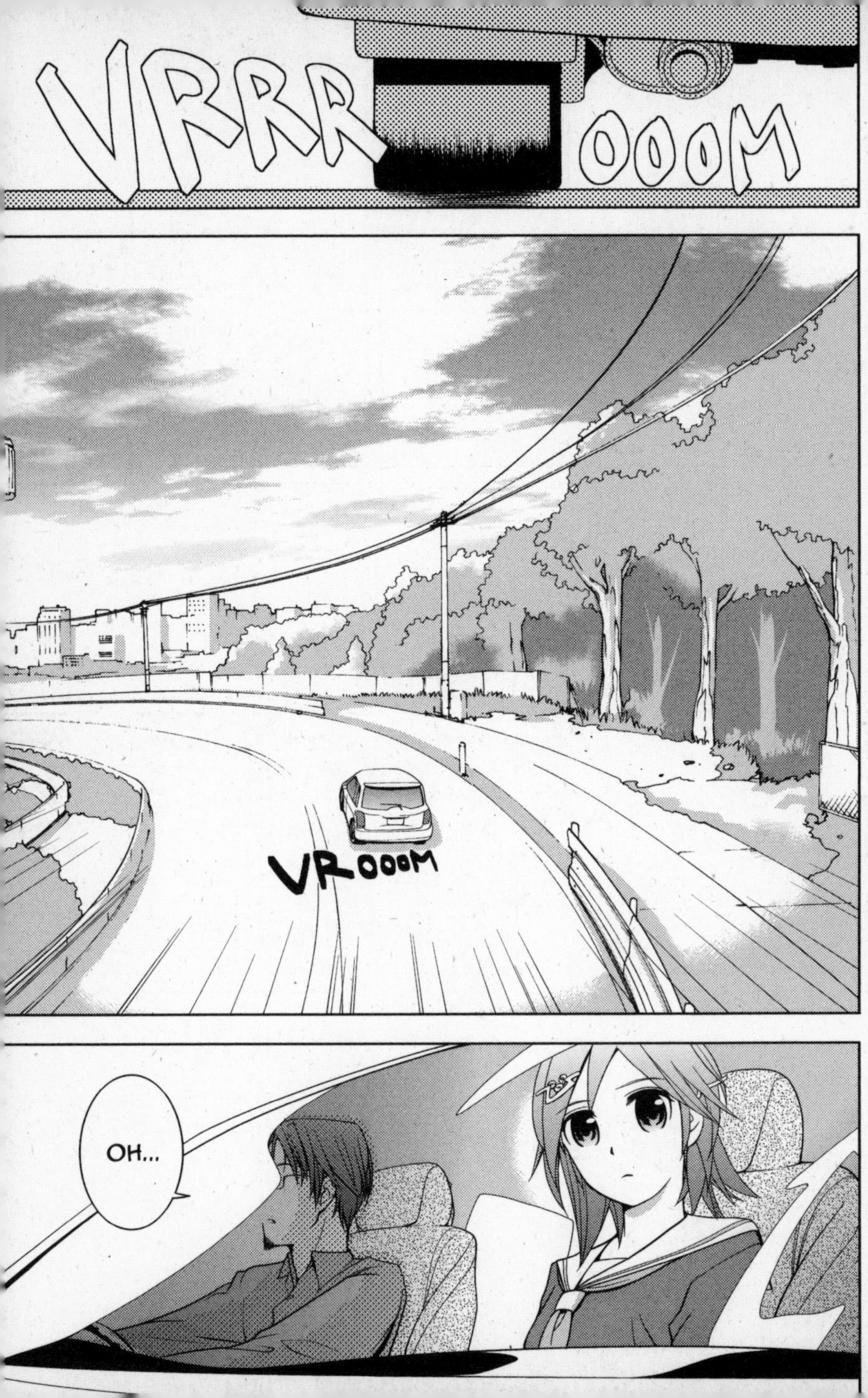
VRRROOOM
VROOOM
OH...

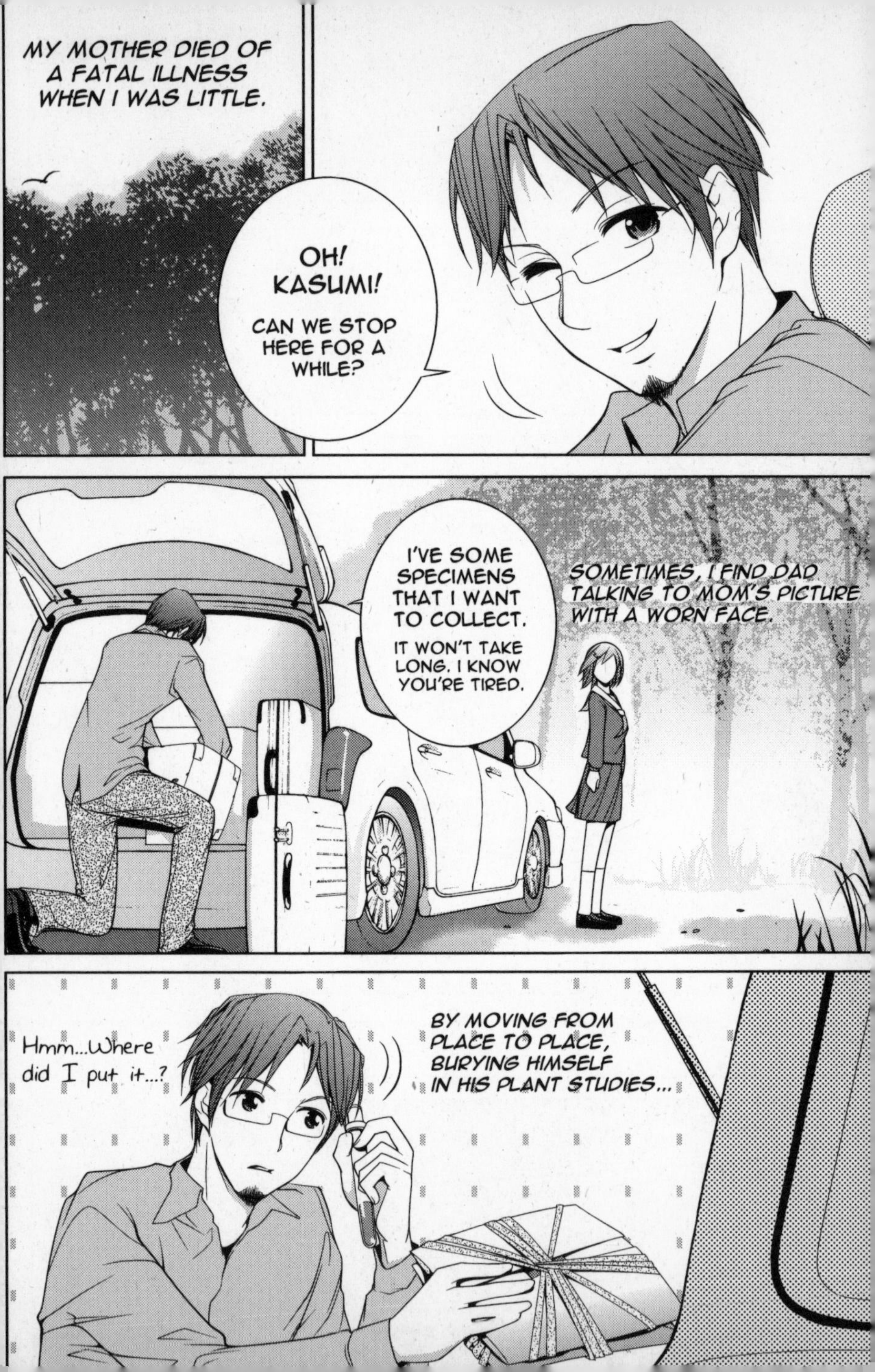
OH! KASUMI!
CAN WE STOP HERE FOR A WHILE?
MY MOTHER DIED OF A FATAL ILLNESS WHEN I WAS LITTLE.
SOMETIMES, I FIND DAD TALKING TO MOM'S PICTURE WITH A WORN FACE.
I'VE SOME SPECIMENS THAT I WANT TO COLLECT.
IT WON'T TAKE LONG. I KNOW YOU'RE TIRED.
BY MOVING FROM PLACE TO PLACE, BURYING HIMSELF IN HIS PLANT STUDIES...
Hmm...Where did I put it...?

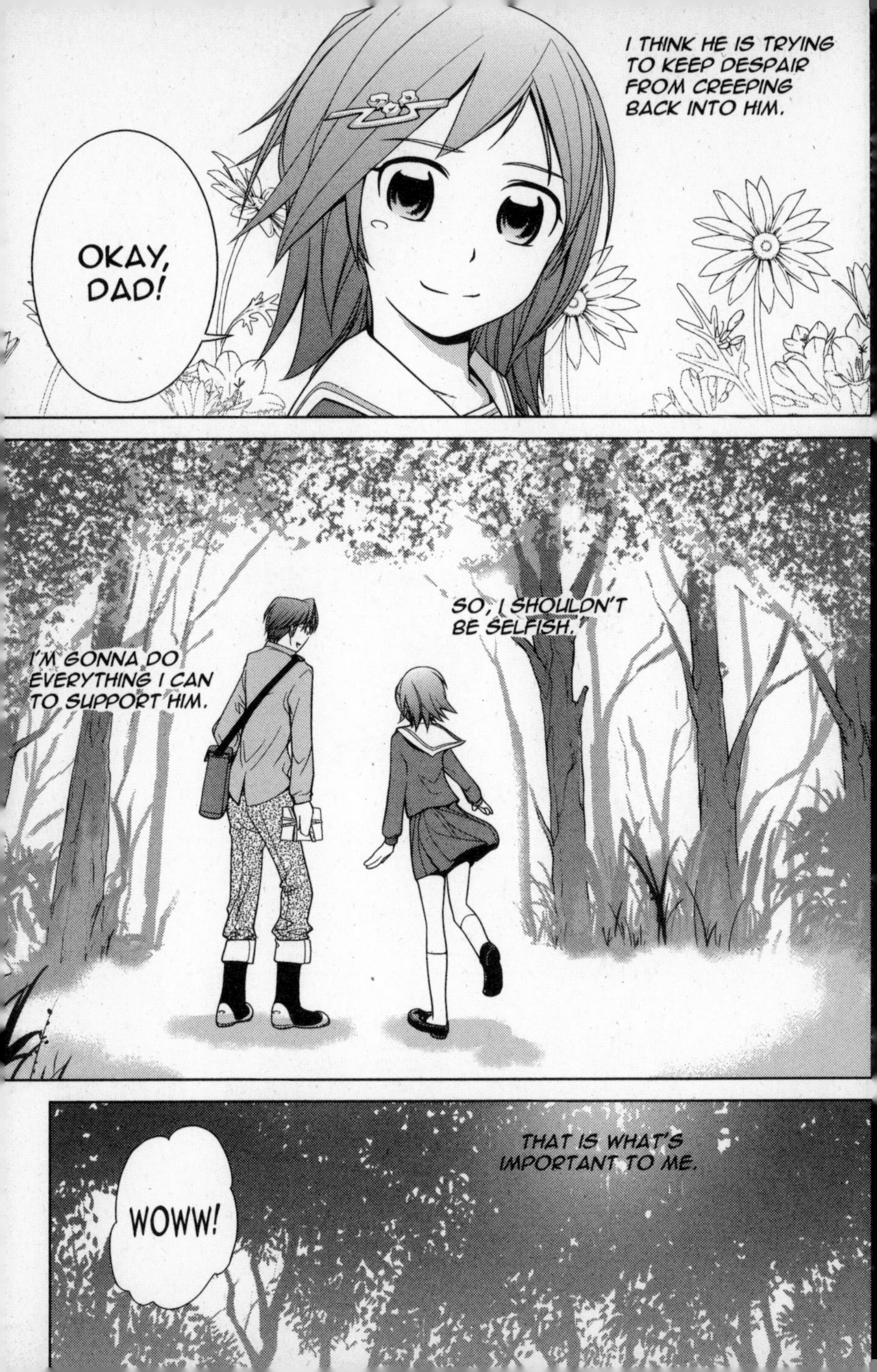
I THINK HE IS TRYING TO KEEP DESPAIR FROM CREEPING BACK INTO HIM.
OKAY, DAD!
SO, I SHOULDN'T BE SELFISH.
I'M GONNA DO EVERYTHING I CAN TO SUPPORT HIM.
THAT IS WHAT'S IMPORTANT TO ME.
WOWW!

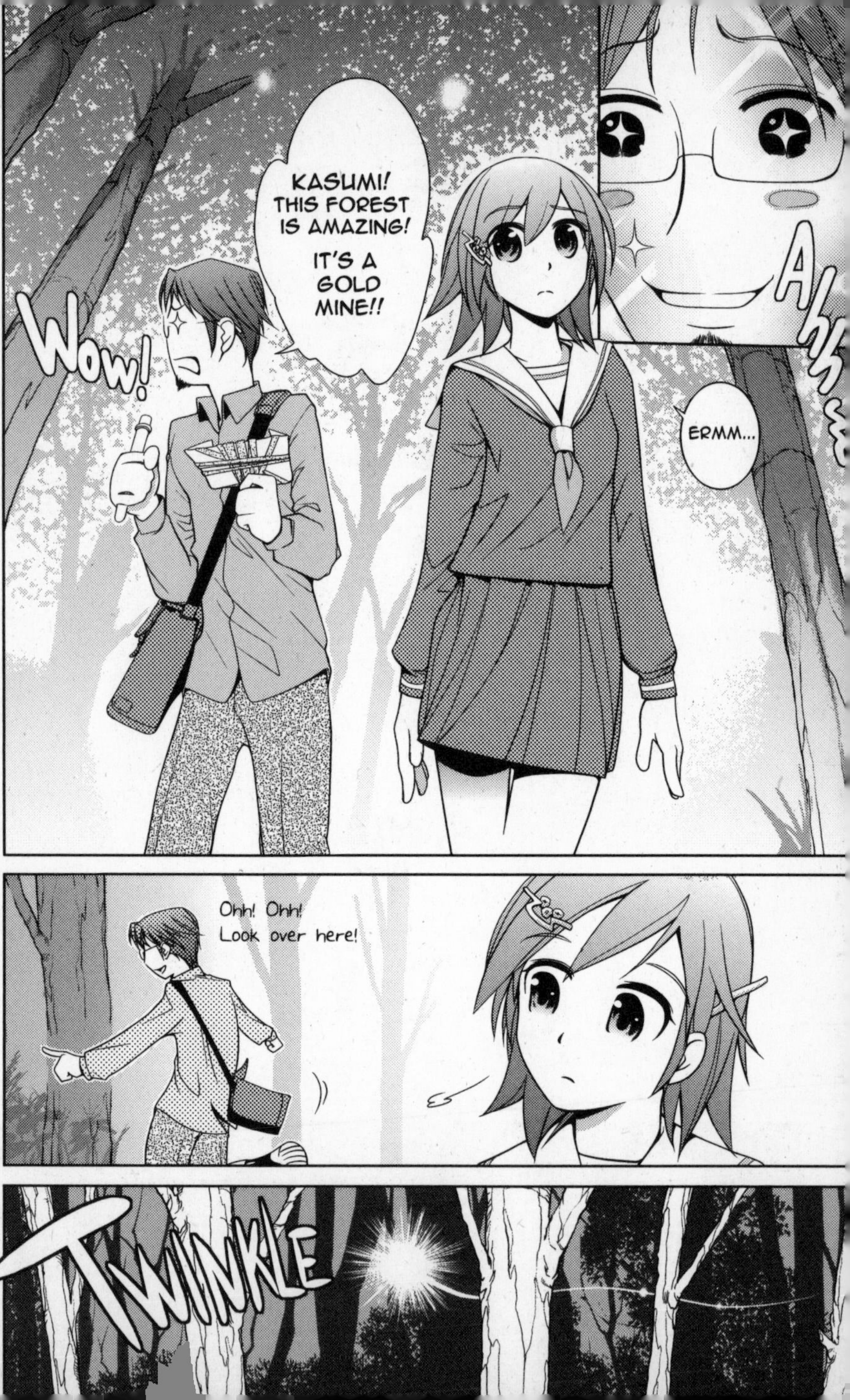
Ahhw
KASUMI! THIS FOREST IS AMAZING!
IT'S A GOLD MINE!!
Wow!
ERMM...
Ohh! Ohh! Look over here!
TWINKLE

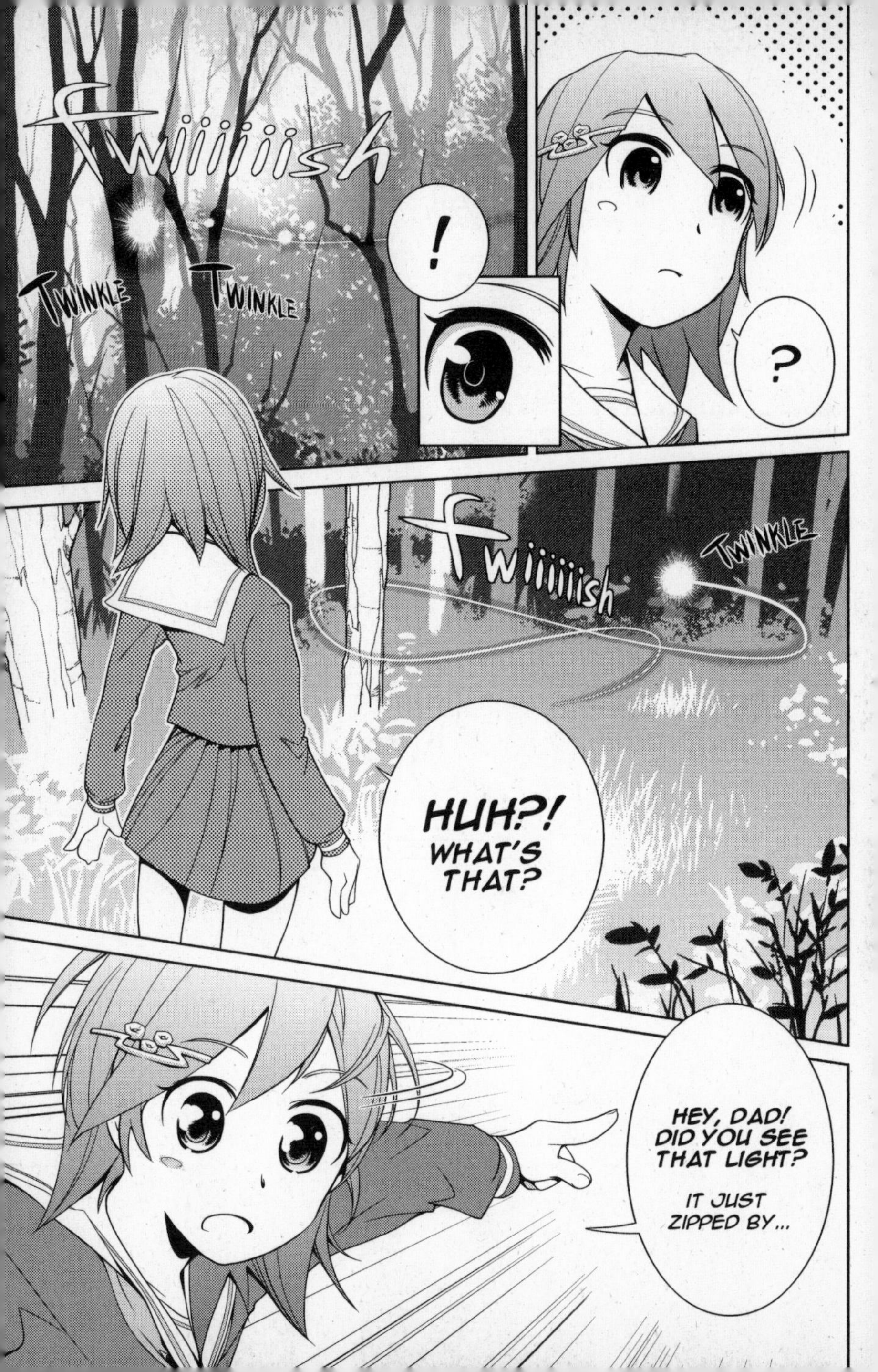
?
!
Fwiiiiiish
TWINKLE
TWINKLE
TWINKLE
Fwiiiiiish
HUH?! WHAT'S THAT?
HEY, DAD! DID YOU SEE THAT LIGHT?
IT JUST ZIPPED BY...

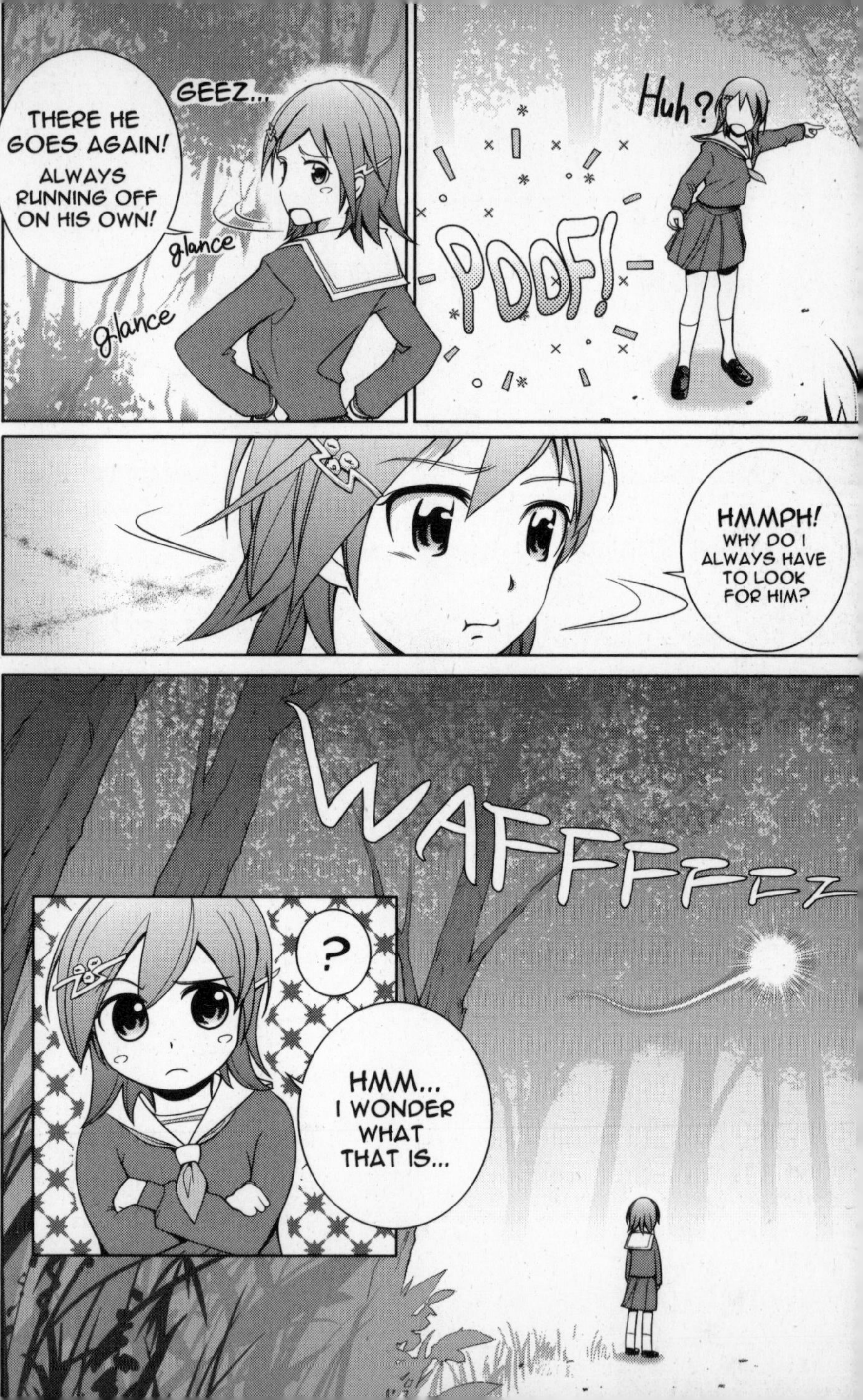
Huh?
POOF!
GEEZ...
THERE HE GOES AGAIN! ALWAYS RUNNING OFF ON HIS OWN!
glance
glance
HMMPH! WHY DO I ALWAYS HAVE TO LOOK FOR HIM?
WAFFFFZZZ
?
HMM... I WONDER WHAT THAT IS...

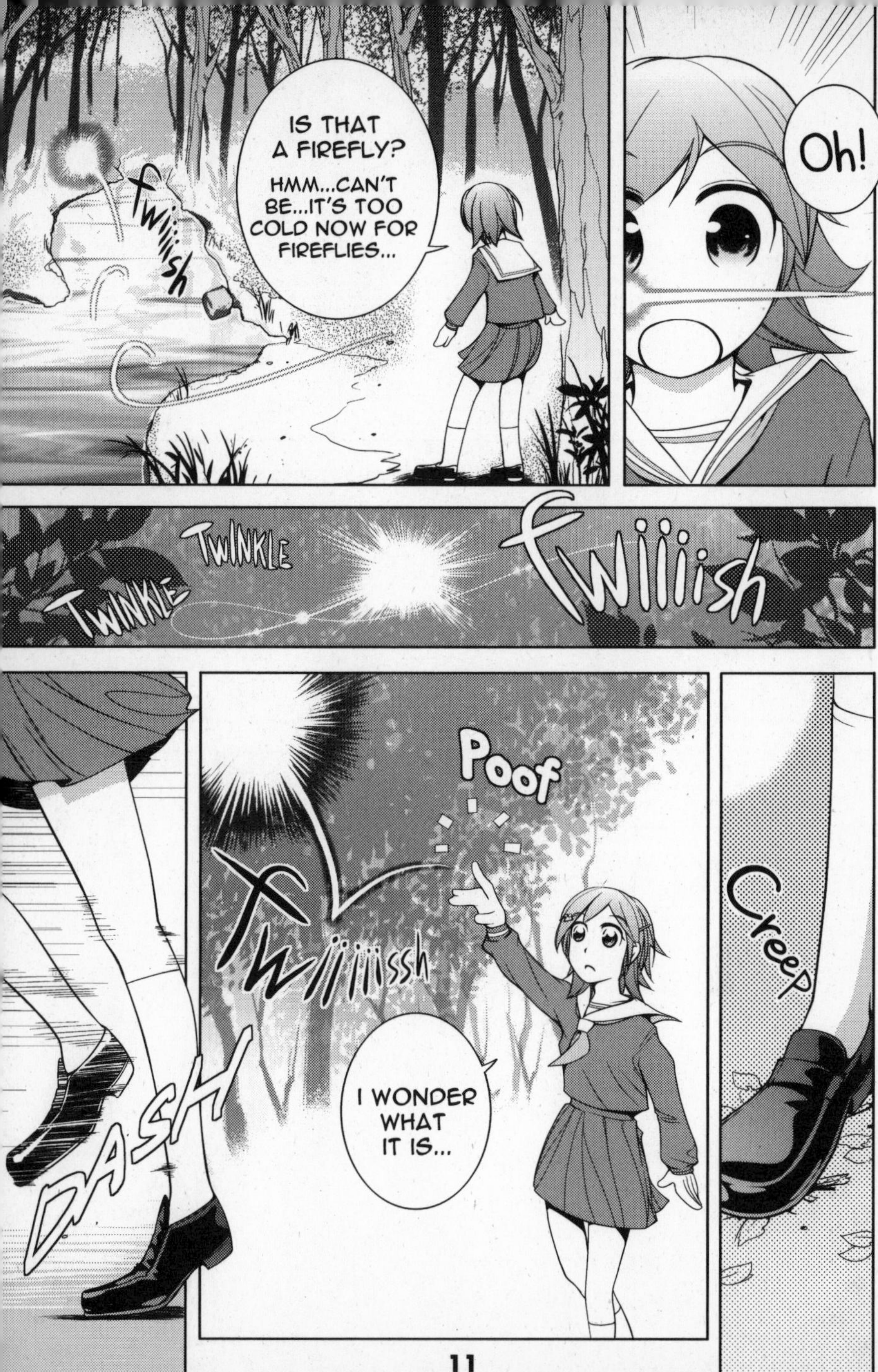
Oh!
IS THAT A FIREFLY?
HMM...CAN'T BE...IT'S TOO COLD NOW FOR FIREFLIES...
fwiiiish
fwiiiish
TWINKLE
TWINKLE
Creep
Poof
fwiiiissh
I WONDER WHAT IT IS...
DASH

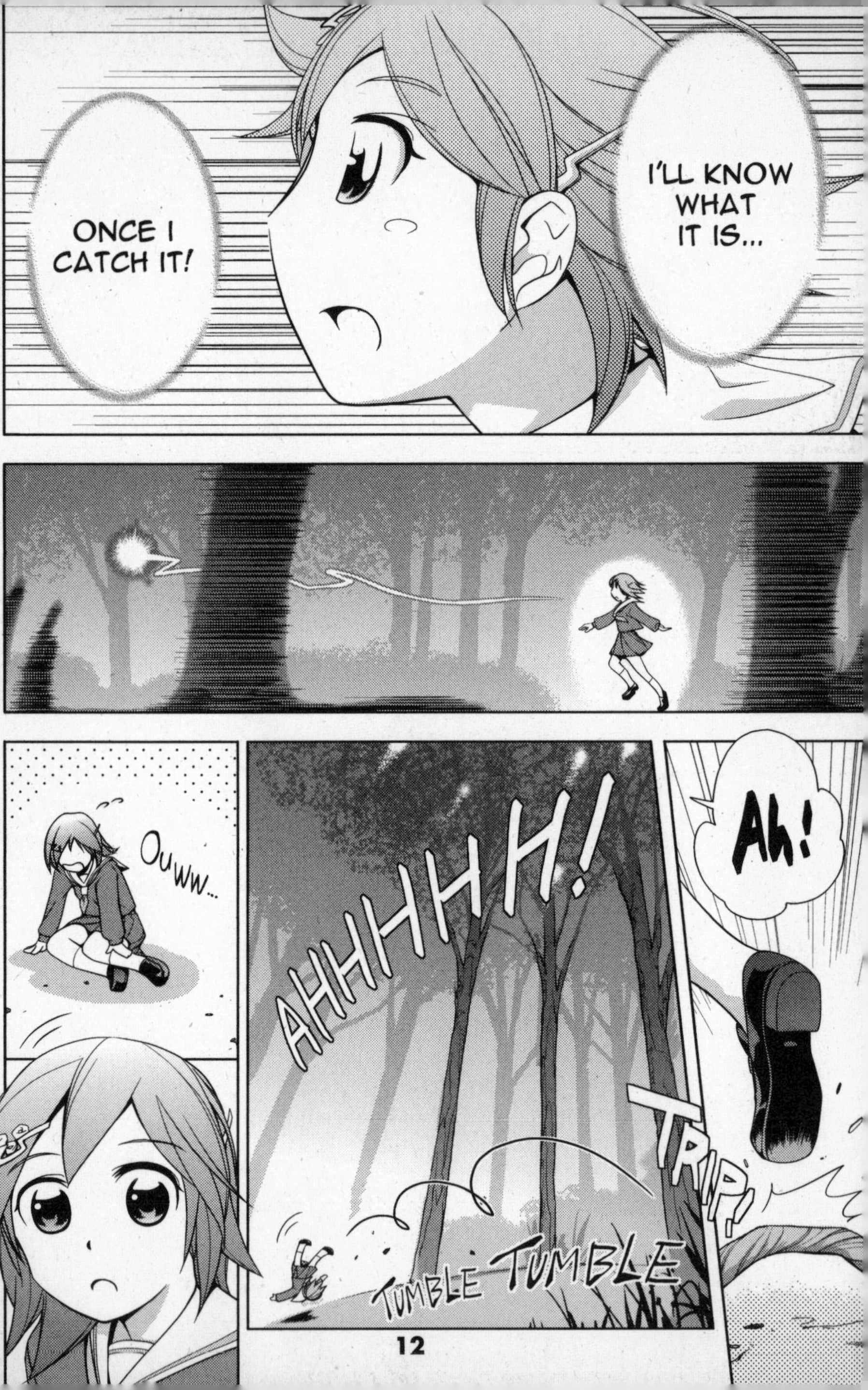
I'LL KNOW WHAT IT IS...
ONCE I CATCH IT!
Ah!
TRIP!
AHHHHHH!
TUMBLE TUMBLE
Ouww...

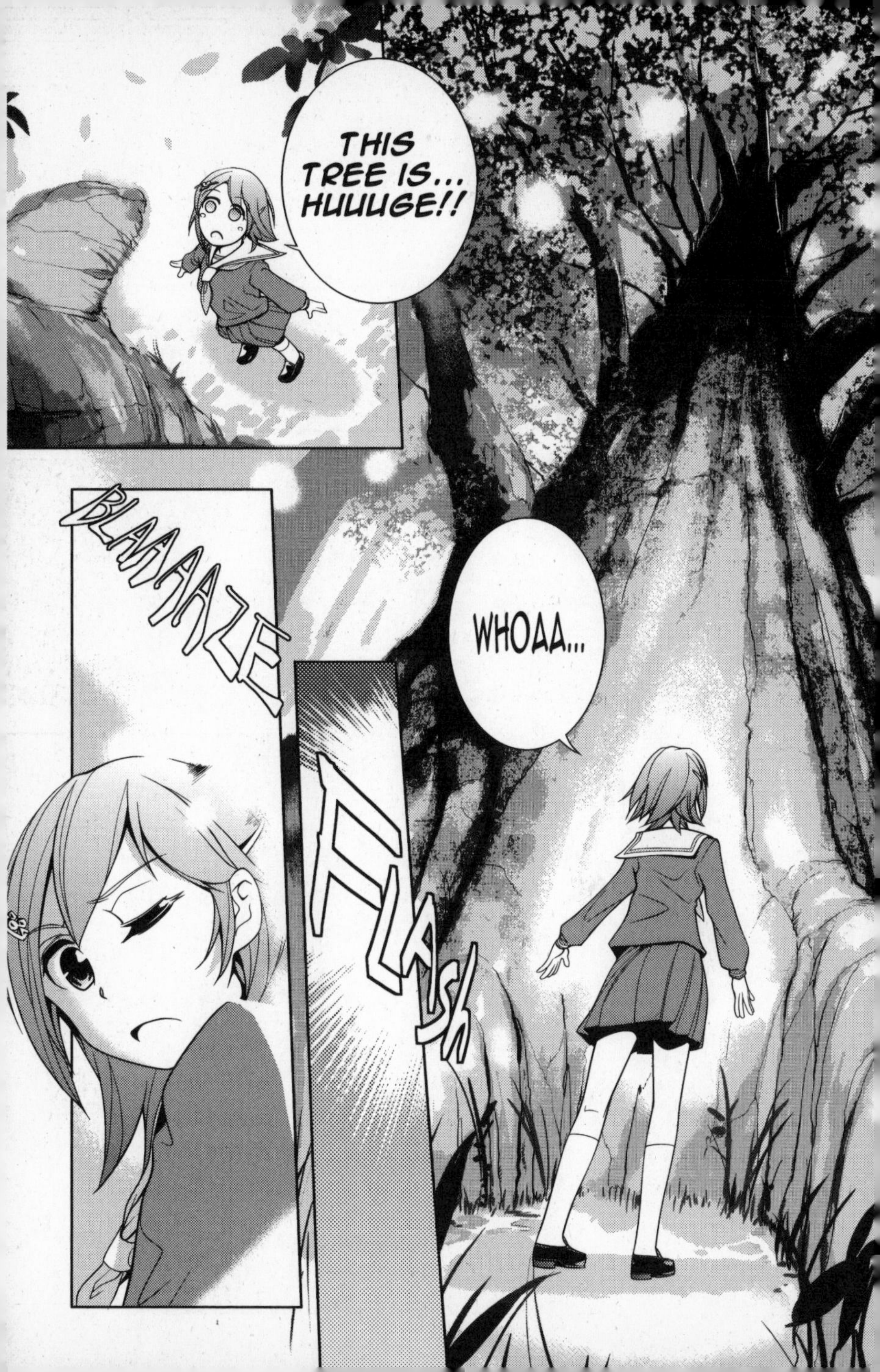
WHOAA...
THIS TREE IS... HUUUGE!!
FLASH
BLAAAAZE

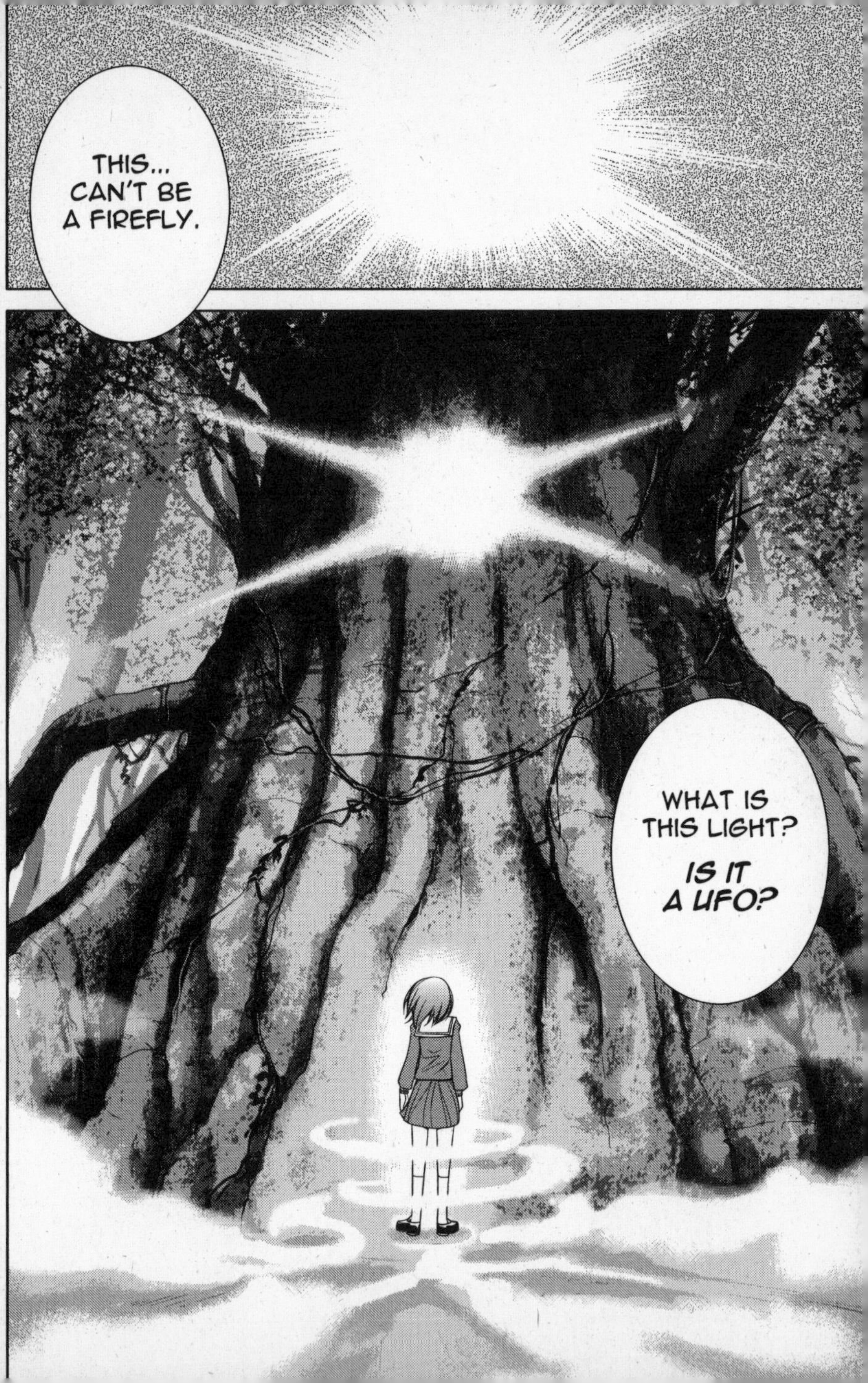
THIS... CAN'T BE A FIREFLY.
WHAT IS THIS LIGHT?
IS IT A UFO?

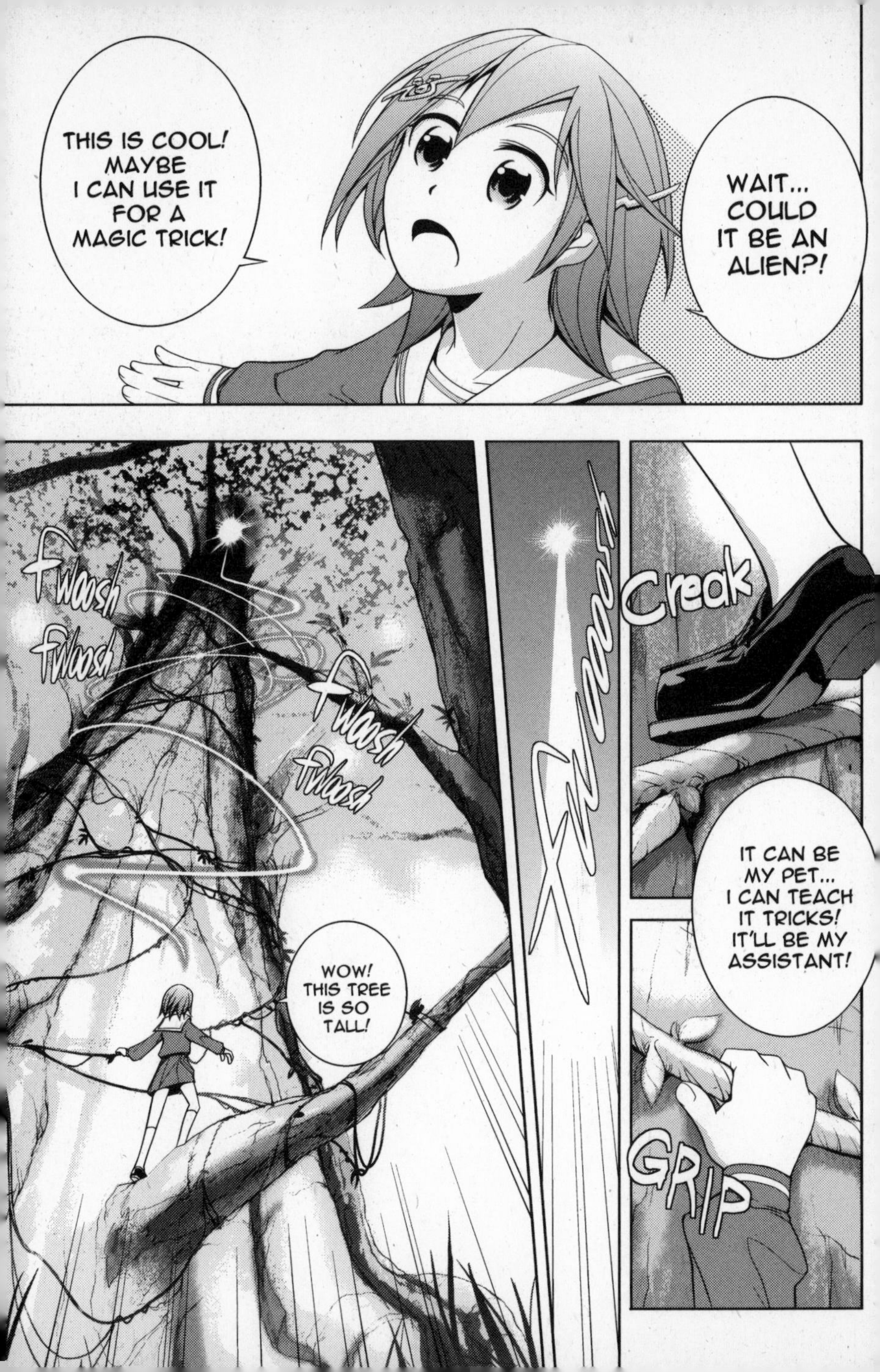
WAIT... COULD IT BE AN ALIEN?!
THIS IS COOL! MAYBE I CAN USE IT FOR A MAGIC TRICK!
Creak
IT CAN BE MY PET... I CAN TEACH IT TRICKS! IT'LL BE MY ASSISTANT!
GRIP
Fwooosh
Fwoosh
fwoosh
Fwoosh
fwoosh
WOW! THIS TREE IS SO TALL!

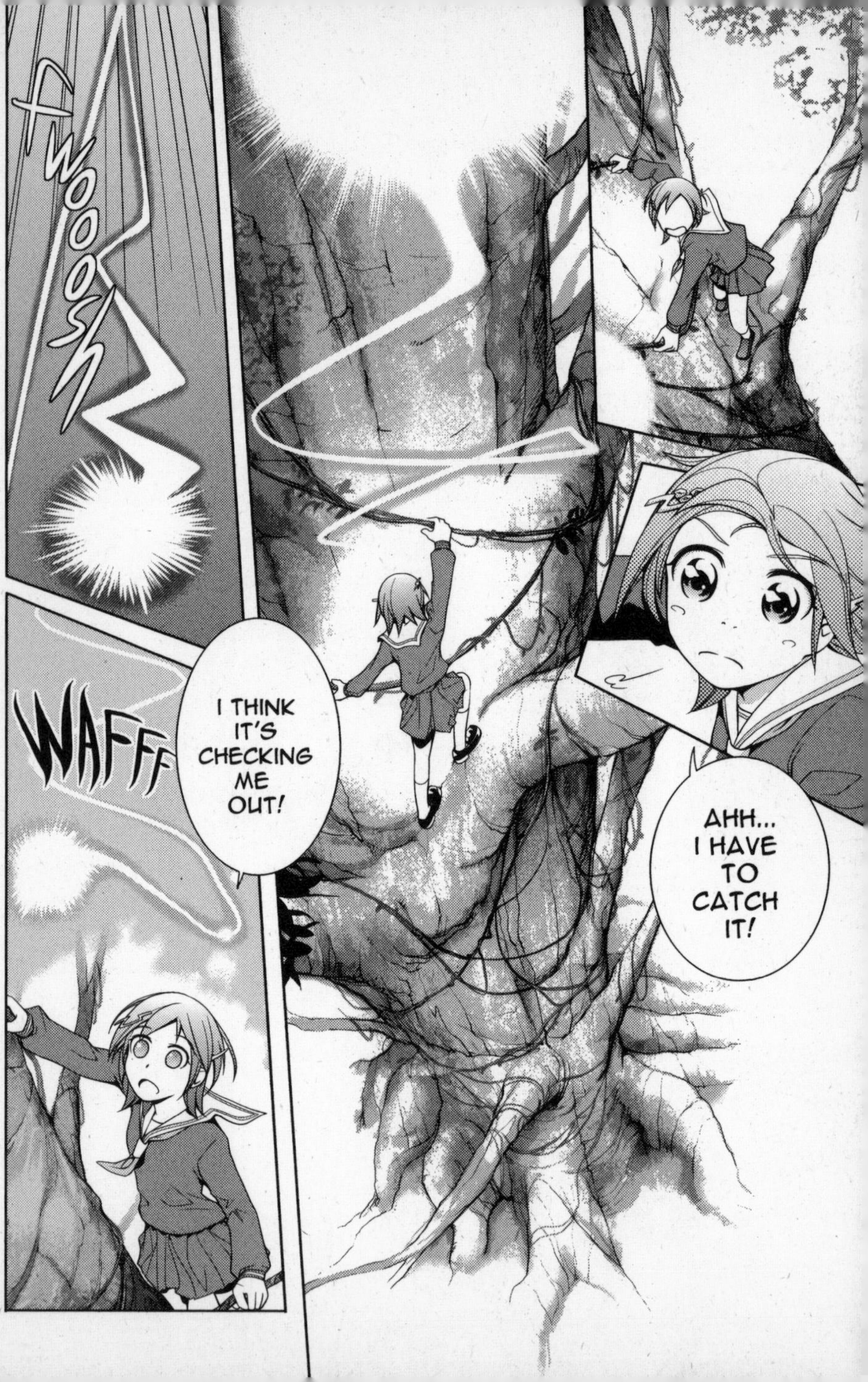
AHH... I HAVE TO CATCH IT!
I THINK IT'S CHECKING ME OUT!
FWOOOSH
WAFFF

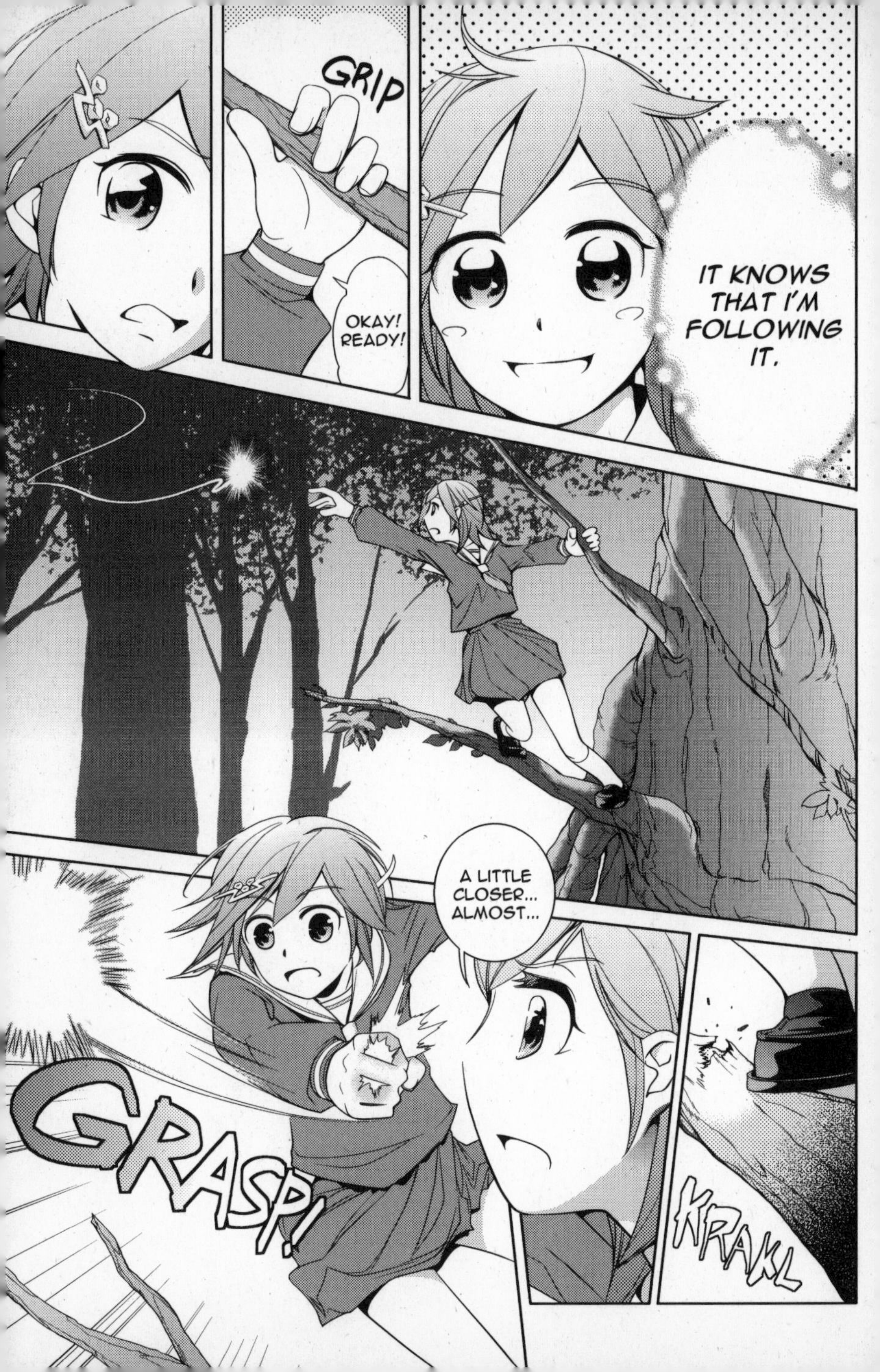
IT KNOWS THAT I'M FOLLOWING IT.
GRIP
OKAY! READY!
KRAKL
A LITTLE CLOSER... ALMOST...
GRASP!

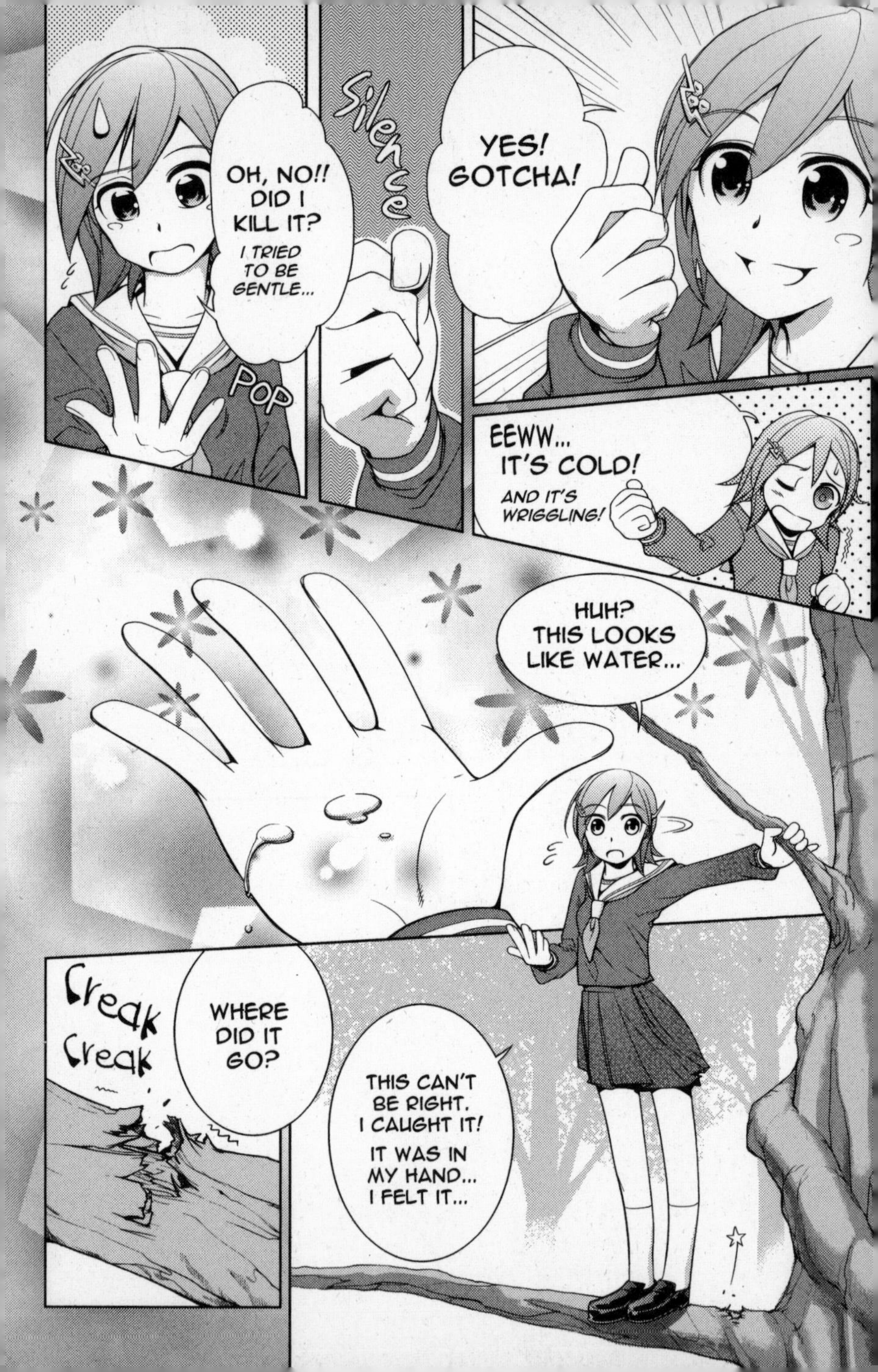
YES! GOTCHA!
Silence
OH, NO!! DID I KILL IT?
I TRIED TO BE GENTLE...
POP
EEWW... IT'S COLD!
AND IT'S WRIGGLING!
HUH? THIS LOOKS LIKE WATER...
WHERE DID IT GO?
THIS CAN'T BE RIGHT. I CAUGHT IT!
IT WAS IN MY HAND... I FELT IT...
Creak Creak

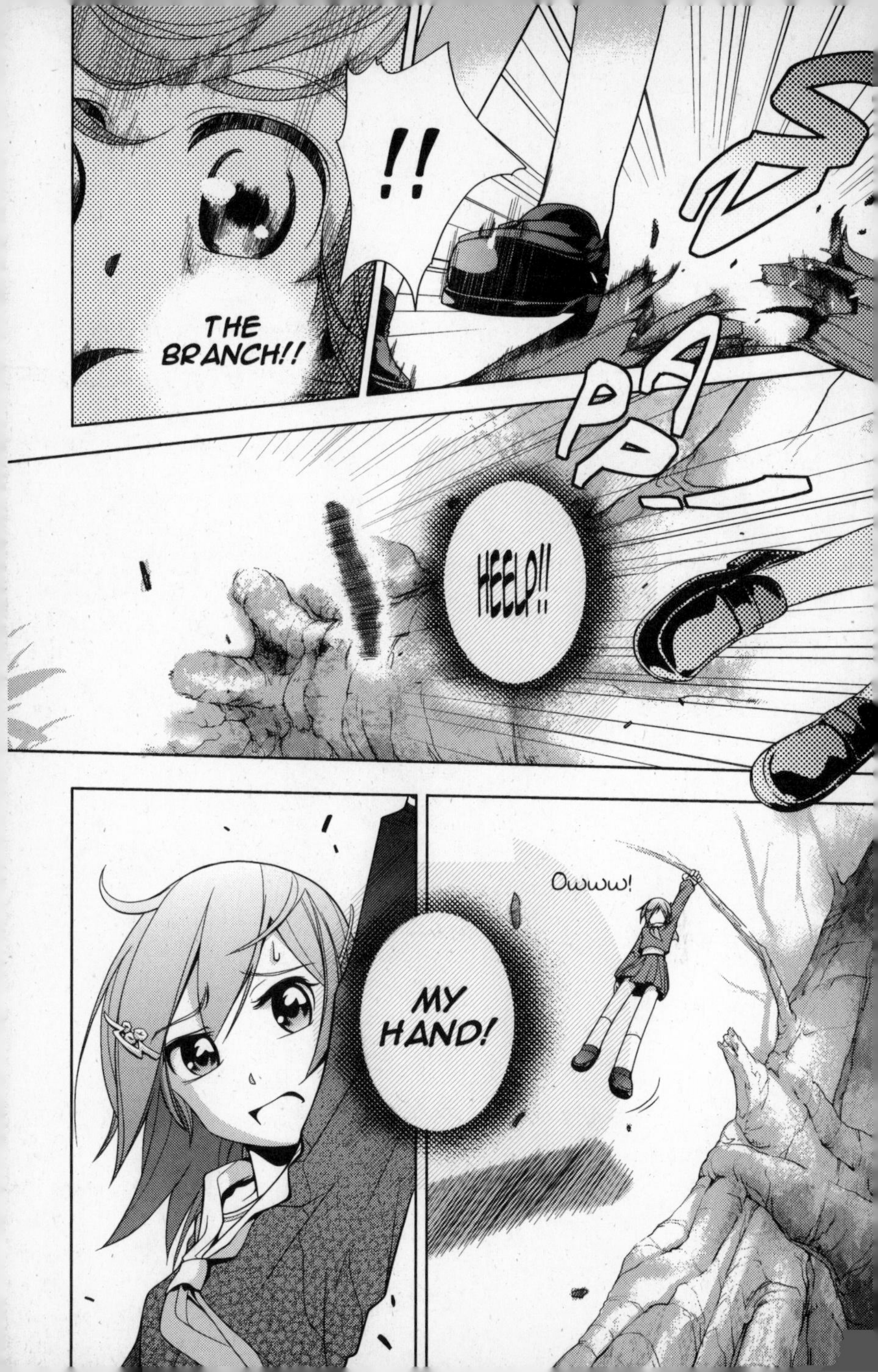
SNAPP—
!!
THE BRANCH!!
HEELP!!
Owww!
MY HAND!

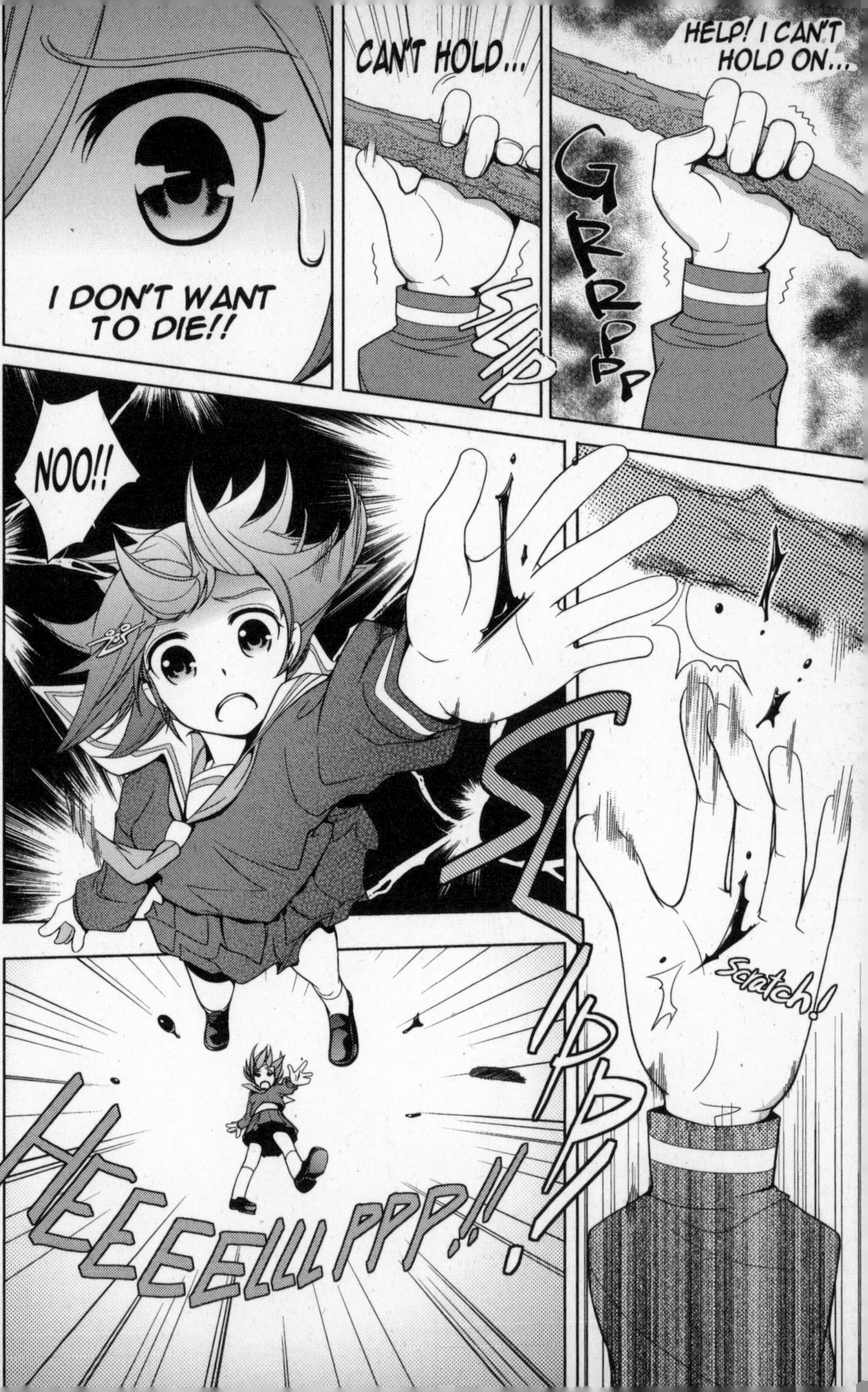
HELP! I CAN'T HOLD ON...
GRRPPP
CAN'T HOLD...
SLIP
I DON'T WANT TO DIE!!
Scratch!
SLIPP
NOO!!
HEEEELLLPPP!!

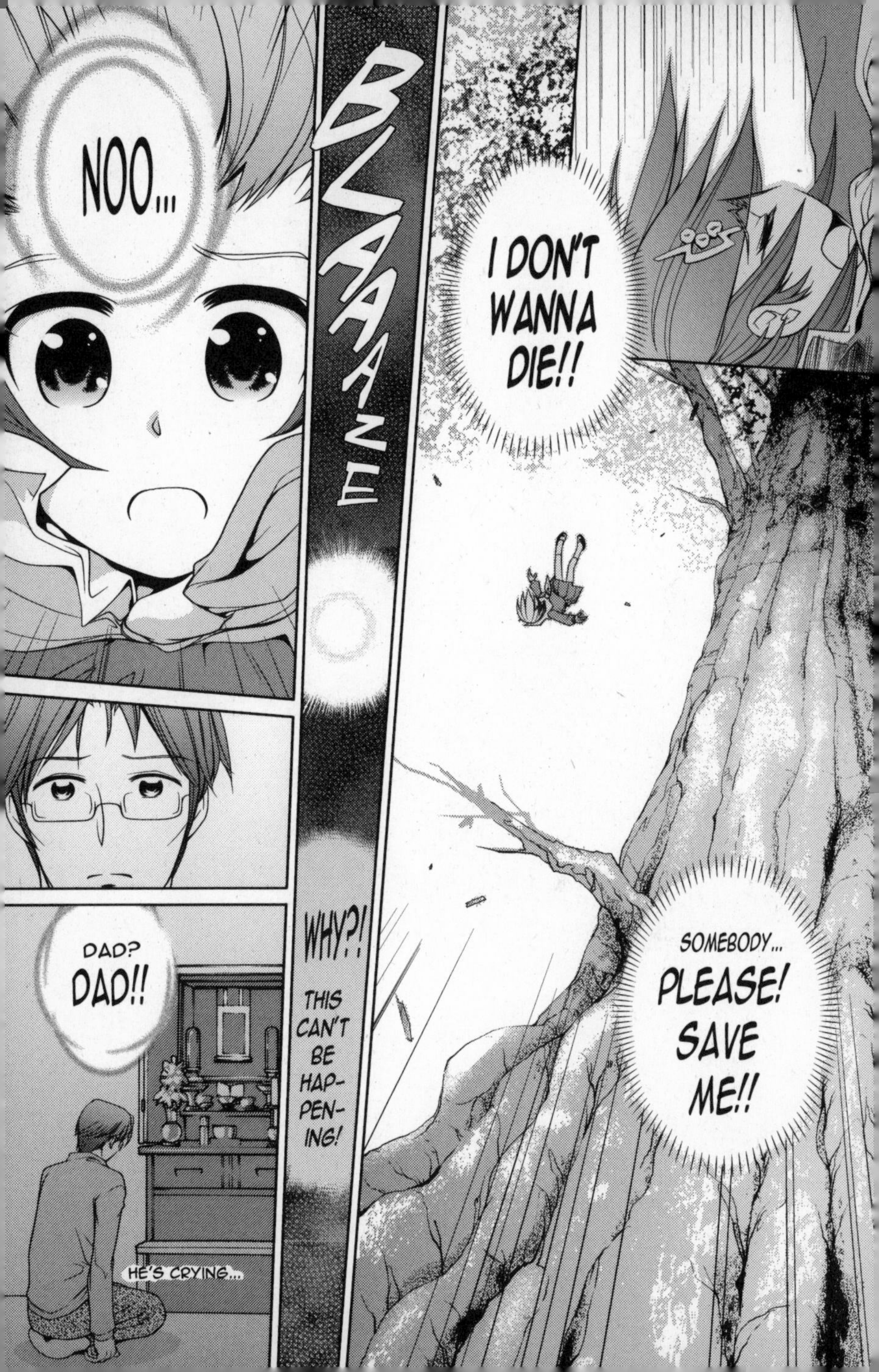
I DON'T WANNA DIE!!
SOMEBODY... PLEASE! SAVE ME!!
BLAAAAZE
WHY?!
THIS CAN'T BE HAP-PEN-ING!
NOO...
DAD? DAD!!
HE'S CRYING...

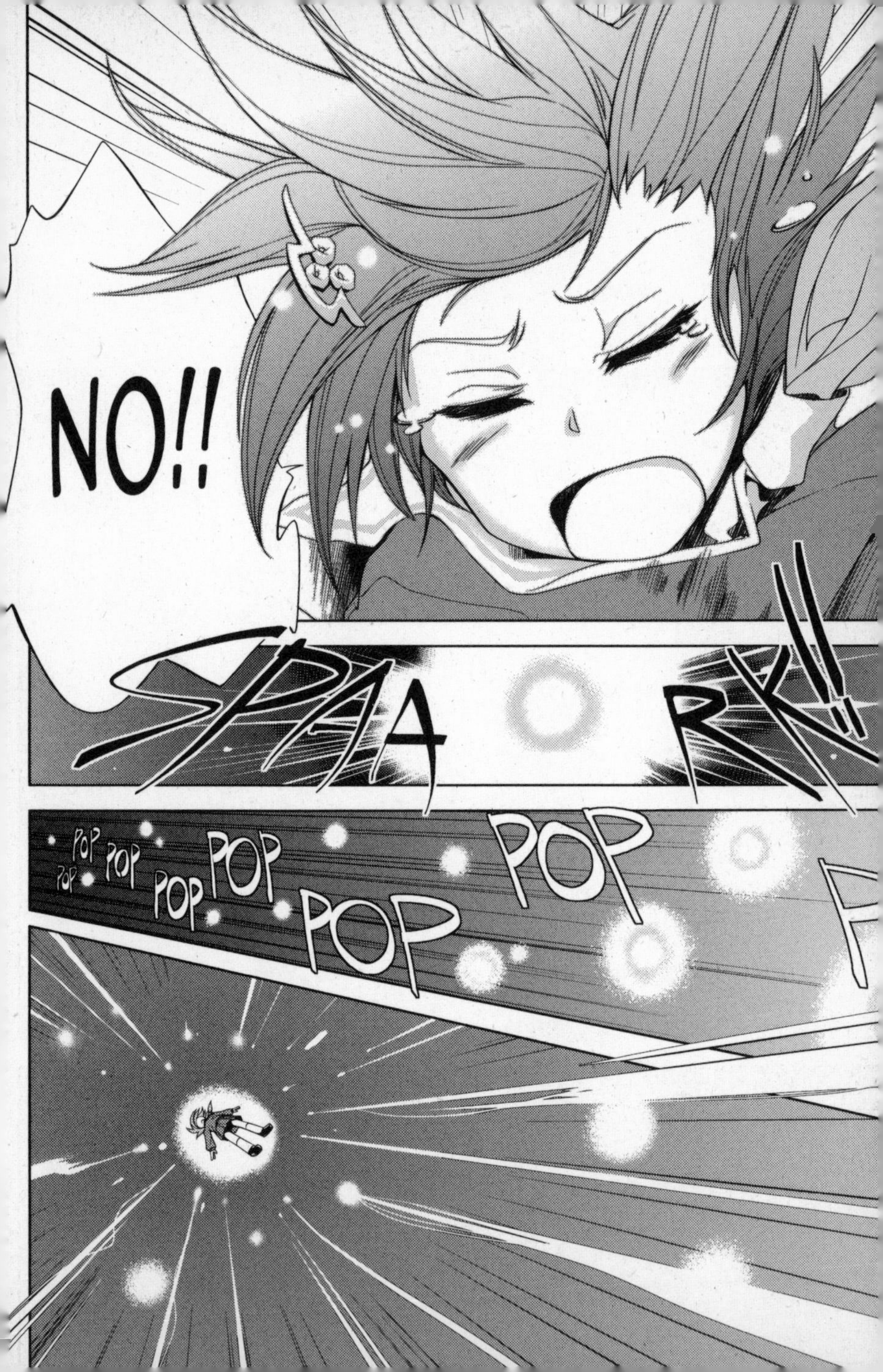
NO!!
SPAA RK!!
POP POP POP POP POP POP POP POP

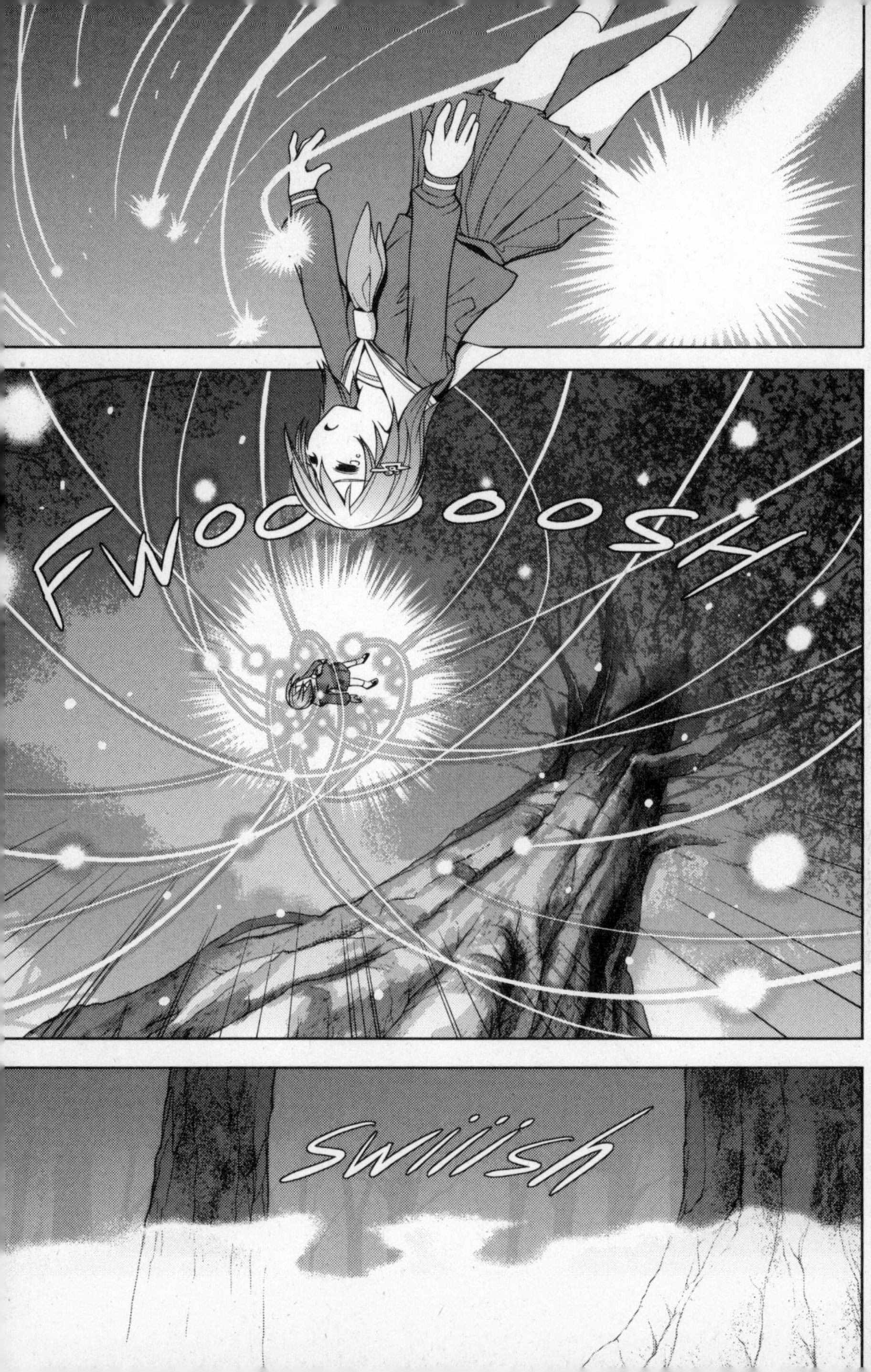
FWOOOOOSH
Swiish

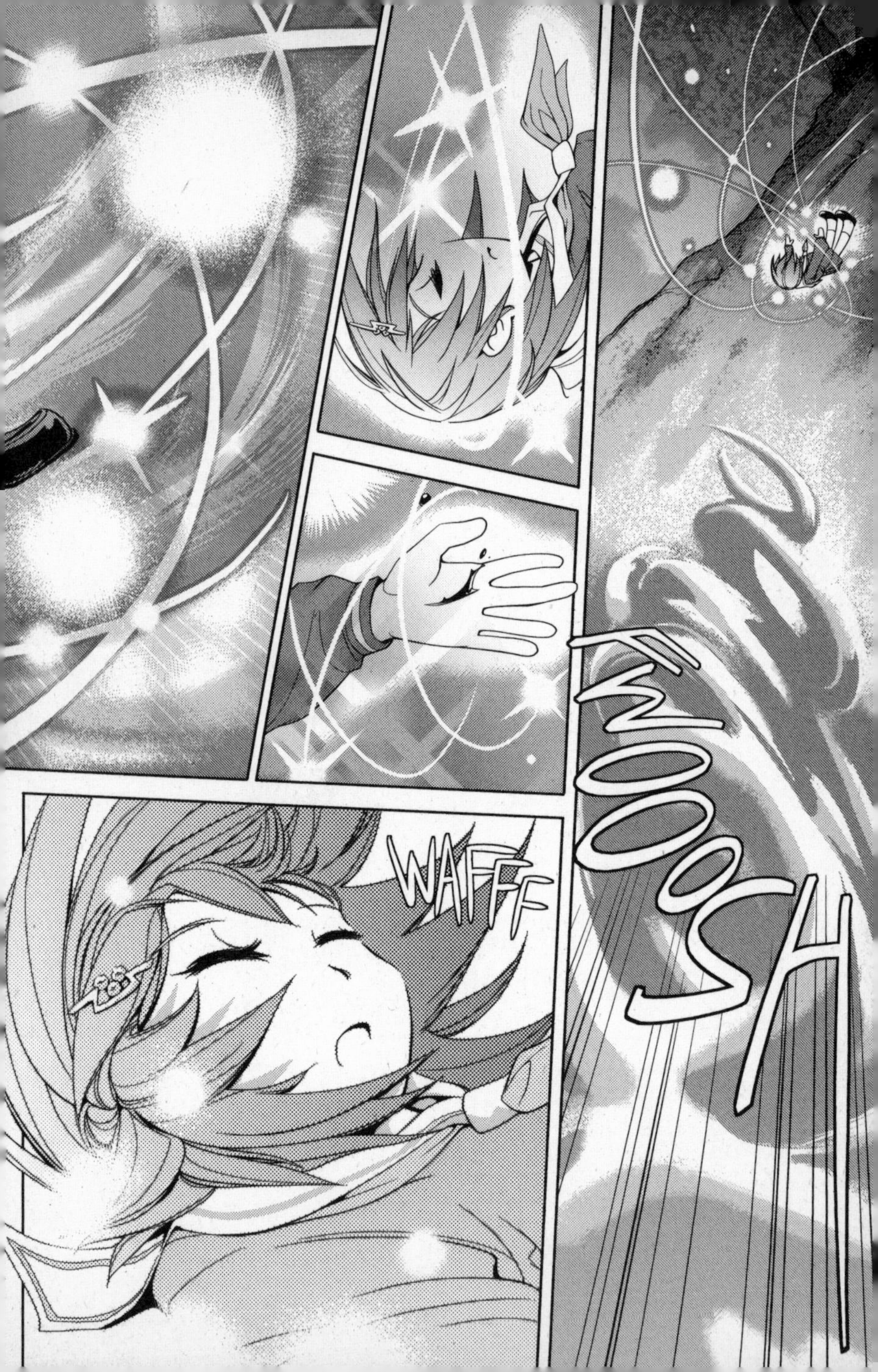
FWOOOSH
WAFFF

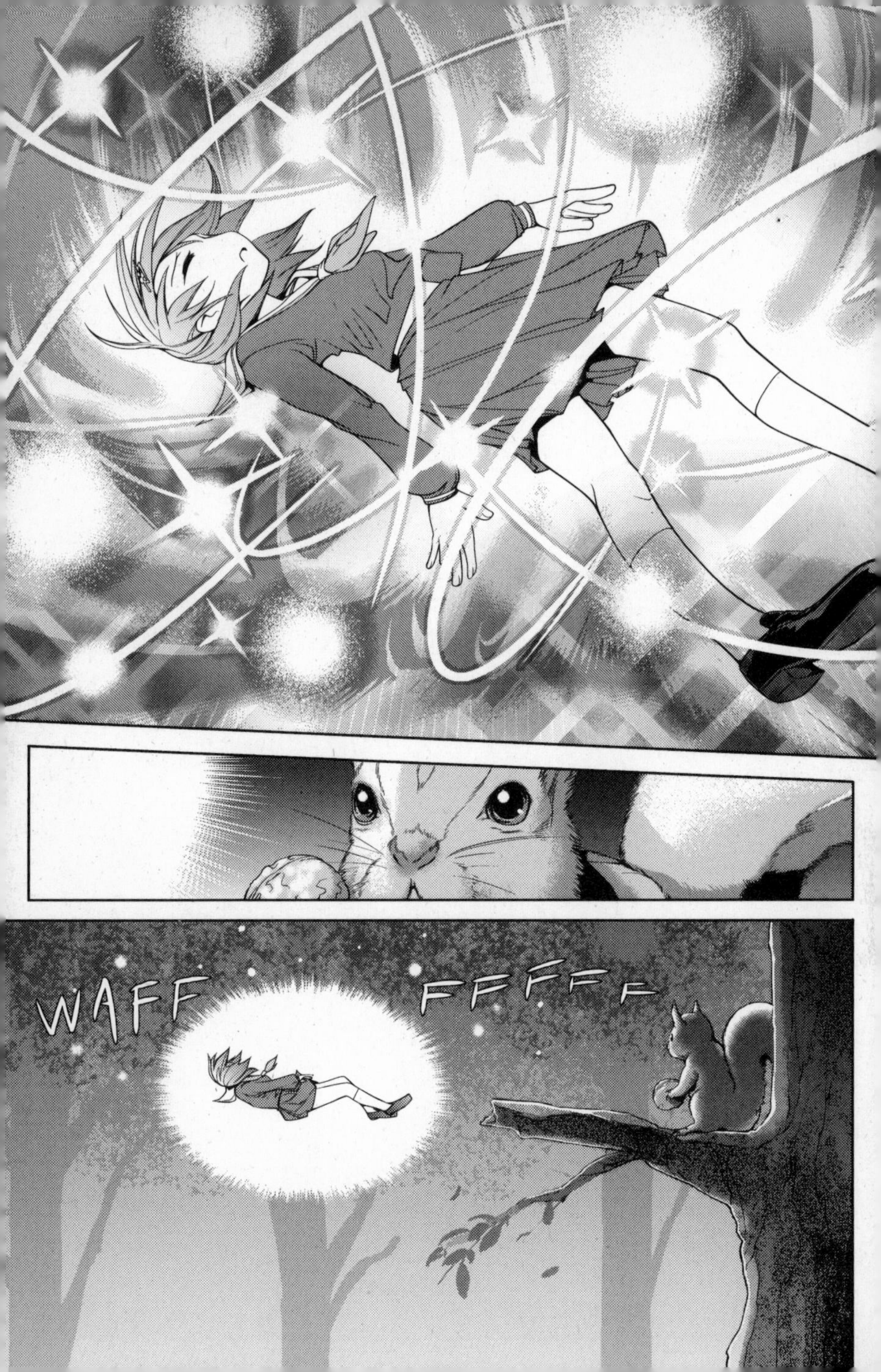
WAFF
FFFFFF

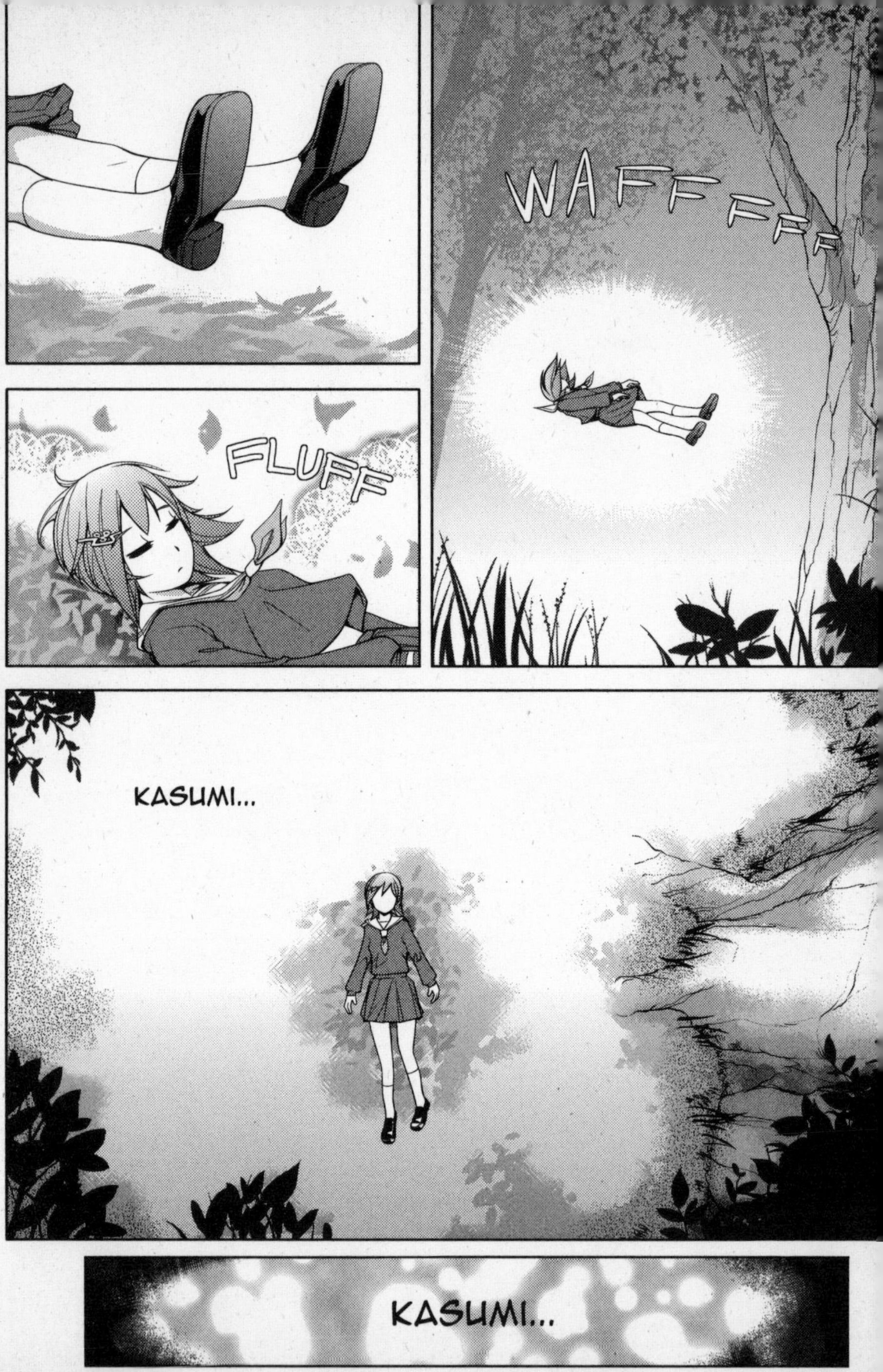
WAFFFFF
FLUFF
KASUMI...
KASUMI...

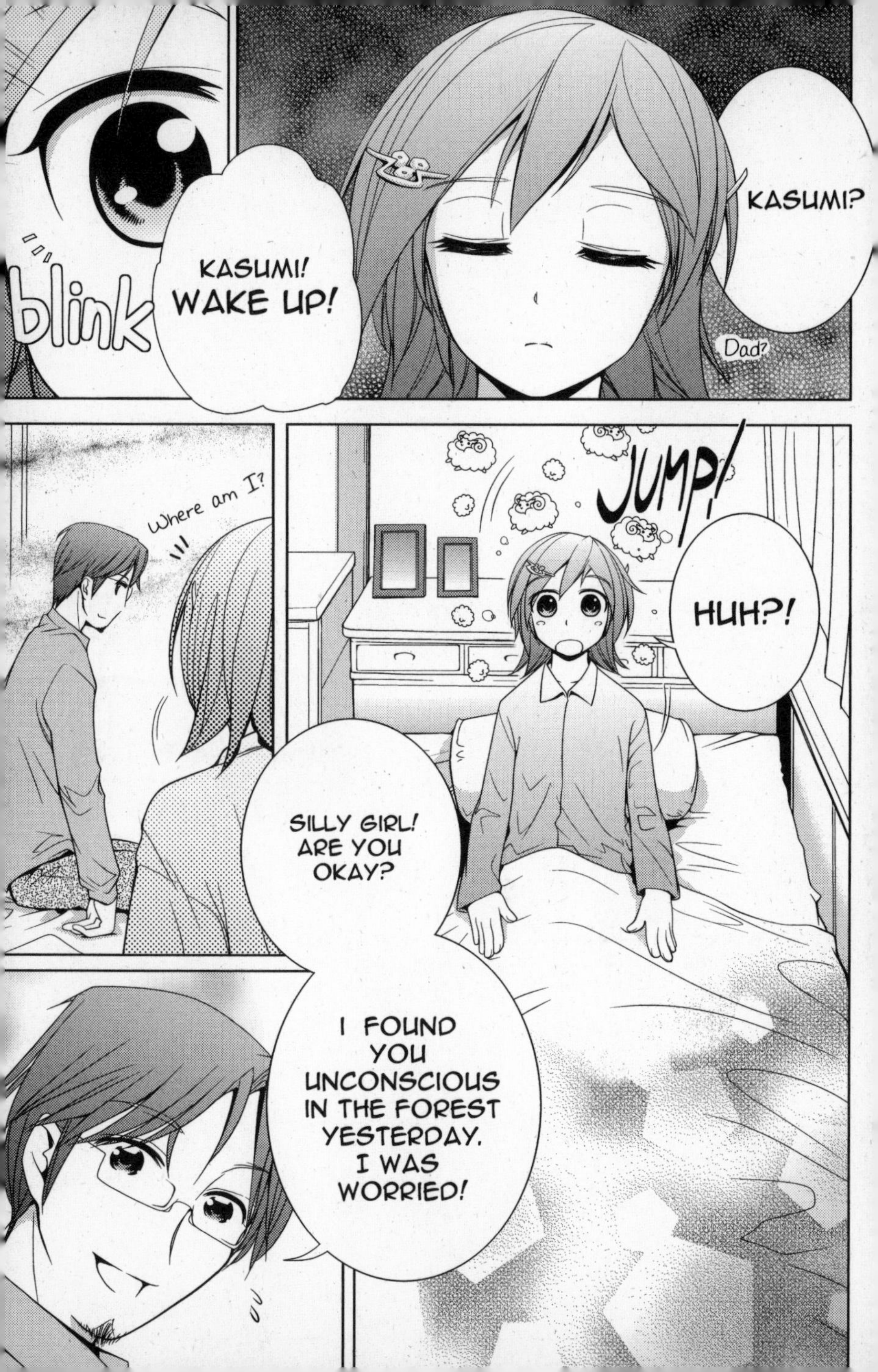
KASUMI?
Dad?
KASUMI! WAKE UP!
blink
JUMP!
HUH?!
Where am I?
SILLY GIRL! ARE YOU OKAY?
I FOUND YOU UNCONSCIOUS IN THE FOREST YESTERDAY. I WAS WORRIED!

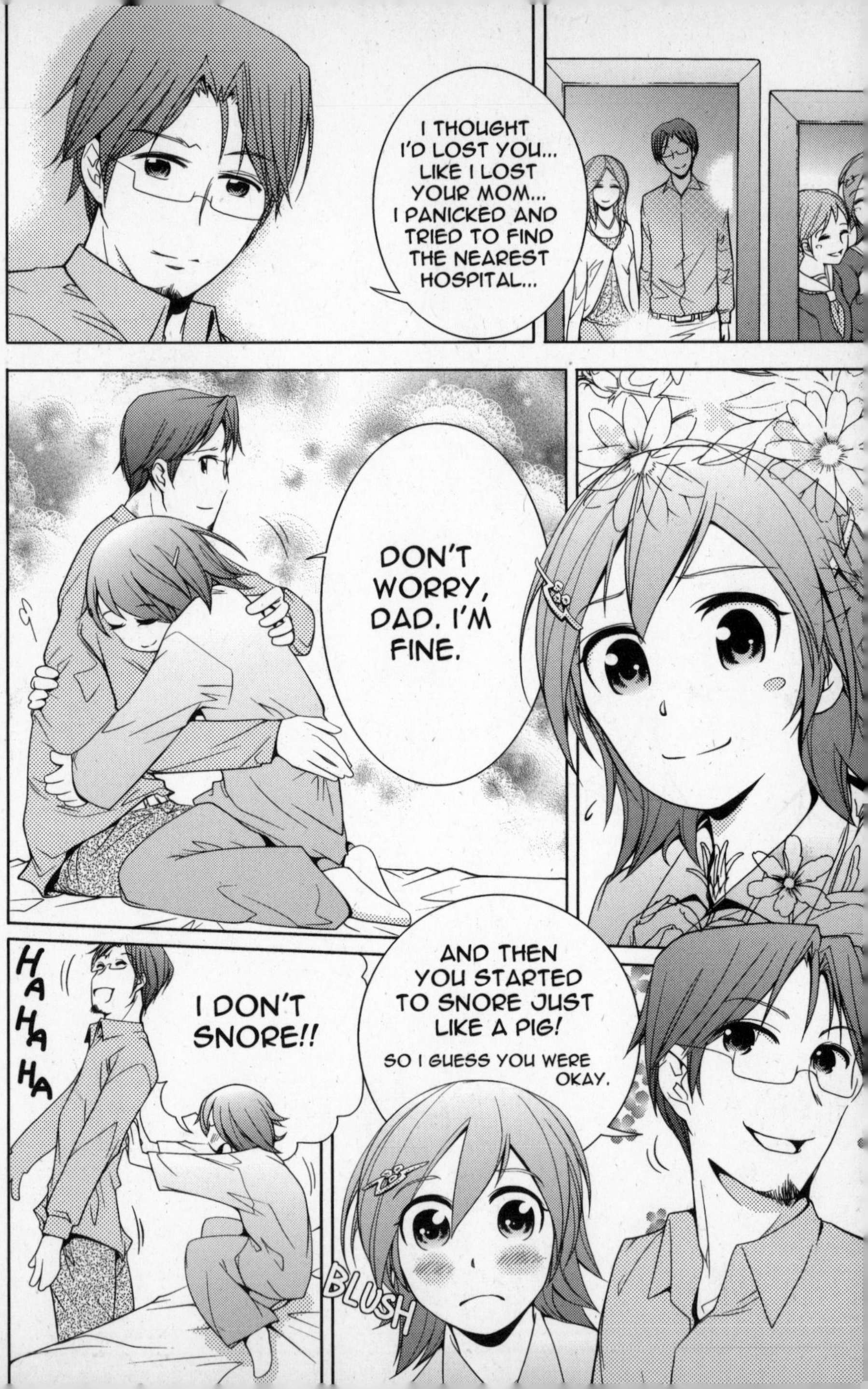
I THOUGHT I'D LOST YOU... LIKE I LOST YOUR MOM... I PANICKED AND TRIED TO FIND THE NEAREST HOSPITAL...
DON'T WORRY, DAD. I'M FINE.
AND THEN YOU STARTED TO SNORE JUST LIKE A PIG!
SO I GUESS YOU WERE OKAY.
BLUSH
I DON'T SNORE!!
HA HA HA HA

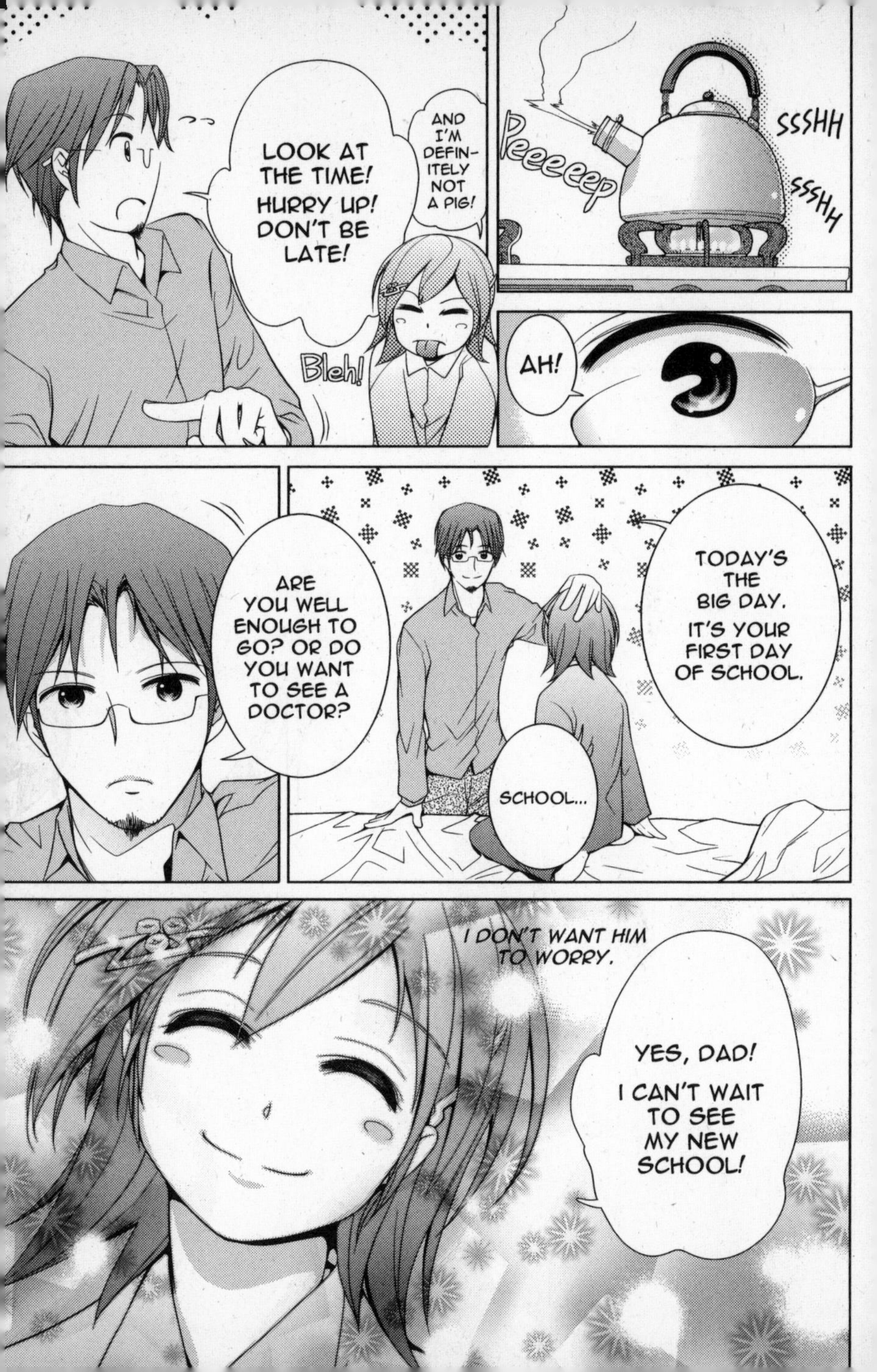

Peeeeep
SSSHH
SSSHH
AH!
AND I'M DEFINITELY NOT A PIG!
LOOK AT THE TIME! HURRY UP! DON'T BE LATE!
Bleh!
TODAY'S THE BIG DAY. IT'S YOUR FIRST DAY OF SCHOOL.
SCHOOL...
ARE YOU WELL ENOUGH TO GO? OR DO YOU WANT TO SEE A DOCTOR?
I DON'T WANT HIM TO WORRY.
YES, DAD! I CAN'T WAIT TO SEE MY NEW SCHOOL!

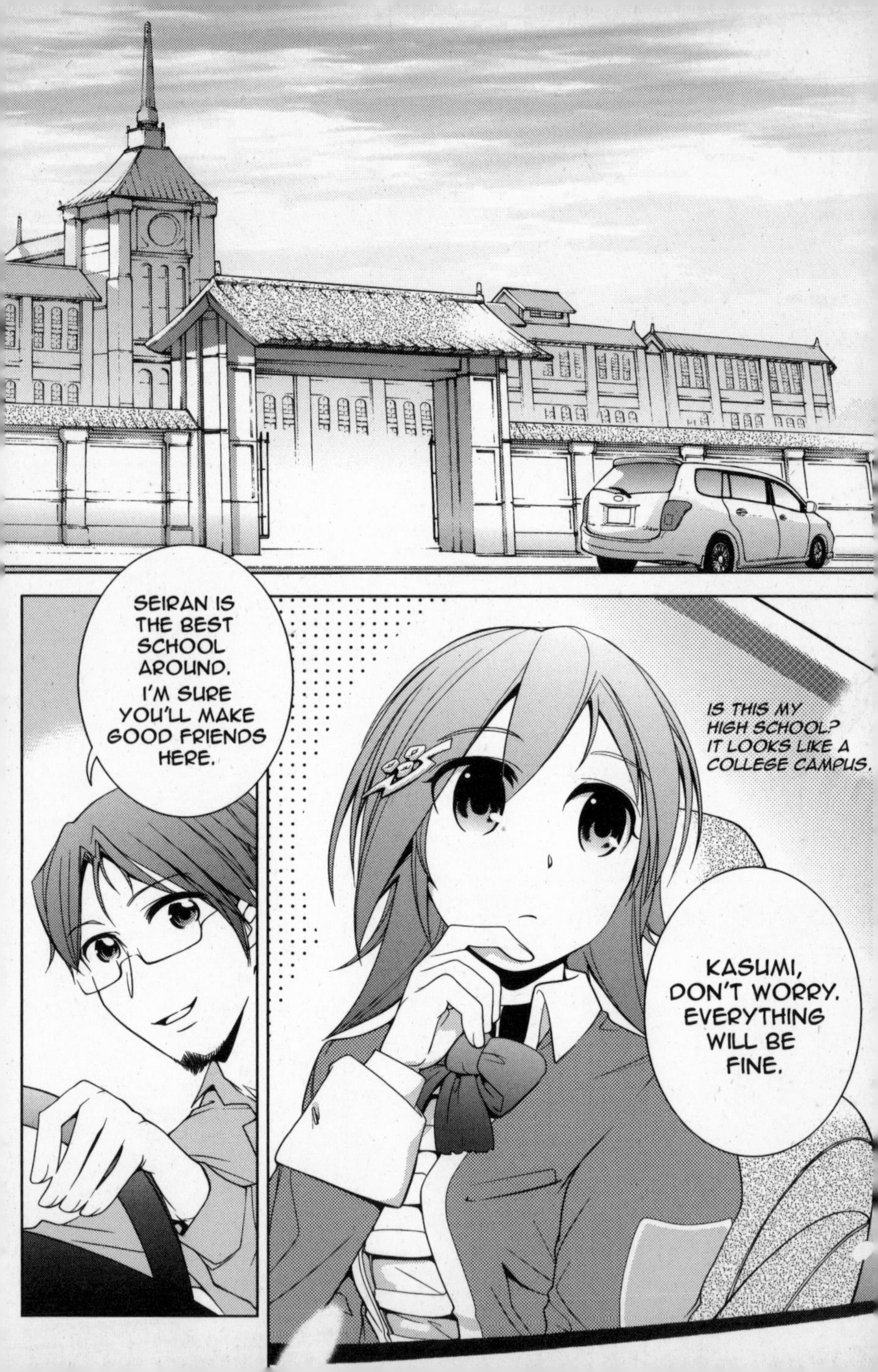
IS THIS MY HIGH SCHOOL? IT LOOKS LIKE A COLLEGE CAMPUS.
KASUMI, DON'T WORRY. EVERYTHING WILL BE FINE.
SEIRAN IS THE BEST SCHOOL AROUND. I'M SURE YOU'LL MAKE GOOD FRIENDS HERE.

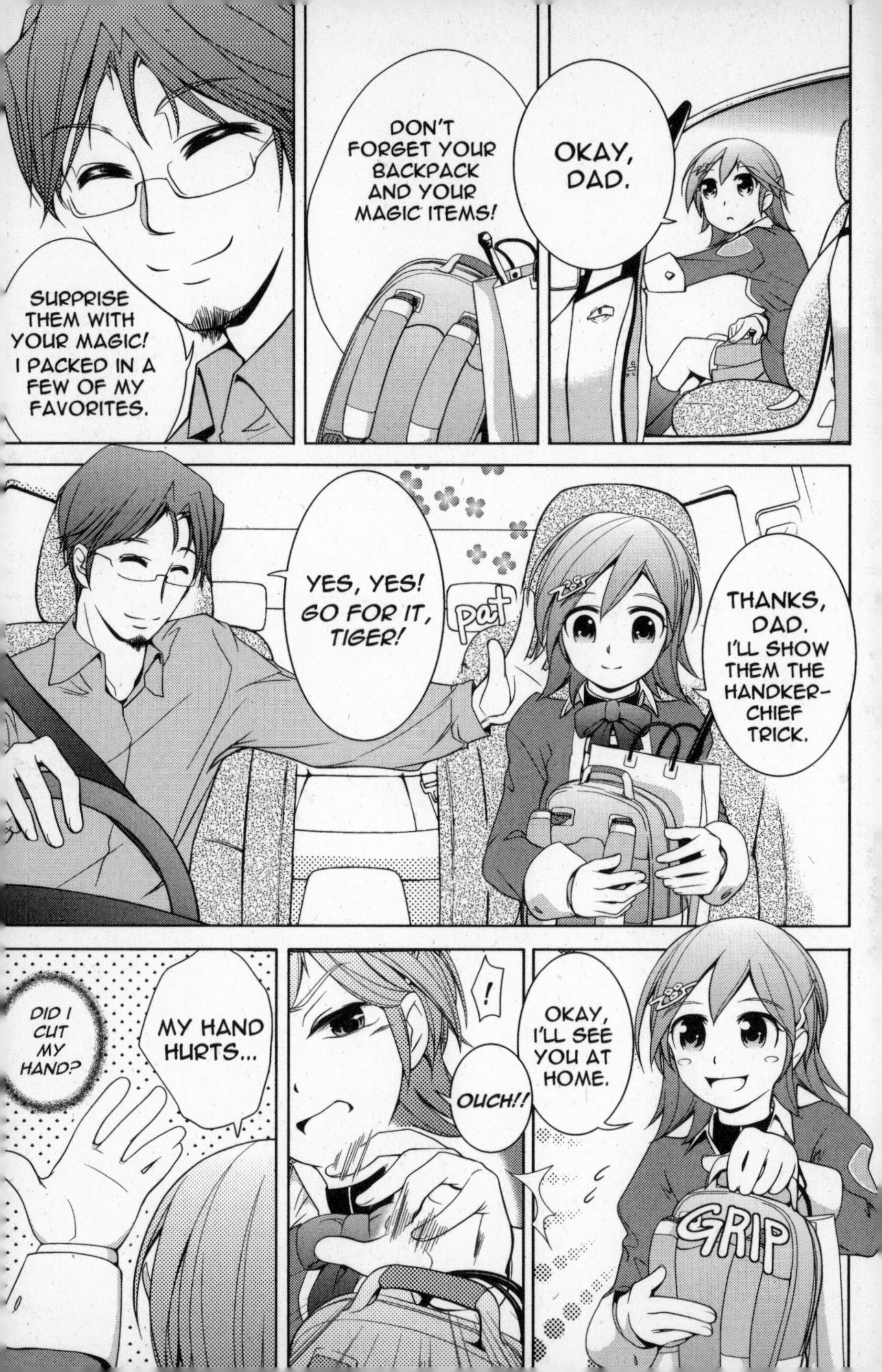
OKAY, DAD.
DON'T FORGET YOUR BACKPACK AND YOUR MAGIC ITEMS!
SURPRISE THEM WITH YOUR MAGIC! I PACKED IN A FEW OF MY FAVORITES.
THANKS, DAD. I'LL SHOW THEM THE HANDKER-CHIEF TRICK.
pat
YES, YES! GO FOR IT, TIGER!
OKAY, I'LL SEE YOU AT HOME.
GRIP
!
OUCH!!
MY HAND HURTS...
DID I CUT MY HAND?

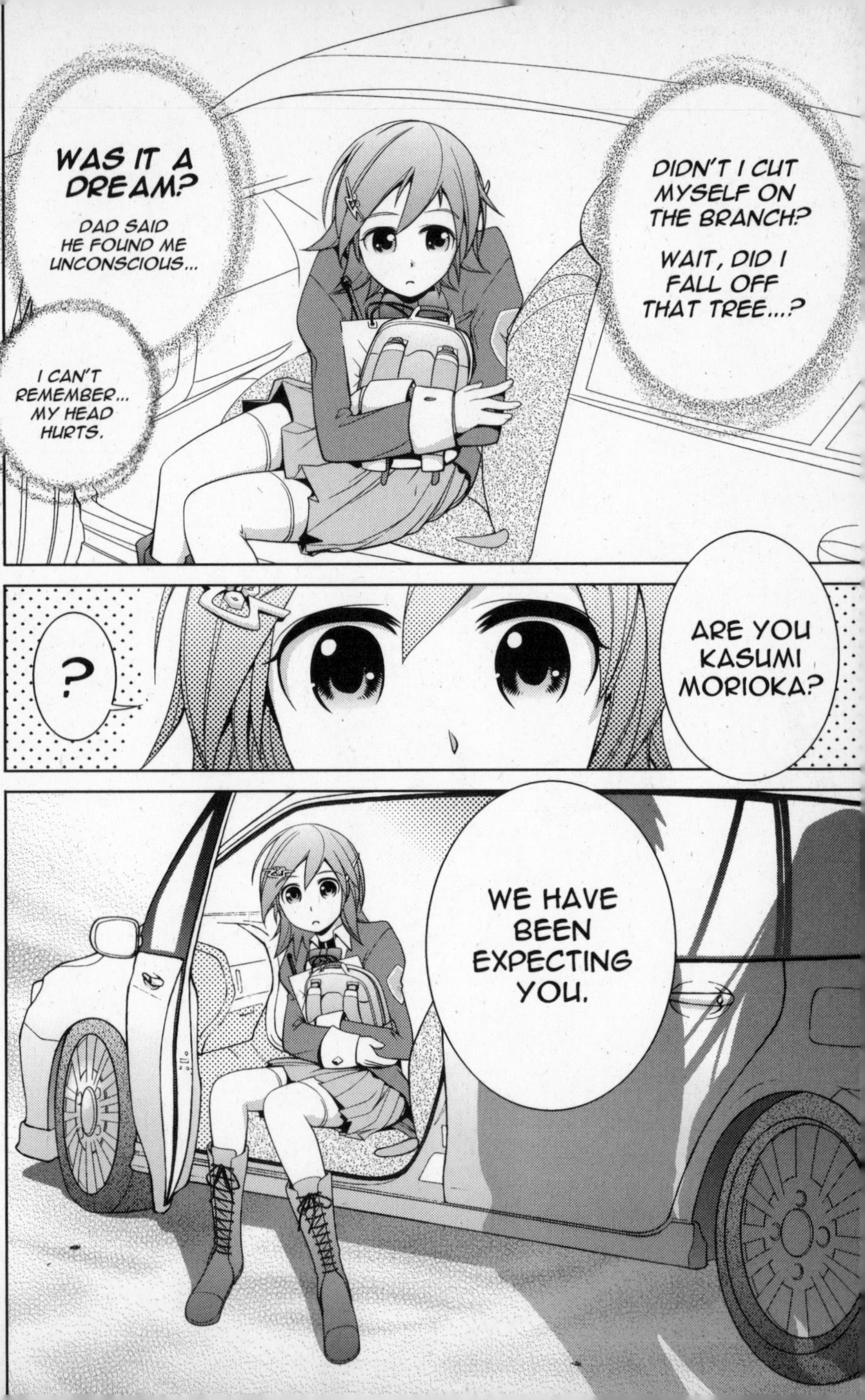
DIDN'T I CUT MYSELF ON THE BRANCH?
WAIT, DID I FALL OFF THAT TREE...?
WAS IT A DREAM?
DAD SAID HE FOUND ME UNCONSCIOUS...
I CAN'T REMEMBER... MY HEAD HURTS.
ARE YOU KASUMI MORIOKA?
?
WE HAVE BEEN EXPECTING YOU.

CHAPTER 2

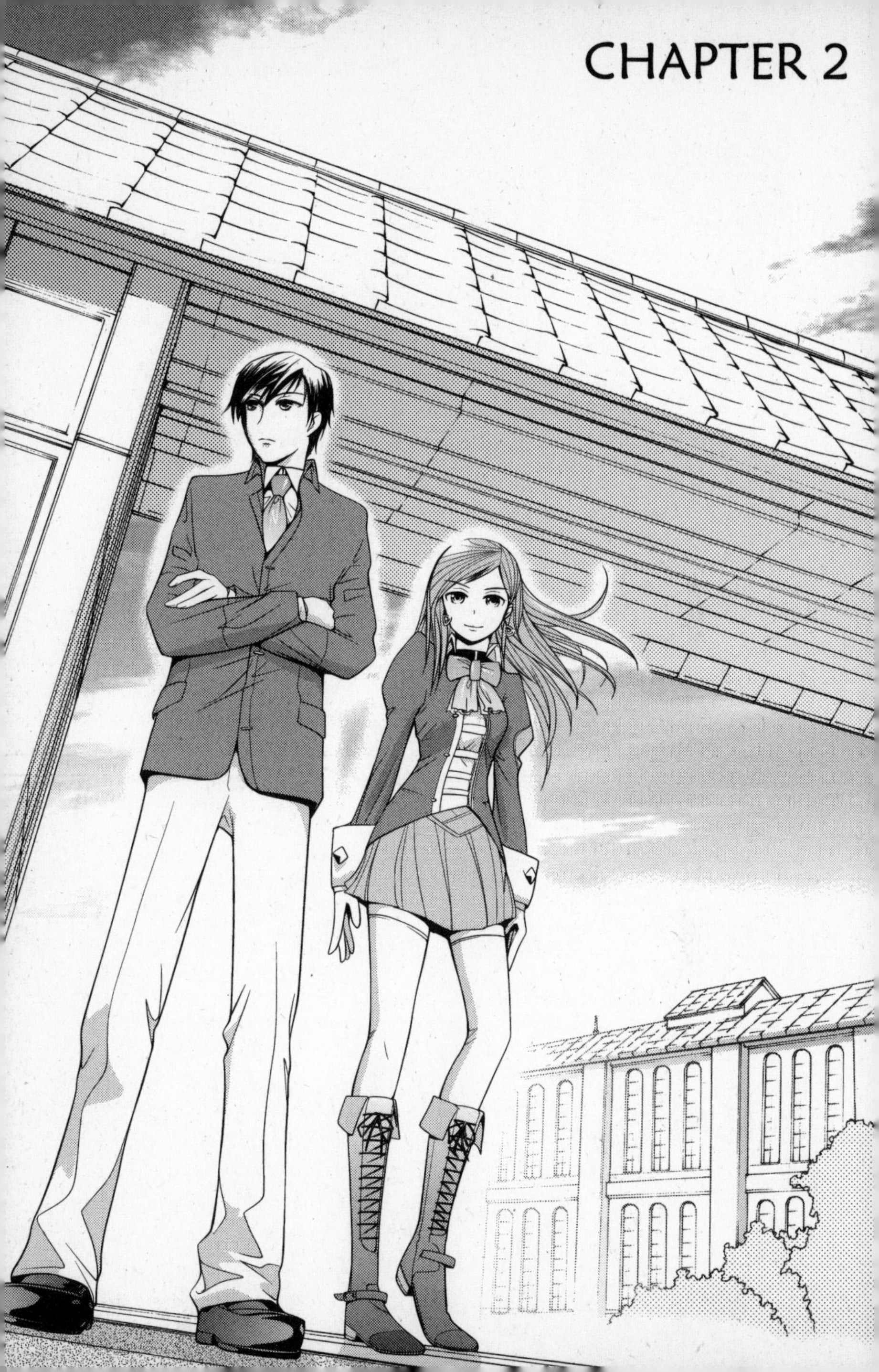

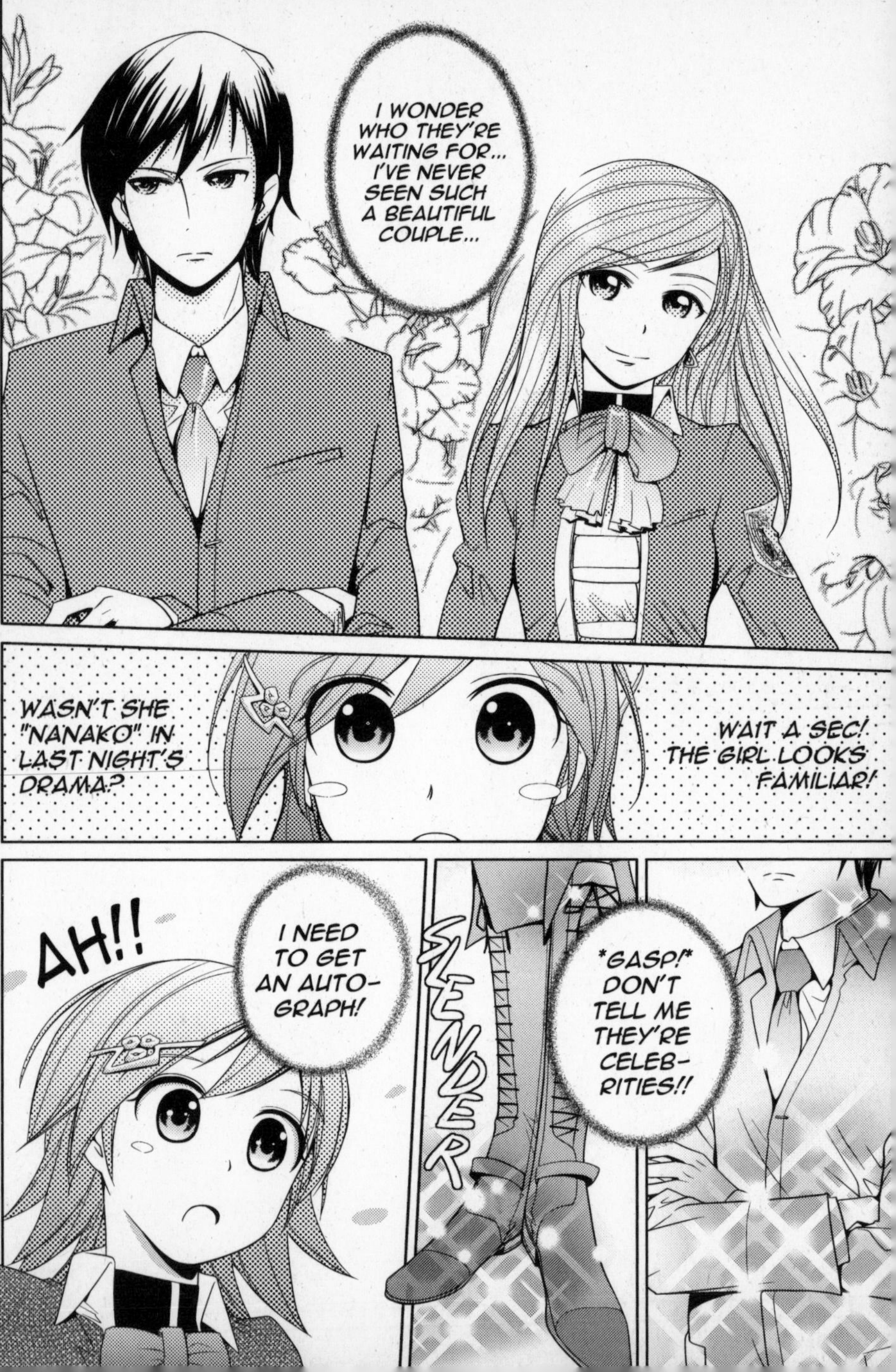
I WONDER WHO THEY'RE WAITING FOR... I'VE NEVER SEEN SUCH A BEAUTIFUL COUPLE...
WAIT A SEC! THE GIRL LOOKS FAMILIAR!
WASN'T SHE "NANAKO" IN LAST NIGHT'S DRAMA?
GASP! DON'T TELL ME THEY'RE CELEBRITIES!!
SLENDER
AH!!
I NEED TO GET AN AUTOGRAPH!

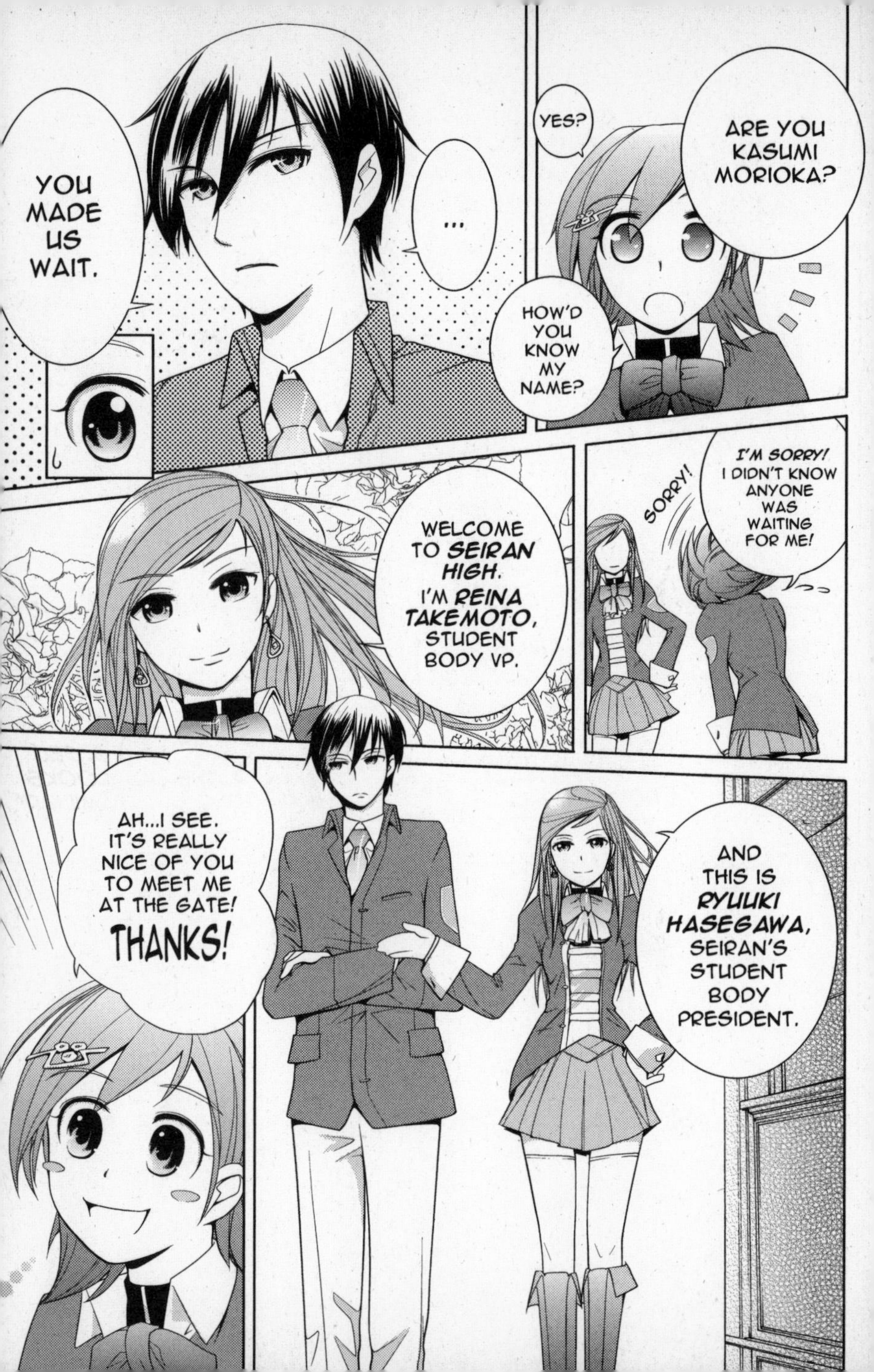
ARE YOU KASUMI MORIOKA?
YES?
HOW'D YOU KNOW MY NAME?
...
YOU MADE US WAIT.
I'M SORRY! I DIDN'T KNOW ANYONE WAS WAITING FOR ME!
SORRY!
WELCOME TO SEIRAN HIGH. I'M REINA TAKEMOTO, STUDENT BODY VP.
AND THIS IS RYUUKI HASEGAWA, SEIRAN'S STUDENT BODY PRESIDENT.
AH...I SEE. IT'S REALLY NICE OF YOU TO MEET ME AT THE GATE!
THANKS!

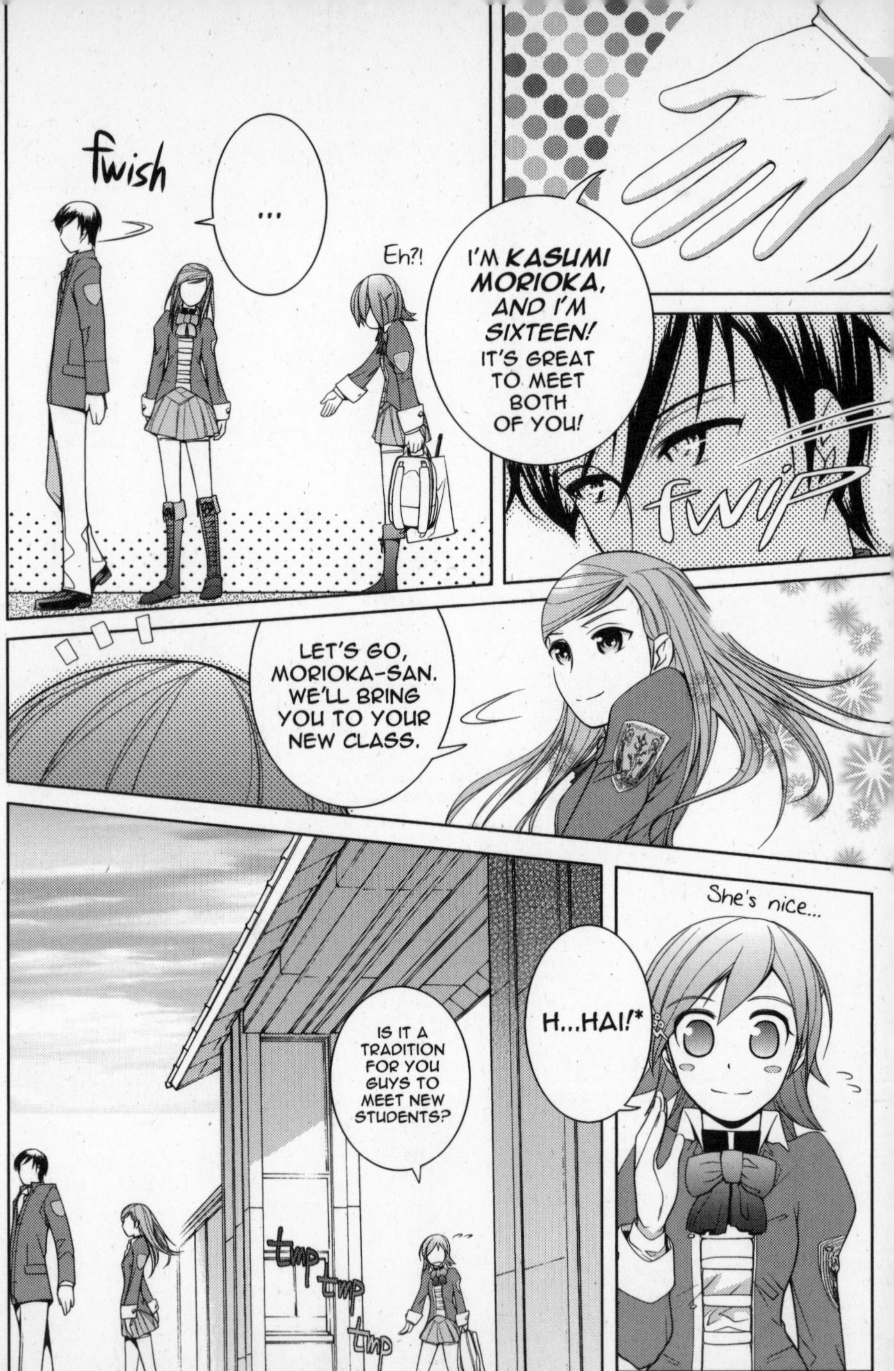
I'M KASUMI MORIOKA, AND I'M SIXTEEN! IT'S GREAT TO MEET BOTH OF YOU!
fwip
fwish
...
Eh?!
LET'S GO, MORIOKA-SAN. WE'LL BRING YOU TO YOUR NEW CLASS.
She's nice...
H...HAI!*
IS IT A TRADITION FOR YOU GUYS TO MEET NEW STUDENTS?
tmp
tmp
tmp

*Hai - means "Yes."

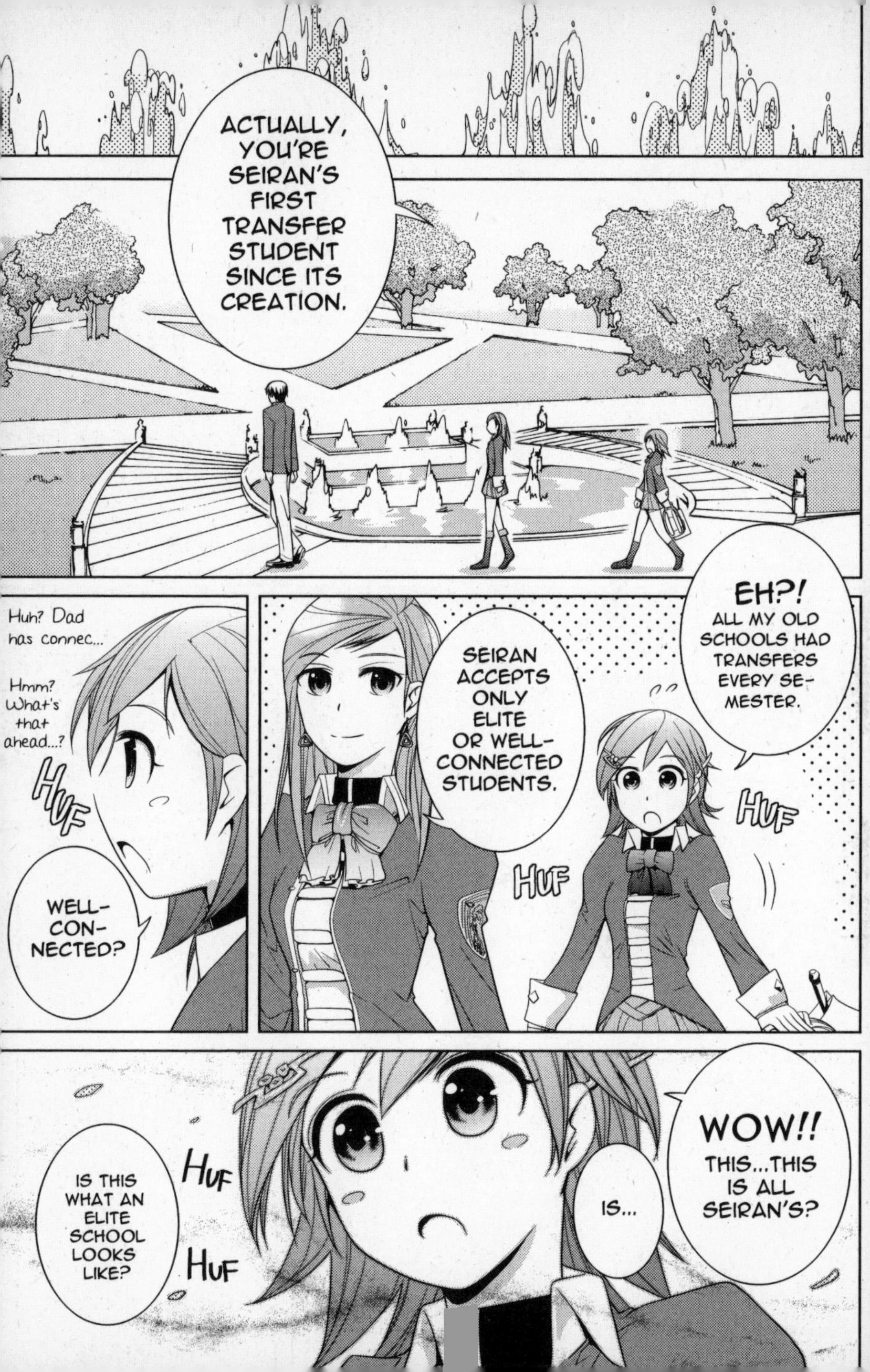
ACTUALLY, YOU'RE SEIRAN'S FIRST TRANSFER STUDENT SINCE ITS CREATION.
EH?! ALL MY OLD SCHOOLS HAD TRANSFERS EVERY SE- MESTER.
HUF
SEIRAN ACCEPTS ONLY ELITE OR WELL-CONNECTED STUDENTS.
HUF
Huh? Dad has connec...
Hmm? What's that ahead...?
HUF
WELL-CON-NECTED?
WOW!! THIS...THIS IS ALL SEIRAN'S?
IS...
HUF
IS THIS WHAT AN ELITE SCHOOL LOOKS LIKE?
HUF

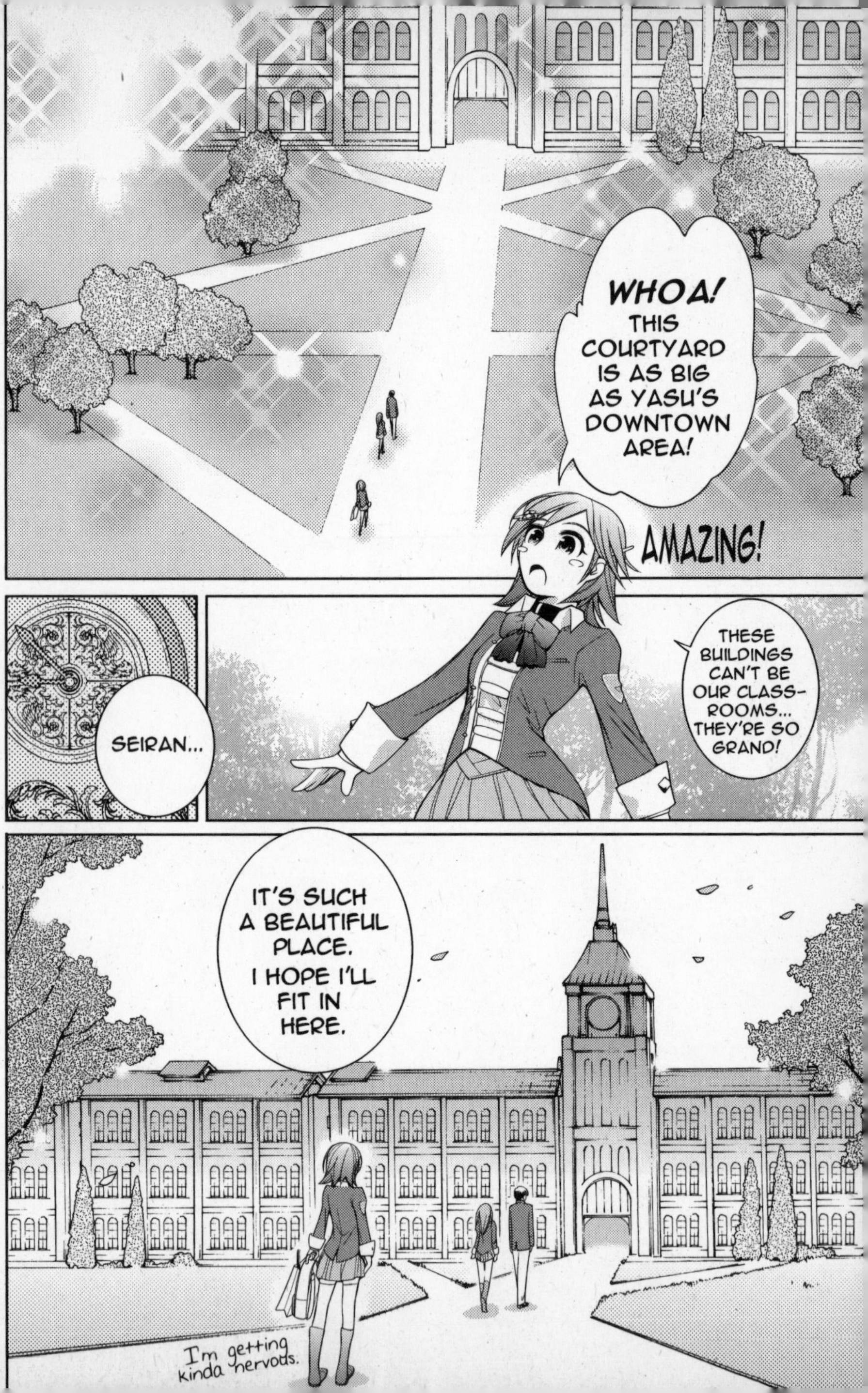
WHOA! THIS COURTYARD IS AS BIG AS YASU'S DOWNTOWN AREA!
AMAZING!
THESE BUILDINGS CAN'T BE OUR CLASS-ROOMS... THEY'RE SO GRAND!
SEIRAN...
IT'S SUCH A BEAUTIFUL PLACE. I HOPE I'LL FIT IN HERE.
I'm getting kinda nervous.

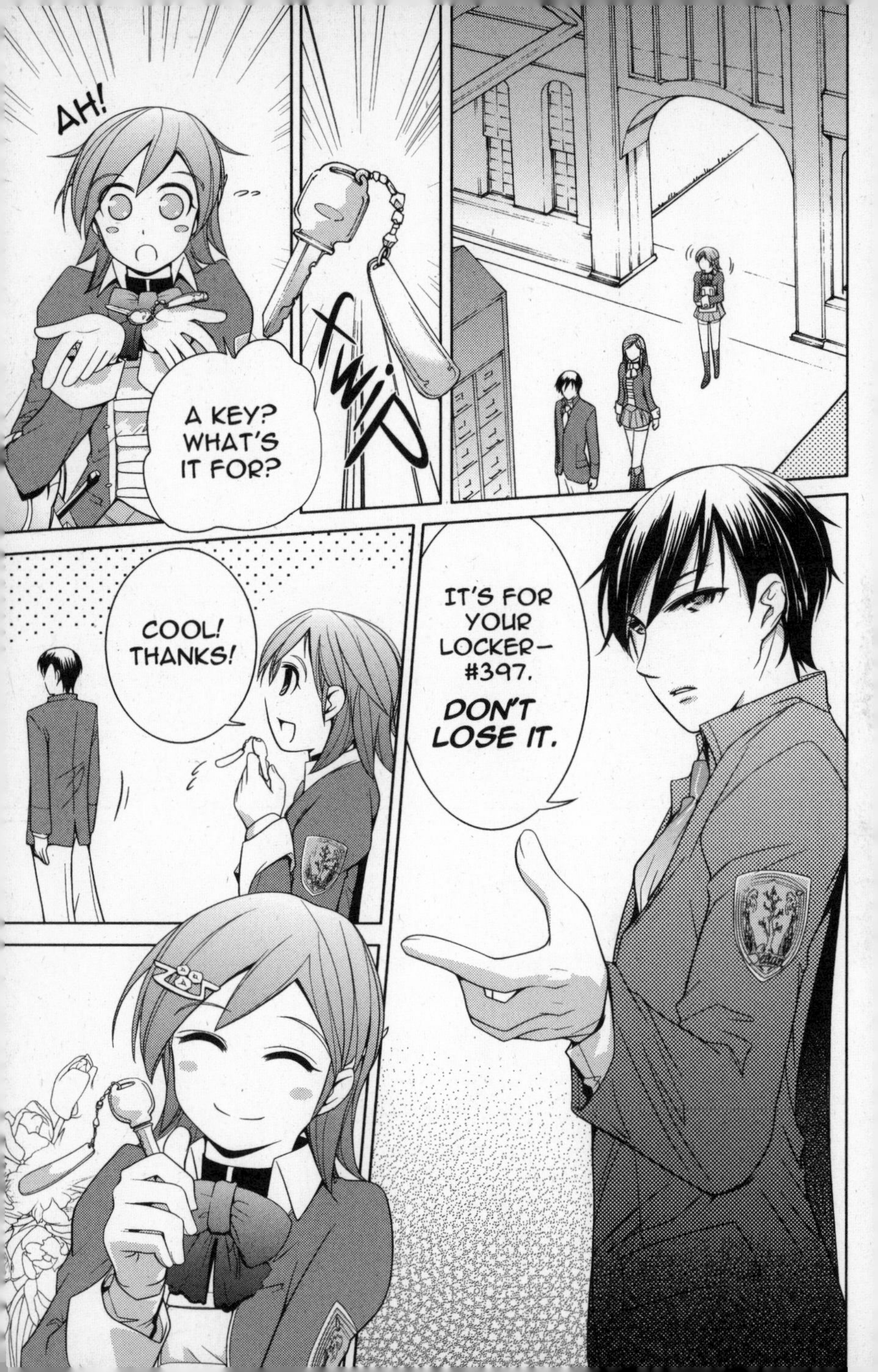
TWIP
AH!
A KEY? WHAT'S IT FOR?
IT'S FOR YOUR LOCKER—#397. DON'T LOSE IT.
COOL! THANKS!

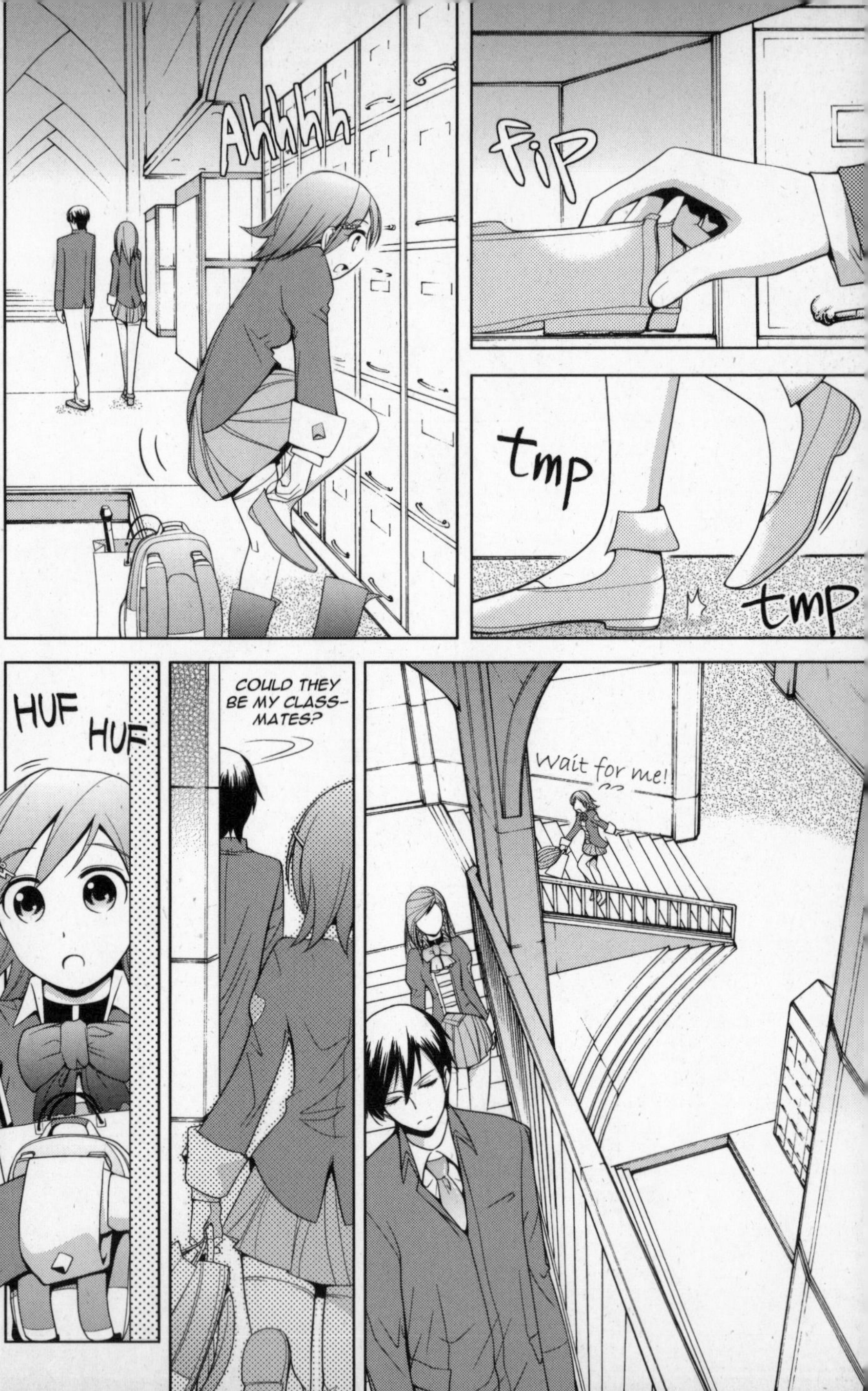

fip
tmp
tmp
Ahhhh
Wait for me!
COULD THEY BE MY CLASS-MATES?
HUF HUF

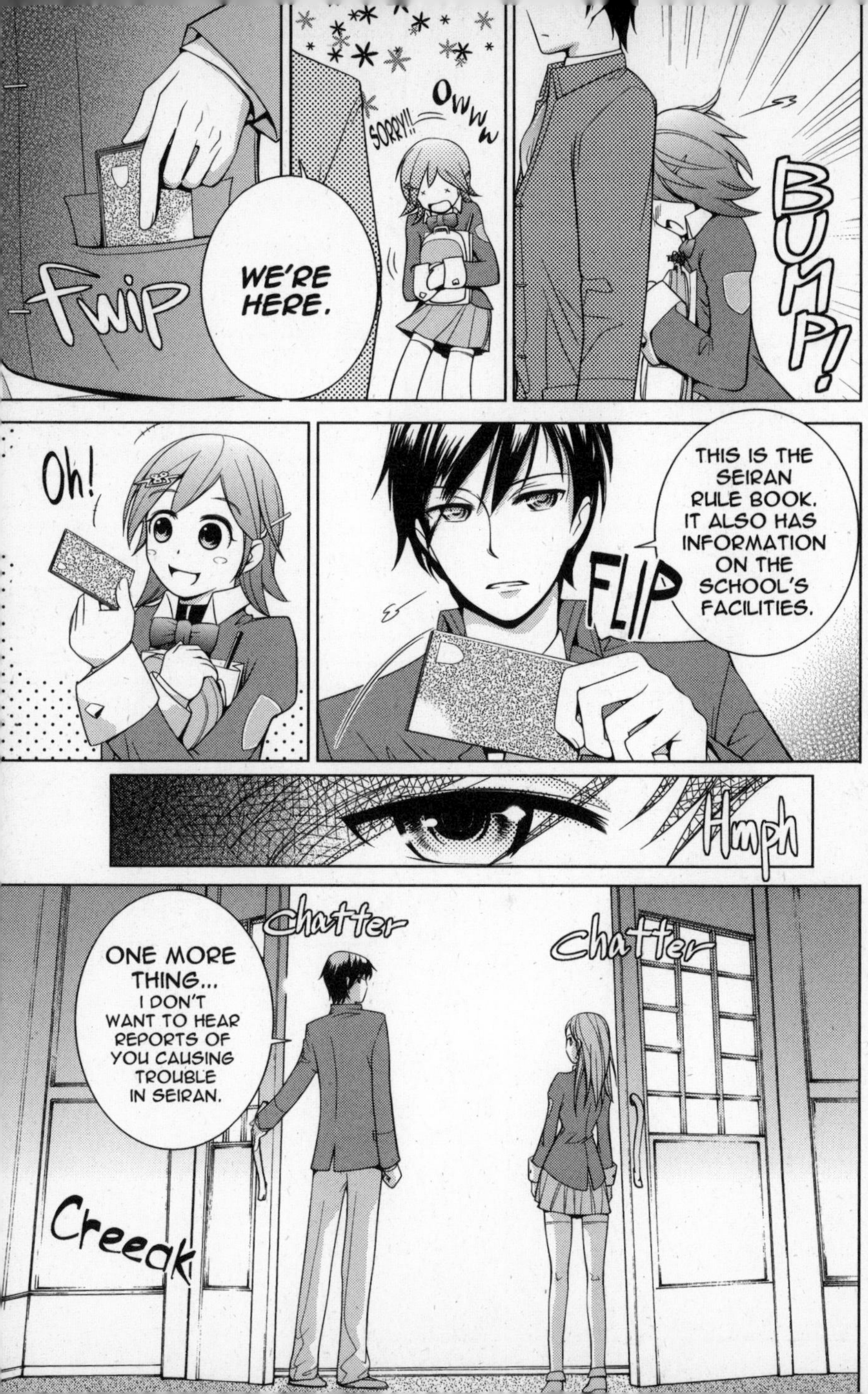
BUMP!
Owww
SORRY!!
WE'RE HERE.
Fwip
THIS IS THE SEIRAN RULE BOOK. IT ALSO HAS INFORMATION ON THE SCHOOL'S FACILITIES.
FLIP
Oh!
Hmph
Chatter
Chatter
ONE MORE THING... I DON'T WANT TO HEAR REPORTS OF YOU CAUSING TROUBLE IN SEIRAN.
Creeak

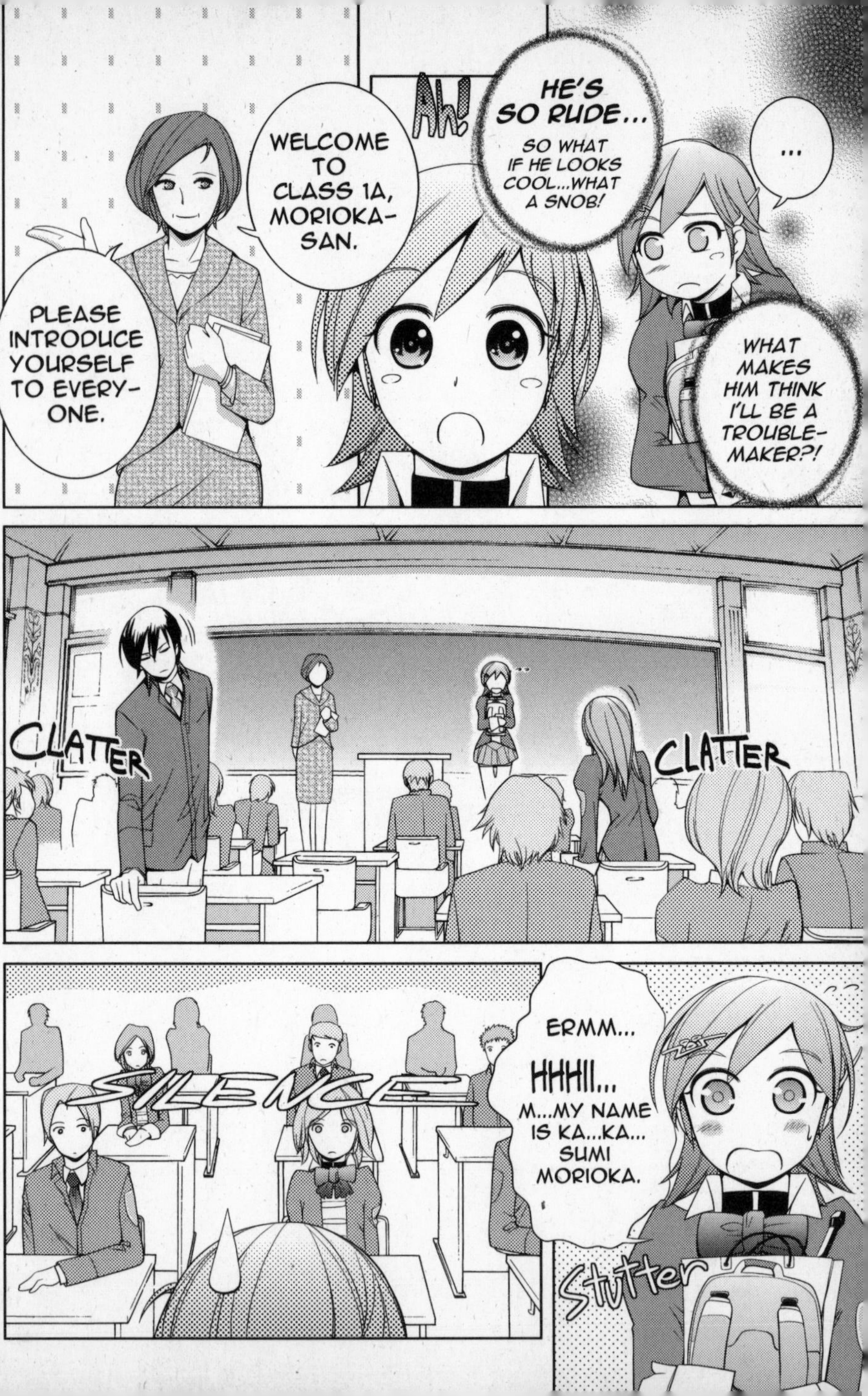
...
HE'S SO RUDE...
SO WHAT IF HE LOOKS COOL...WHAT A SNOB!
Ah!
WHAT MAKES HIM THINK I'LL BE A TROUBLE-MAKER?!
WELCOME TO CLASS 1A, MORIOKA-SAN.
PLEASE INTRODUCE YOURSELF TO EVERY-ONE.
CLATTER
CLATTER
ERMM...
HHHII...
M...MY NAME IS KA...KA... SUMI MORIOKA.
Stutter
SILENCE

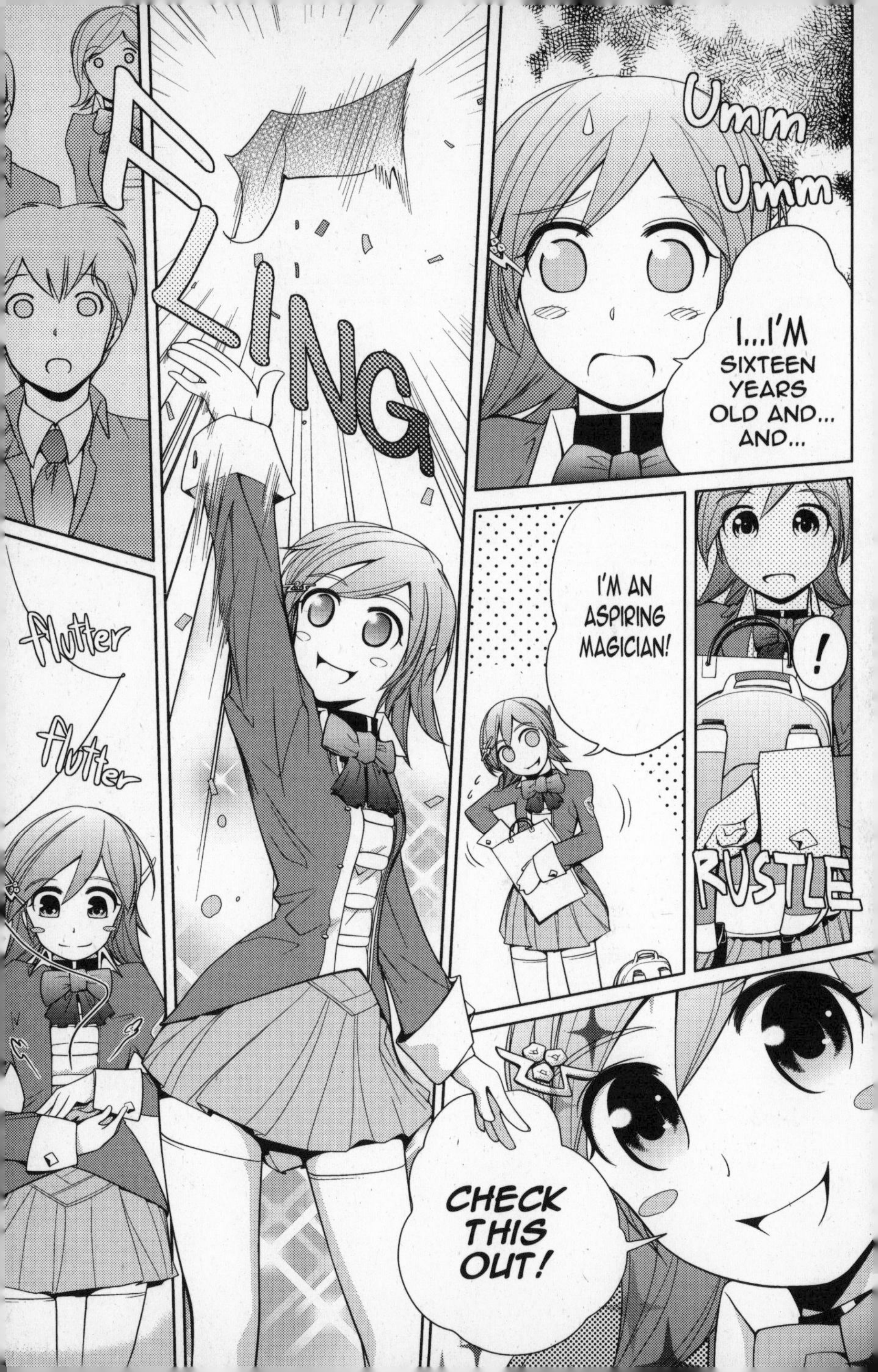
Umm
Umm
I...I'M SIXTEEN YEARS OLD AND... AND...
!
RUSTLE
I'M AN ASPIRING MAGICIAN!
CHECK THIS OUT!
ZING
flutter
flutter

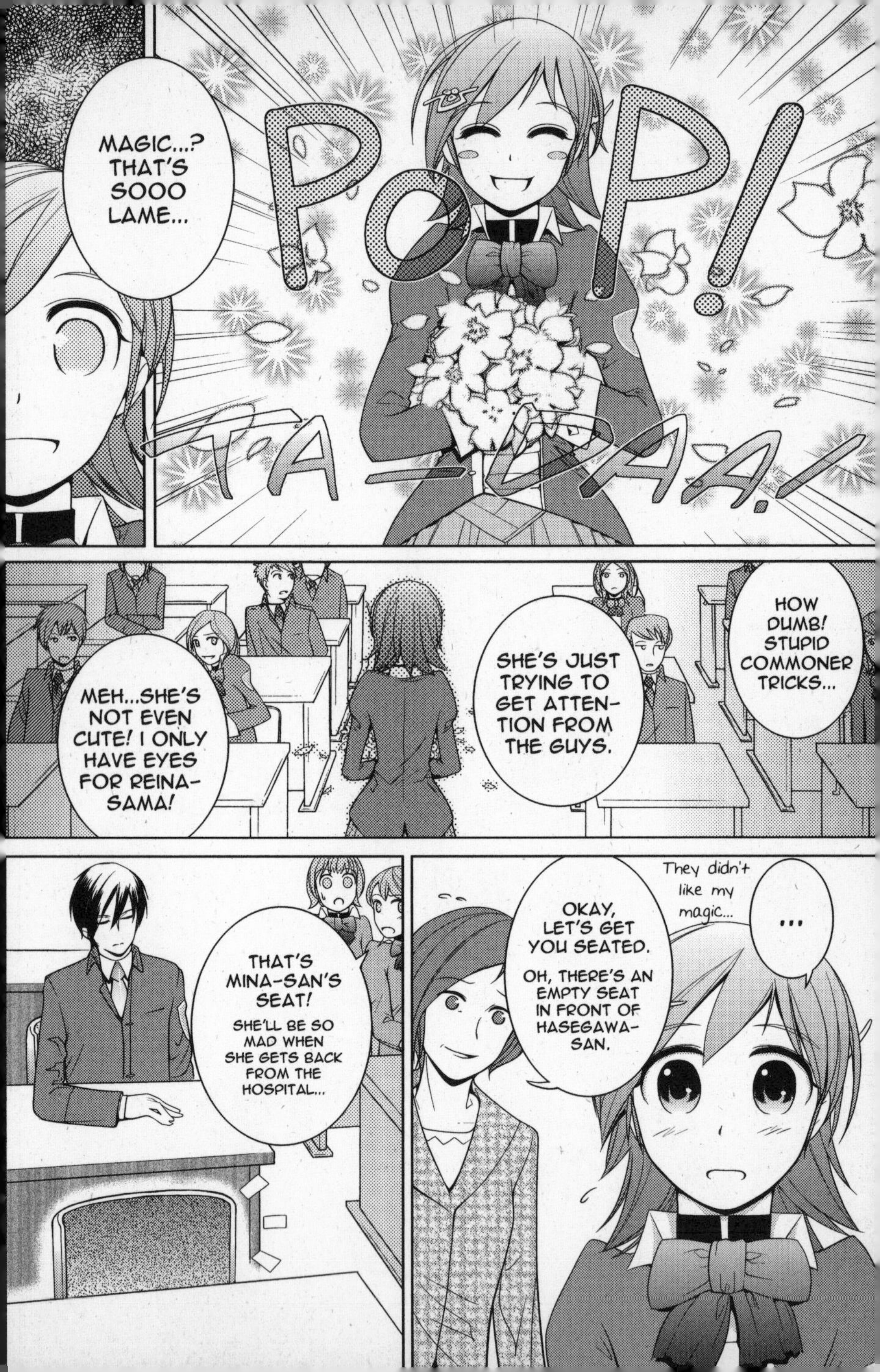
POP!
MAGIC...? THAT'S SOOO LAME...
TA-DAA!
HOW DUMB! STUPID COMMONER TRICKS...
SHE'S JUST TRYING TO GET ATTEN-TION FROM THE GUYS.
MEH...SHE'S NOT EVEN CUTE! I ONLY HAVE EYES FOR REINA-SAMA!
They didn't like my magic...
...
OKAY, LET'S GET YOU SEATED.
OH, THERE'S AN EMPTY SEAT IN FRONT OF HASEGAWA-SAN.
THAT'S MINA-SAN'S SEAT!
SHE'LL BE SO MAD WHEN SHE GETS BACK FROM THE HOSPITAL...

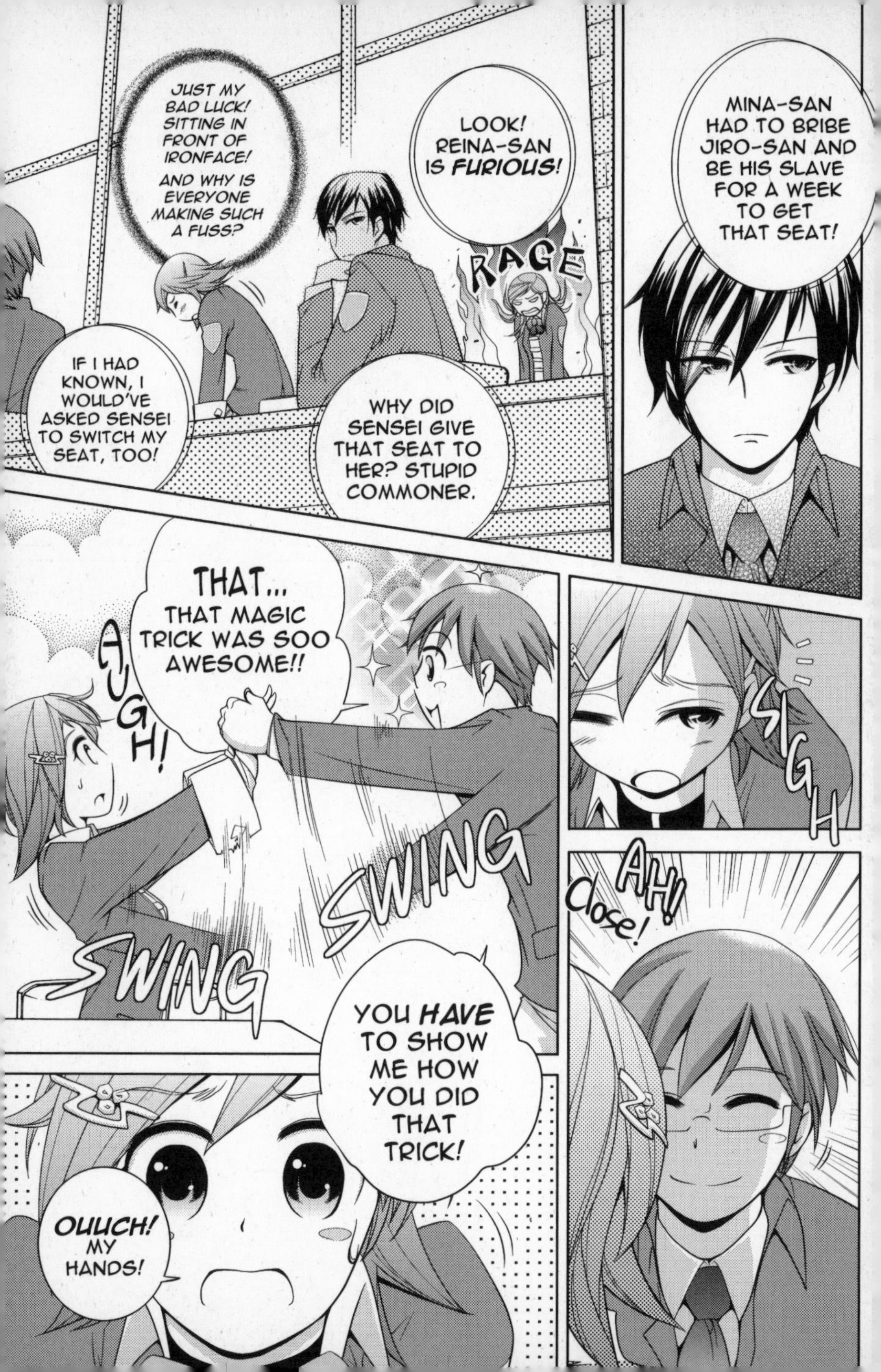
MINA-SAN HAD TO BRIBE JIRO-SAN AND BE HIS SLAVE FOR A WEEK TO GET THAT SEAT!
LOOK! REINA-SAN IS ***FURIOUS***!
JUST MY BAD LUCK! SITTING IN FRONT OF IRONFACE!
AND WHY IS EVERYONE MAKING SUCH A FUSS?
RAGE
WHY DID SENSEI GIVE THAT SEAT TO HER? STUPID COMMONER.
IF I HAD KNOWN, I WOULD'VE ASKED SENSEI TO SWITCH MY SEAT, TOO!
SIGH
AH!
Close!
THAT... THAT MAGIC TRICK WAS SOO AWESOME!!
AUGH!
SWING
SWING
YOU ***HAVE*** TO SHOW ME HOW YOU DID THAT TRICK!
OUUCH! MY HANDS!

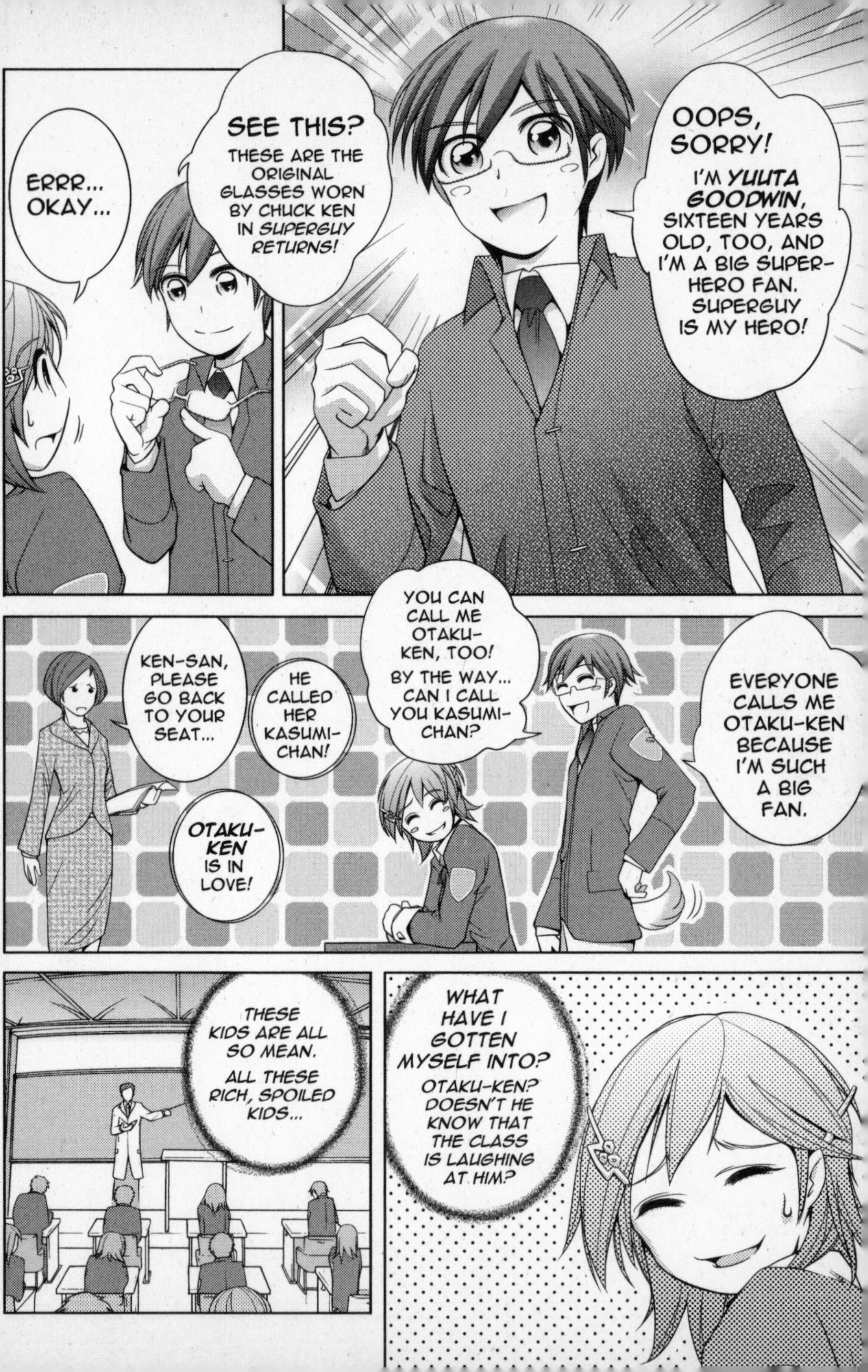
OOPS, SORRY!
I'M YUUTA GOODWIN, SIXTEEN YEARS OLD, TOO, AND I'M A BIG SUPER-HERO FAN. SUPERGUY IS MY HERO!
SEE THIS?
THESE ARE THE ORIGINAL GLASSES WORN BY CHUCK KEN IN SUPERGUY RETURNS!
ERRR... OKAY...
EVERYONE CALLS ME OTAKU-KEN BECAUSE I'M SUCH A BIG FAN.
YOU CAN CALL ME OTAKU-KEN, TOO!
BY THE WAY... CAN I CALL YOU KASUMI-CHAN?
HE CALLED HER KASUMI-CHAN!
KEN-SAN, PLEASE GO BACK TO YOUR SEAT...
OTAKU-KEN IS IN LOVE!
WHAT HAVE I GOTTEN MYSELF INTO?
OTAKU-KEN? DOESN'T HE KNOW THAT THE CLASS IS LAUGHING AT HIM?
THESE KIDS ARE ALL SO MEAN.
ALL THESE RICH, SPOILED KIDS...

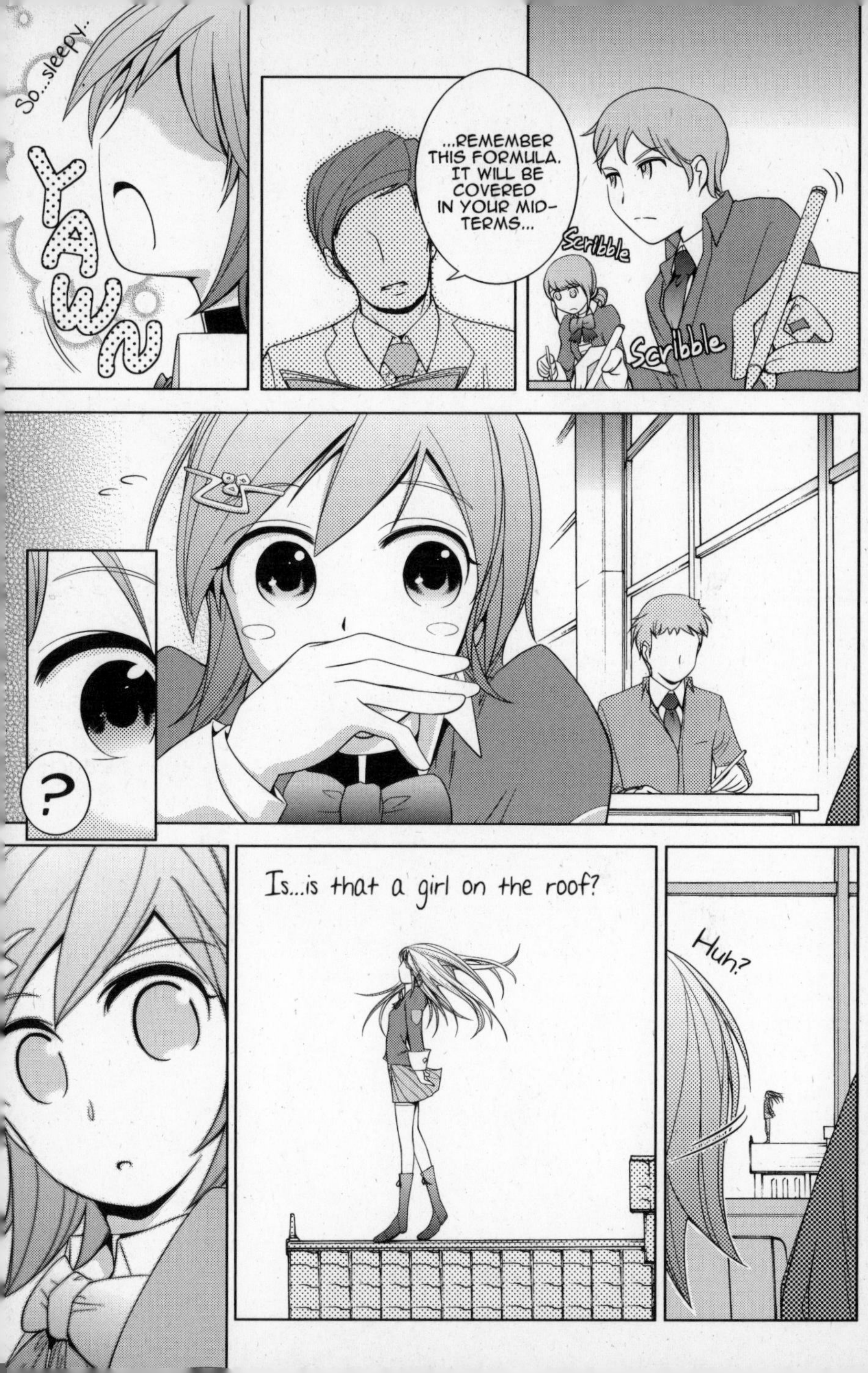
Scribble
Scribble
...REMEMBER THIS FORMULA. IT WILL BE COVERED IN YOUR MID-TERMS...
So...sleepy...
YAWN
?
Huh?
Is...is that a girl on the roof?

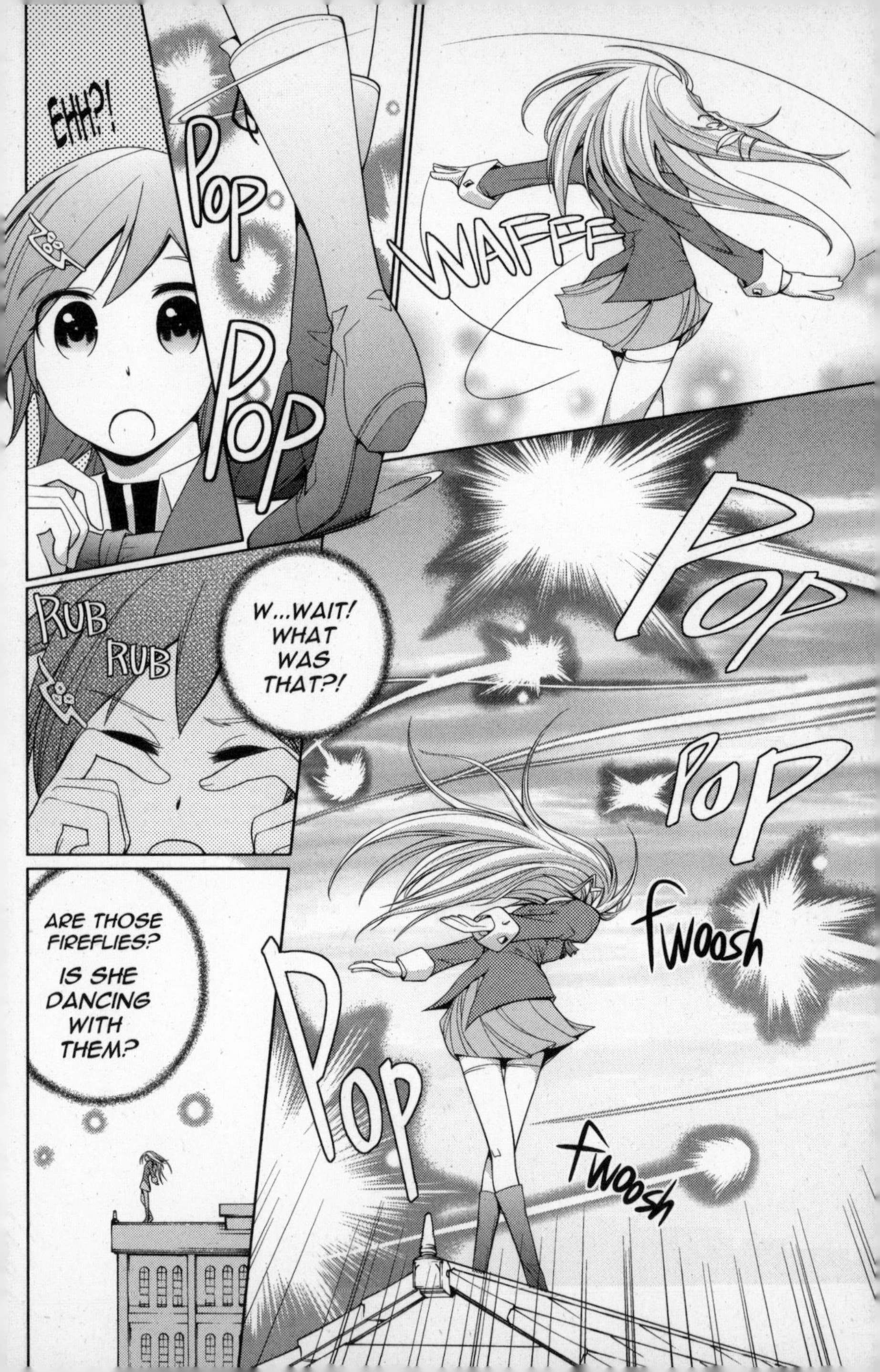
WAFFF
EHH?!
Pop
Pop
Pop
Pop
Pop
fwoosh
Pop
fwoosh
RUB
RUB
W...WAIT! WHAT WAS THAT?!
ARE THOSE FIREFLIES?
IS SHE DANCING WITH THEM?

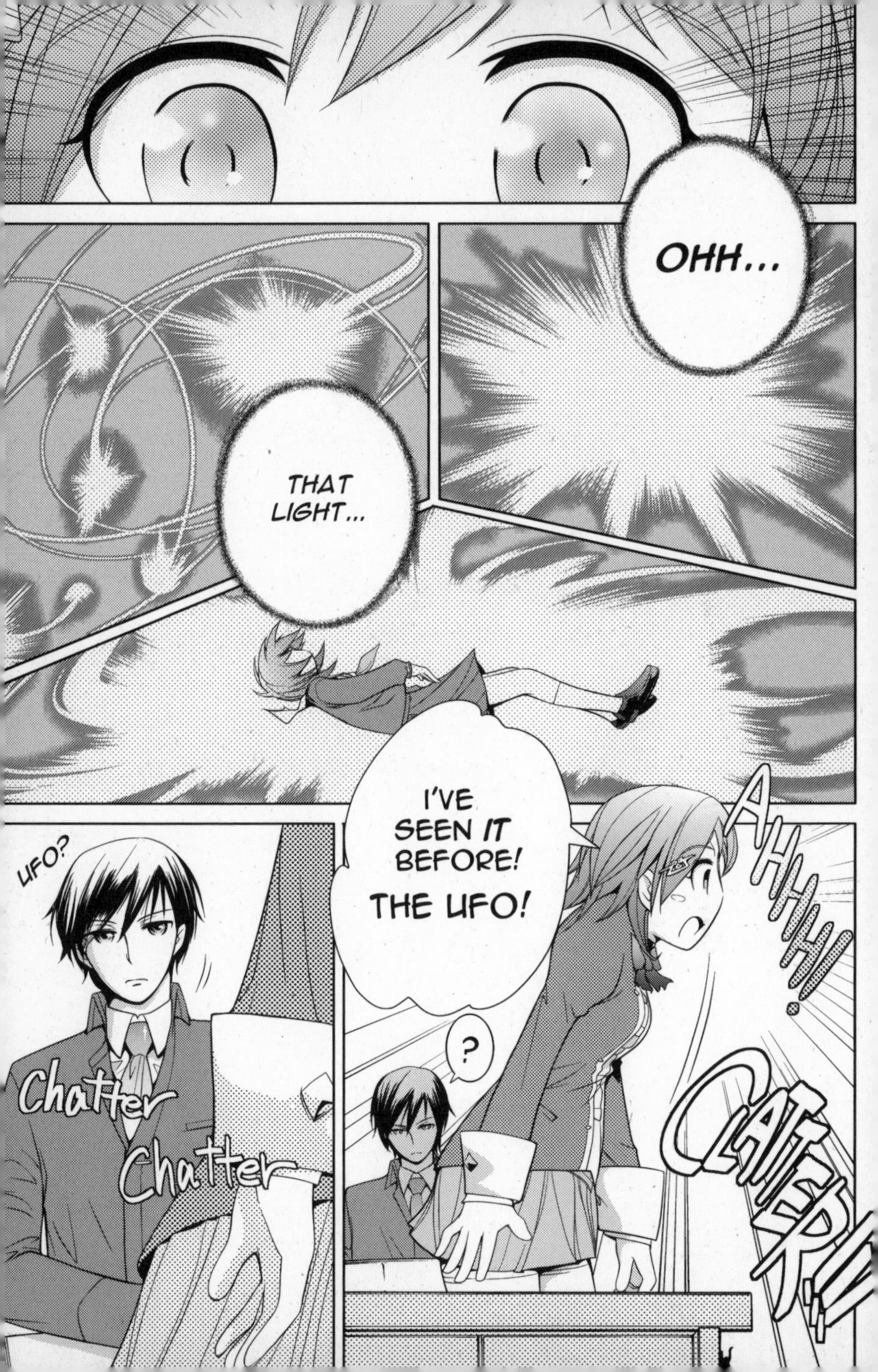
OHH...
THAT LIGHT...
AHHHH!
I'VE SEEN *IT* BEFORE! THE UFO!
?
CLATTER!!
UFO?
Chatter
Chatter

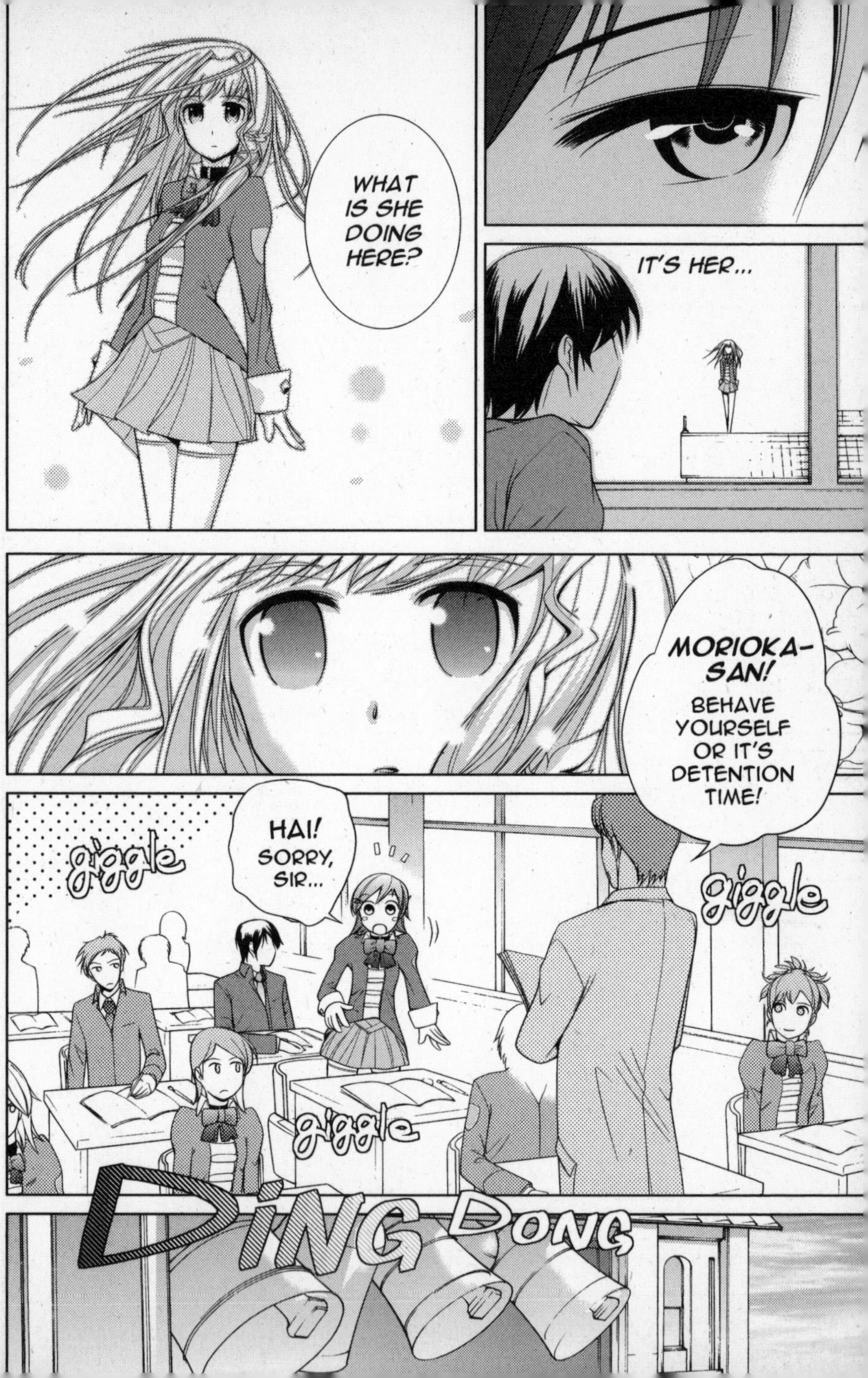
IT'S HER...
WHAT IS SHE DOING HERE?
MORIOKA-SAN! BEHAVE YOURSELF OR IT'S DETENTION TIME!
giggle
HAI! SORRY, SIR...
giggle
giggle
DING DONG

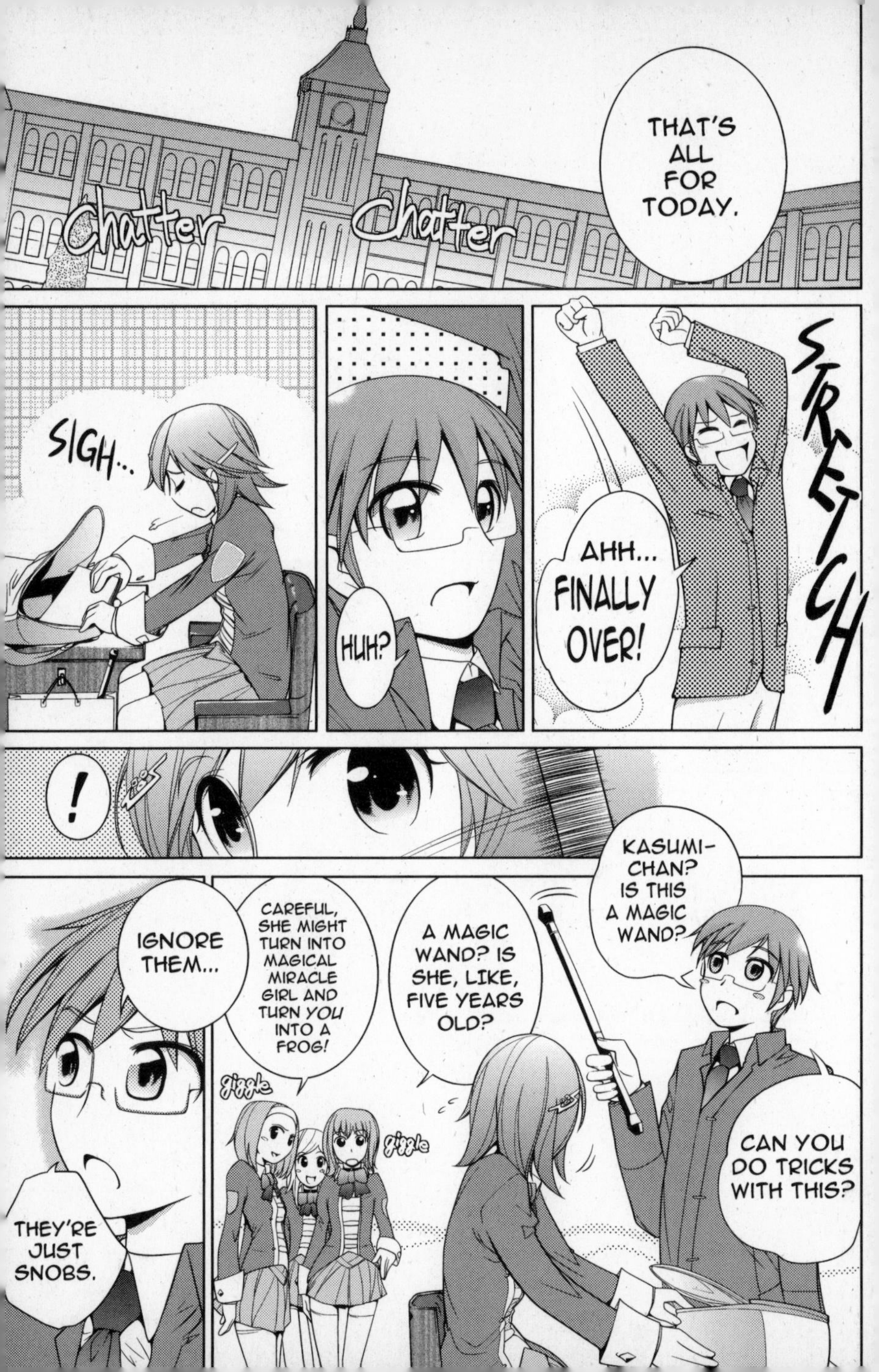
THAT'S ALL FOR TODAY.
Chatter Chatter
STRETCH
AHH... FINALLY OVER!
HUH?
SIGH...
!
KASUMI-CHAN? IS THIS A MAGIC WAND?
CAN YOU DO TRICKS WITH THIS?
A MAGIC WAND? IS SHE, LIKE, FIVE YEARS OLD?
CAREFUL, SHE MIGHT TURN INTO MAGICAL MIRACLE GIRL AND TURN *YOU* INTO A FROG!
giggle
giggle
IGNORE THEM...
THEY'RE JUST SNOBS.

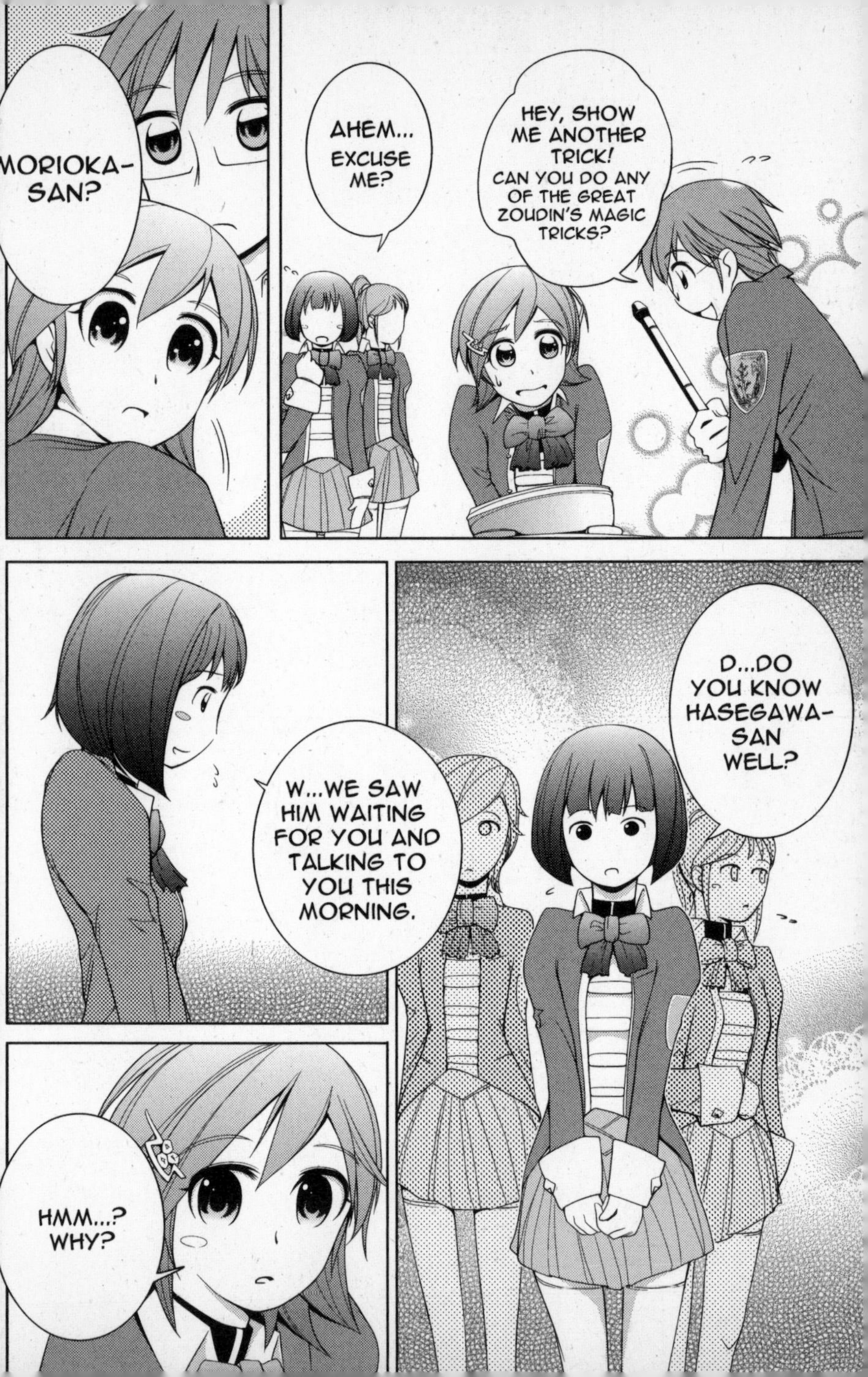
HEY, SHOW ME ANOTHER TRICK! CAN YOU DO ANY OF THE GREAT ZOUDIN'S MAGIC TRICKS?
AHEM... EXCUSE ME?
MORIOKA-SAN?
D...DO YOU KNOW HASEGAWA-SAN WELL?
W...WE SAW HIM WAITING FOR YOU AND TALKING TO YOU THIS MORNING.
HMM...? WHY?

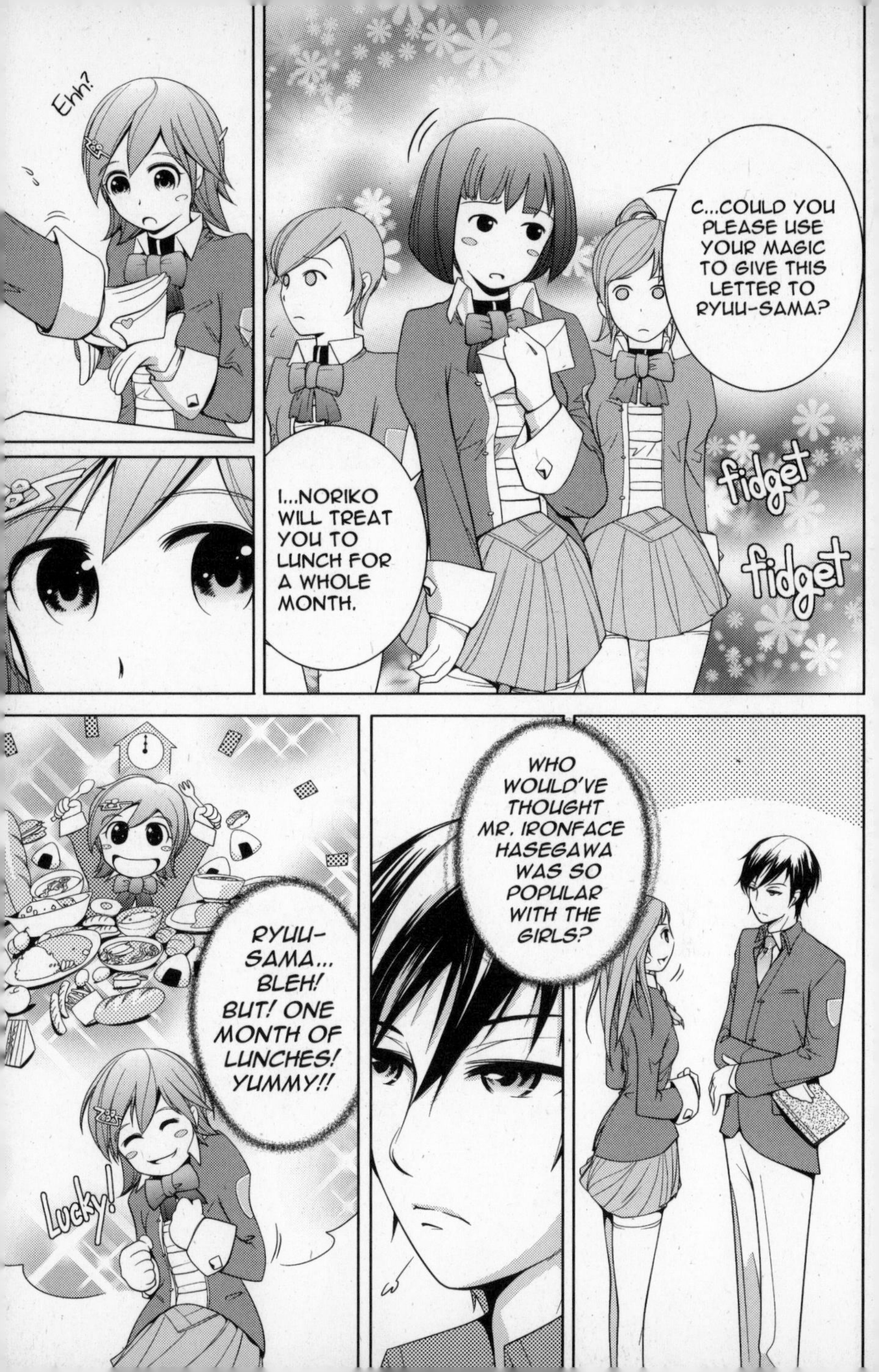
C...COULD YOU PLEASE USE YOUR MAGIC TO GIVE THIS LETTER TO RYUU-SAMA?
fidget
fidget
I...NORIKO WILL TREAT YOU TO LUNCH FOR A WHOLE MONTH.
Ehh?
WHO WOULD'VE THOUGHT MR. IRONFACE HASEGAWA WAS SO POPULAR WITH THE GIRLS?
RYUU-SAMA... BLEH! BUT! ONE MONTH OF LUNCHES! YUMMY!!
Lucky!

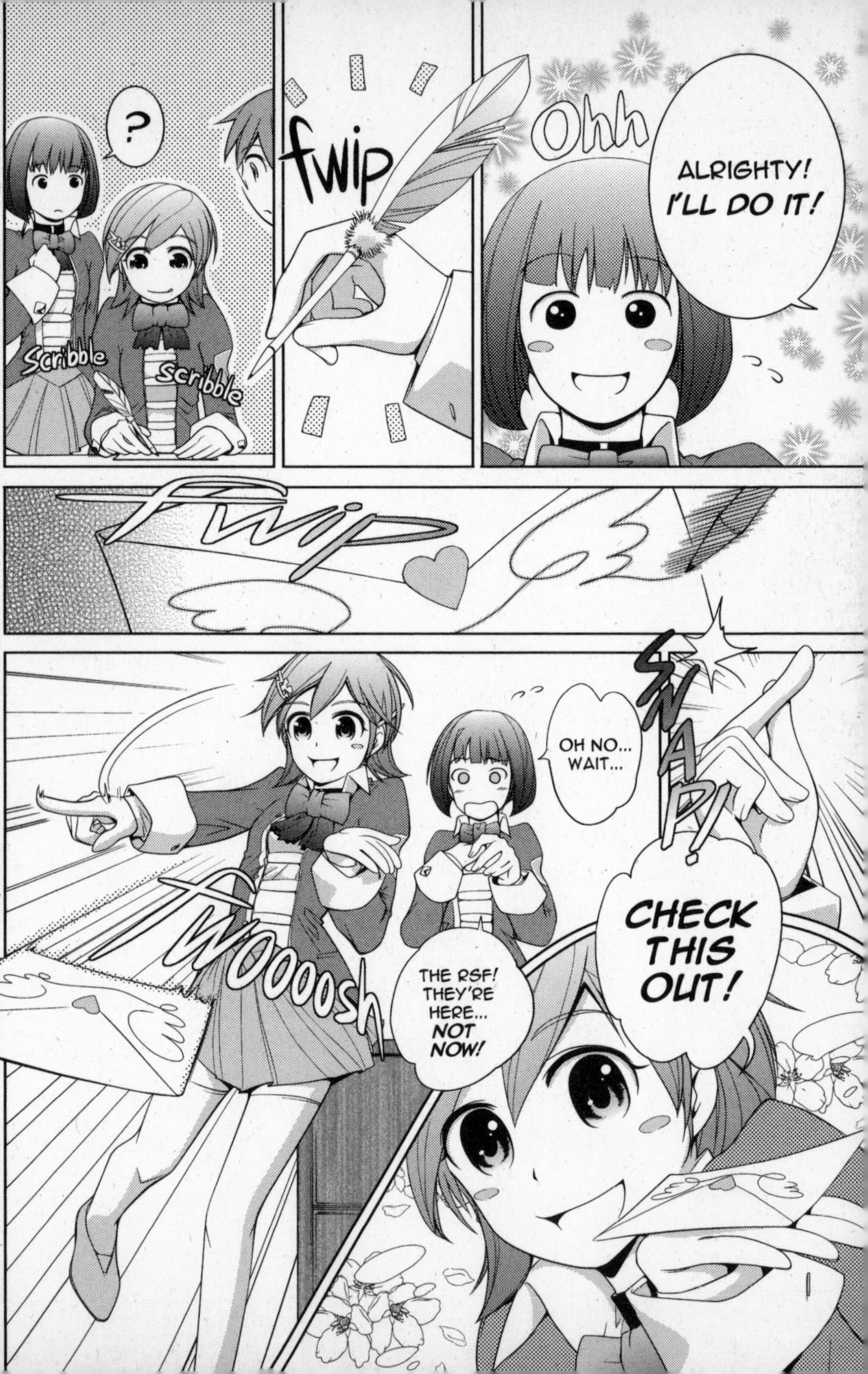

Ohh
ALRIGHTY! I'LL DO IT!
fwip
?
Scribble
scribble
fwip
SNAP!
CHECK THIS OUT!
OH NO... WAIT...
THE RSF! THEY'RE HERE... NOT NOW!
fWOOOosh

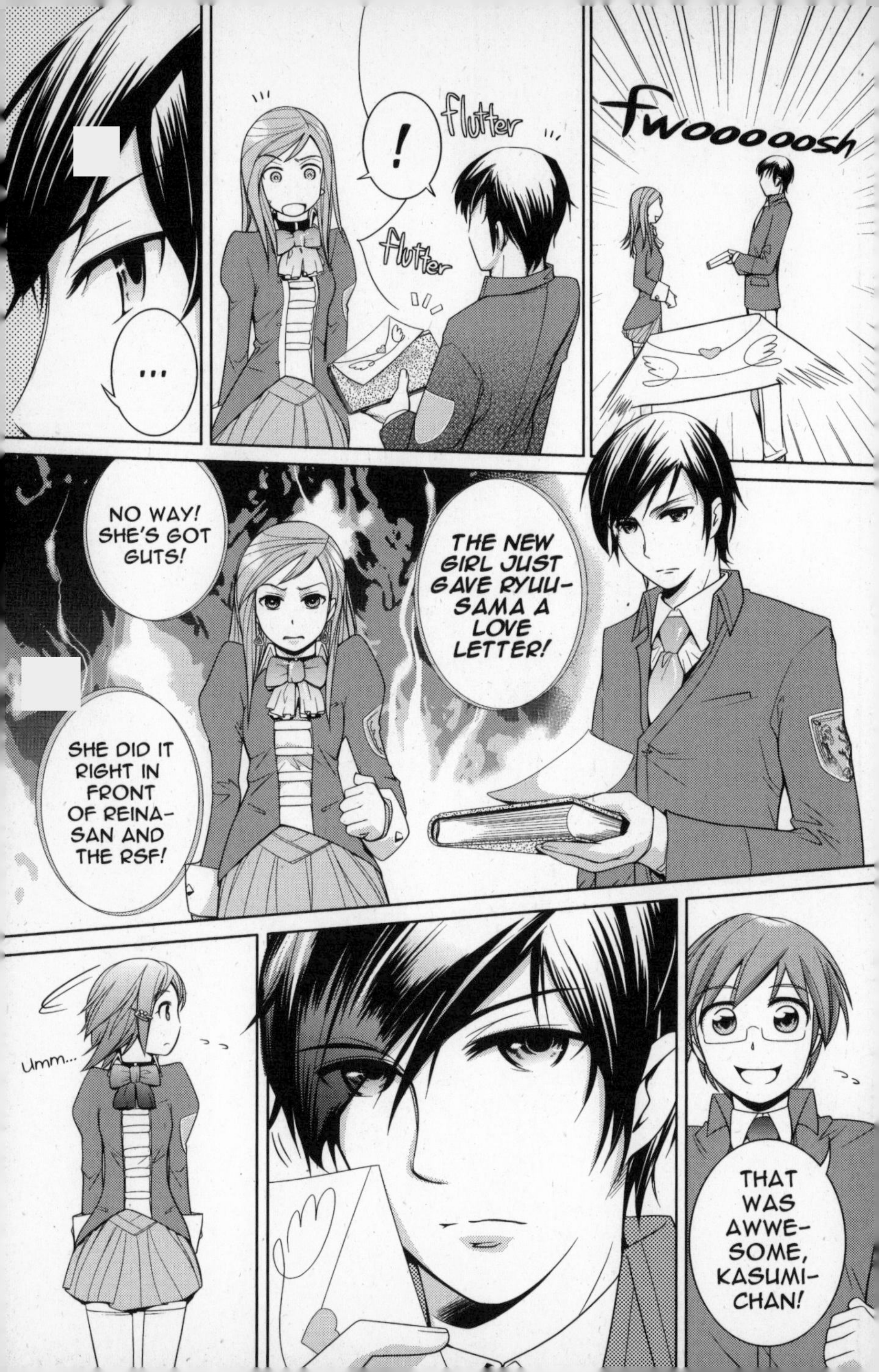
fwoooooosh
flutter
!
flutter
...
THE NEW GIRL JUST GAVE RYUU-SAMA A LOVE LETTER!
NO WAY! SHE'S GOT GUTS!
SHE DID IT RIGHT IN FRONT OF REINA-SAN AND THE RSF!
THAT WAS AWWE-SOME, KASUMI-CHAN!
Umm...

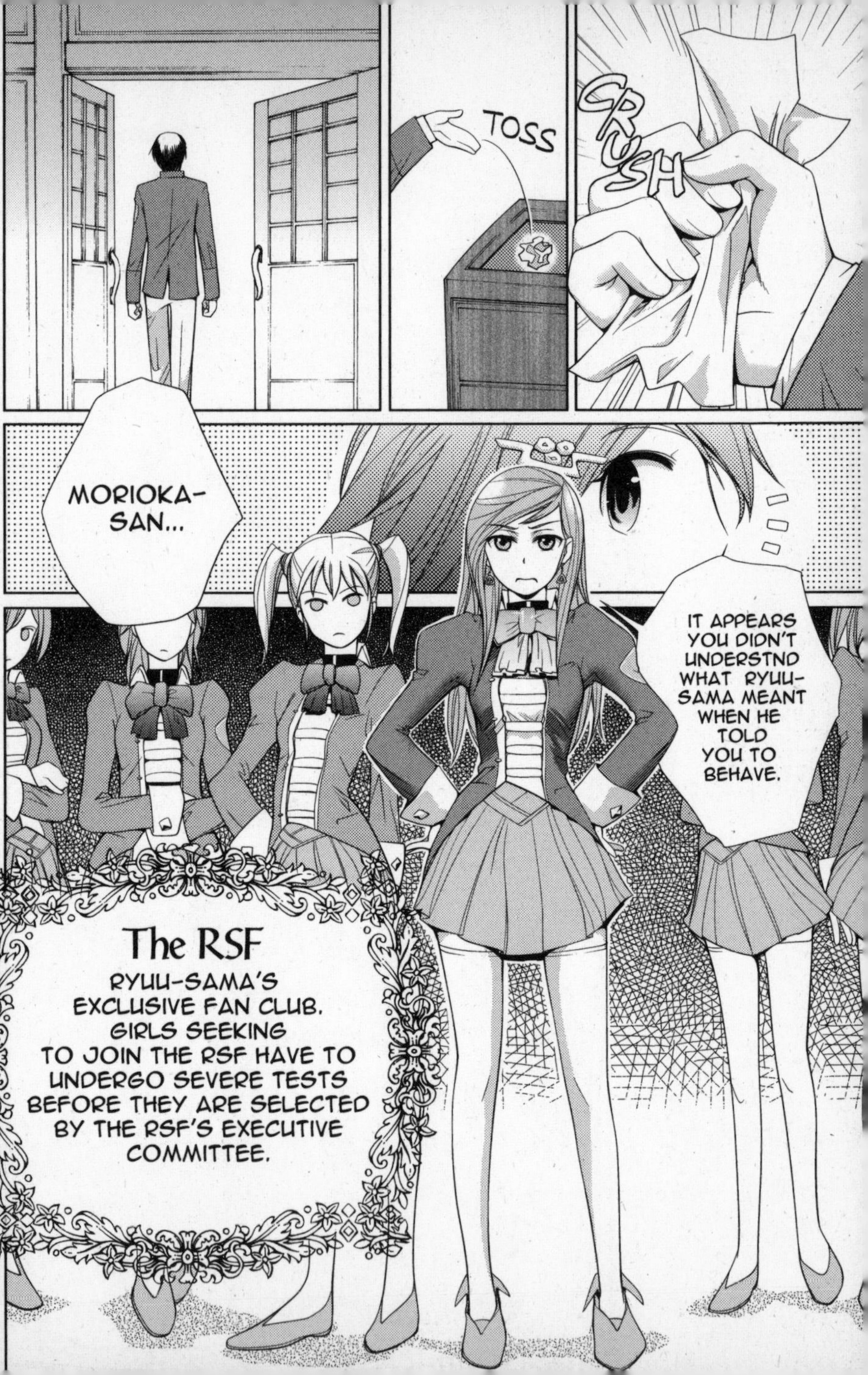
CRUSH
TOSS
MORIOKA-SAN...
IT APPEARS YOU DIDN'T UNDERSTND WHAT RYUU-SAMA MEANT WHEN HE TOLD YOU TO BEHAVE.
The RSF
RYUU-SAMA'S EXCLUSIVE FAN CLUB. GIRLS SEEKING TO JOIN THE RSF HAVE TO UNDERGO SEVERE TESTS BEFORE THEY ARE SELECTED BY THE RSF'S EXECUTIVE COMMITTEE.

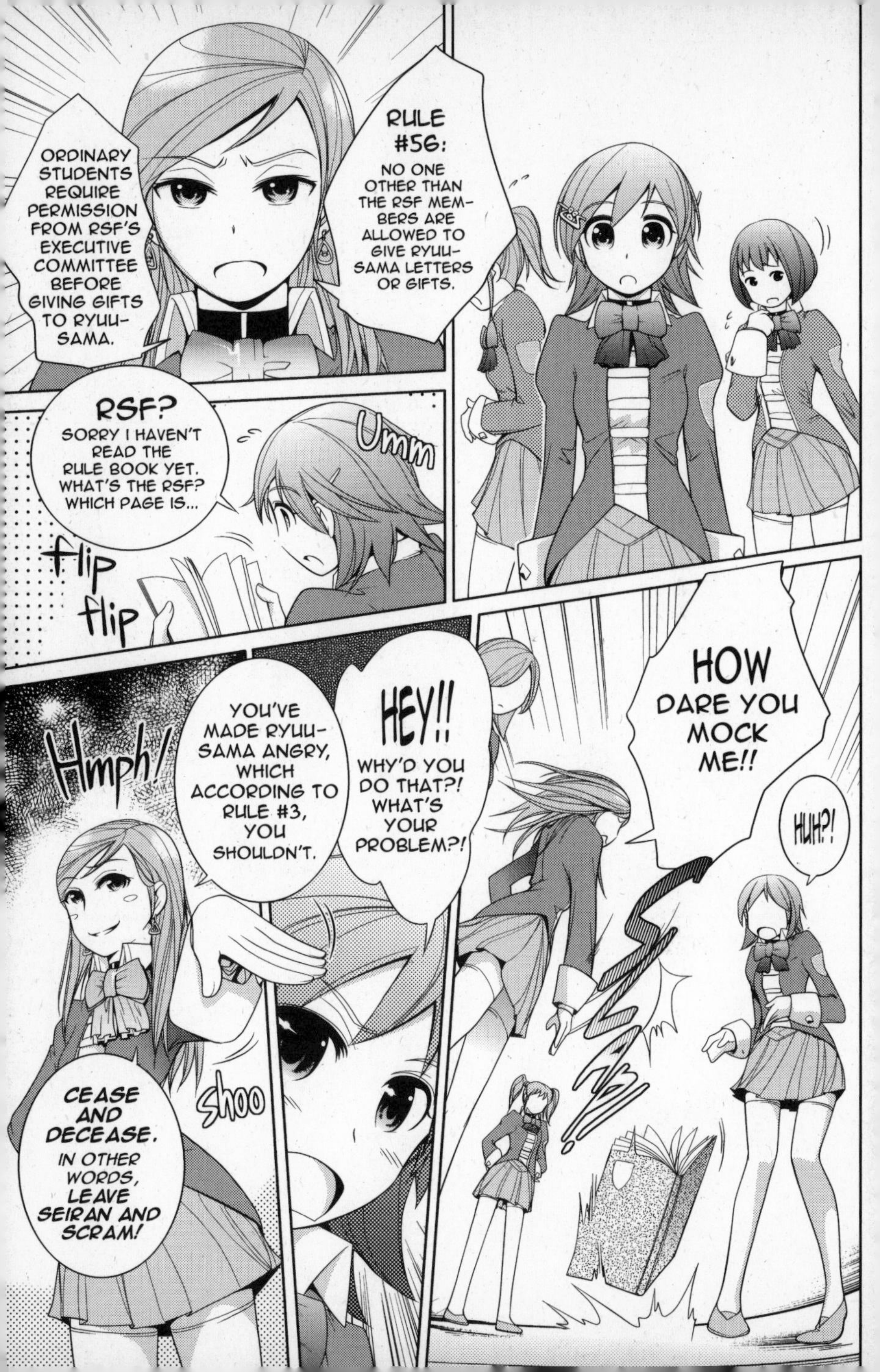
RULE #56: NO ONE OTHER THAN THE RSF MEMBERS ARE ALLOWED TO GIVE RYUU-SAMA LETTERS OR GIFTS.
ORDINARY STUDENTS REQUIRE PERMISSION FROM RSF'S EXECUTIVE COMMITTEE BEFORE GIVING GIFTS TO RYUU-SAMA.
Umm
RSF? SORRY I HAVEN'T READ THE RULE BOOK YET. WHAT'S THE RSF? WHICH PAGE IS...
flip flip
HOW DARE YOU MOCK ME!!
HUH?!
HEY!! WHY'D YOU DO THAT?! WHAT'S YOUR PROBLEM?!
YOU'VE MADE RYUU-SAMA ANGRY, WHICH ACCORDING TO RULE #3, YOU SHOULDN'T.
Hmph!
shoo
CEASE AND DECEASE. IN OTHER WORDS, LEAVE SEIRAN AND SCRAM!

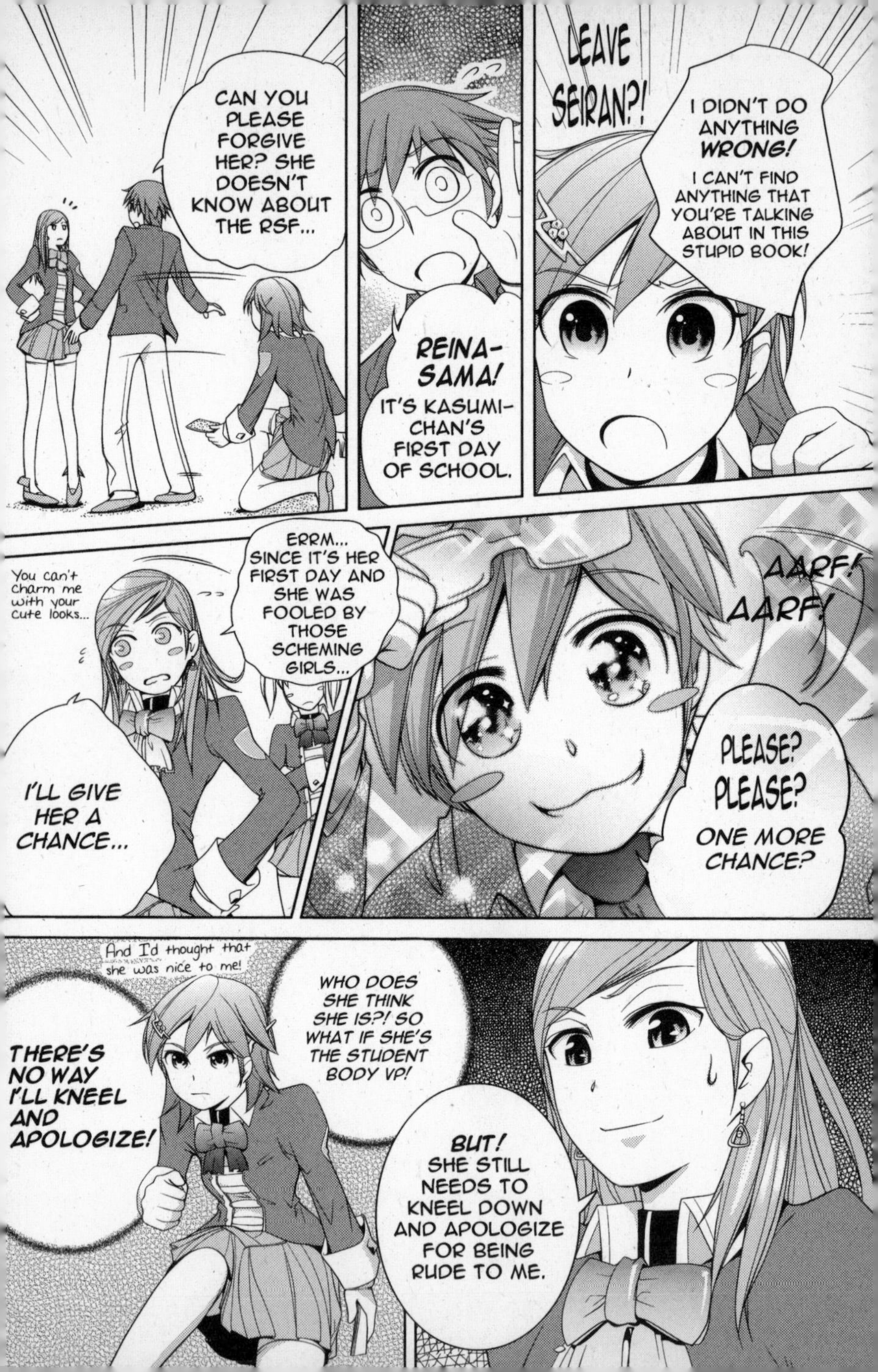
LEAVE SEIRAN?!
I DIDN'T DO ANYTHING WRONG! I CAN'T FIND ANYTHING THAT YOU'RE TALKING ABOUT IN THIS STUPID BOOK!
REINA-SAMA! IT'S KASUMI-CHAN'S FIRST DAY OF SCHOOL.
CAN YOU PLEASE FORGIVE HER? SHE DOESN'T KNOW ABOUT THE RSF...
AARF! AARF!
PLEASE? PLEASE? ONE MORE CHANCE?
ERRM... SINCE IT'S HER FIRST DAY AND SHE WAS FOOLED BY THOSE SCHEMING GIRLS...
You can't charm me with your cute looks...
I'LL GIVE HER A CHANCE...
BUT! SHE STILL NEEDS TO KNEEL DOWN AND APOLOGIZE FOR BEING RUDE TO ME.
WHO DOES SHE THINK SHE IS?! SO WHAT IF SHE'S THE STUDENT BODY VP!
And I'd thought that she was nice to me!
THERE'S NO WAY I'LL KNEEL AND APOLOGIZE!

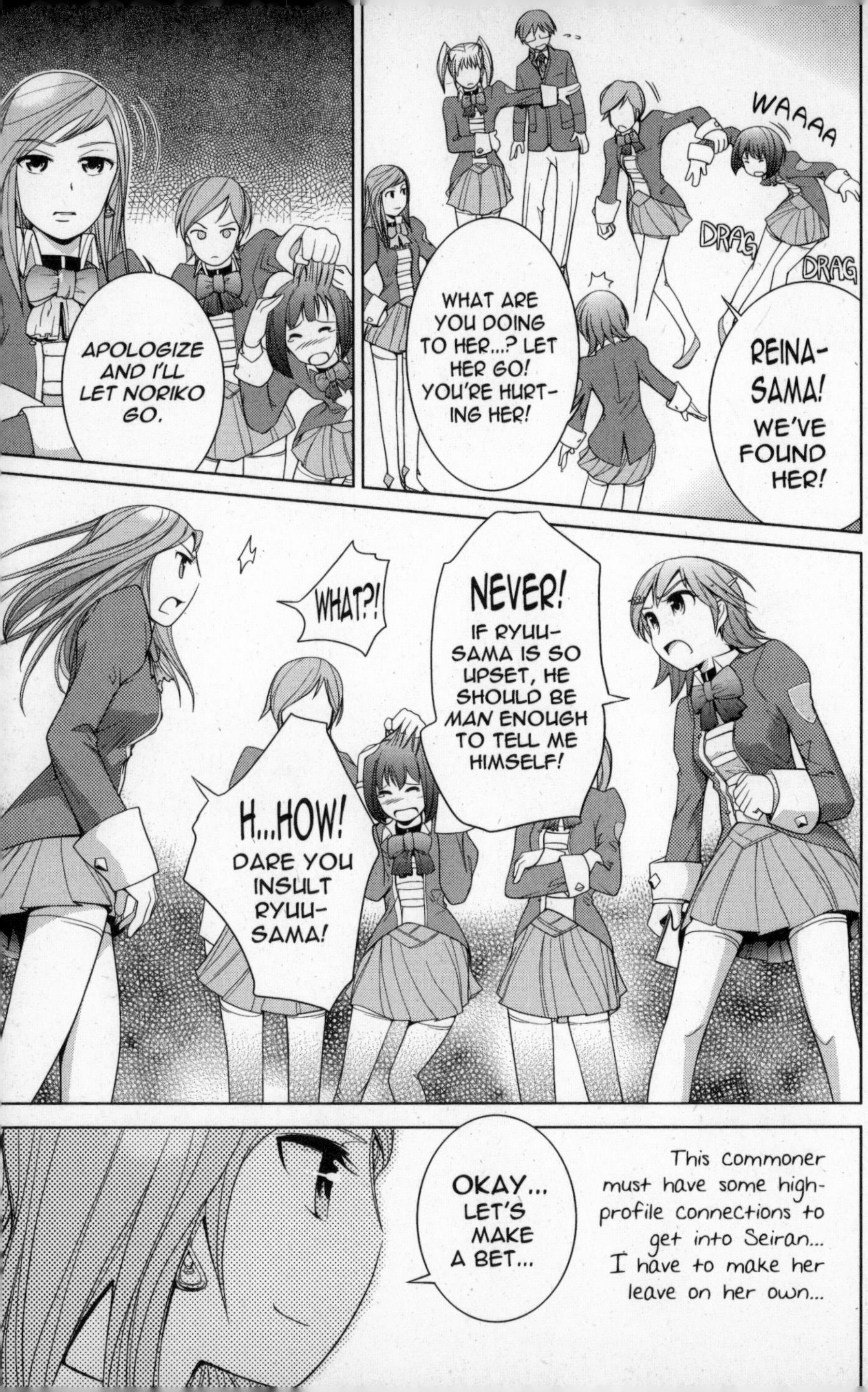
WAAAA
DRAG
DRAG
REINA-SAMA! WE'VE FOUND HER!
WHAT ARE YOU DOING TO HER...? LET HER GO! YOU'RE HURT-ING HER!
APOLOGIZE AND I'LL LET NORIKO GO.
NEVER! IF RYUU-SAMA IS SO UPSET, HE SHOULD BE MAN ENOUGH TO TELL ME HIMSELF!
WHAT?!
H...HOW! DARE YOU INSULT RYUU-SAMA!
This commoner must have some high-profile connections to get into Seiran... I have to make her leave on her own...
OKAY... LET'S MAKE A BET...

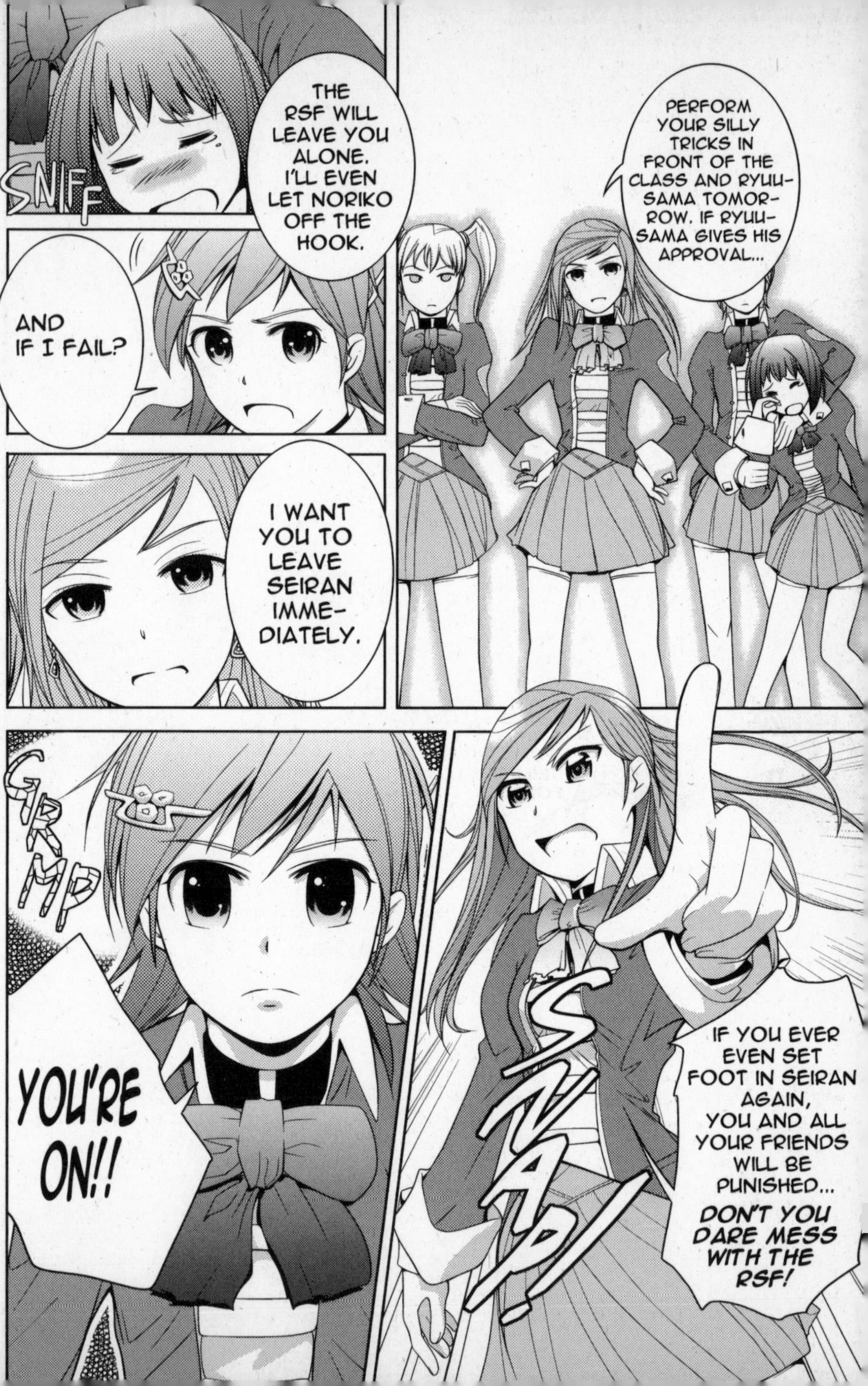
PERFORM YOUR SILLY TRICKS IN FRONT OF THE CLASS AND RYUU-SAMA TOMORROW. IF RYUU-SAMA GIVES HIS APPROVAL...
SNIFF
THE RSF WILL LEAVE YOU ALONE. I'LL EVEN LET NORIKO OFF THE HOOK.
AND IF I FAIL?
I WANT YOU TO LEAVE SEIRAN IMMEDIATELY.
IF YOU EVER EVEN SET FOOT IN SEIRAN AGAIN, YOU AND ALL YOUR FRIENDS WILL BE PUNISHED... *DON'T YOU DARE MESS WITH THE RSF!*
SNAP!
GRRMP
YOU'RE ON!!

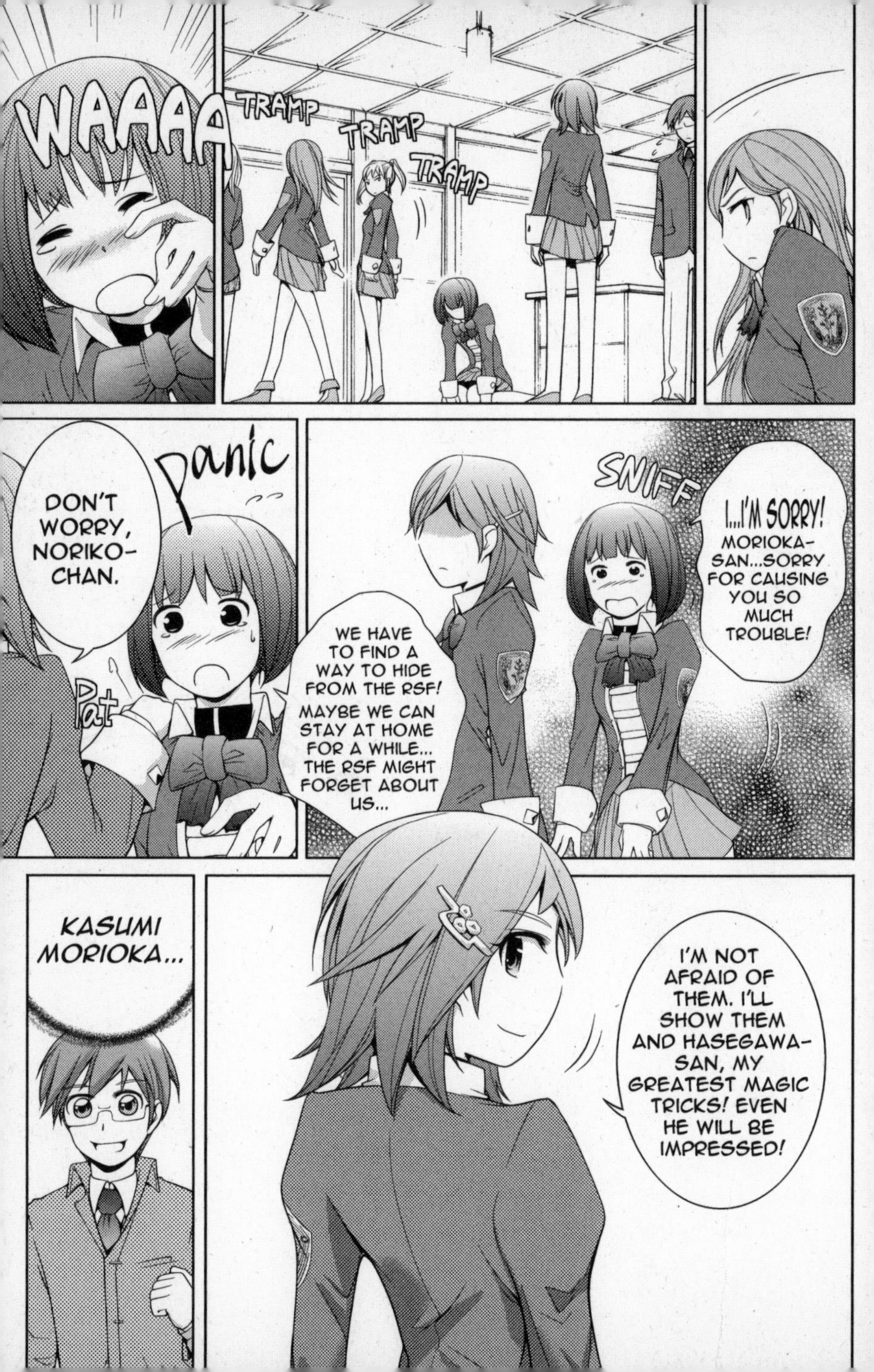
TRAMP
TRAMP
TRAMP
WAAAA
SNIFF
I...I'M SORRY! MORIOKA-SAN...SORRY FOR CAUSING YOU SO MUCH TROUBLE!
WE HAVE TO FIND A WAY TO HIDE FROM THE RSF! MAYBE WE CAN STAY AT HOME FOR A WHILE... THE RSF MIGHT FORGET ABOUT US...
panic
DON'T WORRY, NORIKO-CHAN.
Pat
I'M NOT AFRAID OF THEM. I'LL SHOW THEM AND HASEGAWA-SAN, MY GREATEST MAGIC TRICKS! EVEN HE WILL BE IMPRESSED!
KASUMI MORIOKA...

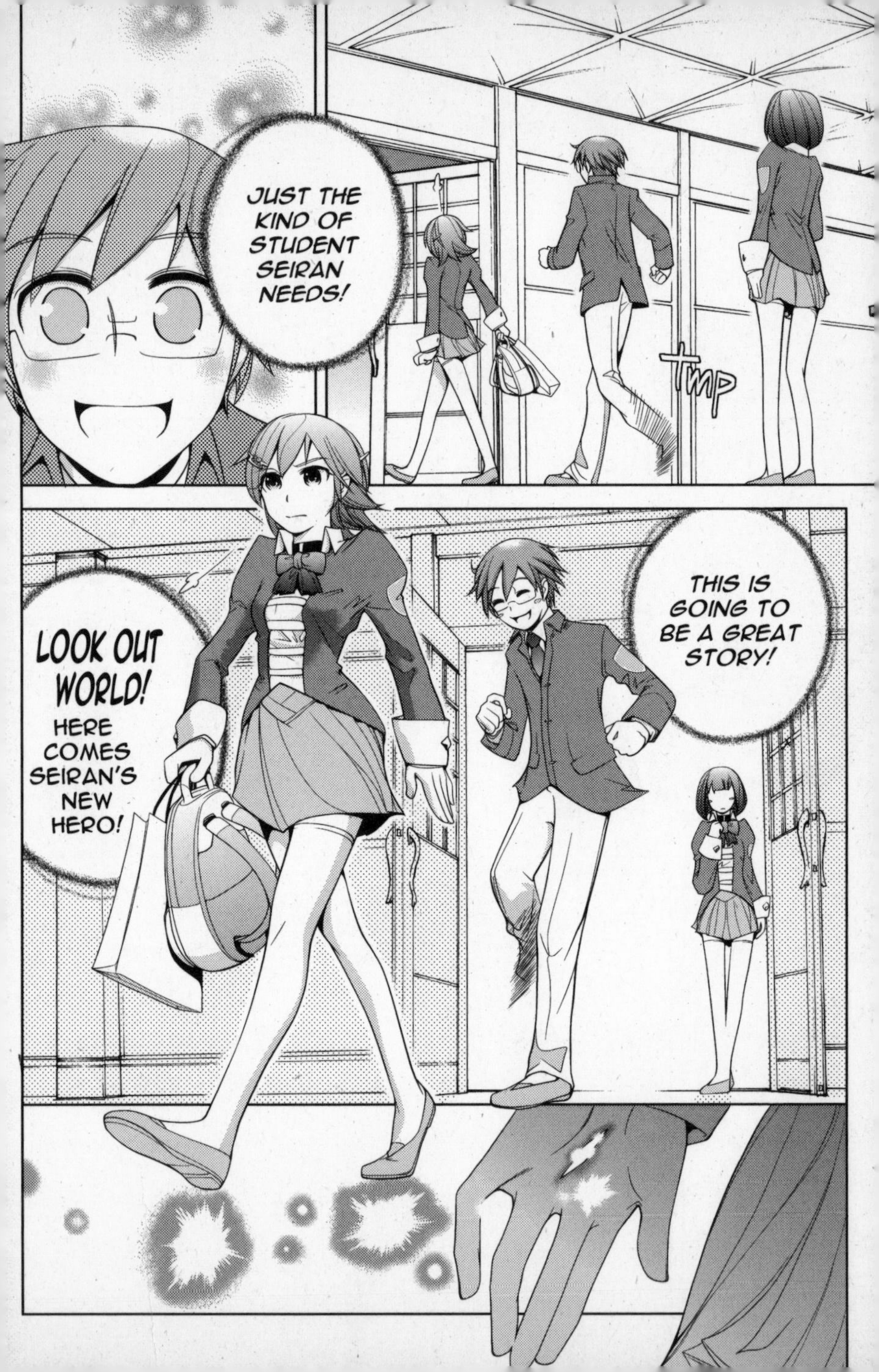
tmp
JUST THE KIND OF STUDENT SEIRAN NEEDS!
THIS IS GOING TO BE A GREAT STORY!
LOOK OUT WORLD! HERE COMES SEIRAN'S NEW HERO!

CHAPTER 3

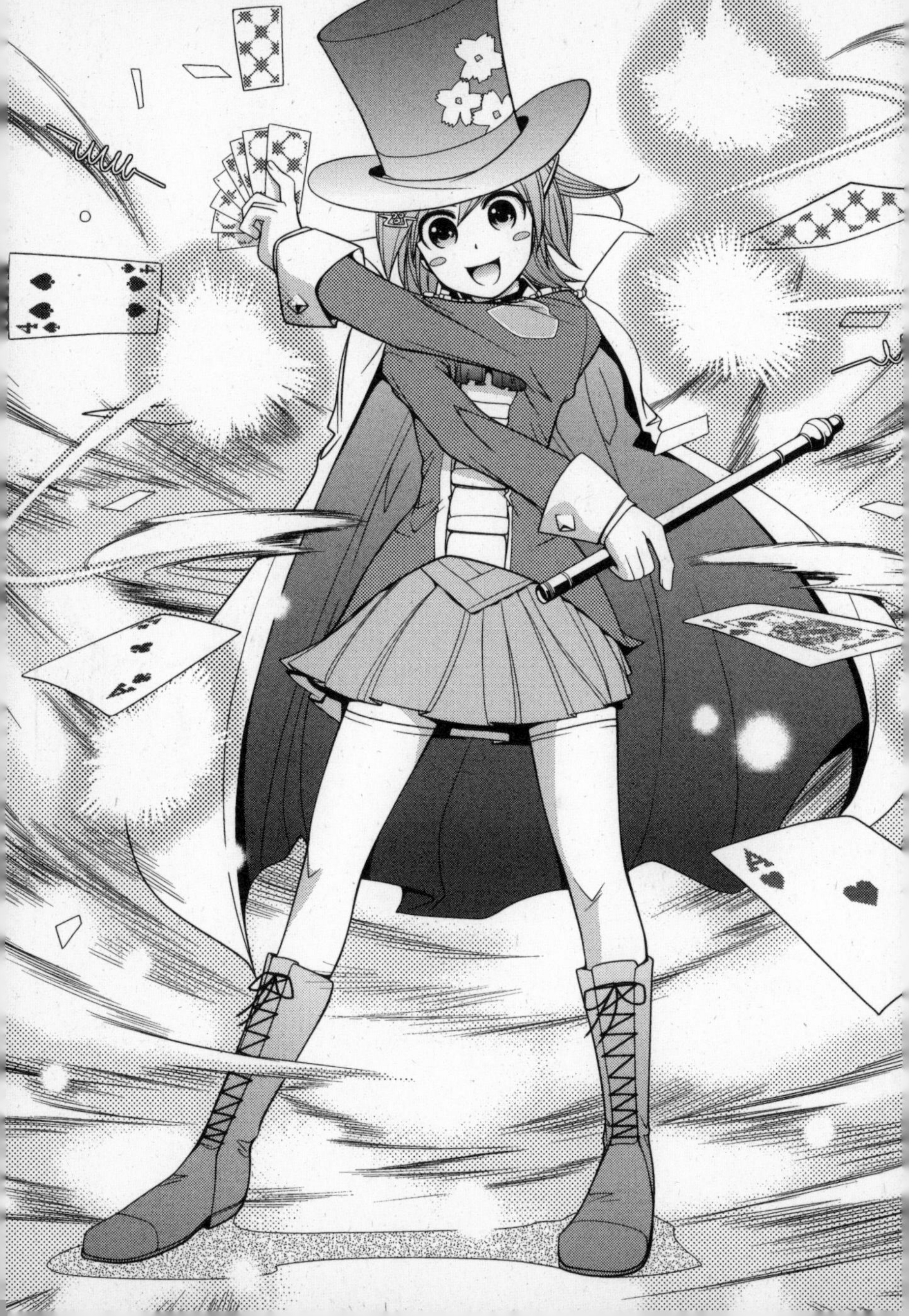

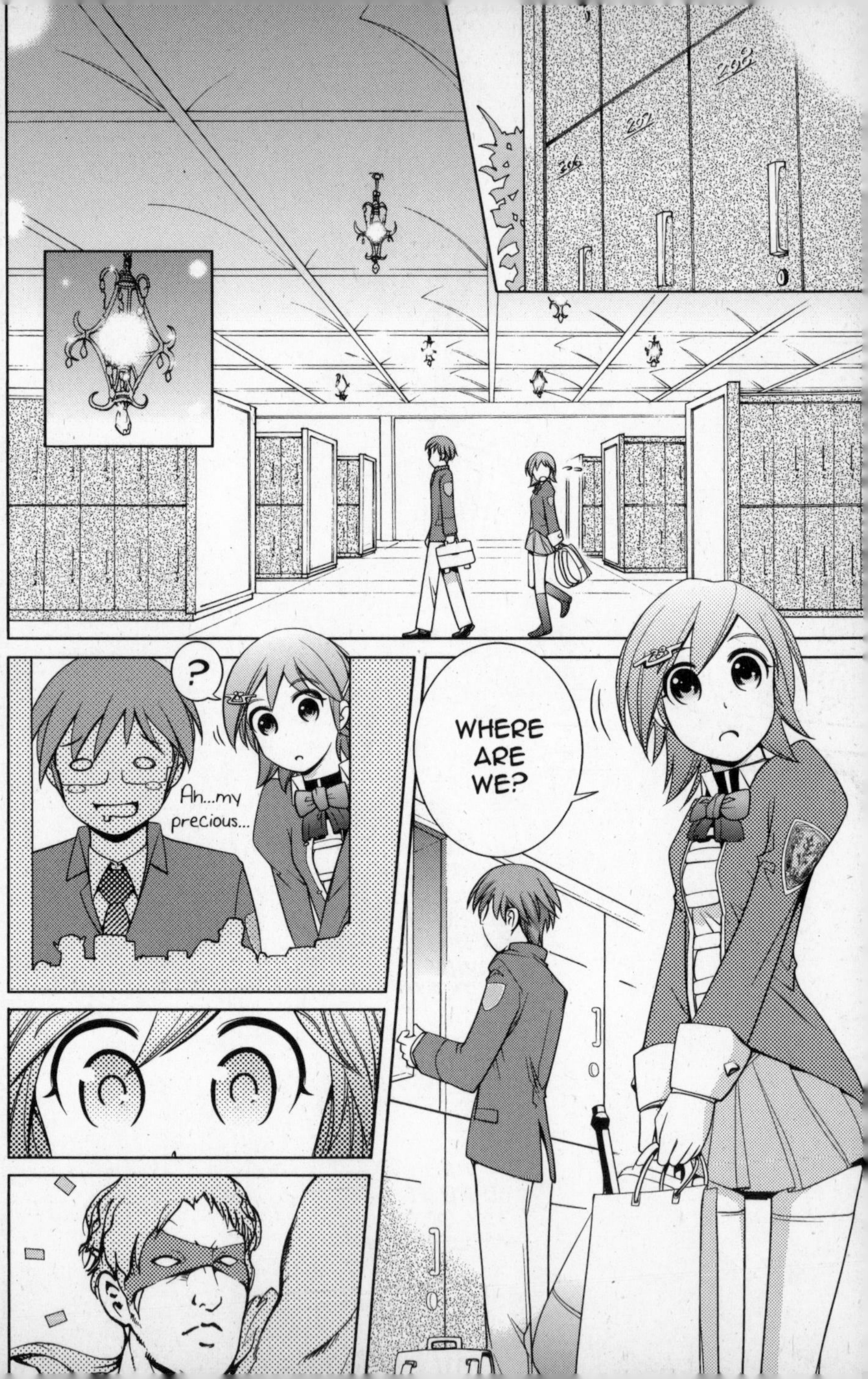
WHERE ARE WE?
?
Ah...my precious...

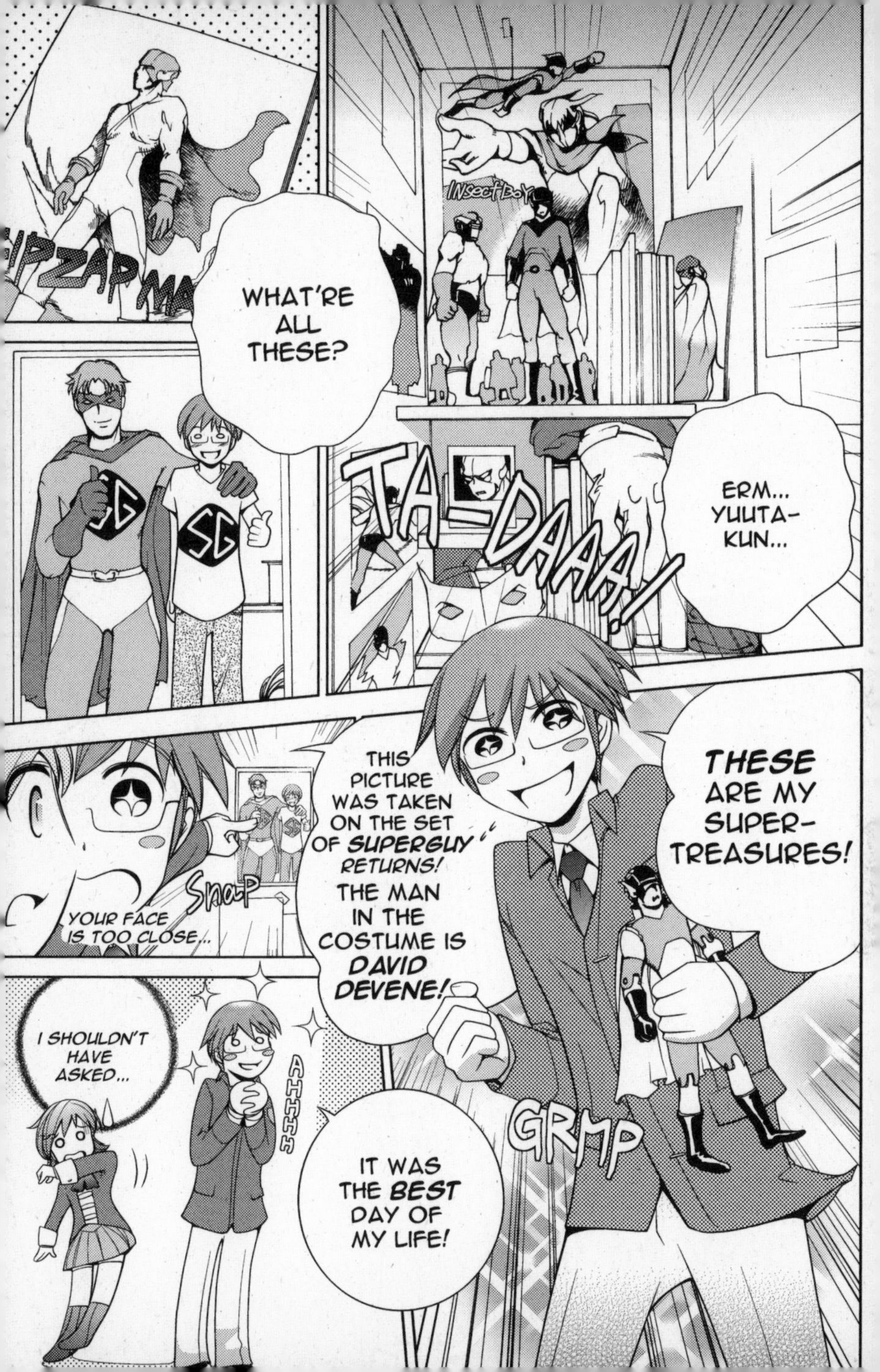
WHAT'RE ALL THESE?
INSECTBOY
ERM... YUUTA-KUN...
TA-DAAA!
THESE ARE MY SUPER-TREASURES!
GRMP
THIS PICTURE WAS TAKEN ON THE SET OF SUPERGUY RETURNS! THE MAN IN THE COSTUME IS DAVID DEVENE!
SNAP
YOUR FACE IS TOO CLOSE...
IT WAS THE BEST DAY OF MY LIFE!
AHHHHH
I SHOULDN'T HAVE ASKED...

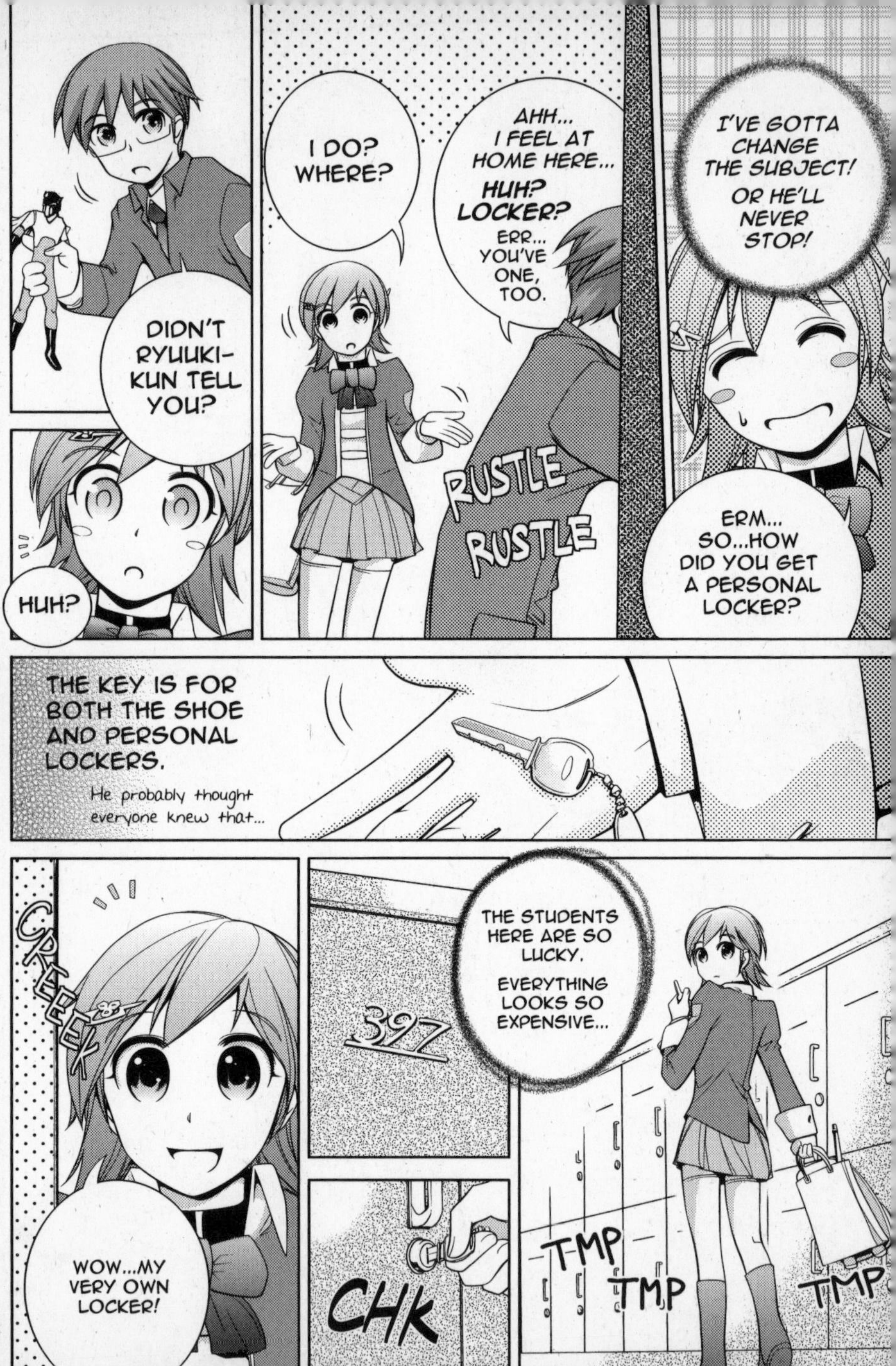
I'VE GOTTA CHANGE THE SUBJECT!
OR HE'LL NEVER STOP!
ERM... SO...HOW DID YOU GET A PERSONAL LOCKER?
AHH... I FEEL AT HOME HERE...
HUH? LOCKER?
ERR... YOU'VE ONE, TOO.
I DO? WHERE?
RUSTLE
RUSTLE
DIDN'T RYUUKI-KUN TELL YOU?
HUH?
THE KEY IS FOR BOTH THE SHOE AND PERSONAL LOCKERS.
He probably thought everyone knew that...
THE STUDENTS HERE ARE SO LUCKY.
EVERYTHING LOOKS SO EXPENSIVE...
TMP
TMP
TMP
397
CHK
CREEEK
WOW...MY VERY OWN LOCKER!

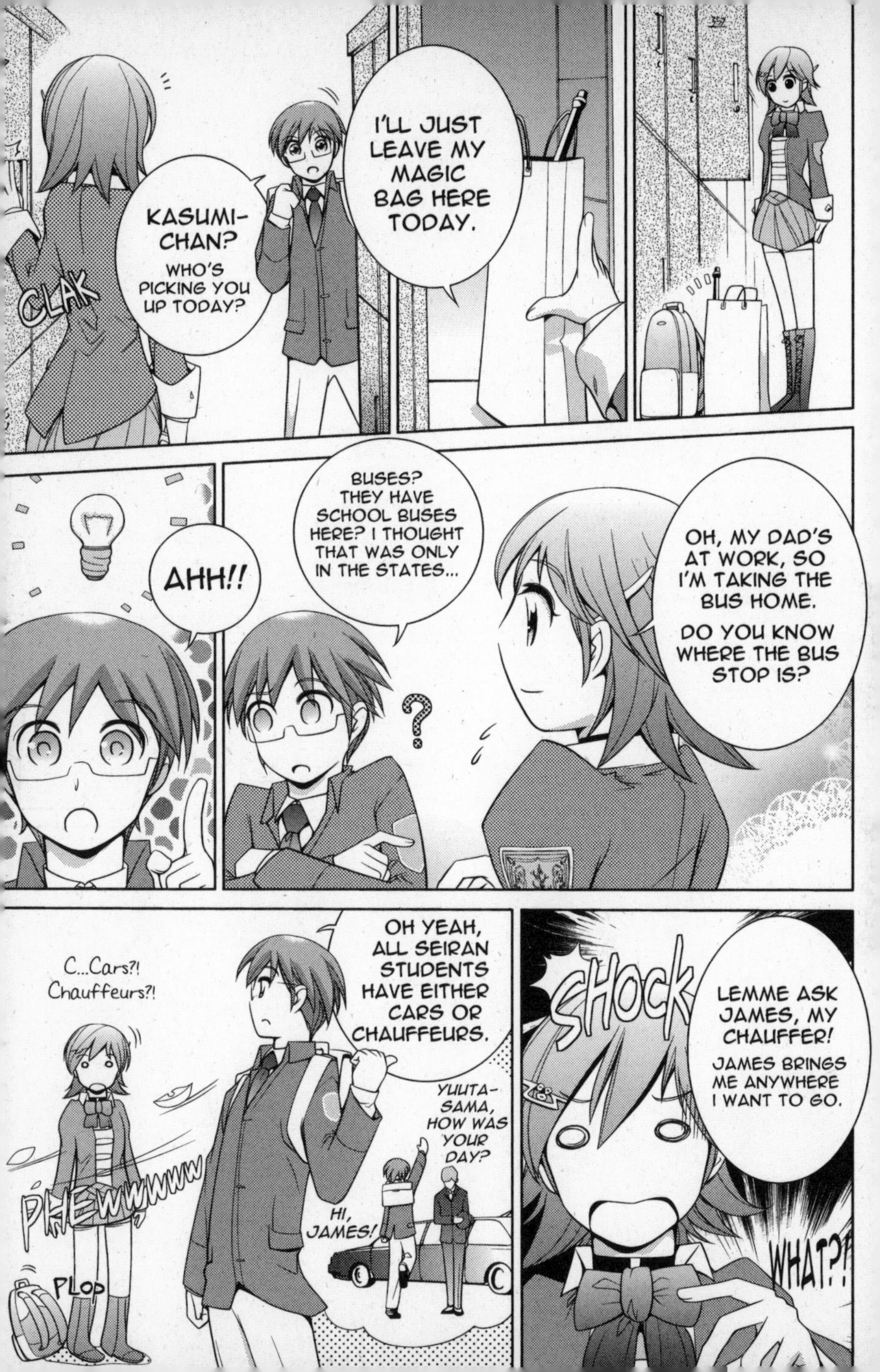
I'LL JUST LEAVE MY MAGIC BAG HERE TODAY.
KASUMI-CHAN?
WHO'S PICKING YOU UP TODAY?
CLAK
OH, MY DAD'S AT WORK, SO I'M TAKING THE BUS HOME.
DO YOU KNOW WHERE THE BUS STOP IS?
BUSES? THEY HAVE SCHOOL BUSES HERE? I THOUGHT THAT WAS ONLY IN THE STATES...
AHH!!
SHOCK
LEMME ASK JAMES, MY CHAUFFER!
JAMES BRINGS ME ANYWHERE I WANT TO GO.
WHAT?!
OH YEAH, ALL SEIRAN STUDENTS HAVE EITHER CARS OR CHAUFFEURS.
C...Cars?! Chauffeurs?!
YUUTA-SAMA, HOW WAS YOUR DAY?
HI, JAMES!
PHEWWWWWW
PLOP

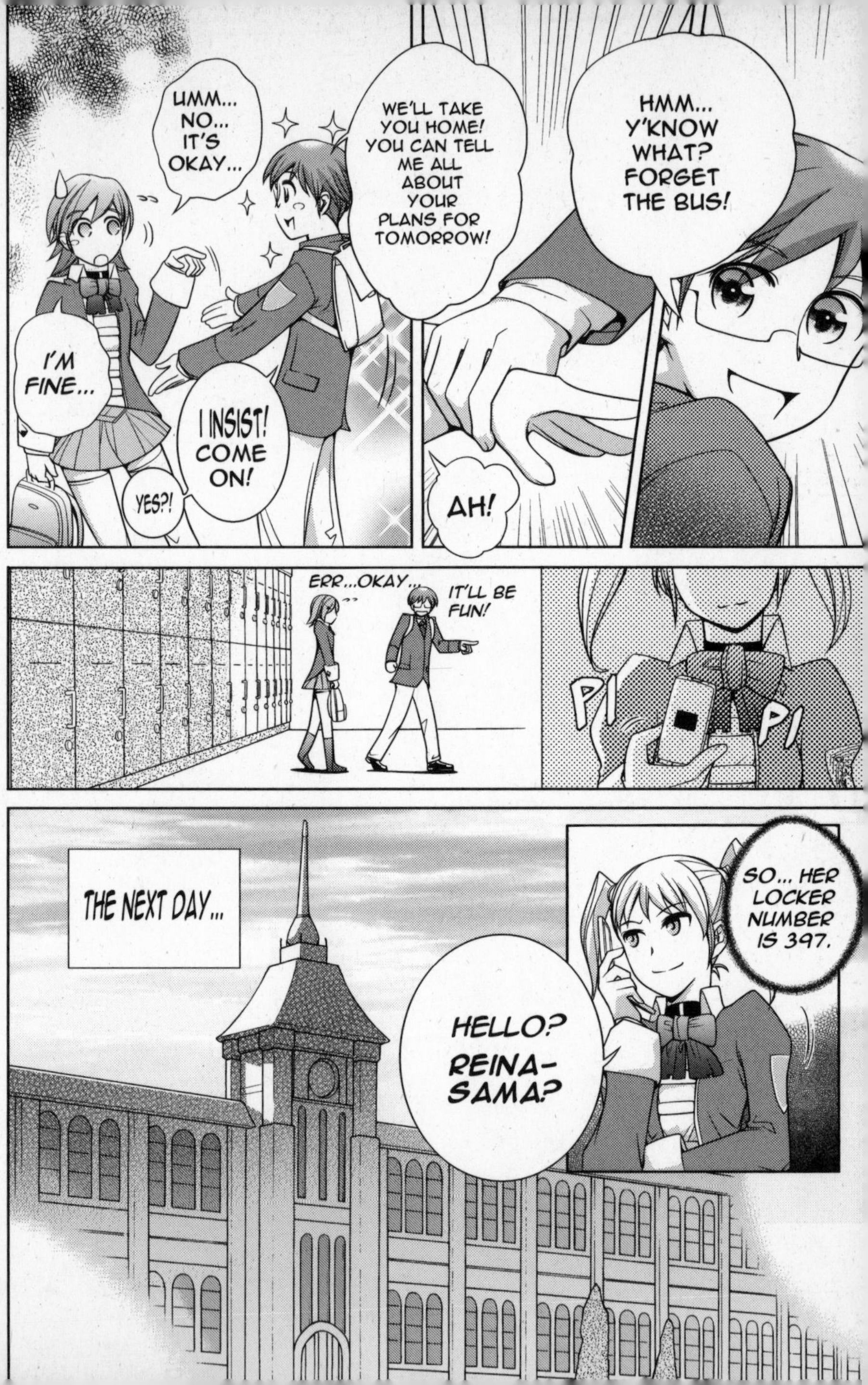
HMM... Y'KNOW WHAT? FORGET THE BUS!
AH!
WE'LL TAKE YOU HOME! YOU CAN TELL ME ALL ABOUT YOUR PLANS FOR TOMORROW!
UMM... NO... IT'S OKAY...
I'M FINE...
I INSIST! COME ON!
YES?!
PI
PI
IT'LL BE FUN!
ERR...OKAY...
SO... HER LOCKER NUMBER IS 397.
HELLO? REINA-SAMA?
THE NEXT DAY...

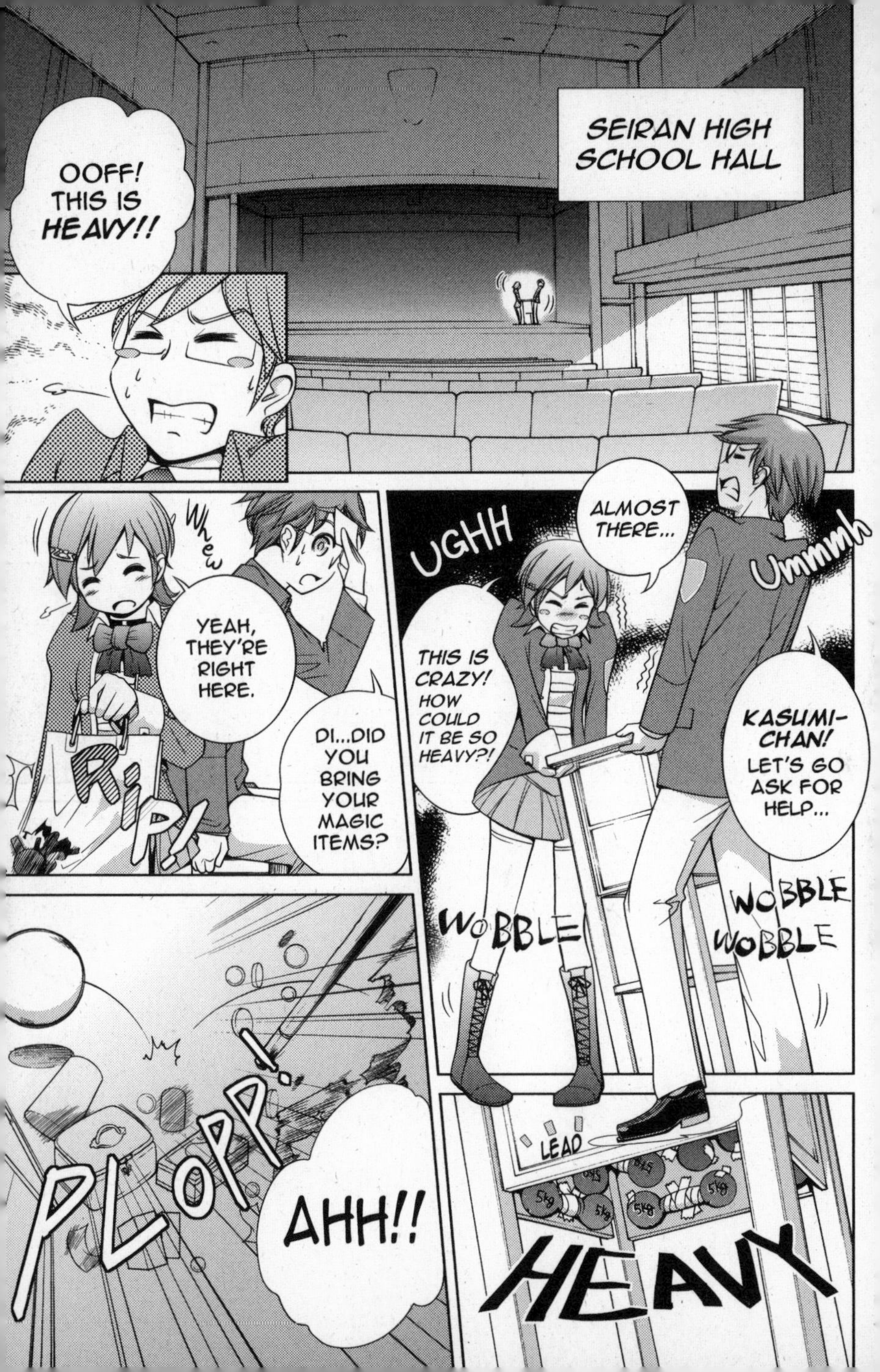
SEIRAN HIGH SCHOOL HALL
OOFF! THIS IS HEAVY!!
ALMOST THERE...
UGHH
Ummmh
THIS IS CRAZY! HOW COULD IT BE SO HEAVY?!
KASUMI-CHAN! LET'S GO ASK FOR HELP...
WOBBLE
WOBBLE WOBBLE
LEAD
5kg
HEAVY
Whew
DI...DID YOU BRING YOUR MAGIC ITEMS?
YEAH, THEY'RE RIGHT HERE.
RiP!
PLOPP
AHH!!

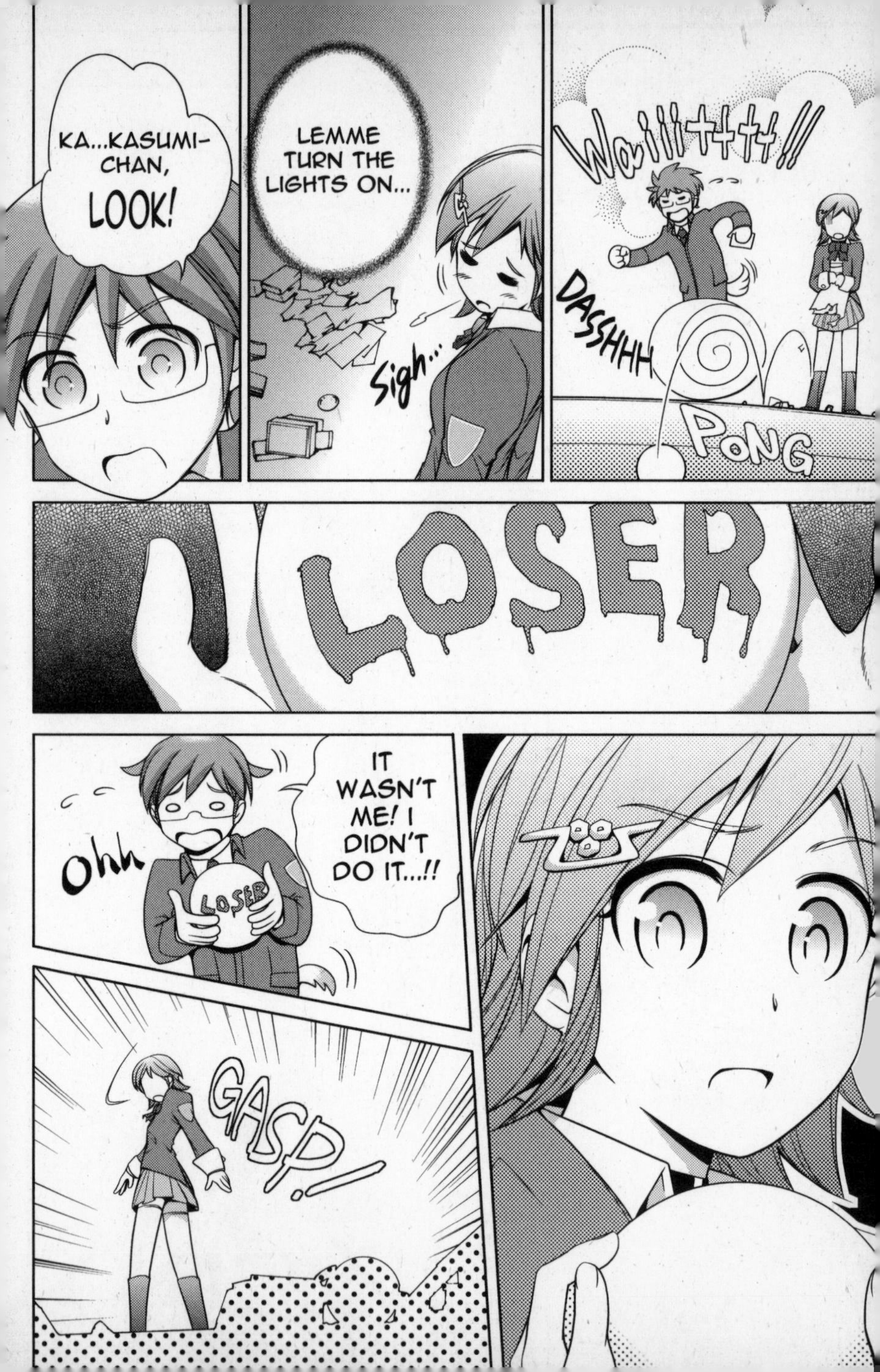
Waiiitttt!!
DASSHHH
PONG
LEMME TURN THE LIGHTS ON...
Sigh...
KA...KASUMI-CHAN, LOOK!
LOSER
IT WASN'T ME! I DIDN'T DO IT...!!
Ohh
LOSER
GASP!

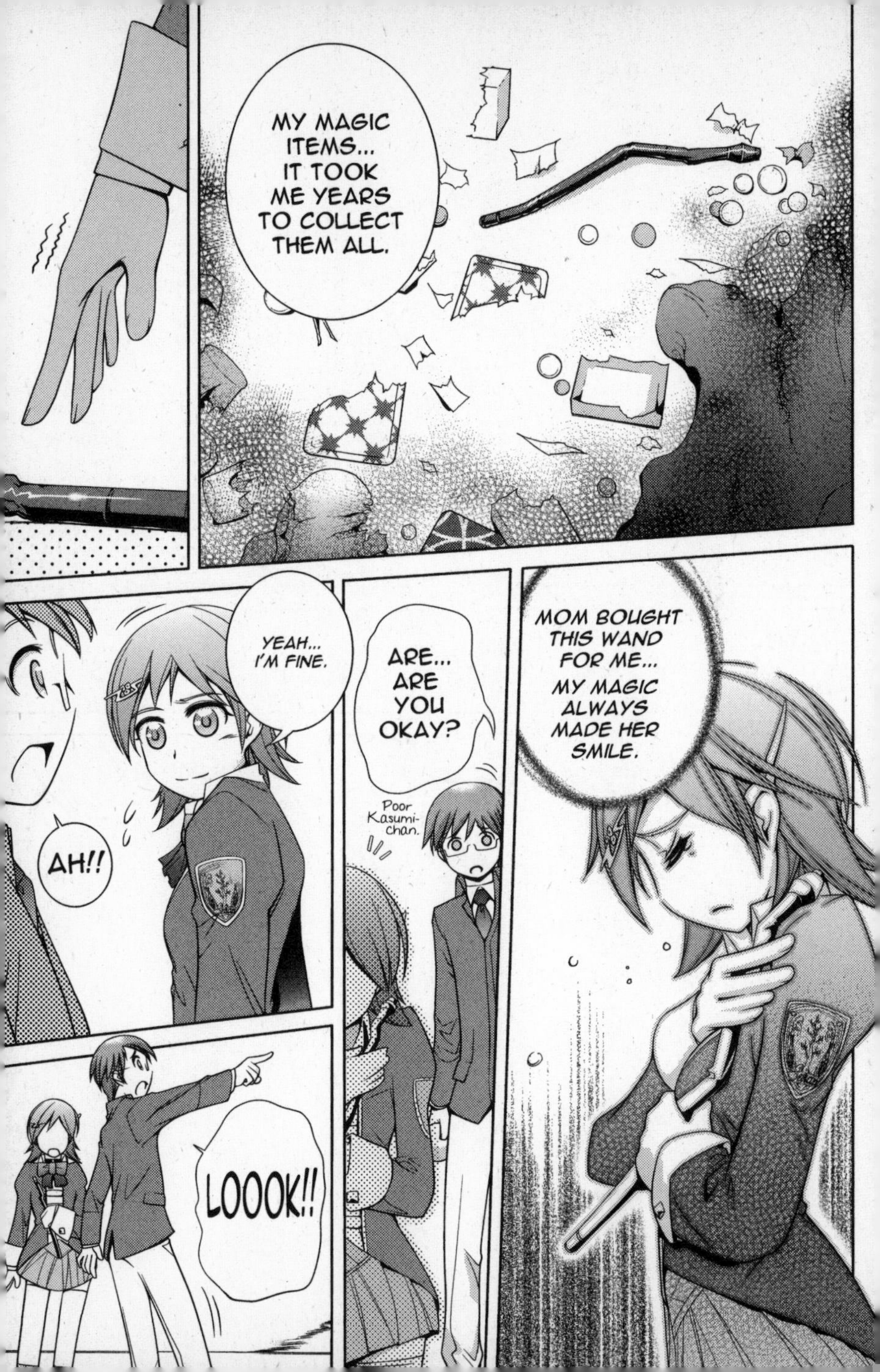
MY MAGIC ITEMS... IT TOOK ME YEARS TO COLLECT THEM ALL.
MOM BOUGHT THIS WAND FOR ME... MY MAGIC ALWAYS MADE HER SMILE.
ARE... ARE YOU OKAY?
Poor Kasumi-chan.
YEAH... I'M FINE.
AH!!
LOOOK!!

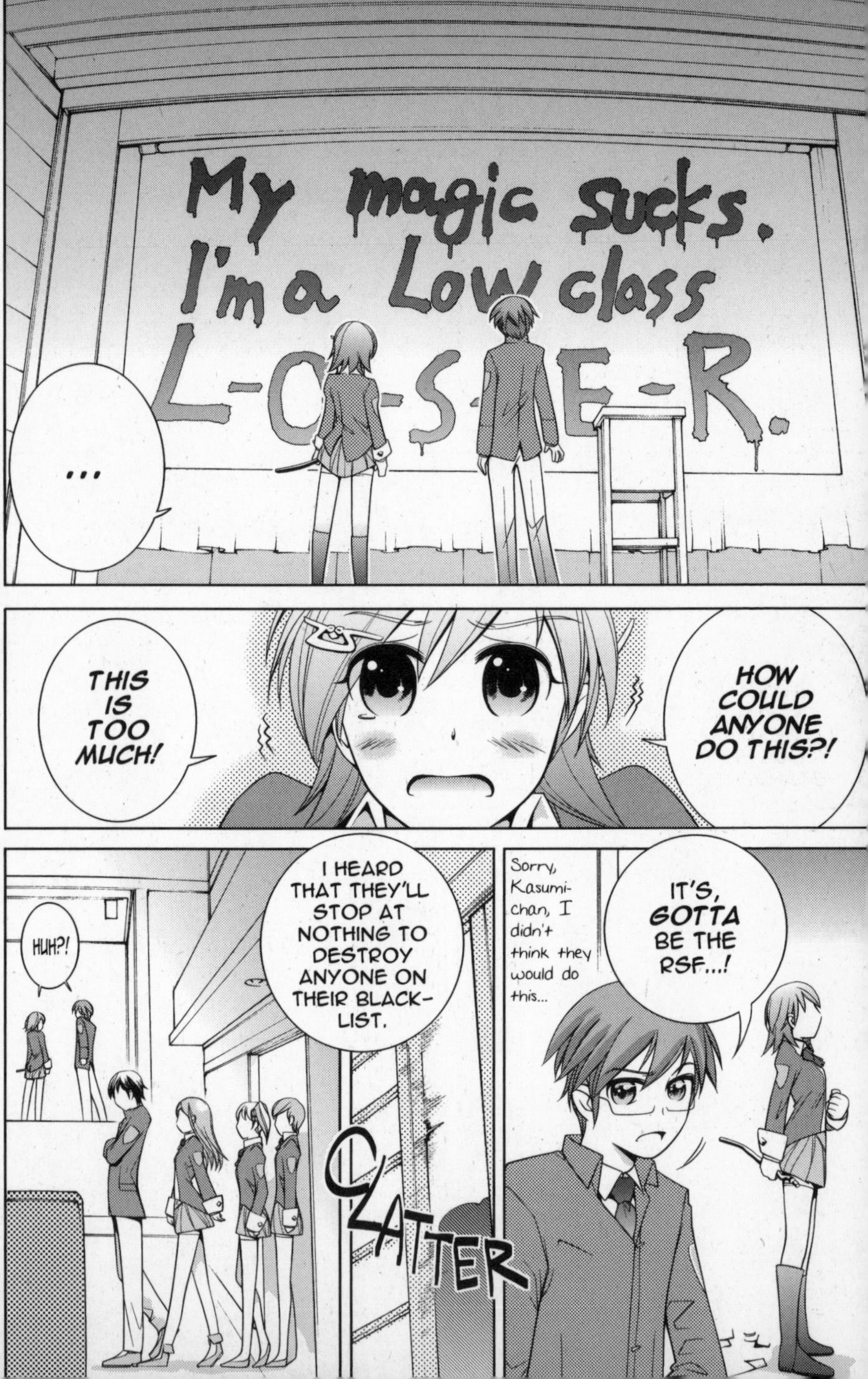
My magic sucks. I'm a Low class L-O-S-E-R.
...
HOW COULD ANYONE DO THIS?!
THIS IS TOO MUCH!
IT'S, GOTTA BE THE RSF...!
Sorry, Kasumi-chan, I didn't think they would do this...
I HEARD THAT THEY'LL STOP AT NOTHING TO DESTROY ANYONE ON THEIR BLACK-LIST.
HUH?!
CLATTER

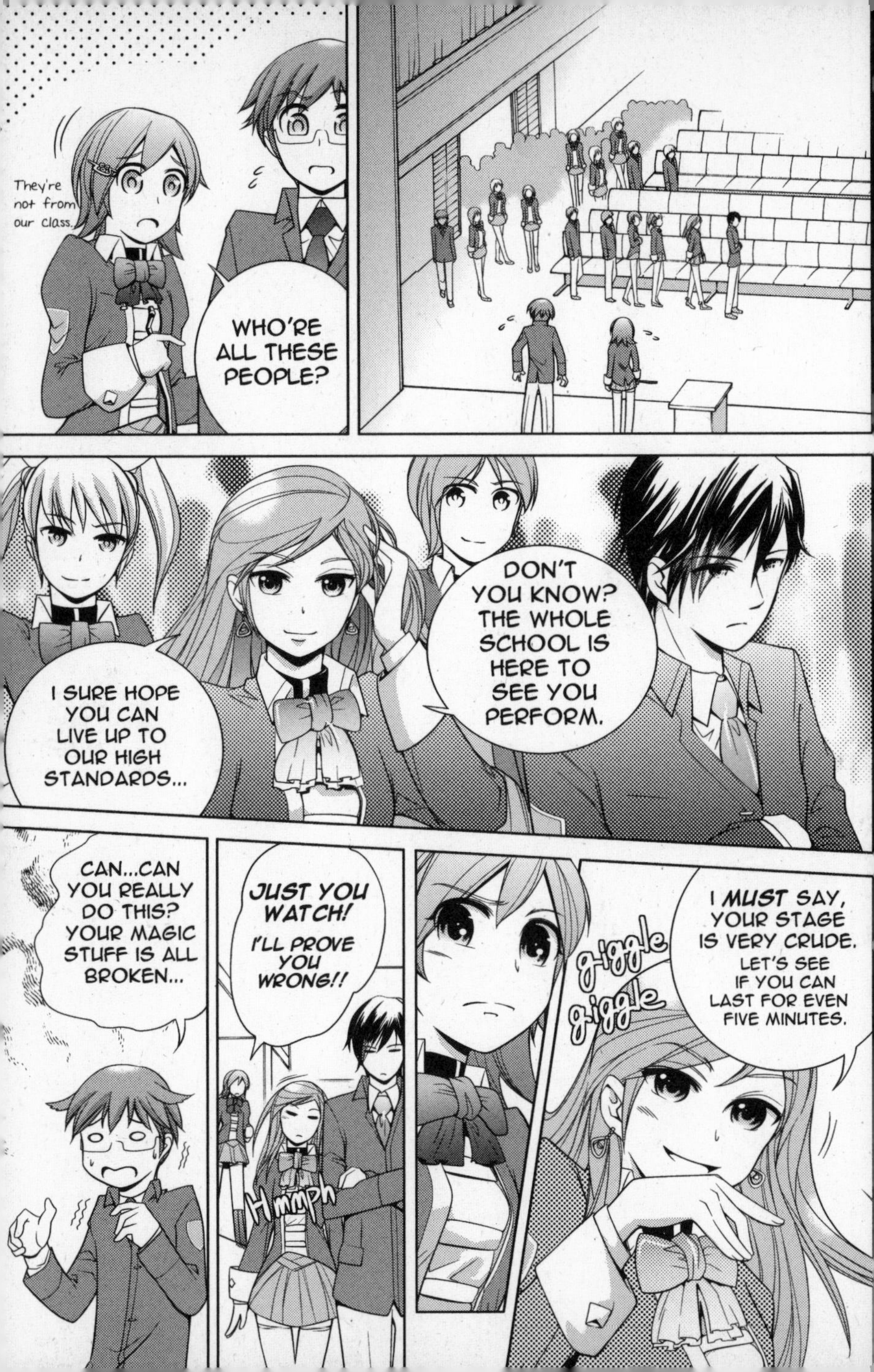
WHO'RE ALL THESE PEOPLE?
They're not from our class.
DON'T YOU KNOW? THE WHOLE SCHOOL IS HERE TO SEE YOU PERFORM.
I SURE HOPE YOU CAN LIVE UP TO OUR HIGH STANDARDS...
I MUST SAY, YOUR STAGE IS VERY CRUDE. LET'S SEE IF YOU CAN LAST FOR EVEN FIVE MINUTES.
giggle
giggle
JUST YOU WATCH!
I'LL PROVE YOU WRONG!!
Hmmph
CAN...CAN YOU REALLY DO THIS? YOUR MAGIC STUFF IS ALL BROKEN...

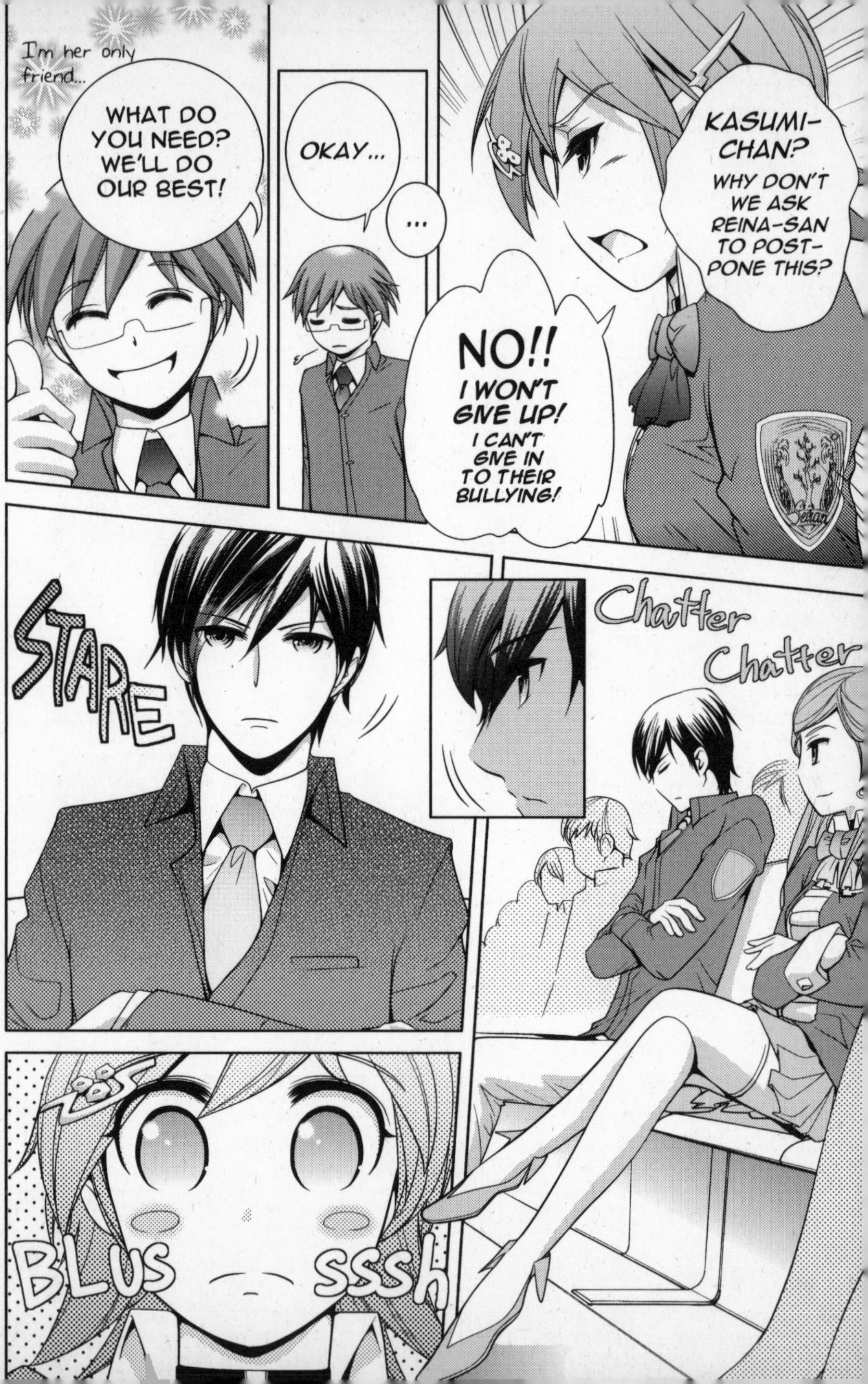
KASUMI-CHAN? WHY DON'T WE ASK REINA-SAN TO POST-PONE THIS?
NO!! I WON'T GIVE UP! I CAN'T GIVE IN TO THEIR BULLYING!
OKAY...
...
I'm her only friend...
WHAT DO YOU NEED? WE'LL DO OUR BEST!
Chatter Chatter
STARE
BLUS SSSh

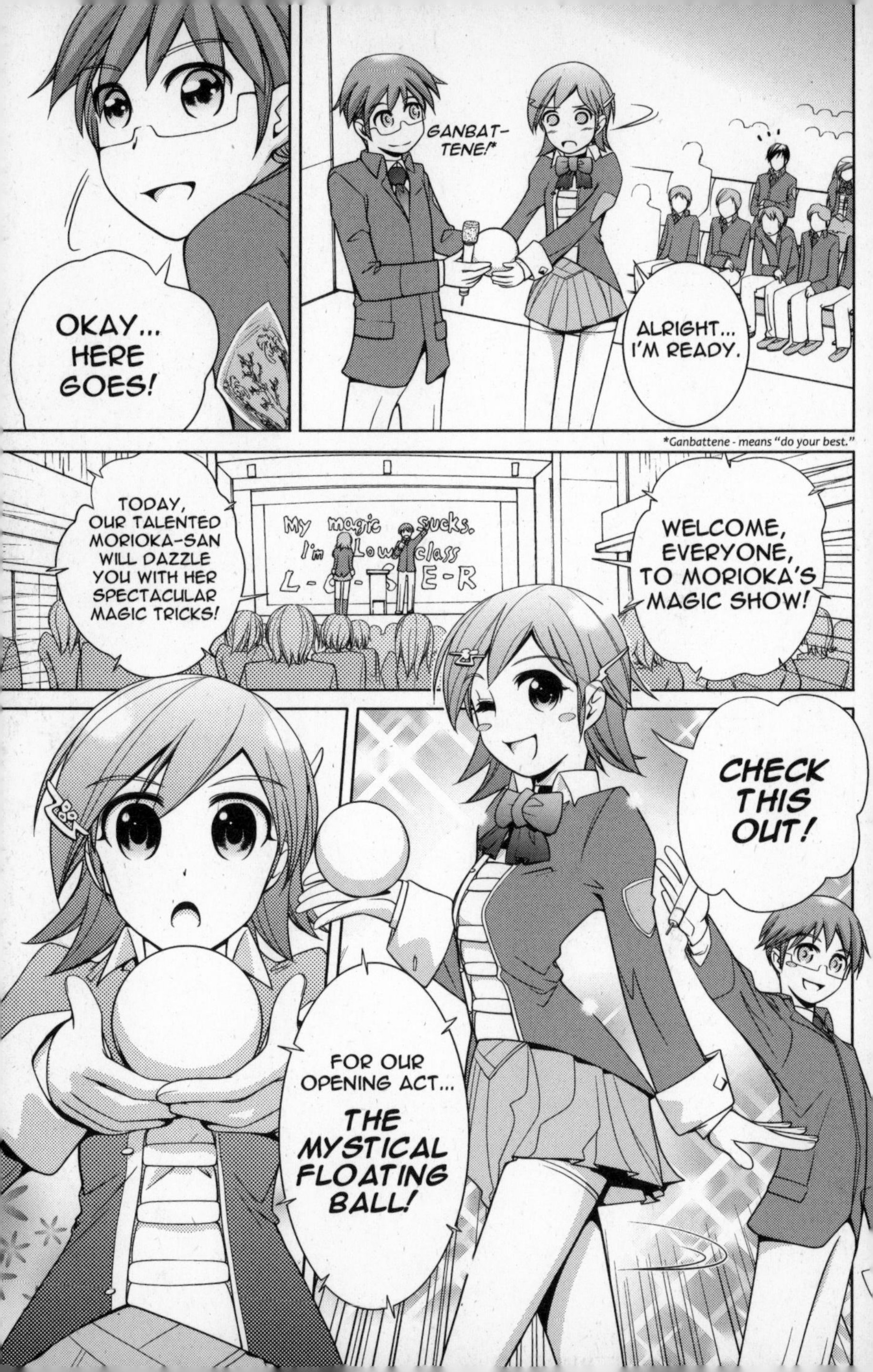
GANBAT-TENE!*
ALRIGHT... I'M READY.
OKAY... HERE GOES!
WELCOME, EVERYONE, TO MORIOKA'S MAGIC SHOW!
TODAY, OUR TALENTED MORIOKA-SAN WILL DAZZLE YOU WITH HER SPECTACULAR MAGIC TRICKS!
CHECK THIS OUT!
FOR OUR OPENING ACT...
THE MYSTICAL FLOATING BALL!

*Ganbattene - means "do your best."

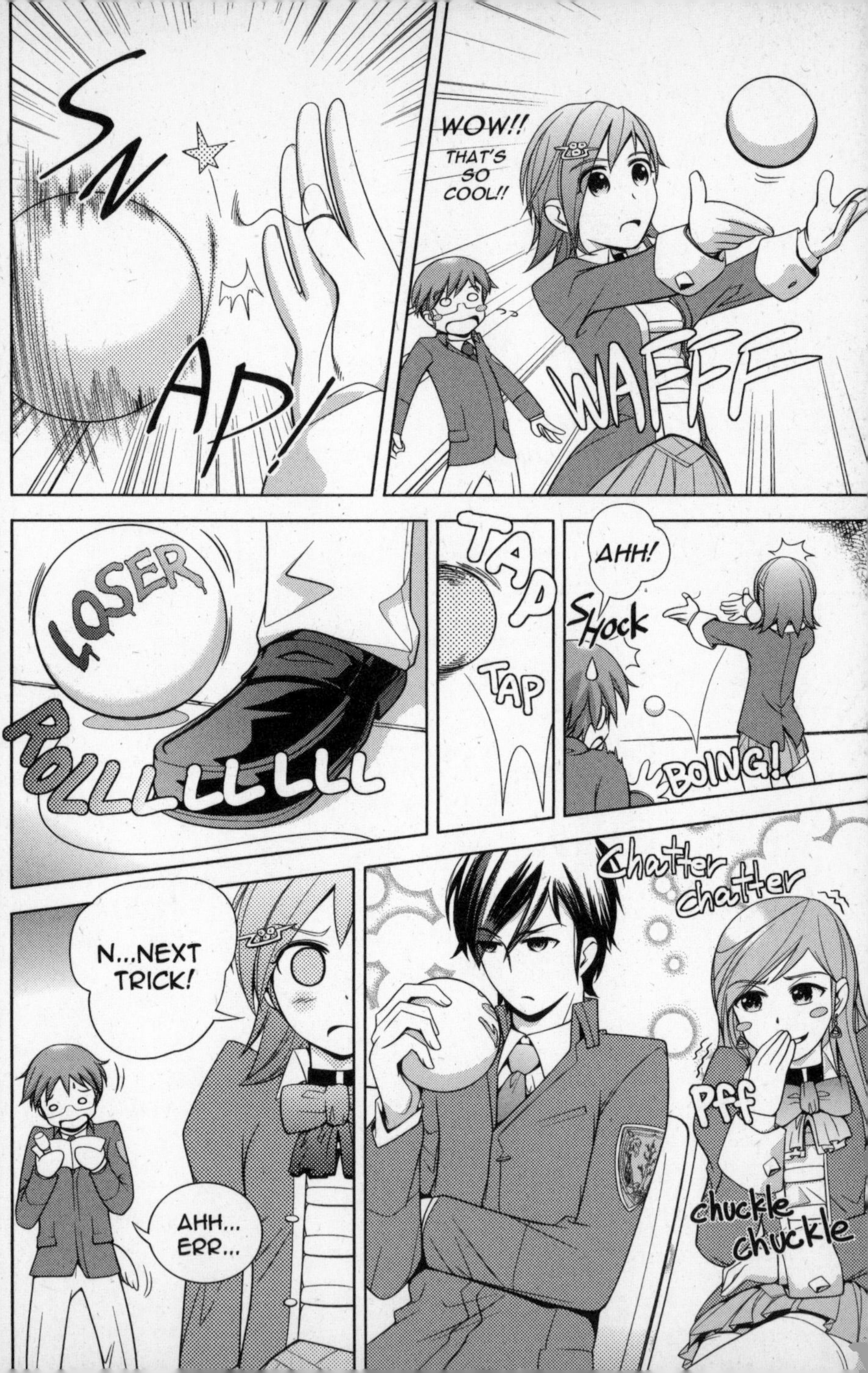
WOW!! THAT'S SO COOL!!
WAFFF
SNAP!
AHH!
SHOCK
BOING!
TAP
TAP
LOSER
ROLLLLLLLL
Chatter chatter
Pff
chuckle chuckle
N...NEXT TRICK!
AHH... ERR...

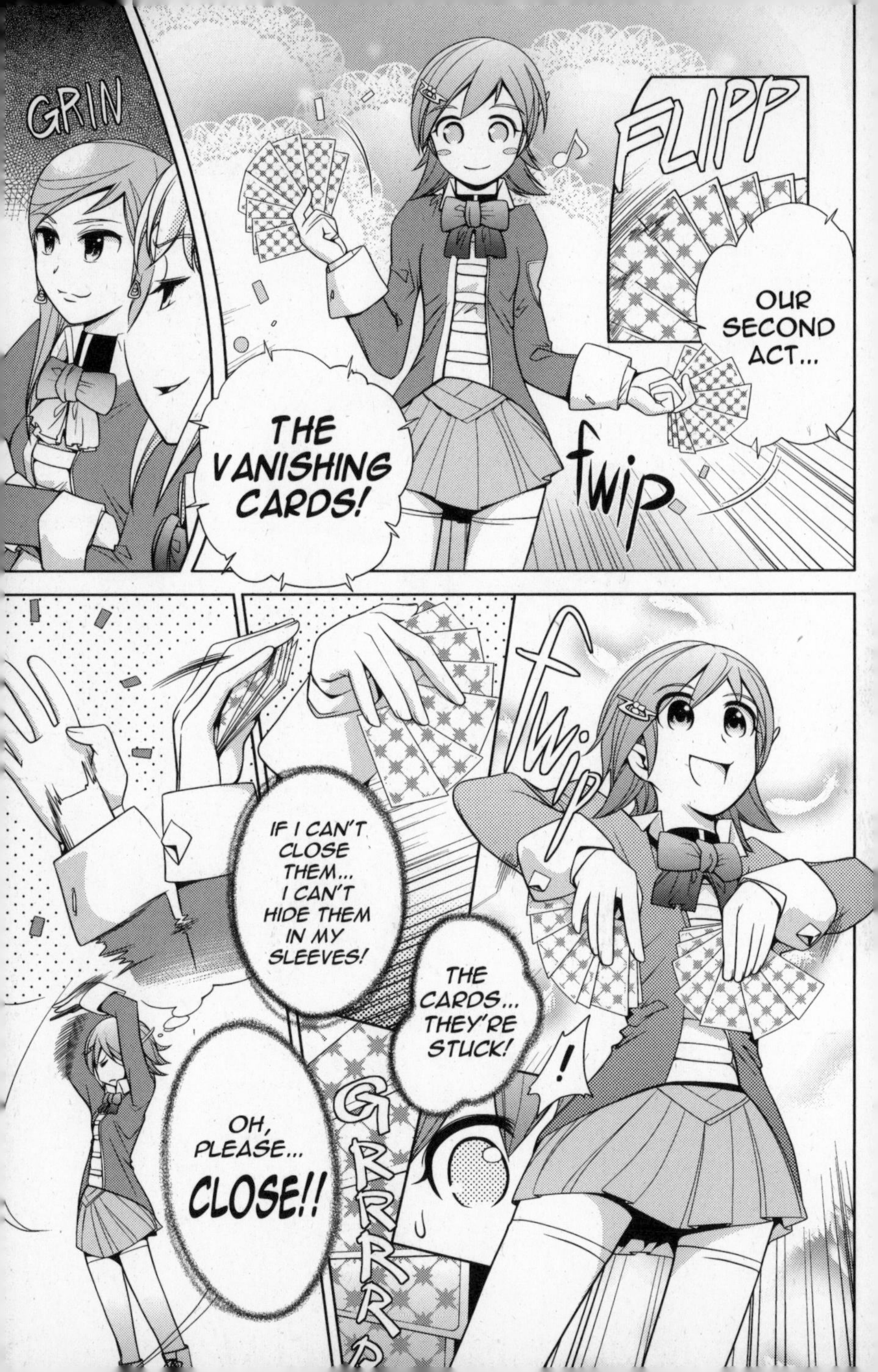
FLIPP
OUR SECOND ACT...
fwip
THE VANISHING CARDS!
GRIN
fwip
!
THE CARDS... THEY'RE STUCK!
IF I CAN'T CLOSE THEM... I CAN'T HIDE THEM IN MY SLEEVES!
GRRRR
OH, PLEASE... CLOSE!!

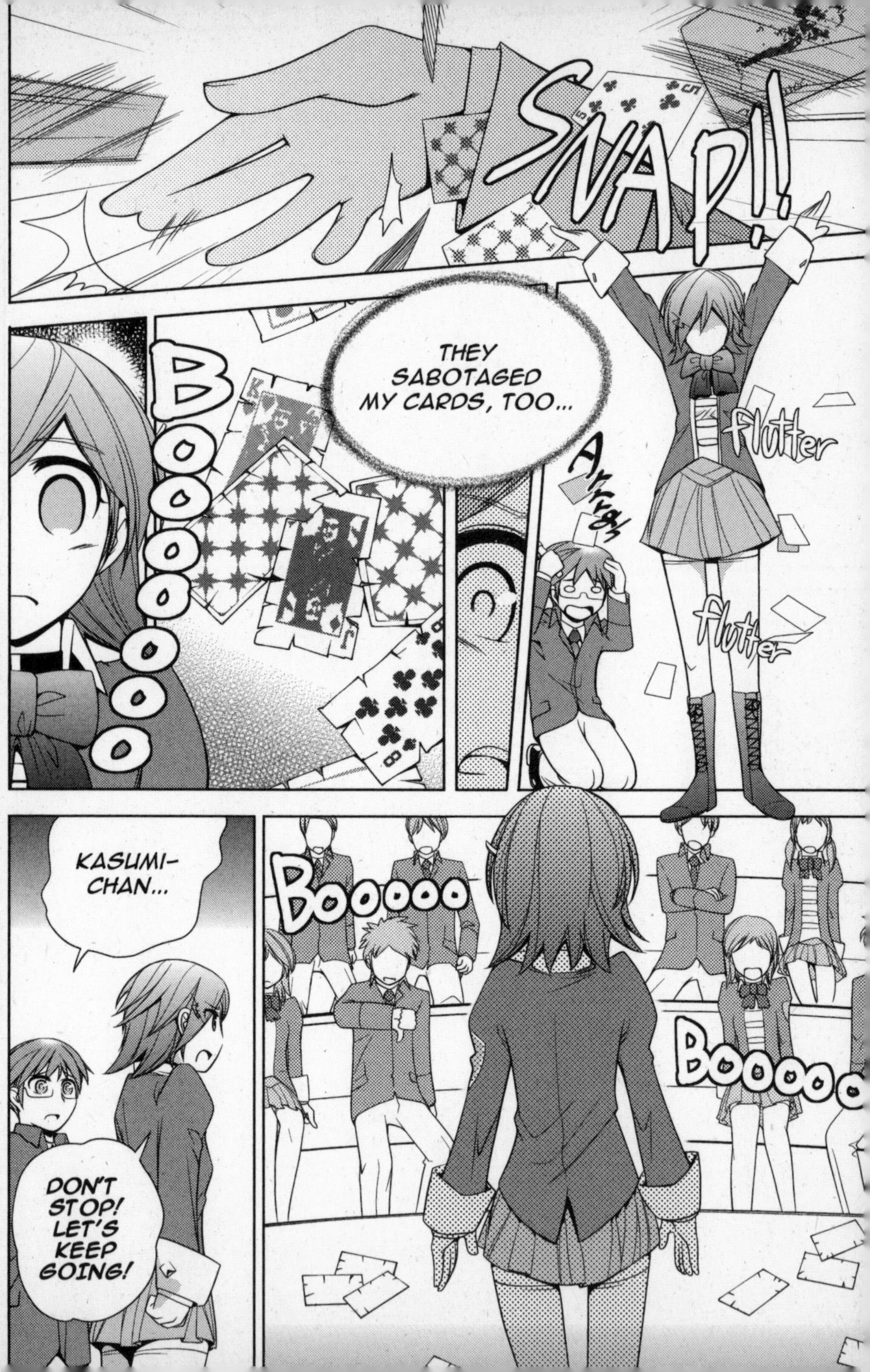
SNAP!!
Arrrgh
flutter
flutter
THEY SABOTAGED MY CARDS, TOO...
Booooooooo
Booooo
Boooooo
KASUMI-CHAN...
DON'T STOP! LET'S KEEP GOING!

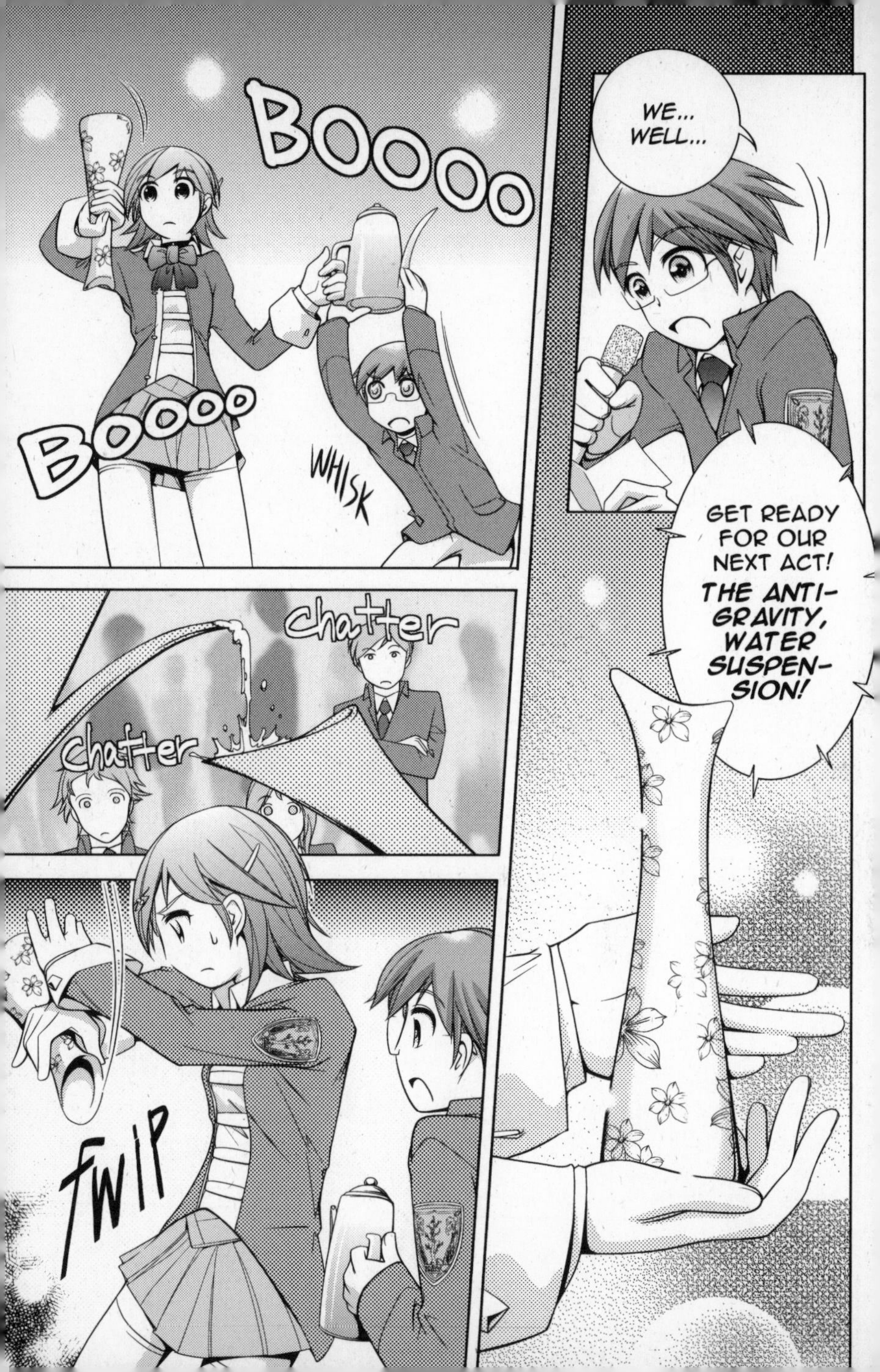
WE... WELL...
BOOOO
BOOOO
WHISK
GET READY FOR OUR NEXT ACT! THE ANTI-GRAVITY, WATER SUSPENSION!
Chatter
Chatter
FWIP

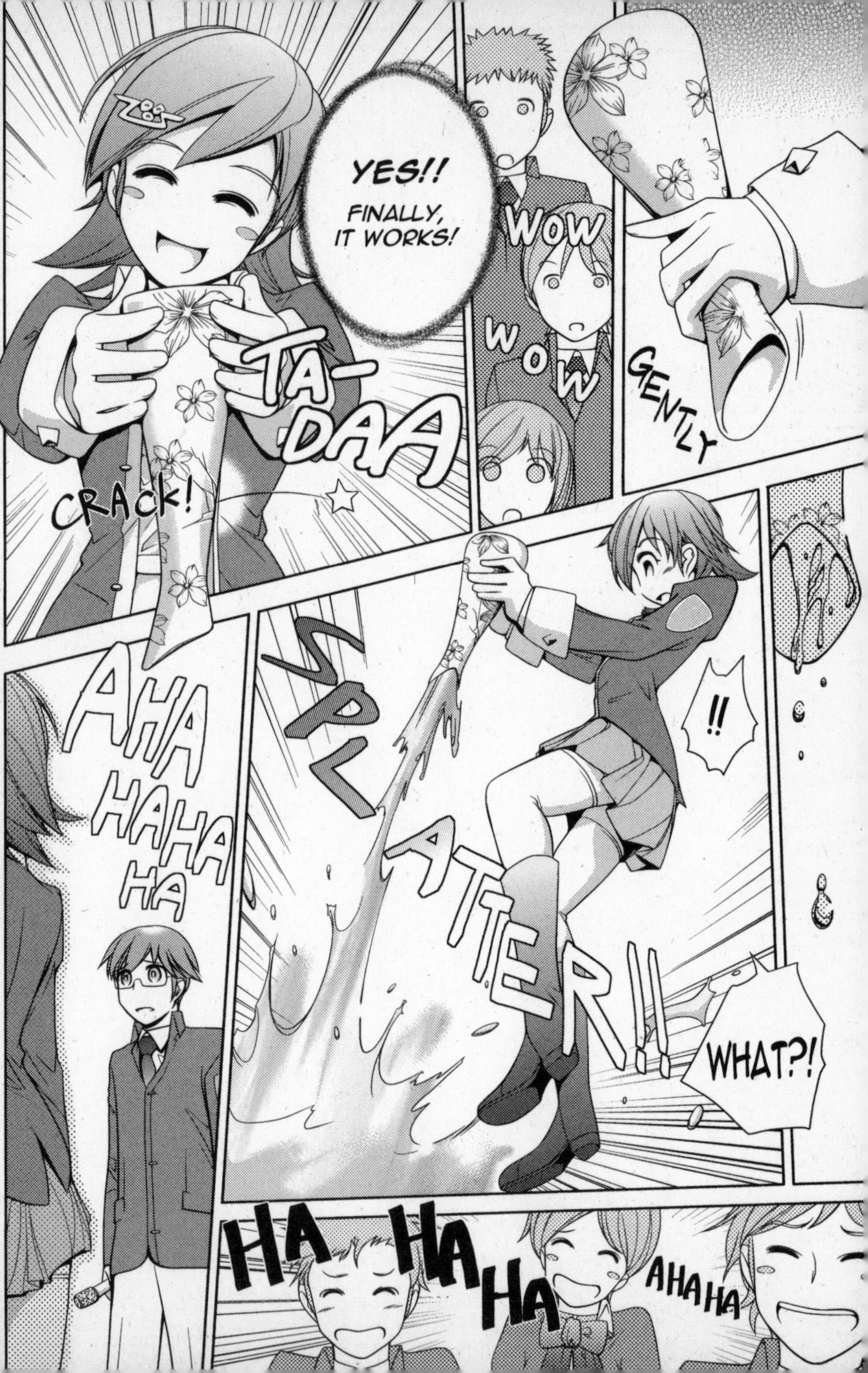
GENTLY
WOW
WOW
WOW
YES!!
FINALLY, IT WORKS!
TA-DAA
CRACK!
!!
SPLATTER!!
WHAT?!
HA HA HA
AHAHA
AHA HAHA HA HA

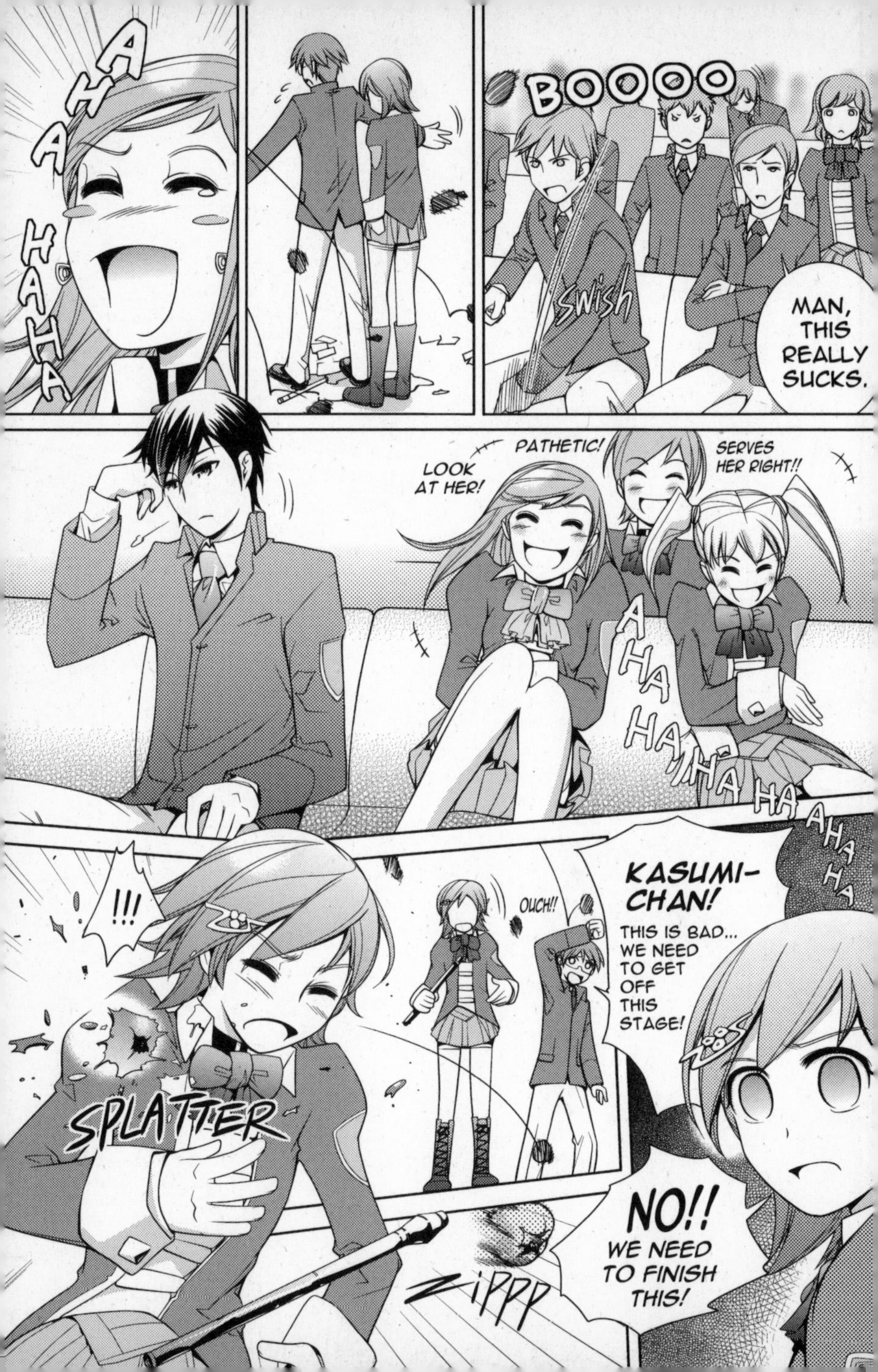
BOOOO
SWISH
MAN, THIS REALLY SUCKS.
AHAHAHAHAHA
SERVES HER RIGHT!!
PATHETIC!
LOOK AT HER!
AHAHAHAHAHAHA
KASUMI-CHAN!
THIS IS BAD... WE NEED TO GET OFF THIS STAGE!
NO!! WE NEED TO FINISH THIS!
OUCH!!
!!!
SPLATTER
ZIPPP

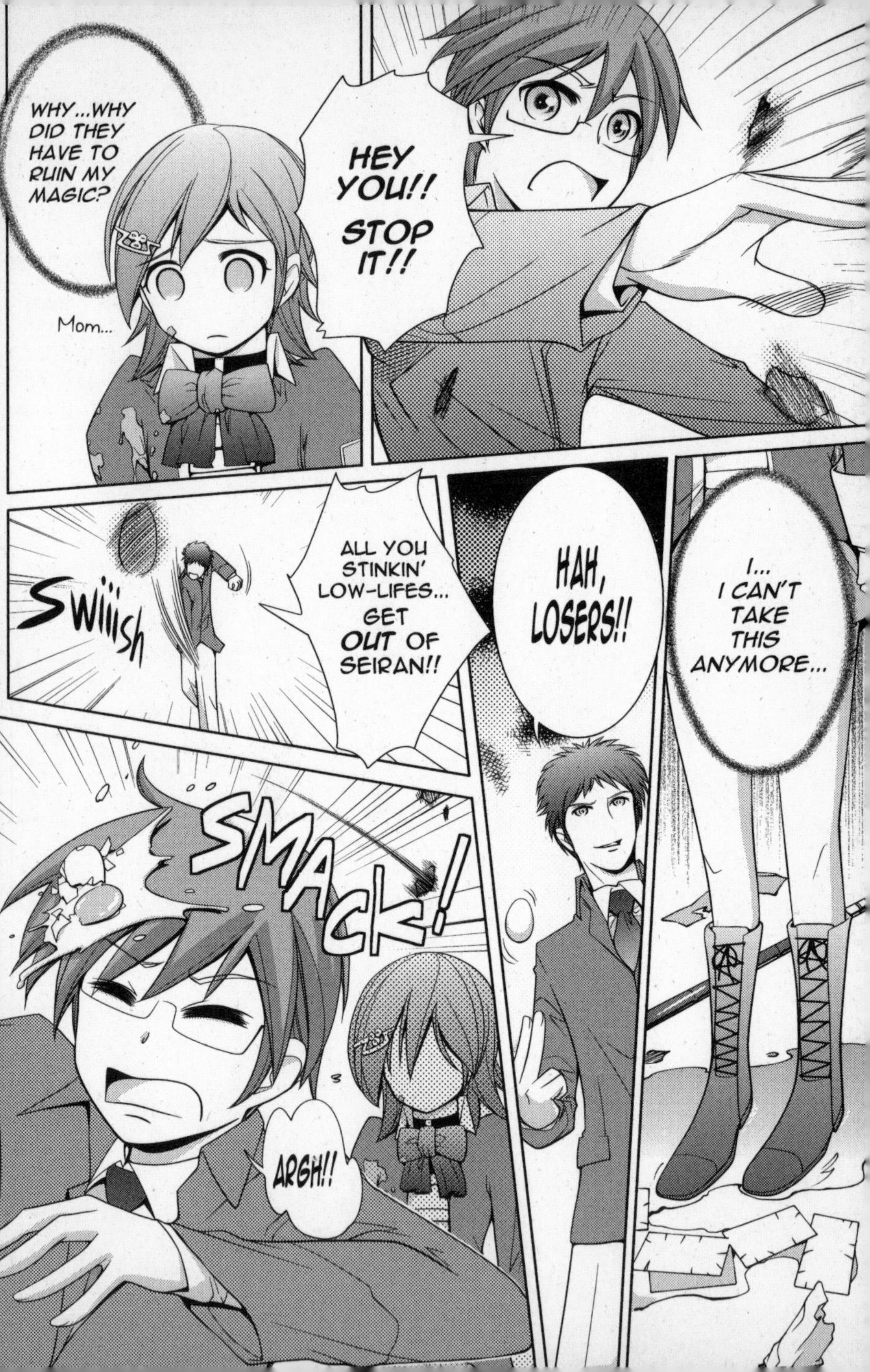
HEY YOU!! STOP IT!!
WHY...WHY DID THEY HAVE TO RUIN MY MAGIC?
Mom...
I... I CAN'T TAKE THIS ANYMORE...
HAH, LOSERS!!
ALL YOU STINKIN' LOW-LIFES... GET OUT OF SEIRAN!!
Swiiish
SMACK!
ARGH!!

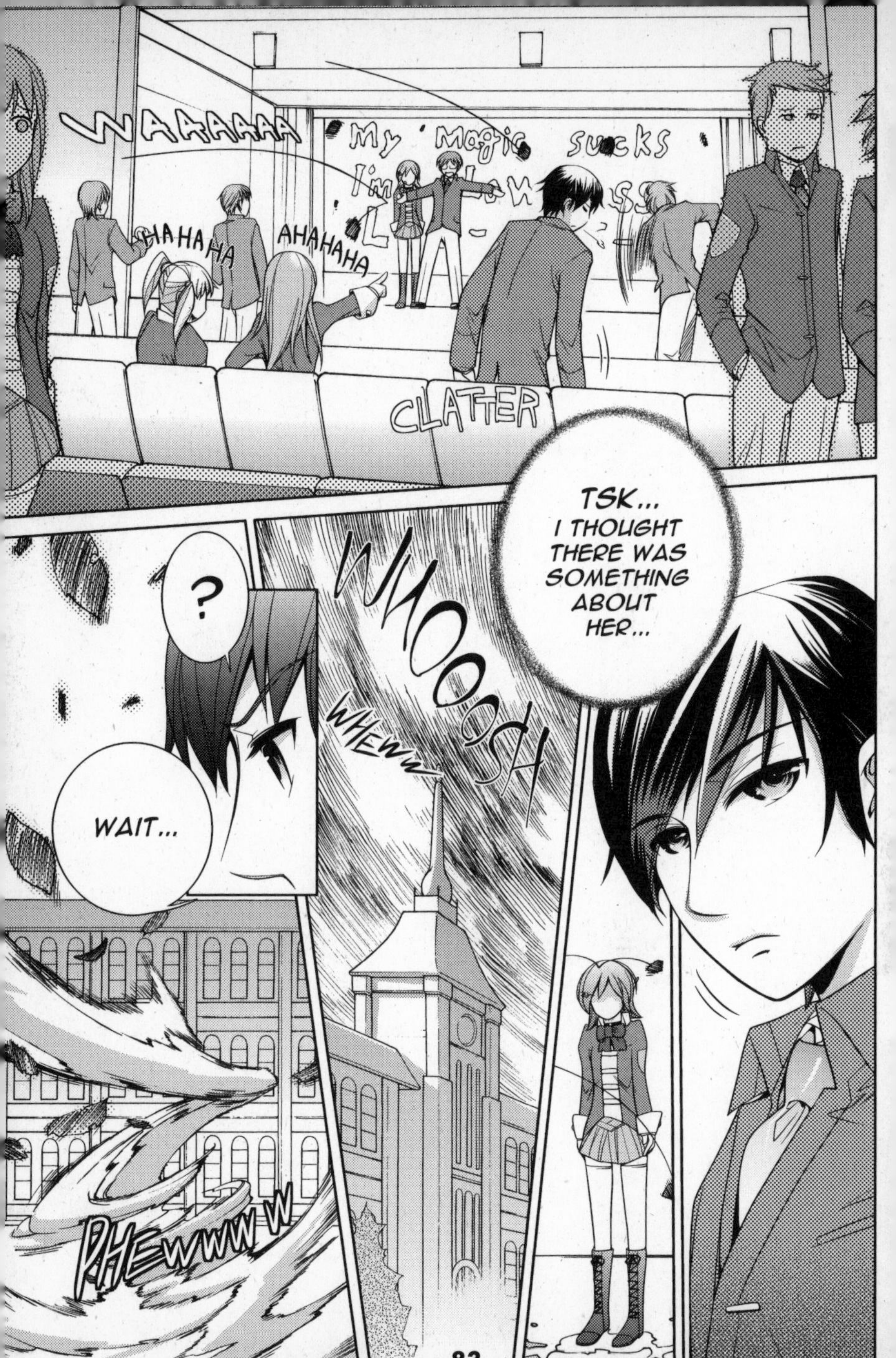
My magic sucks
WAAAAAA
AHAHAHA
HAHAHA
CLATTER
TSK... I THOUGHT THERE WAS SOMETHING ABOUT HER...
WHOOOSH
WHEWW
?
WAIT...
PHEWWWW

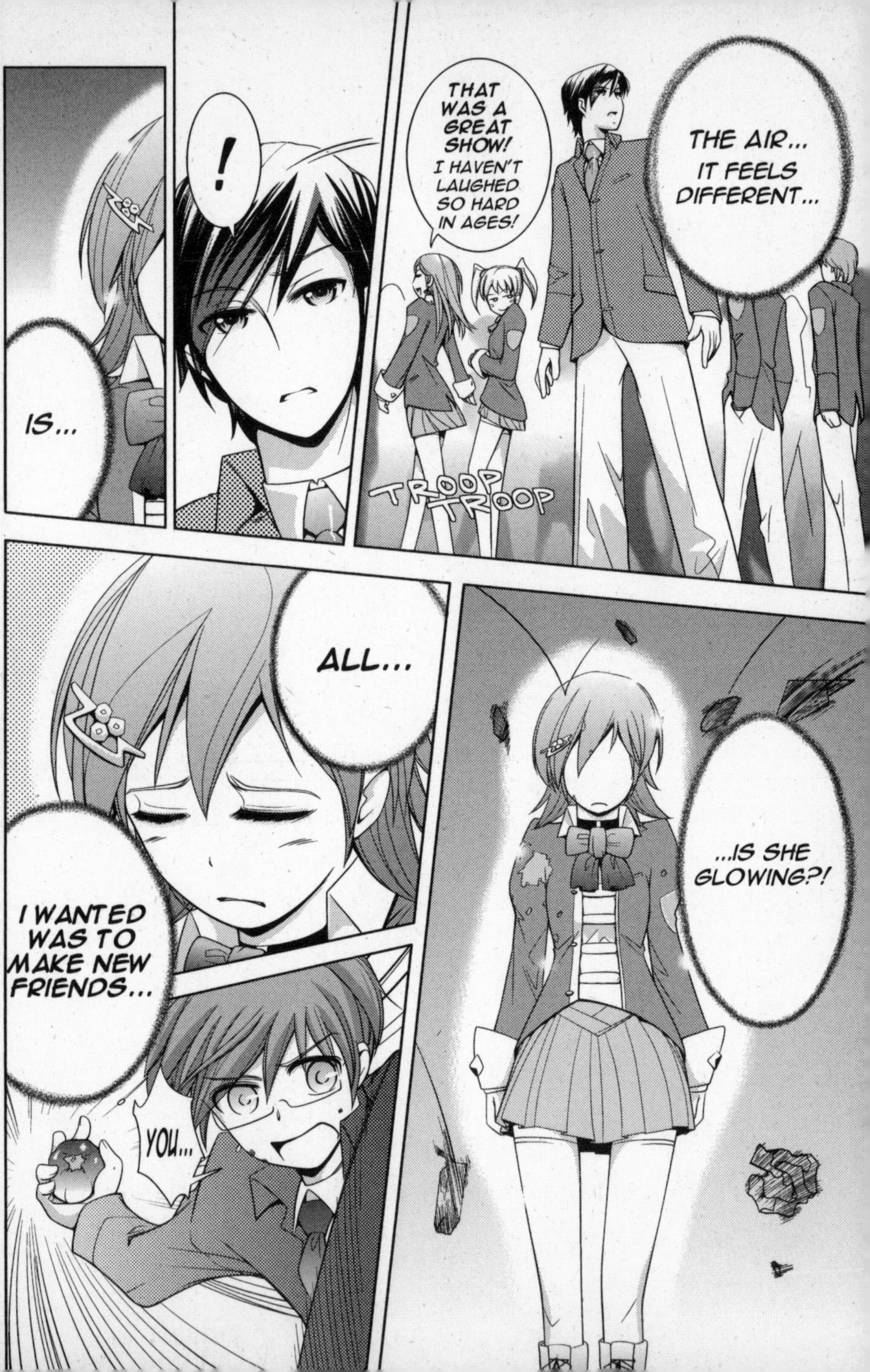
THE AIR... IT FEELS DIFFERENT...
THAT WAS A GREAT SHOW! I HAVEN'T LAUGHED SO HARD IN AGES!
TROOP TROOP
!
IS...
...IS SHE GLOWING?!
ALL...
I WANTED WAS TO MAKE NEW FRIENDS...
YOU...

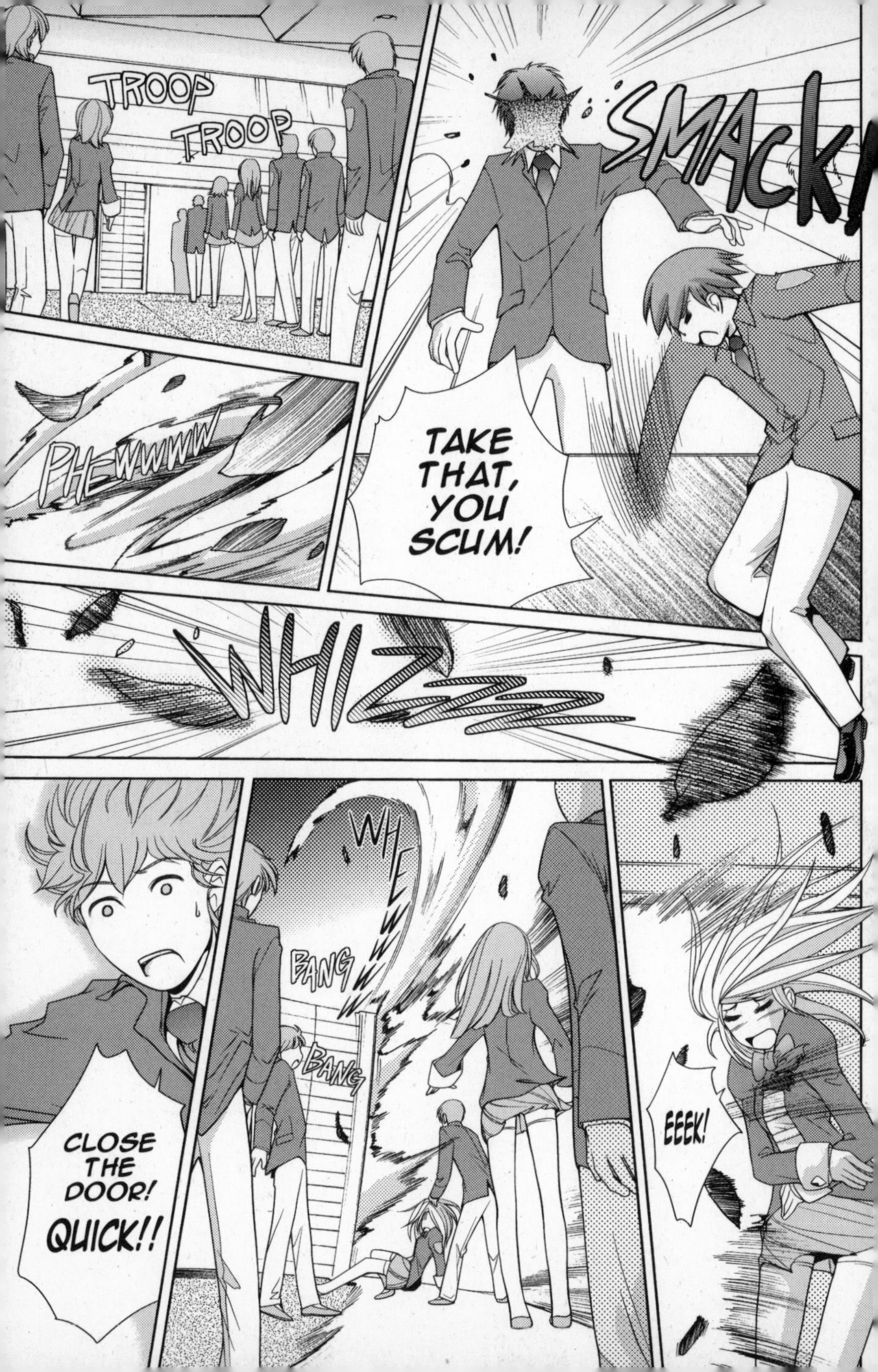
SMACK!
TAKE THAT, YOU SCUM!
TROOP
TROOP
PHEWWWW
WHIZZZZ
EEEK!
WHEEWWWWW
BANG
BANG
CLOSE THE DOOR! QUICK!!

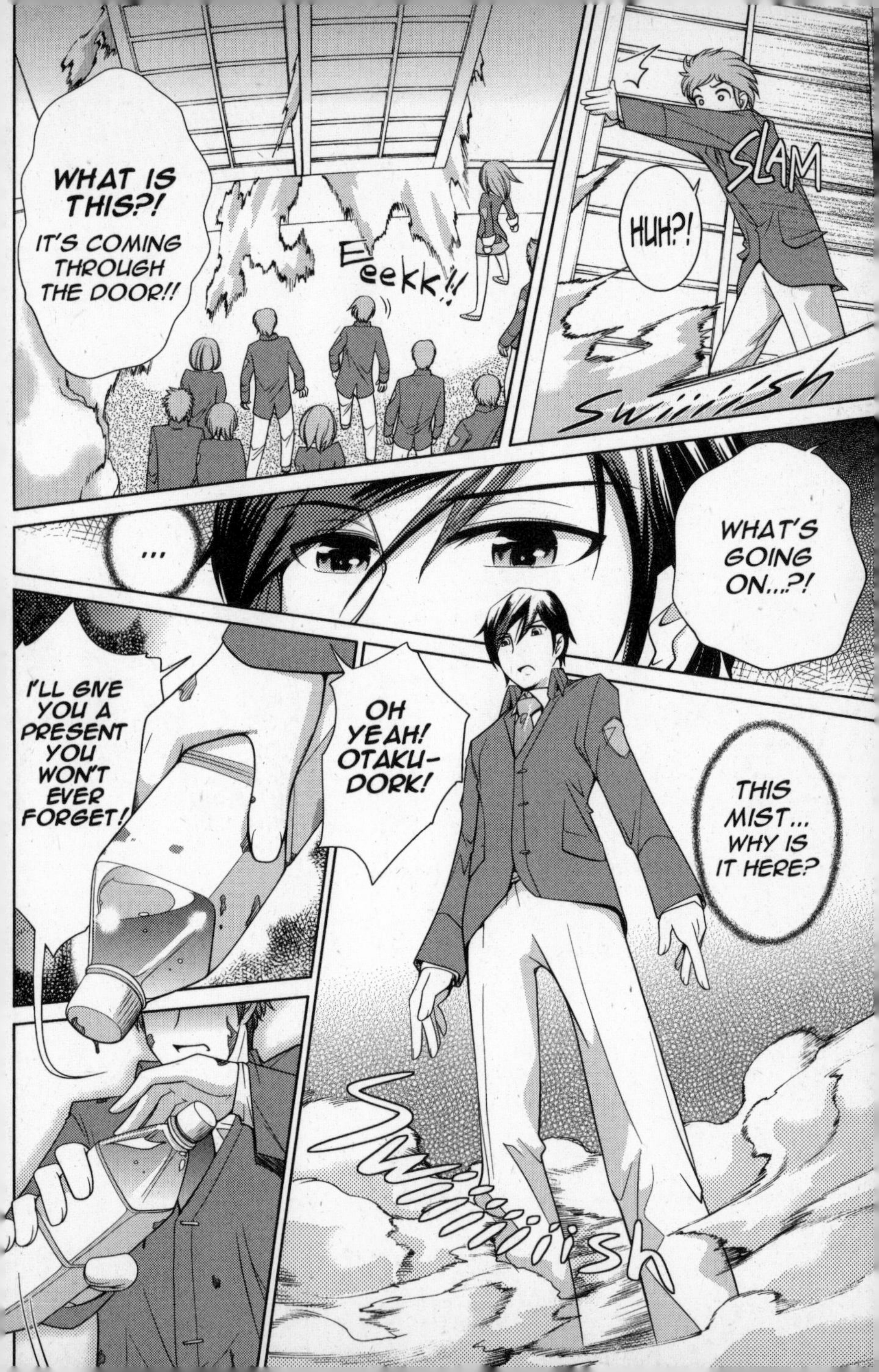
HUH?!
SLAM
Swiiiiish
WHAT IS THIS?! IT'S COMING THROUGH THE DOOR!!
Eeekk!!
WHAT'S GOING ON...?!
...
THIS MIST... WHY IS IT HERE?
Swiiiiiish
OH YEAH! OTAKU-DORK!
I'LL GIVE YOU A PRESENT YOU WON'T EVER FORGET!

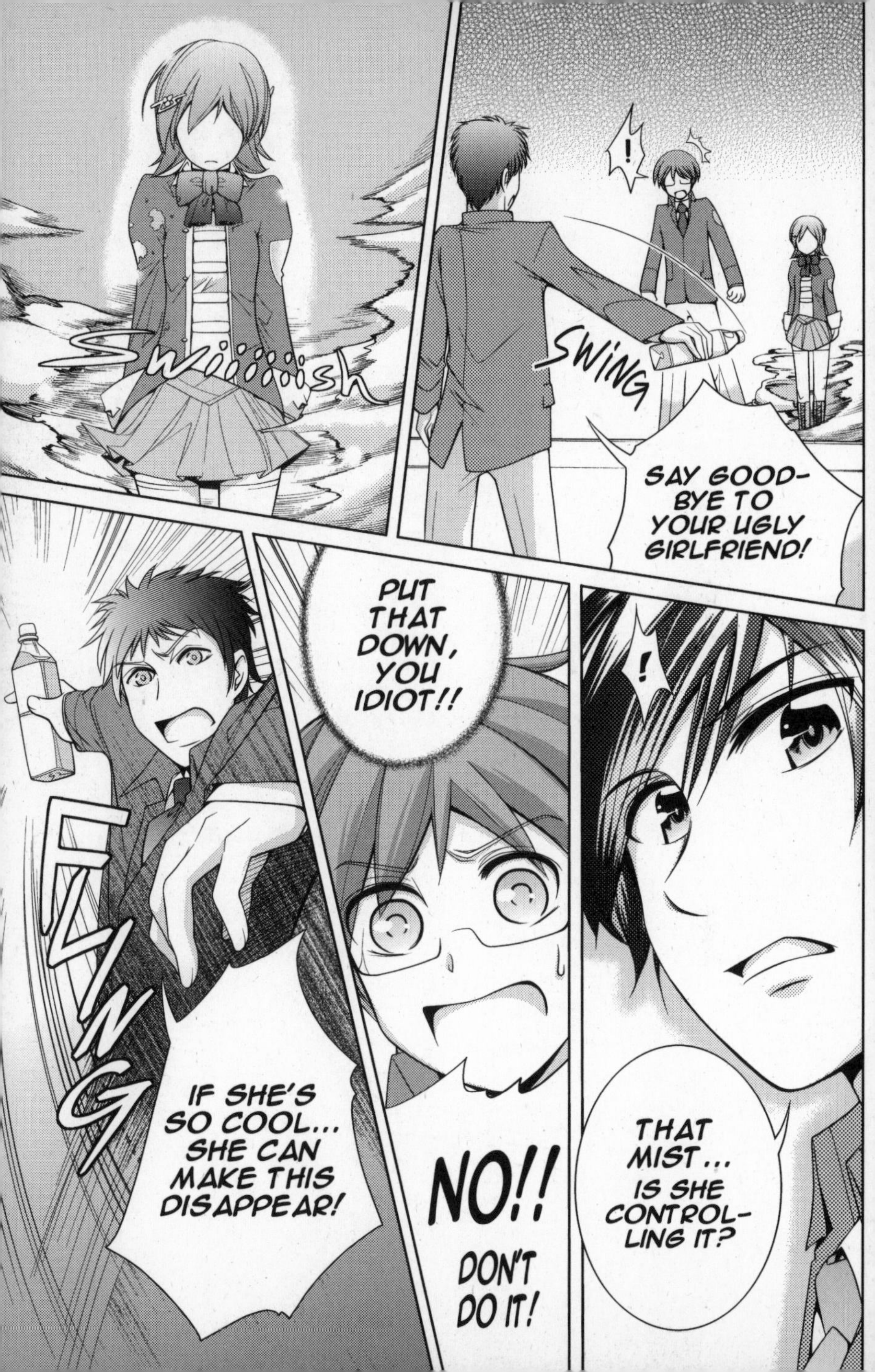
!
SWING
SAY GOOD-BYE TO YOUR UGLY GIRLFRIEND!
Swiiiiiish
!
THAT MIST... IS SHE CONTROL-LING IT?
PUT THAT DOWN, YOU IDIOT!!
NO!!
DON'T DO IT!
FLING
IF SHE'S SO COOL... SHE CAN MAKE THIS DISAPPEAR!

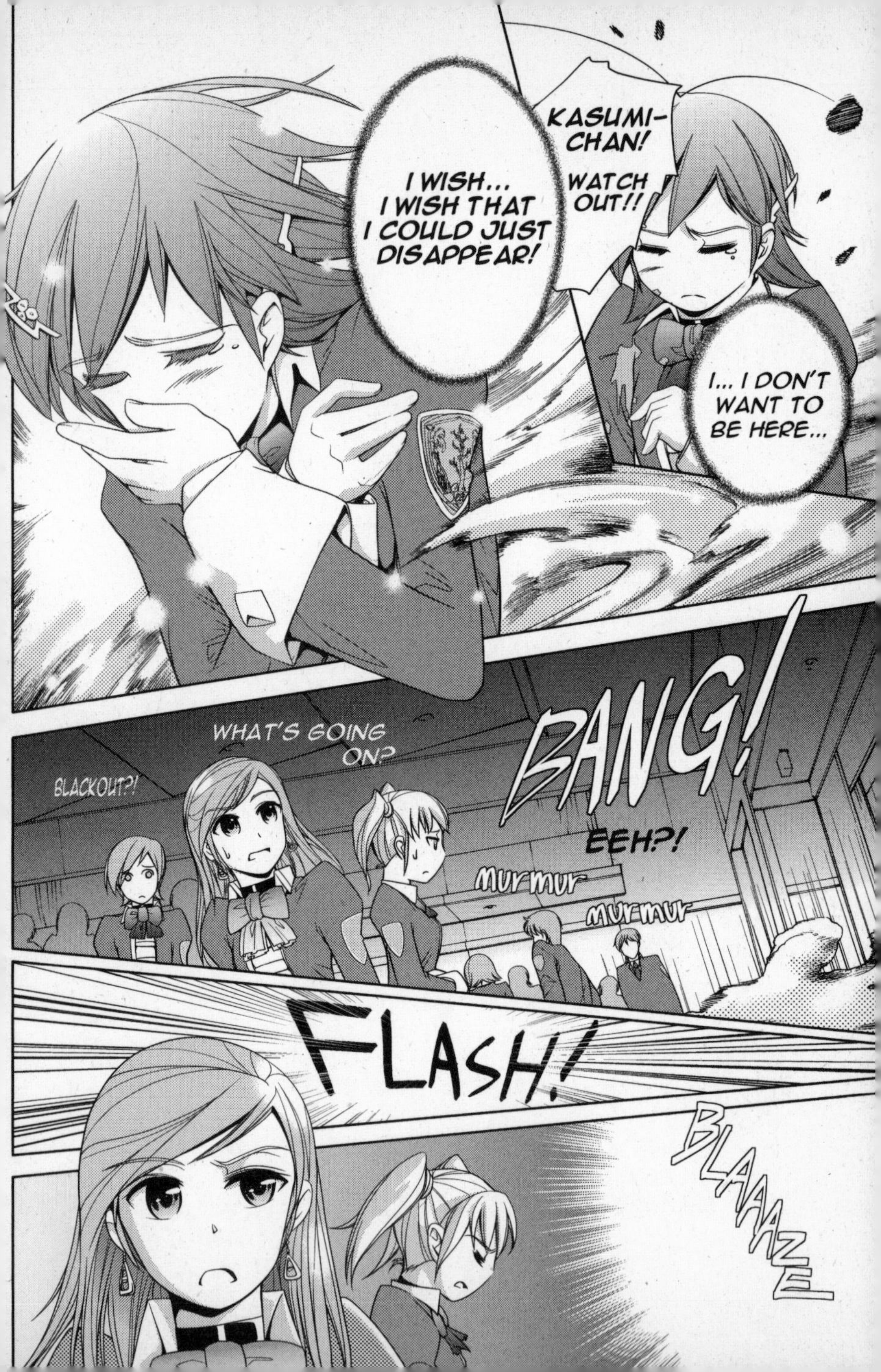
KASUMI-CHAN!
WATCH OUT!!
I WISH... I WISH THAT I COULD JUST DISAPPEAR!
I... I DON'T WANT TO BE HERE...
BANG!
EEH?!
murmur
murmur
WHAT'S GOING ON?
BLACKOUT?!
FLASH!
BLAAAZE

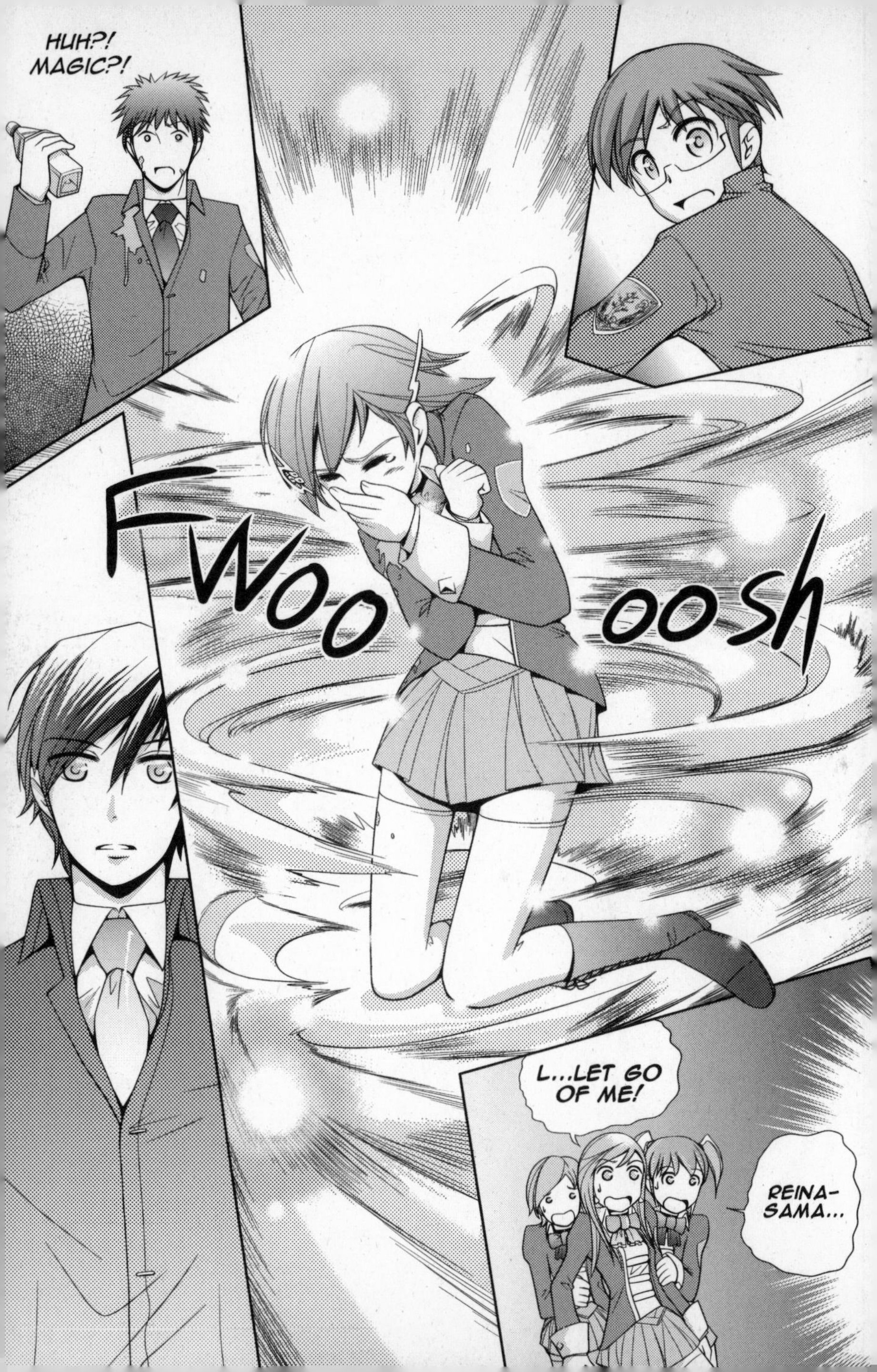
HUH?! MAGIC?!
FWOOOOSH
L...LET GO OF ME!
REINA-SAMA...

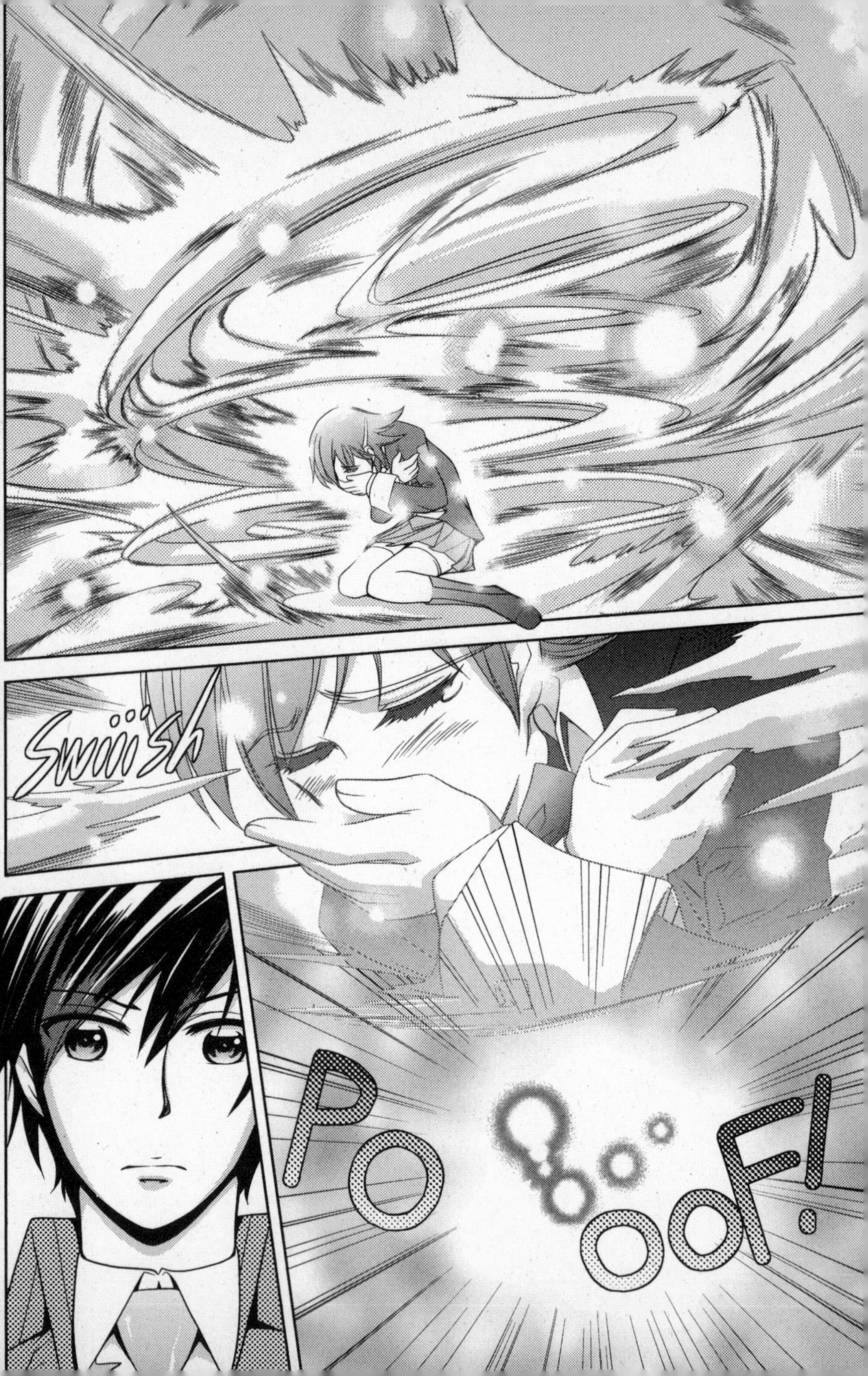
Swiiish
POOOOF!

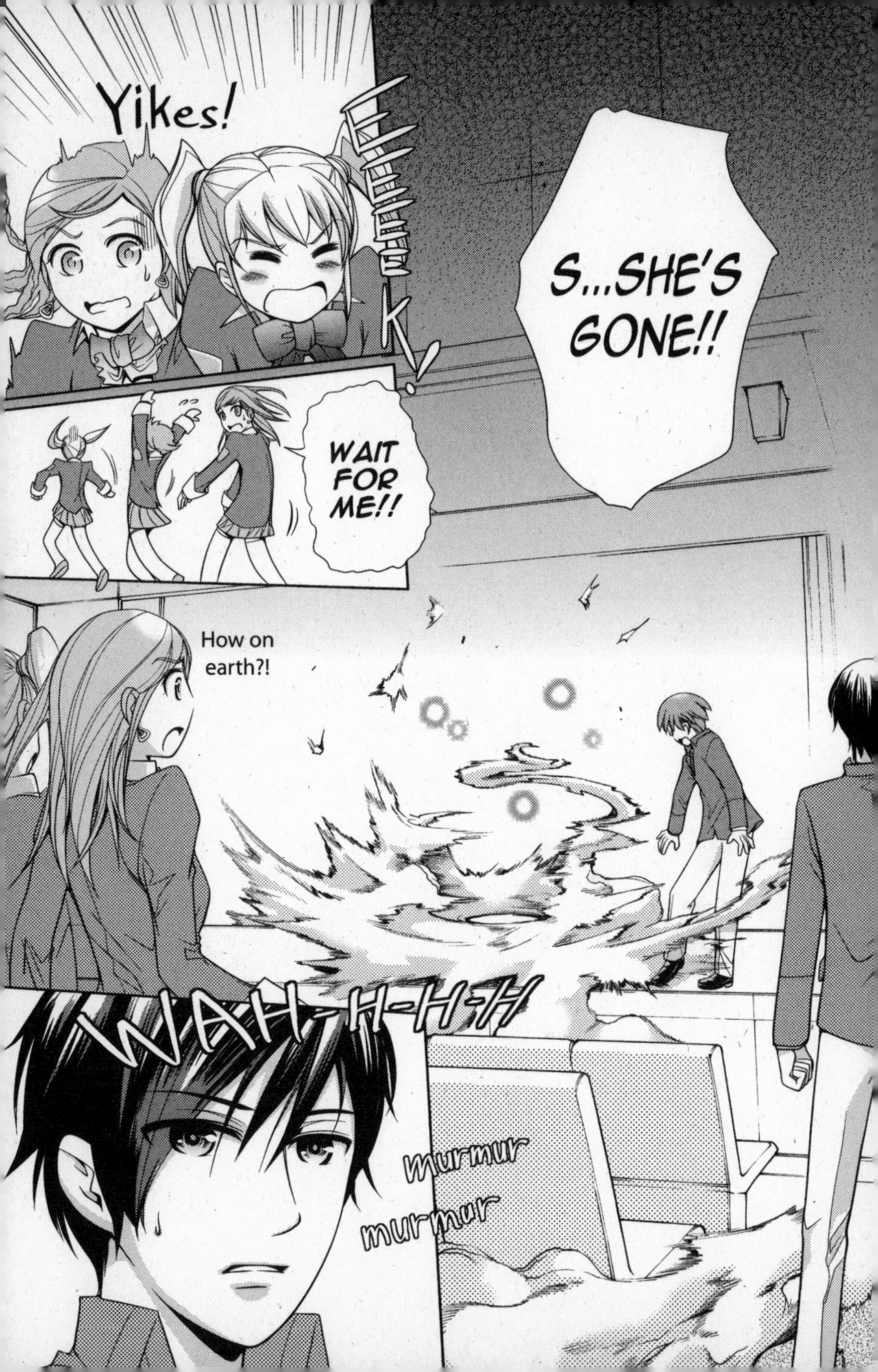
S...SHE'S GONE!!
Yikes!
EEEEEK!
WAIT FOR ME!!
How on earth?!
WAH-H-H-H
murmur
murmur

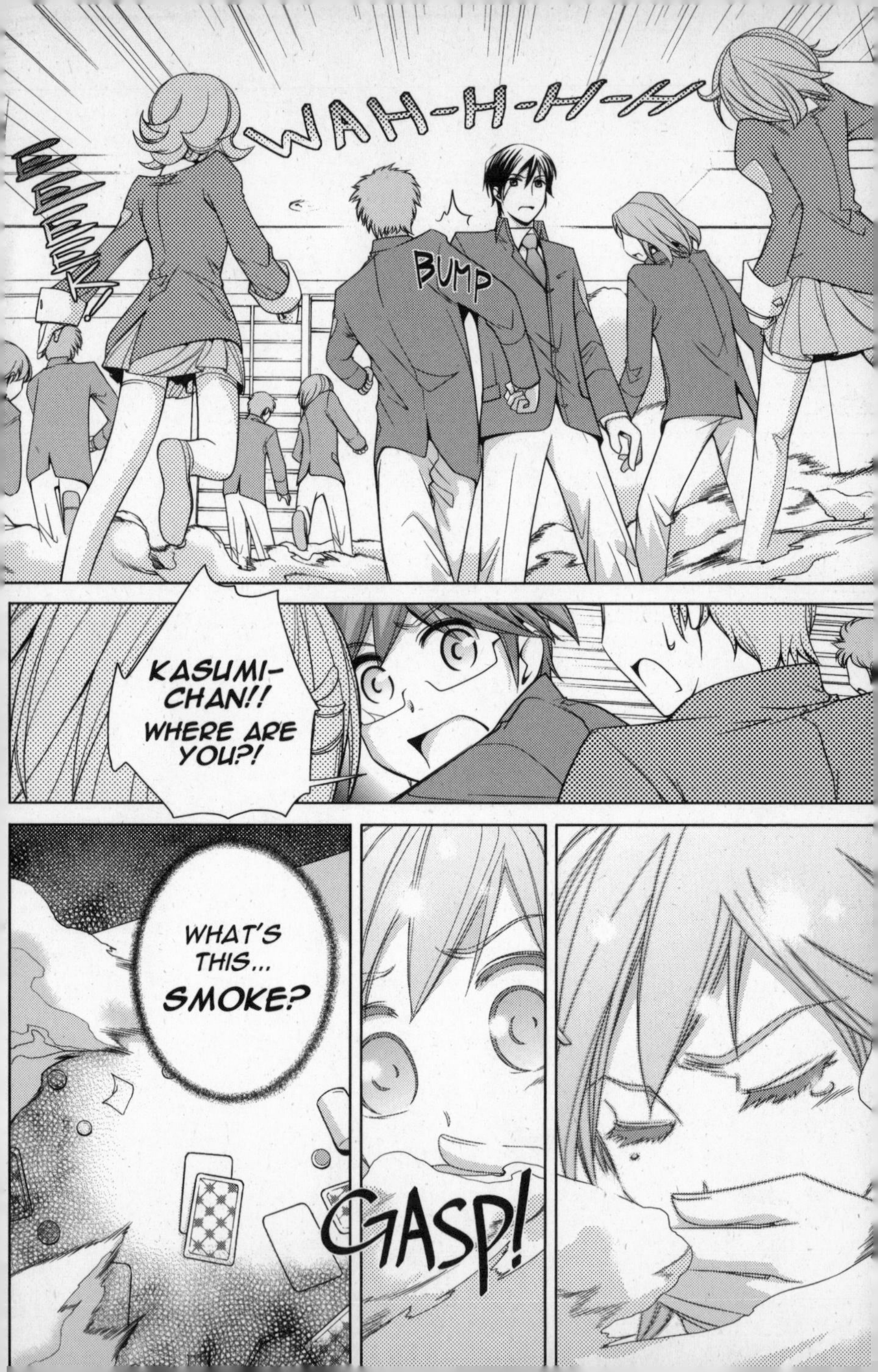
WAH-H-H-H
BUMP
EEEEK!
KASUMI-CHAN!! WHERE ARE YOU?!
GASP!
WHAT'S THIS... SMOKE?

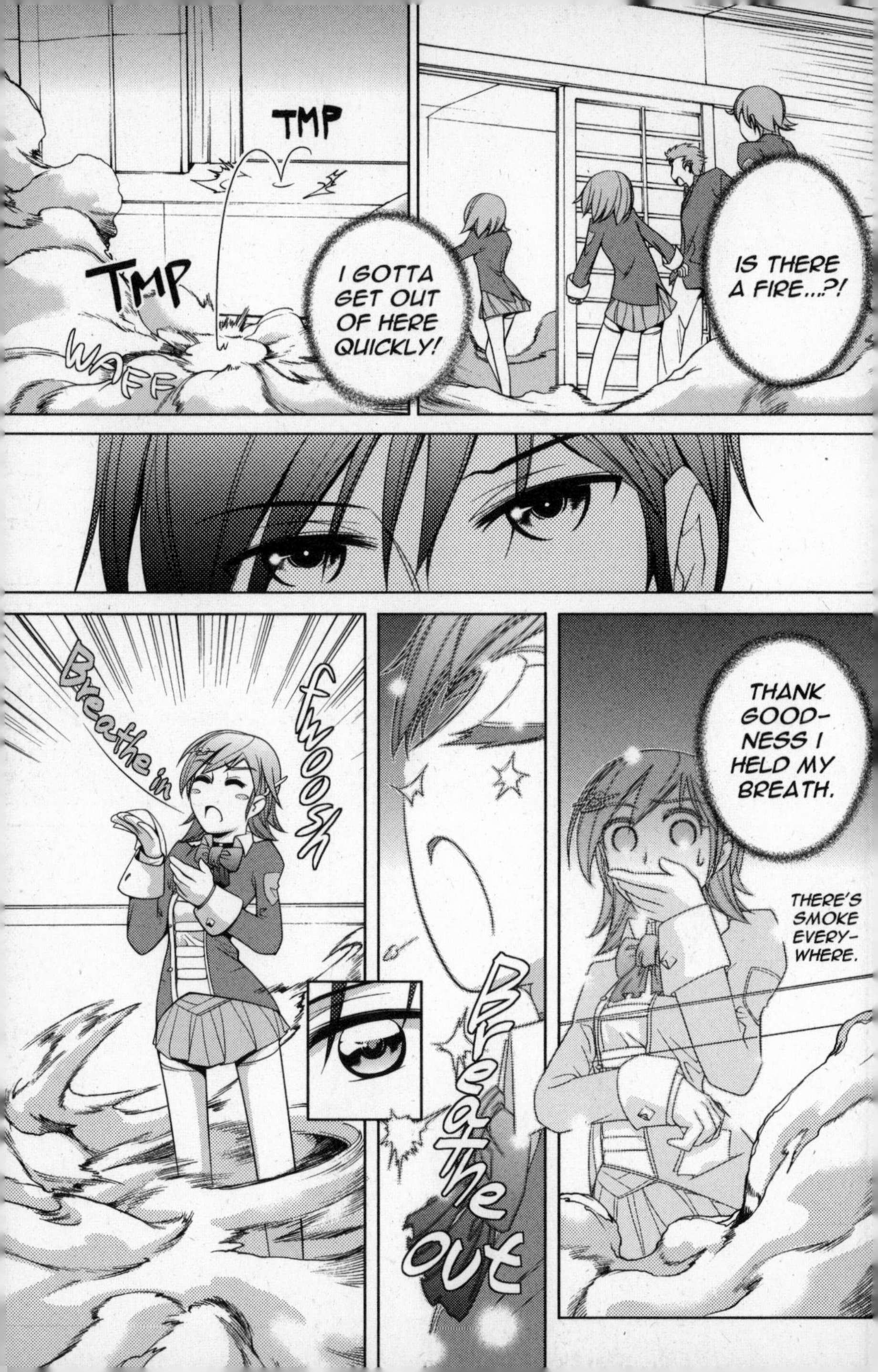
IS THERE A FIRE...?!
I GOTTA GET OUT OF HERE QUICKLY!
TMP
TMP
WAFF
THANK GOODNESS I HELD MY BREATH.
THERE'S SMOKE EVERYWHERE.
Breathe out
fwoosh
Breathe in

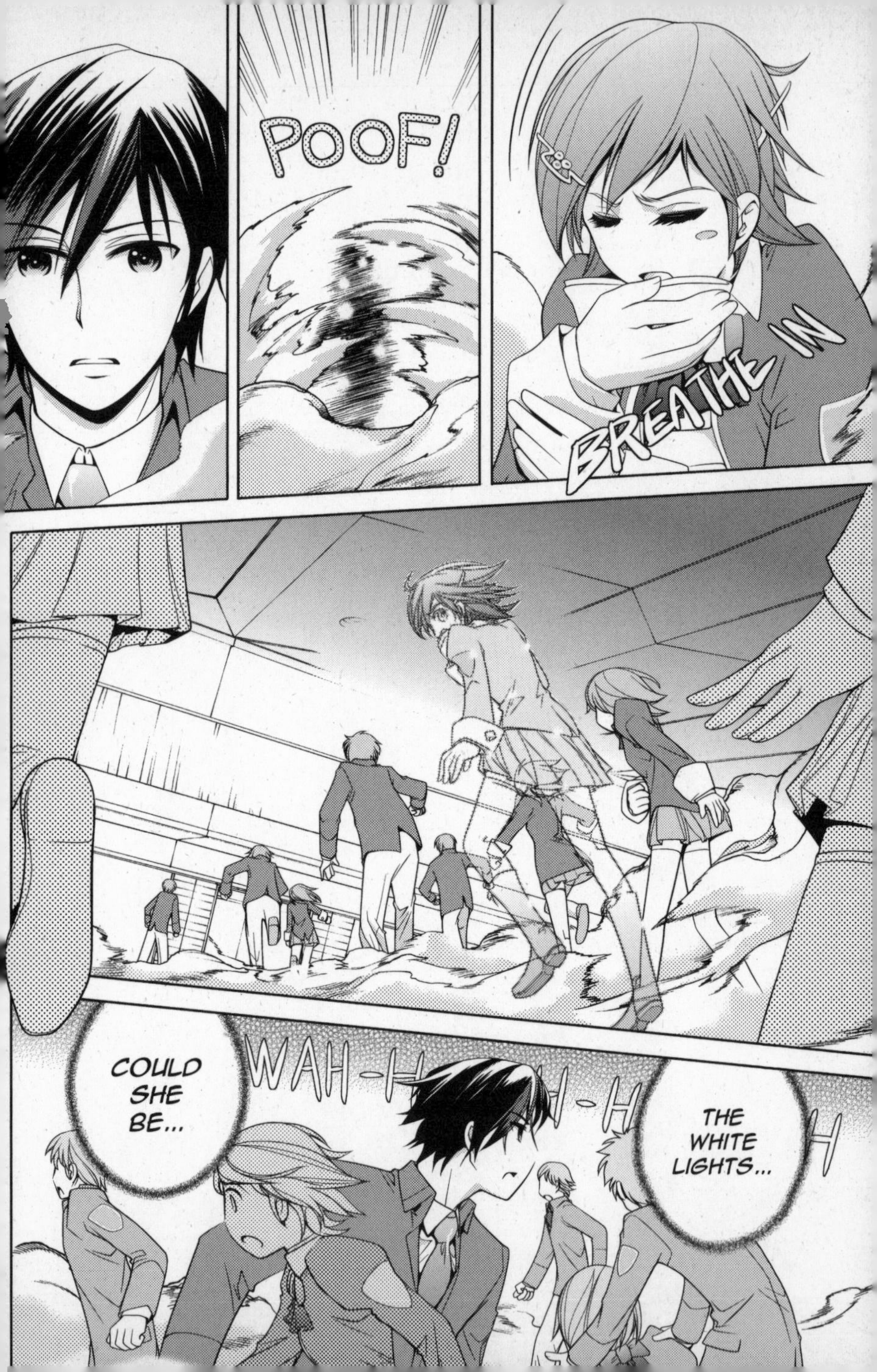
BREATHE IN
POOF!
THE WHITE LIGHTS...
WAH-H-H-H-H
COULD SHE BE...

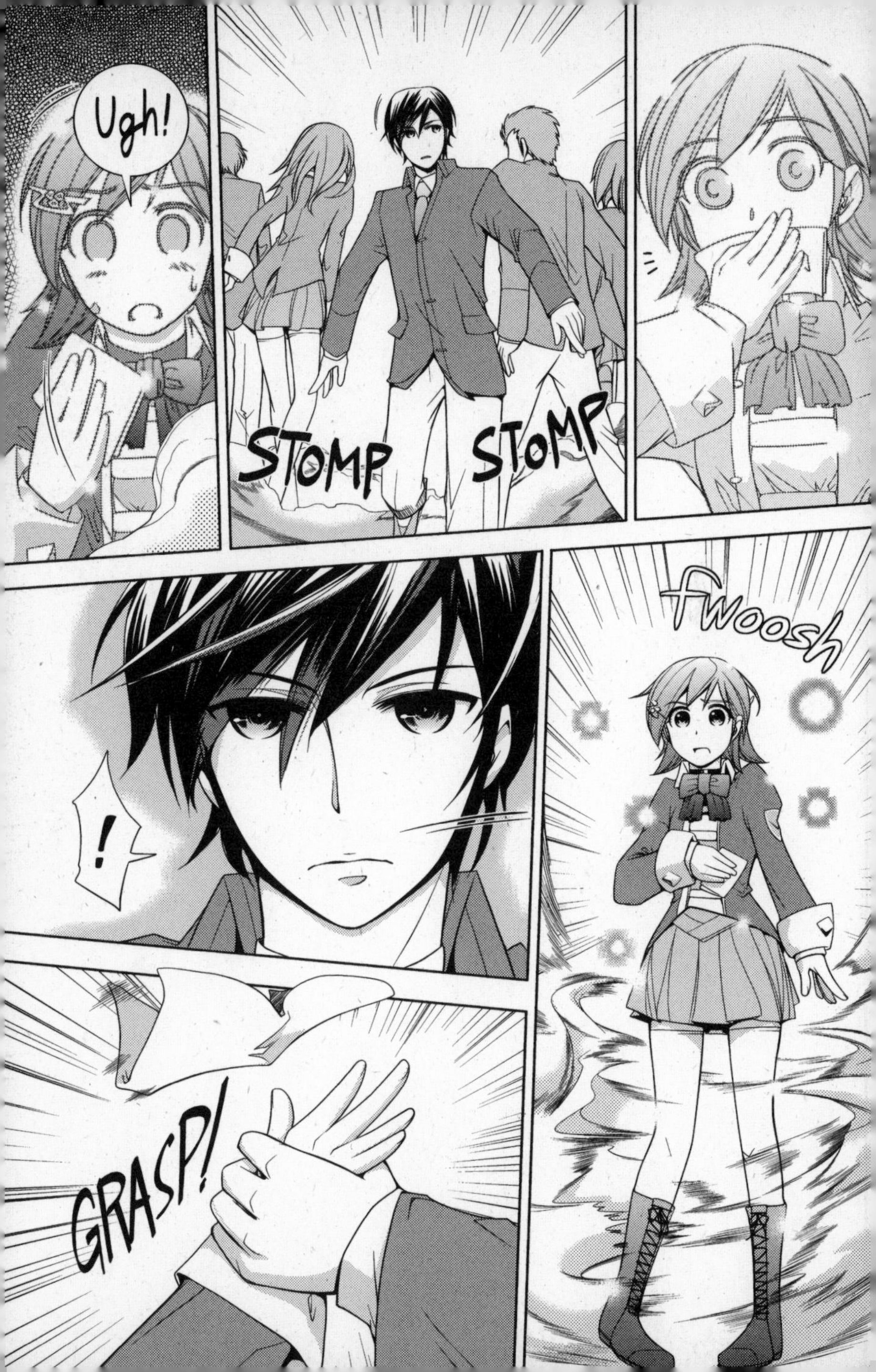
STOMP STOMP
Ugh!
fwoosh
!
GRASP!

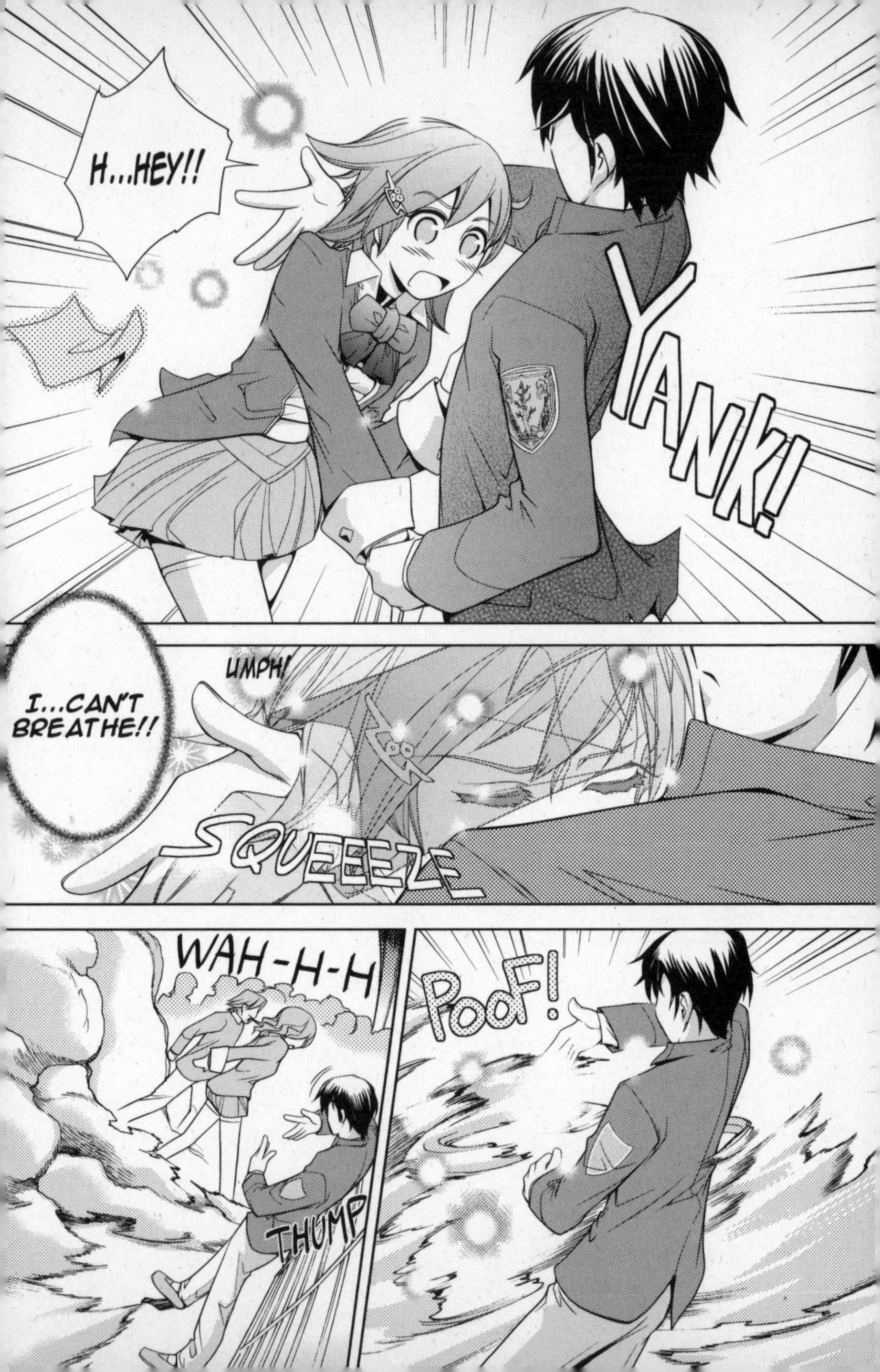
YANK!
H...HEY!!
UMPH!
I...CAN'T BREATHE!!
SQUEEEZE
POOF!
WAH-H-H
THUMP

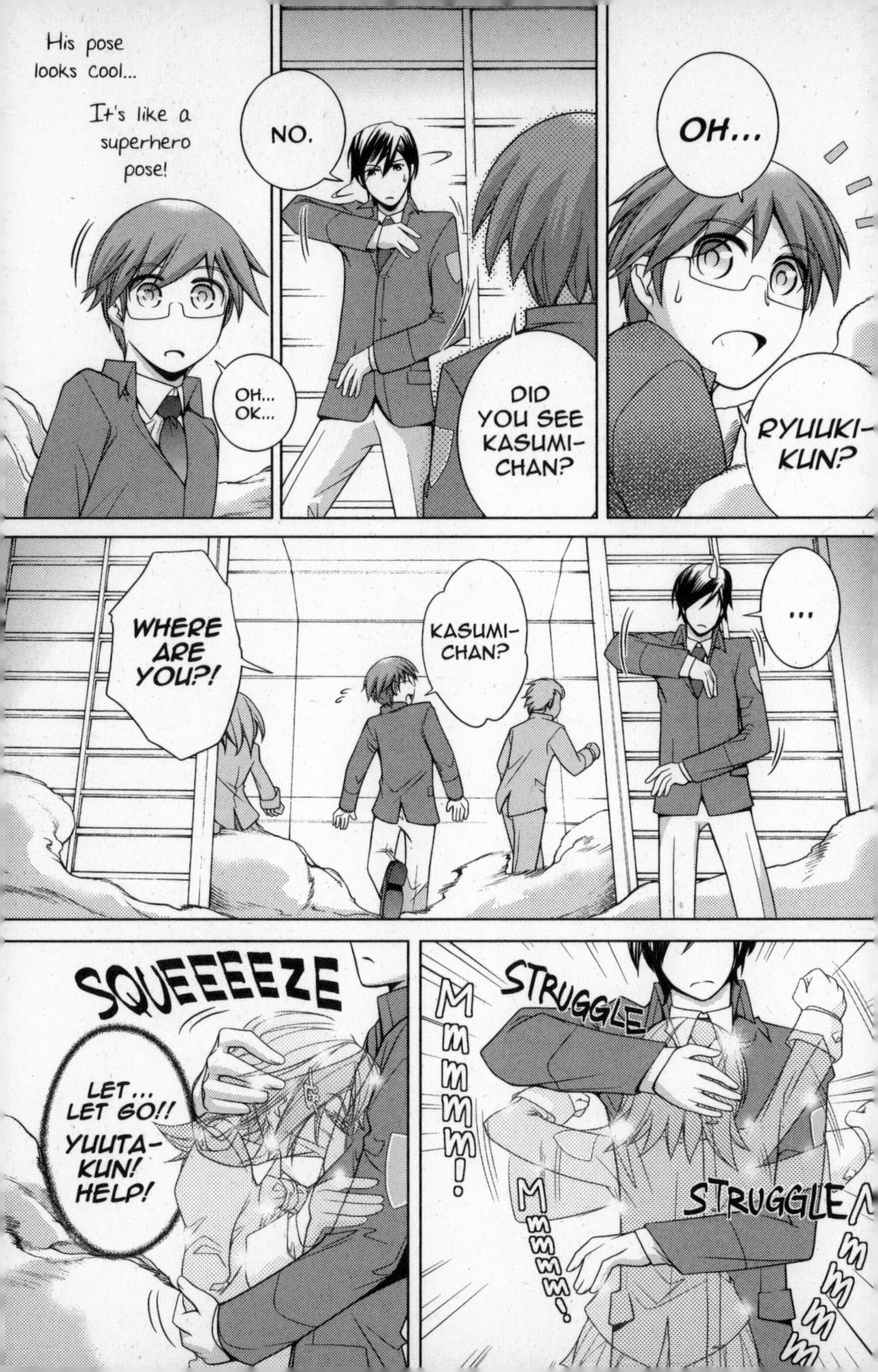
OH...
RYUUKI-KUN?
DID YOU SEE KASUMI-CHAN?
NO.
OH... OK...
His pose looks cool...
It's like a superhero pose!
...
KASUMI-CHAN?
WHERE ARE YOU?!
STRUGGLE
MMMMM!
STRUGGLE
Mmmmm!
SQUEEEEEZE
LET... LET GO!! YUUTA-KUN! HELP!

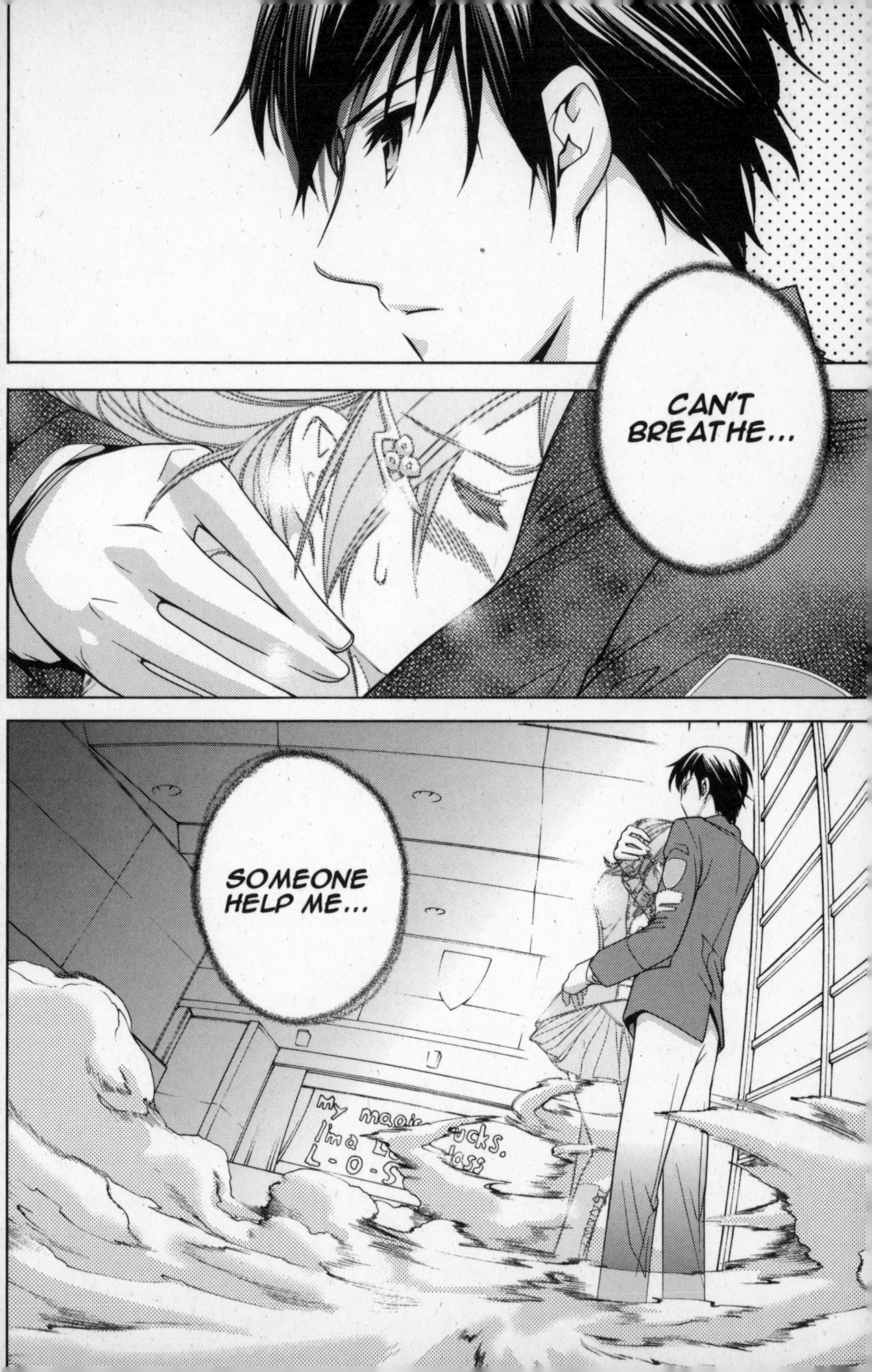
CAN'T BREATHE...
SOMEONE HELP ME...

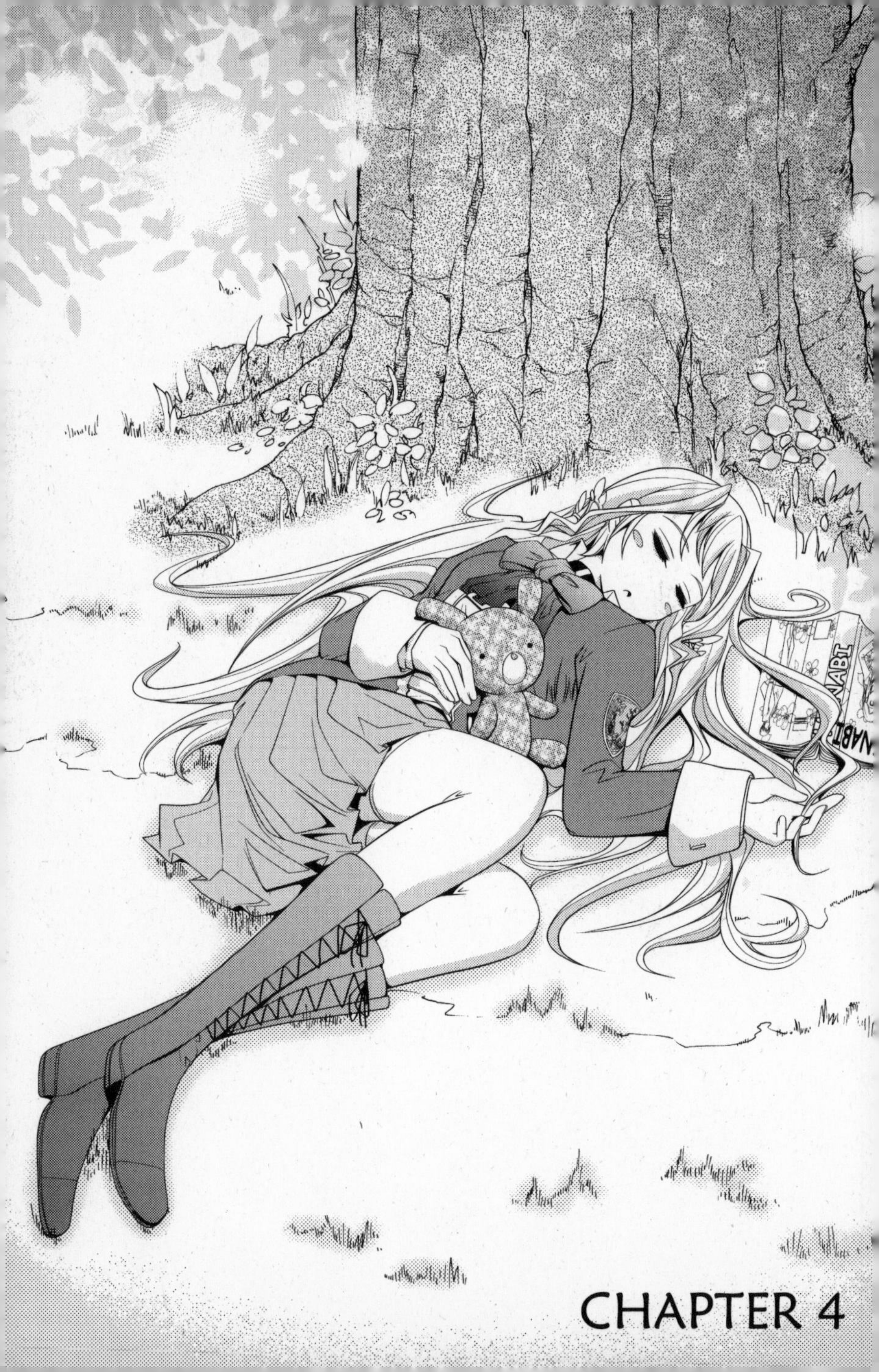

CHAPTER 4

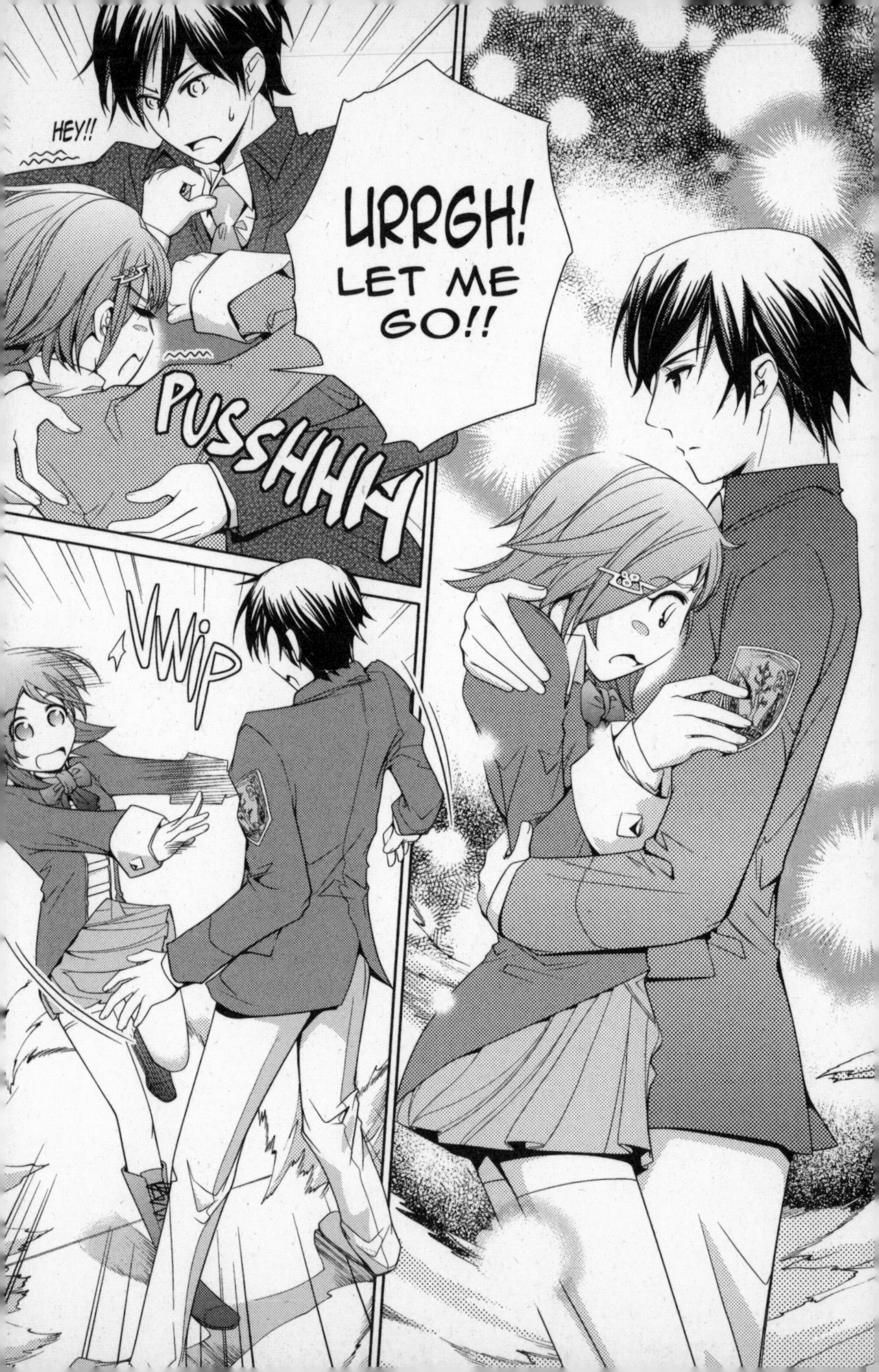
URRGH! LET ME GO!!
HEY!!
PUSSHHH
VWIP

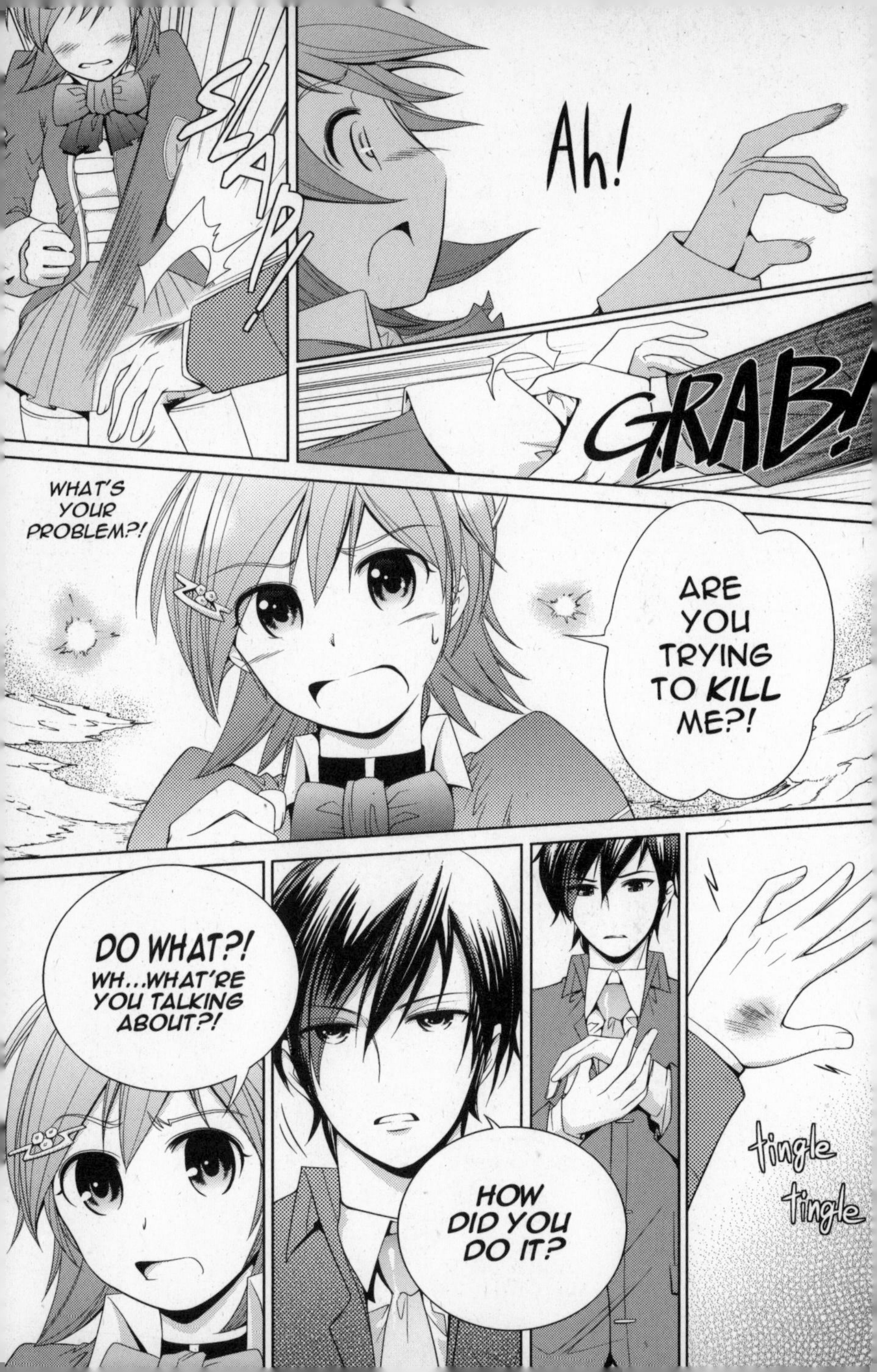
Ah!
GRAB!
SLAP!
WHAT'S YOUR PROBLEM?!
ARE YOU TRYING TO KILL ME?!
tingle tingle
HOW DID YOU DO IT?
DO WHAT?! WH...WHAT'RE YOU TALKING ABOUT?!

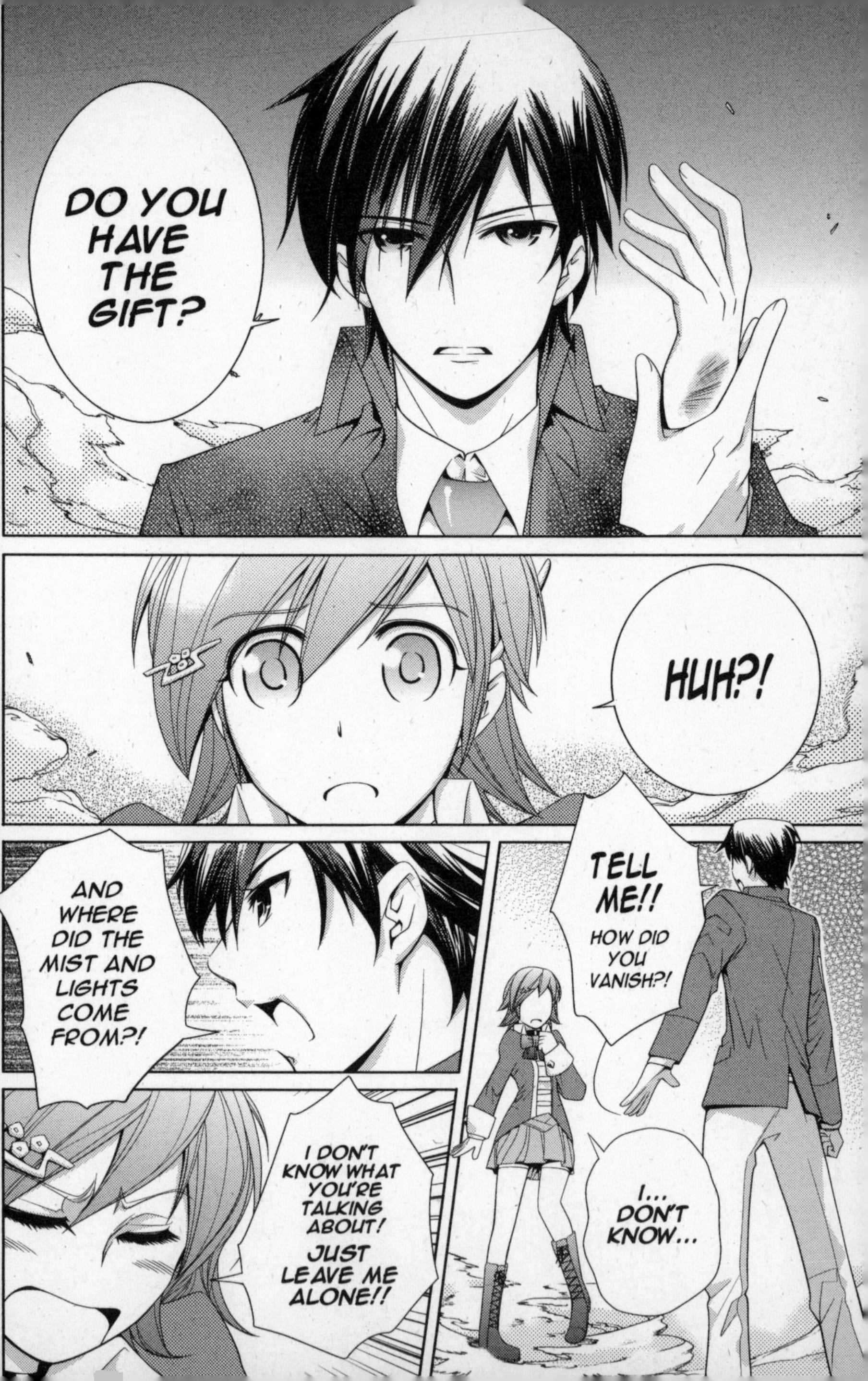
DO YOU HAVE THE GIFT?
HUH?!
TELL ME!!
HOW DID YOU VANISH?!
I... DON'T KNOW...
AND WHERE DID THE MIST AND LIGHTS COME FROM?!
I DON'T KNOW WHAT YOU'RE TALKING ABOUT!
JUST LEAVE ME ALONE!!

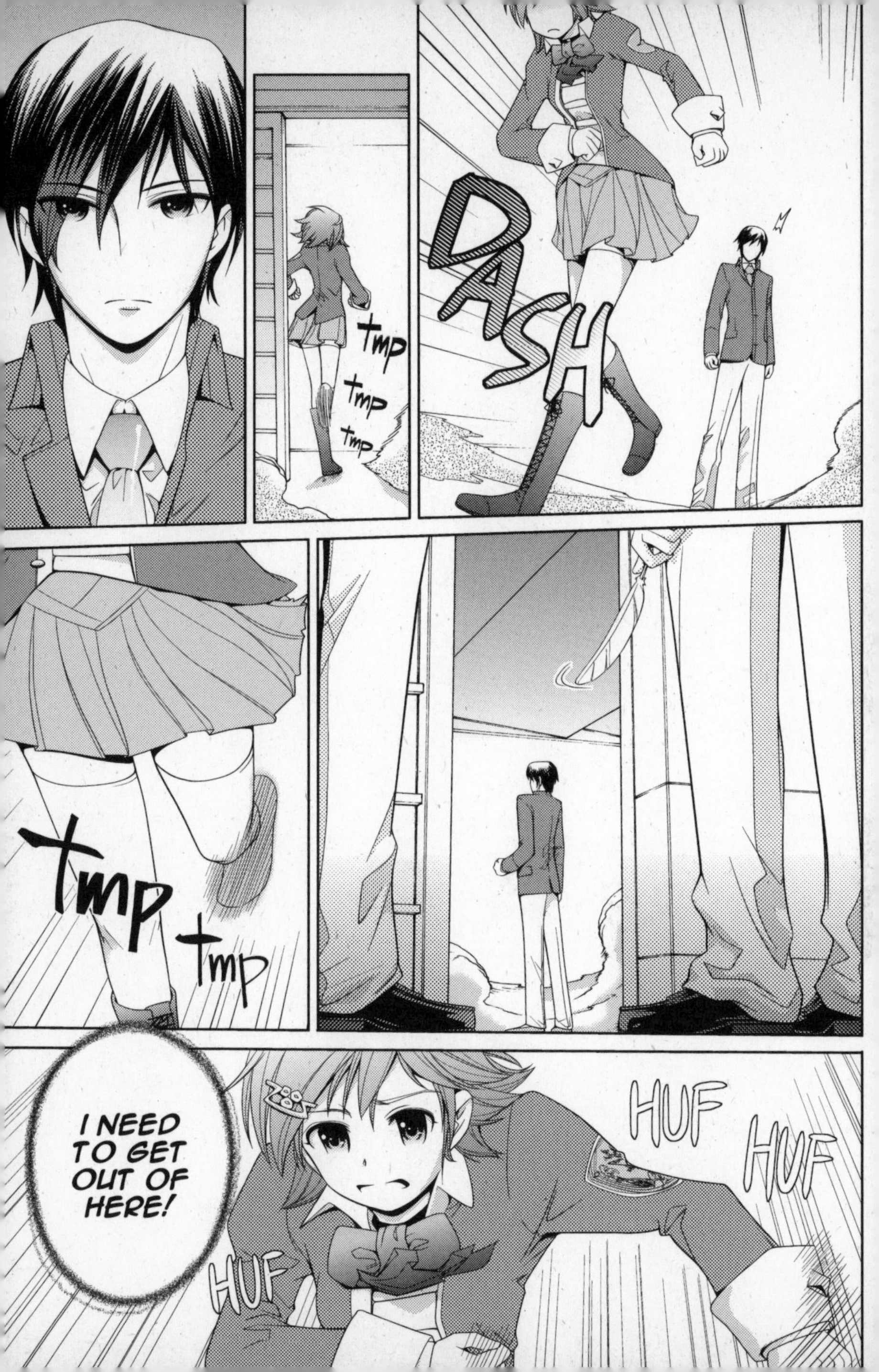
DASH
tmp
tmp
tmp
tmp
tmp
HUF
HUF
I NEED TO GET OUT OF HERE!
HUF

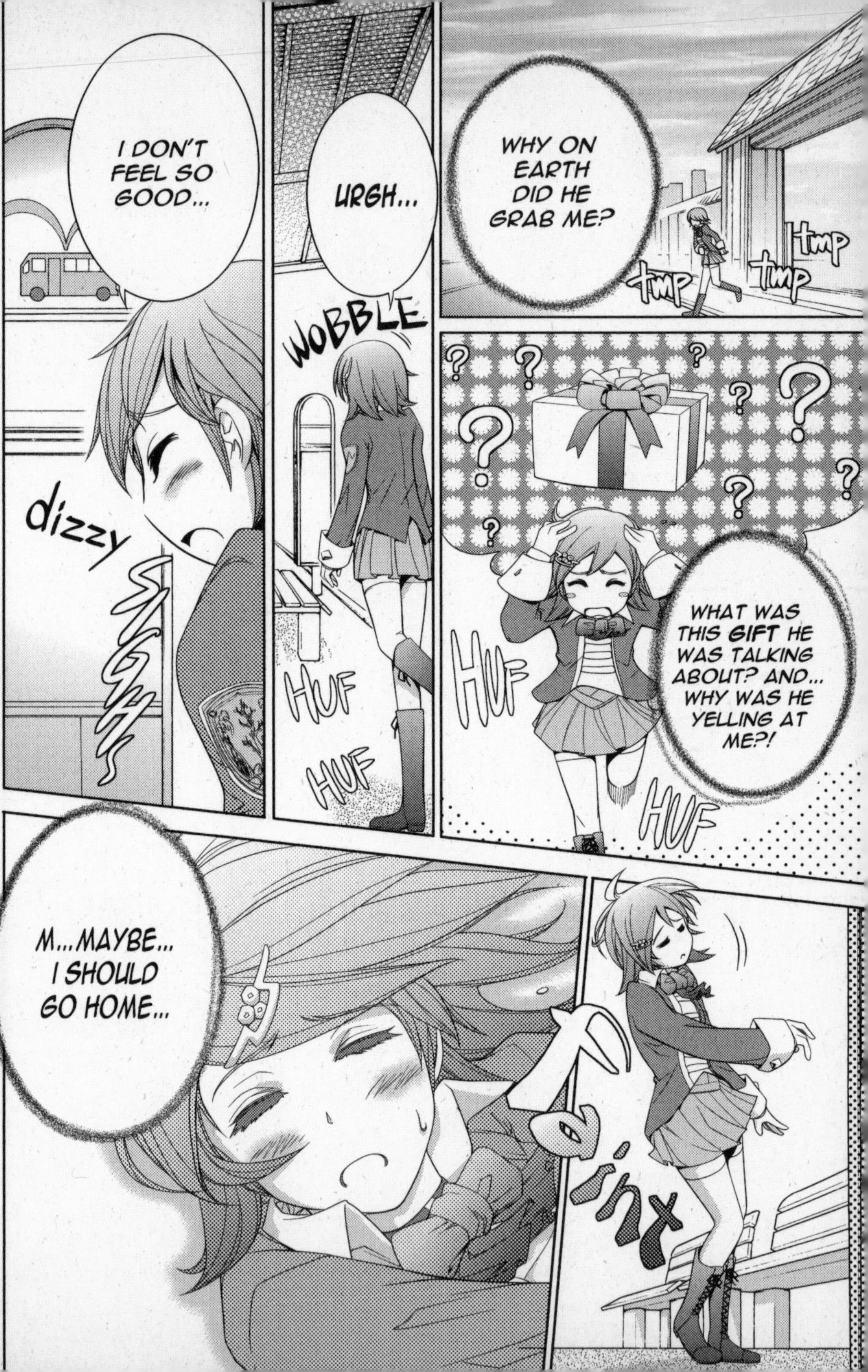
WHY ON EARTH DID HE GRAB ME?
tmp
tmp
tmp
WHAT WAS THIS **GIFT** HE WAS TALKING ABOUT? AND... WHY WAS HE YELLING AT ME?!
HUF
HUF
URGH...
WOBBLE
HUF
HUF
I DON'T FEEL SO GOOD...
dizzy
M...MAYBE... I SHOULD GO HOME...

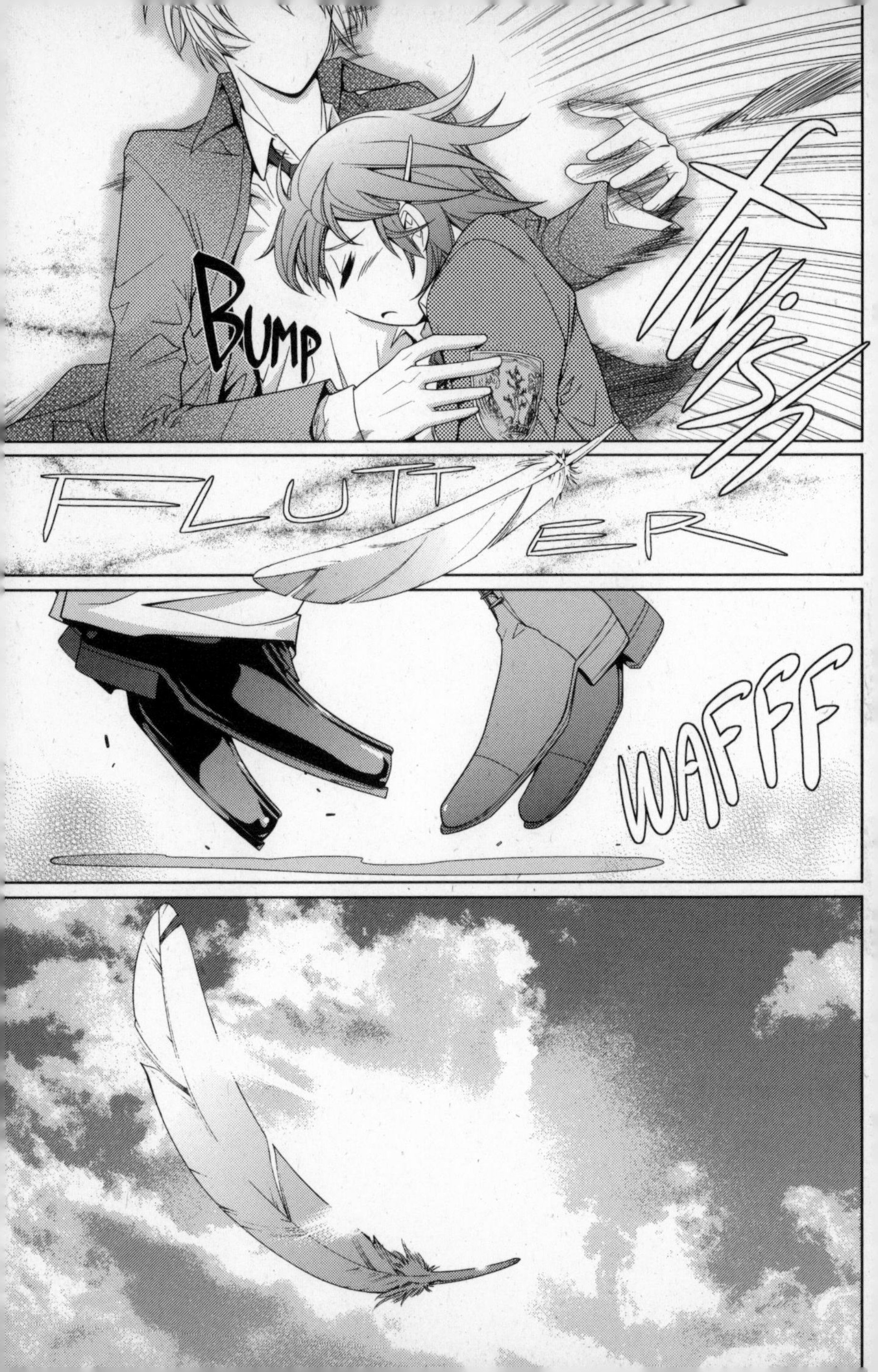
SWISH
BUMP
FLUTTER
WAFFF

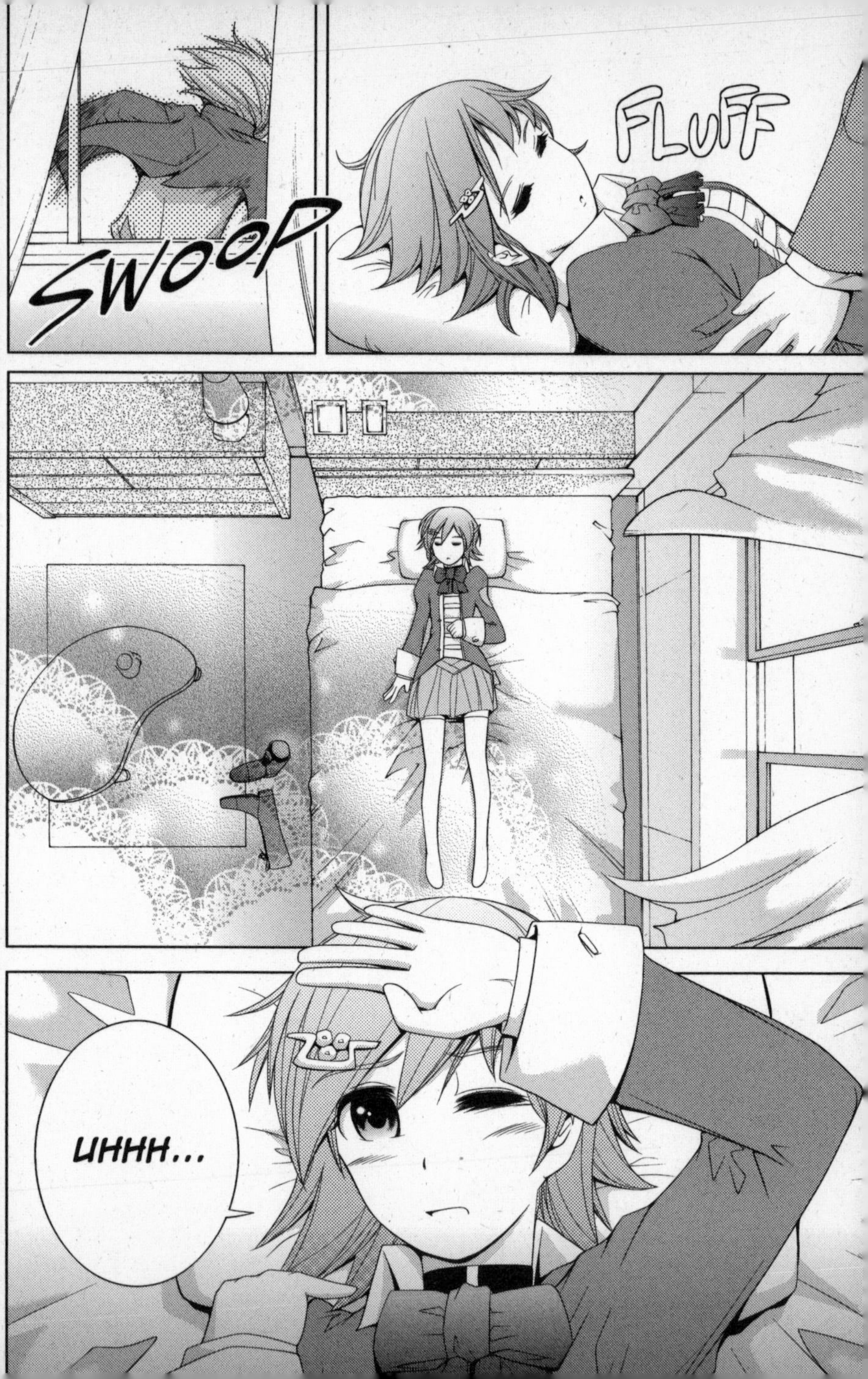
FLUFF
SWOOP
UHHH...

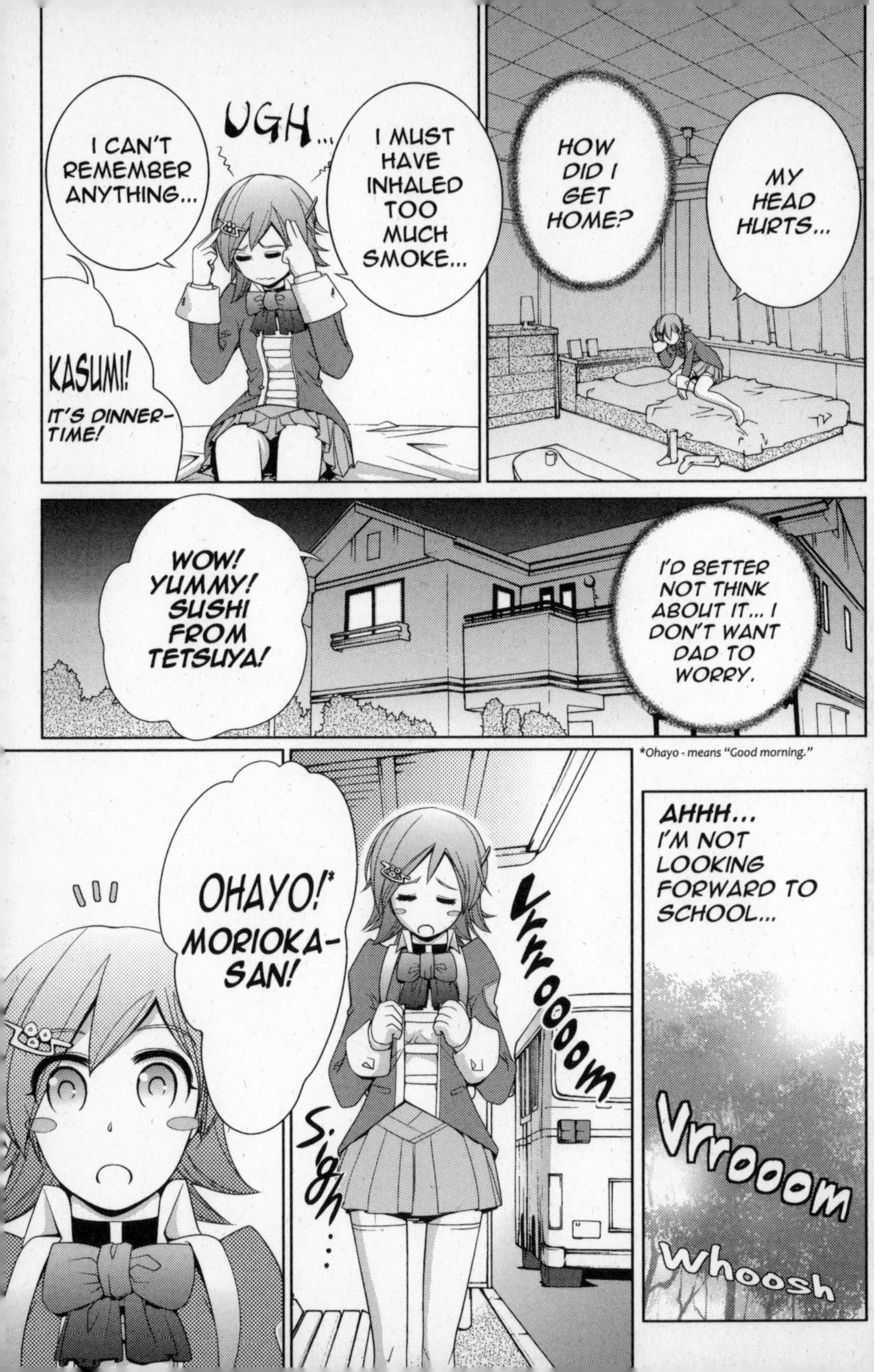
MY HEAD HURTS...
HOW DID I GET HOME?
I MUST HAVE INHALED TOO MUCH SMOKE...
UGH...
I CAN'T REMEMBER ANYTHING...
KASUMI!
IT'S DINNER-TIME!
I'D BETTER NOT THINK ABOUT IT... I DON'T WANT DAD TO WORRY.
WOW! YUMMY! SUSHI FROM TETSUYA!
AHHH... I'M NOT LOOKING FORWARD TO SCHOOL...
Vrrooom
Whoosh
Vrrroooom
Sigh...
OHAYO!* MORIOKA-SAN!

*Ohayo - means "Good morning."

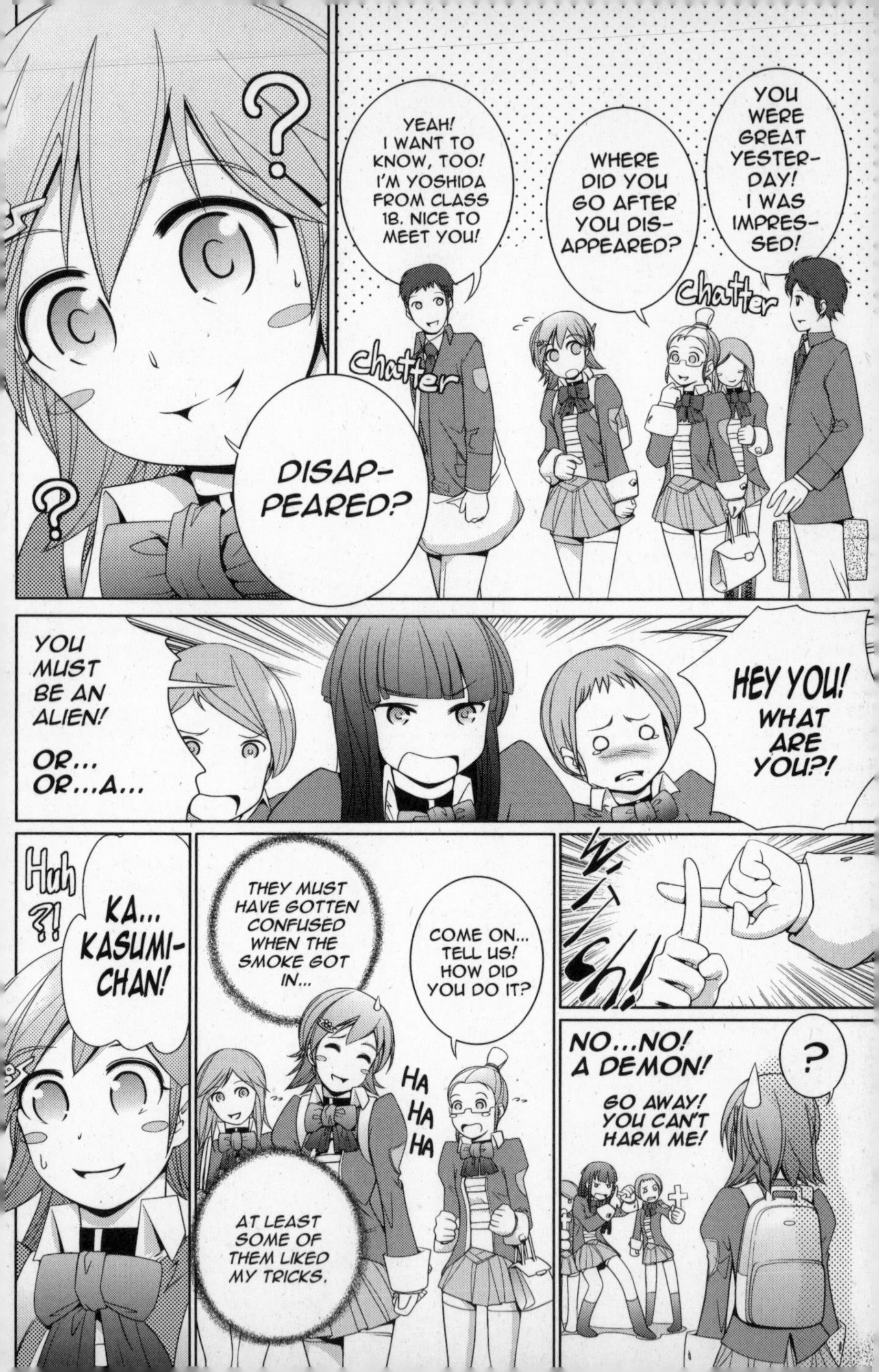
YOU WERE GREAT YESTER-DAY! I WAS IMPRES-SED!
Chatter
WHERE DID YOU GO AFTER YOU DIS-APPEARED?
YEAH! I WANT TO KNOW, TOO! I'M YOSHIDA FROM CLASS 1B. NICE TO MEET YOU!
Chatter
DISAP-PEARED?
HEY YOU! WHAT ARE YOU?!
YOU MUST BE AN ALIEN!
OR... OR...A...
WITCH!!
?
NO...NO! A DEMON!
GO AWAY! YOU CAN'T HARM ME!
COME ON... TELL US! HOW DID YOU DO IT?
THEY MUST HAVE GOTTEN CONFUSED WHEN THE SMOKE GOT IN...
HA HA HA
AT LEAST SOME OF THEM LIKED MY TRICKS.
KA... KASUMI-CHAN!
Huh?!

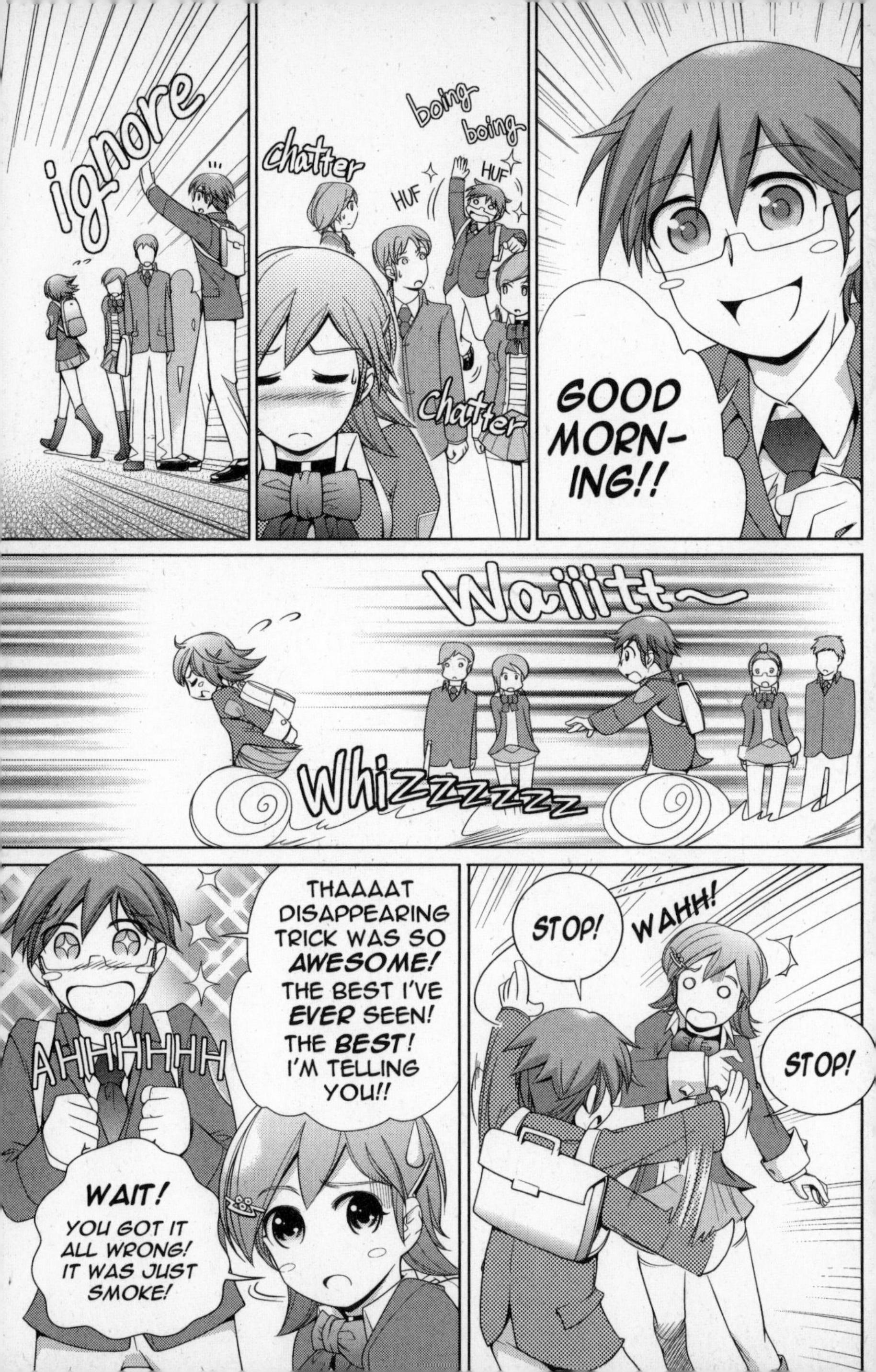
GOOD MORNING!!
boing boing
HUF
HUF
chatter
Chatter
ignore
Waiiitt~
Whizzzzzzz
STOP!
WAHH!
STOP!
THAAAAT DISAPPEARING TRICK WAS SO AWESOME! THE BEST I'VE EVER SEEN! THE BEST! I'M TELLING YOU!!
AHHHHHH
WAIT! YOU GOT IT ALL WRONG! IT WAS JUST SMOKE!

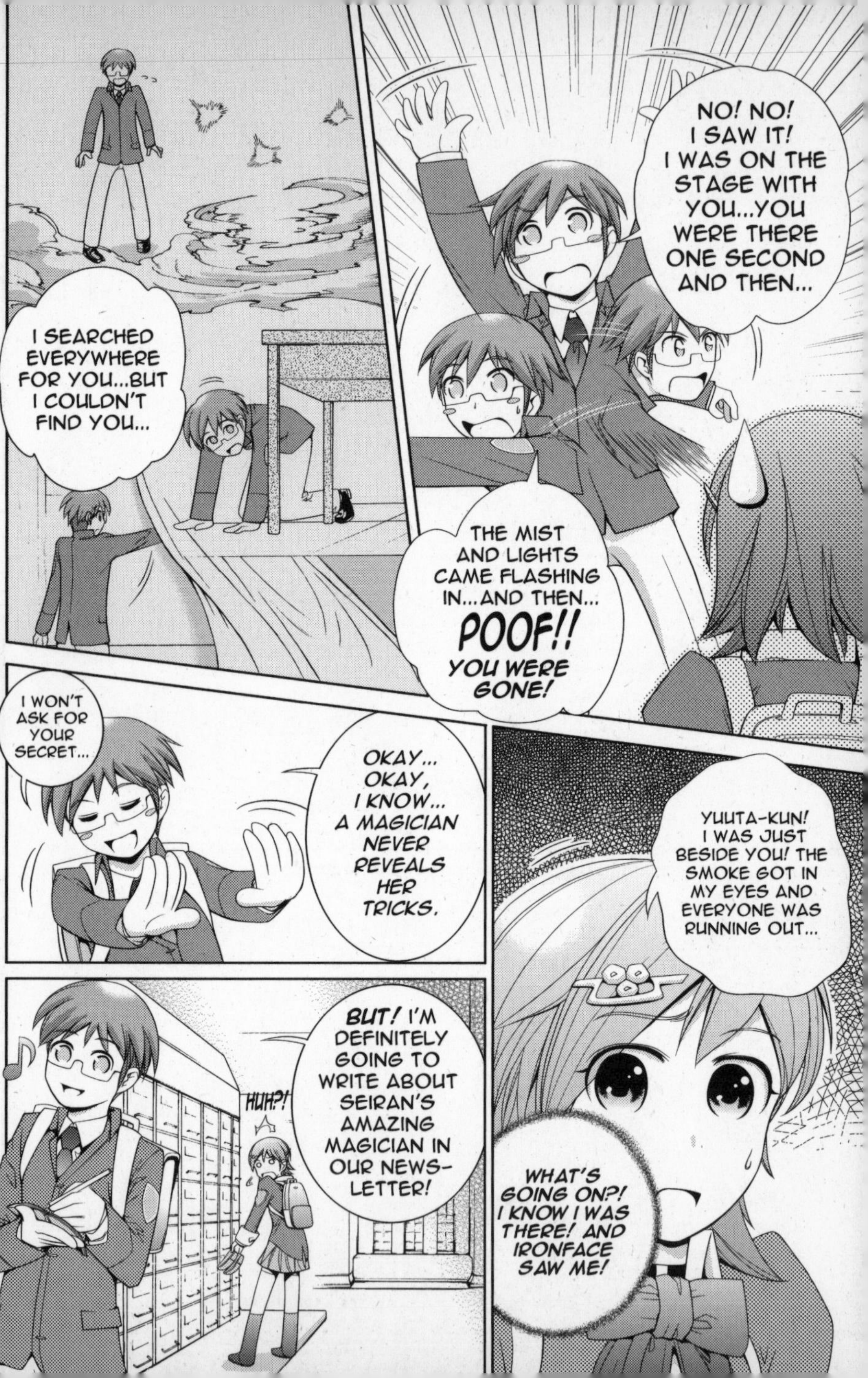
NO! NO! I SAW IT! I WAS ON THE STAGE WITH YOU...YOU WERE THERE ONE SECOND AND THEN...
THE MIST AND LIGHTS CAME FLASHING IN...AND THEN... POOF!! YOU WERE GONE!
I SEARCHED EVERYWHERE FOR YOU...BUT I COULDN'T FIND YOU...
YUUTA-KUN! I WAS JUST BESIDE YOU! THE SMOKE GOT IN MY EYES AND EVERYONE WAS RUNNING OUT...
WHAT'S GOING ON?! I KNOW I WAS THERE! AND IRONFACE SAW ME!
OKAY... OKAY, I KNOW... A MAGICIAN NEVER REVEALS HER TRICKS.
I WON'T ASK FOR YOUR SECRET...
BUT! I'M DEFINITELY GOING TO WRITE ABOUT SEIRAN'S AMAZING MAGICIAN IN OUR NEWS-LETTER!
HUH?!

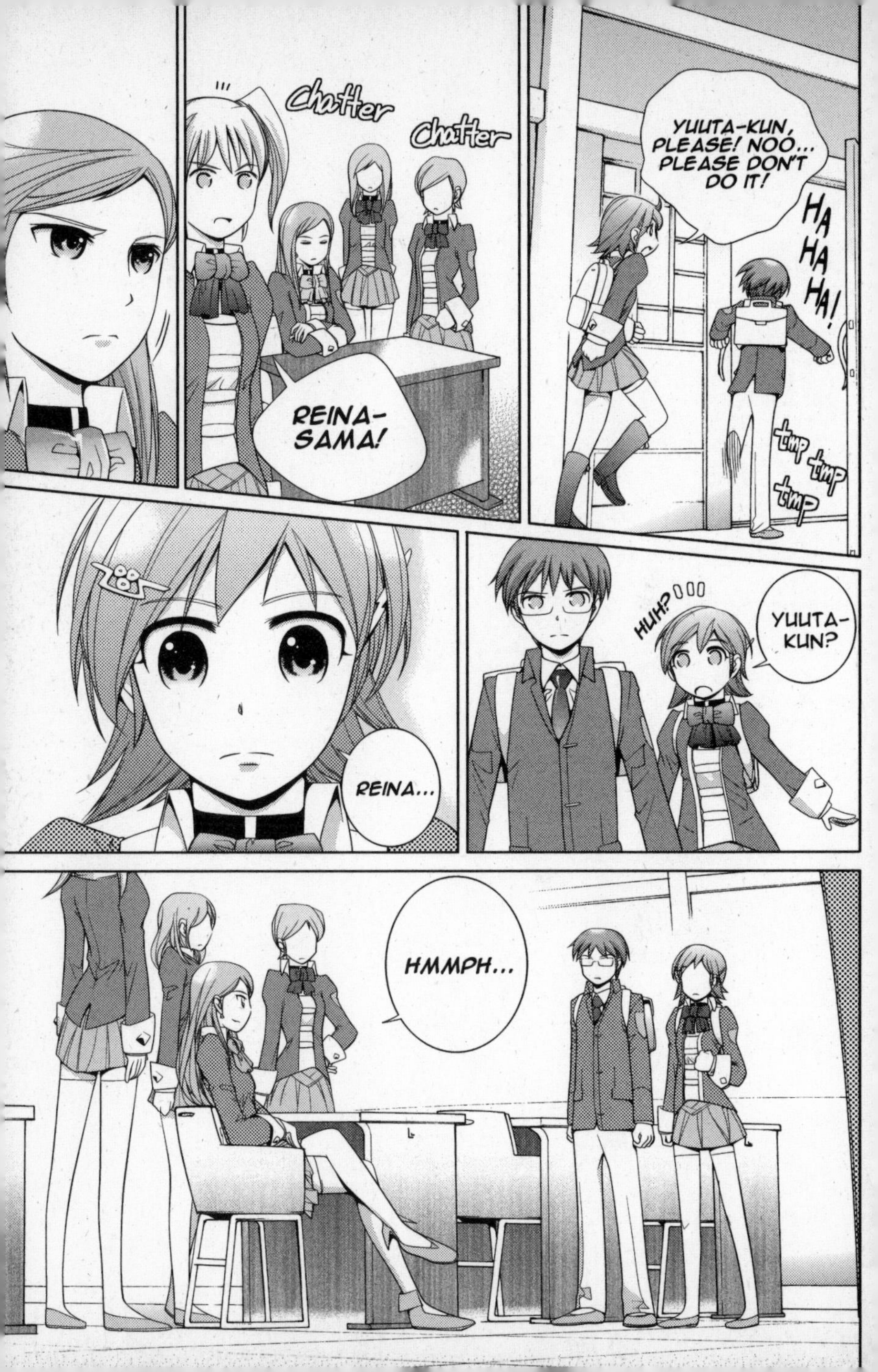
YUUTA-KUN, PLEASE! NOO... PLEASE DON'T DO IT!
HA HA HA!
tmp tmp tmp
Chatter
Chatter
REINA-SAMA!
YUUTA-KUN?
HUH?
REINA...
HMMPH...

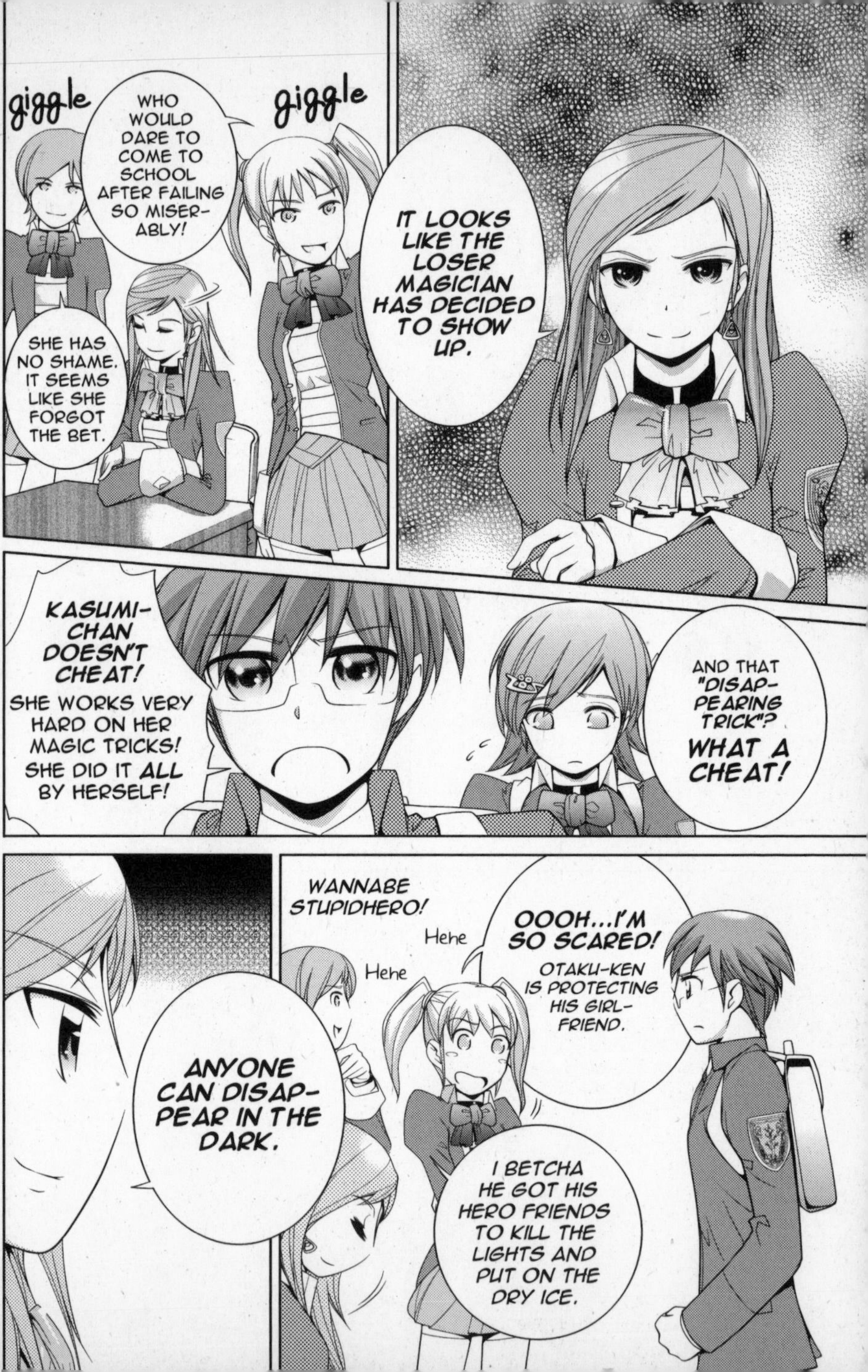
IT LOOKS LIKE THE LOSER MAGICIAN HAS DECIDED TO SHOW UP.
giggle
WHO WOULD DARE TO COME TO SCHOOL AFTER FAILING SO MISER-ABLY!
giggle
SHE HAS NO SHAME. IT SEEMS LIKE SHE FORGOT THE BET.
AND THAT "DISAP-PEARING TRICK"? WHAT A CHEAT!
KASUMI-CHAN DOESN'T CHEAT!
SHE WORKS VERY HARD ON HER MAGIC TRICKS!
SHE DID IT ALL BY HERSELF!
OOOH...I'M SO SCARED!
OTAKU-KEN IS PROTECTING HIS GIRL-FRIEND.
WANNABE STUPIDHERO!
Hehe
Hehe
I BETCHA HE GOT HIS HERO FRIENDS TO KILL THE LIGHTS AND PUT ON THE DRY ICE.
ANYONE CAN DISAP-PEAR IN THE DARK.

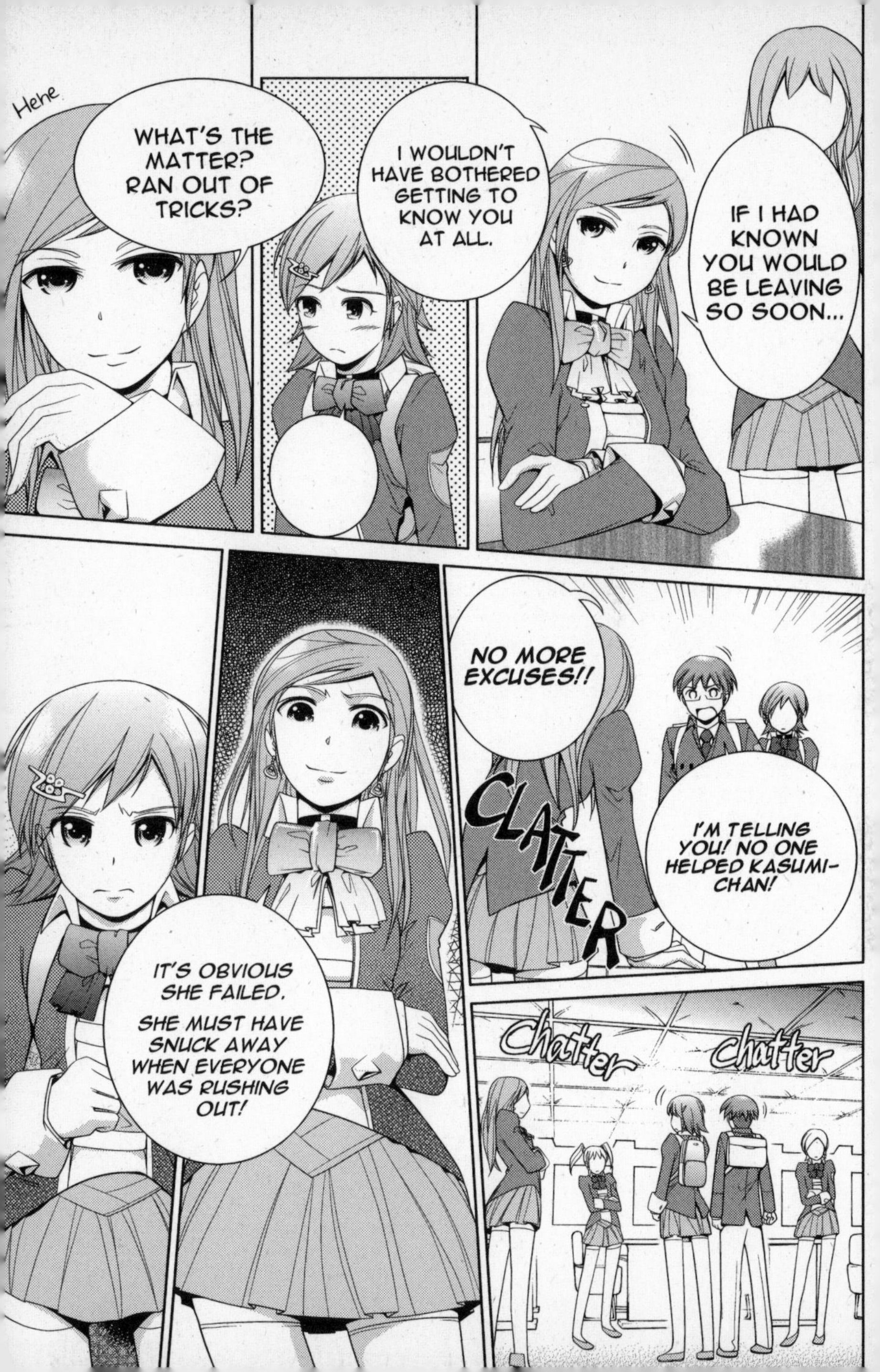
IF I HAD KNOWN YOU WOULD BE LEAVING SO SOON...
I WOULDN'T HAVE BOTHERED GETTING TO KNOW YOU AT ALL.
Hehe
WHAT'S THE MATTER? RAN OUT OF TRICKS?
NO MORE EXCUSES!!
CLATTER
I'M TELLING YOU! NO ONE HELPED KASUMI-CHAN!
Chatter
Chatter
IT'S OBVIOUS SHE FAILED.
SHE MUST HAVE SNUCK AWAY WHEN EVERYONE WAS RUSHING OUT!

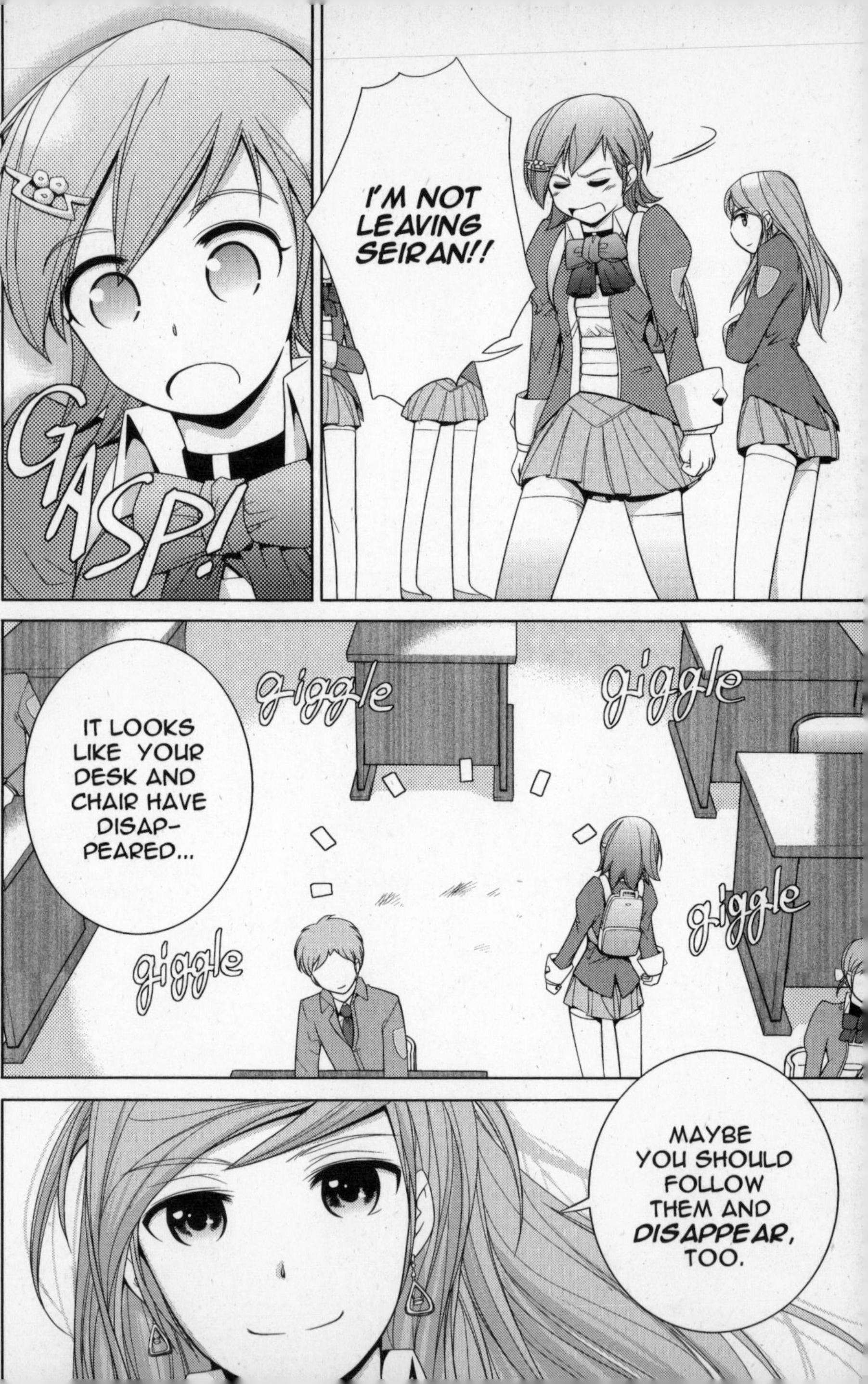
I'M NOT LEAVING SEIRAN!!
GASP!
giggle
giggle
IT LOOKS LIKE YOUR DESK AND CHAIR HAVE DISAP-PEARED...
giggle
giggle
MAYBE YOU SHOULD FOLLOW THEM AND DISAPPEAR, TOO.

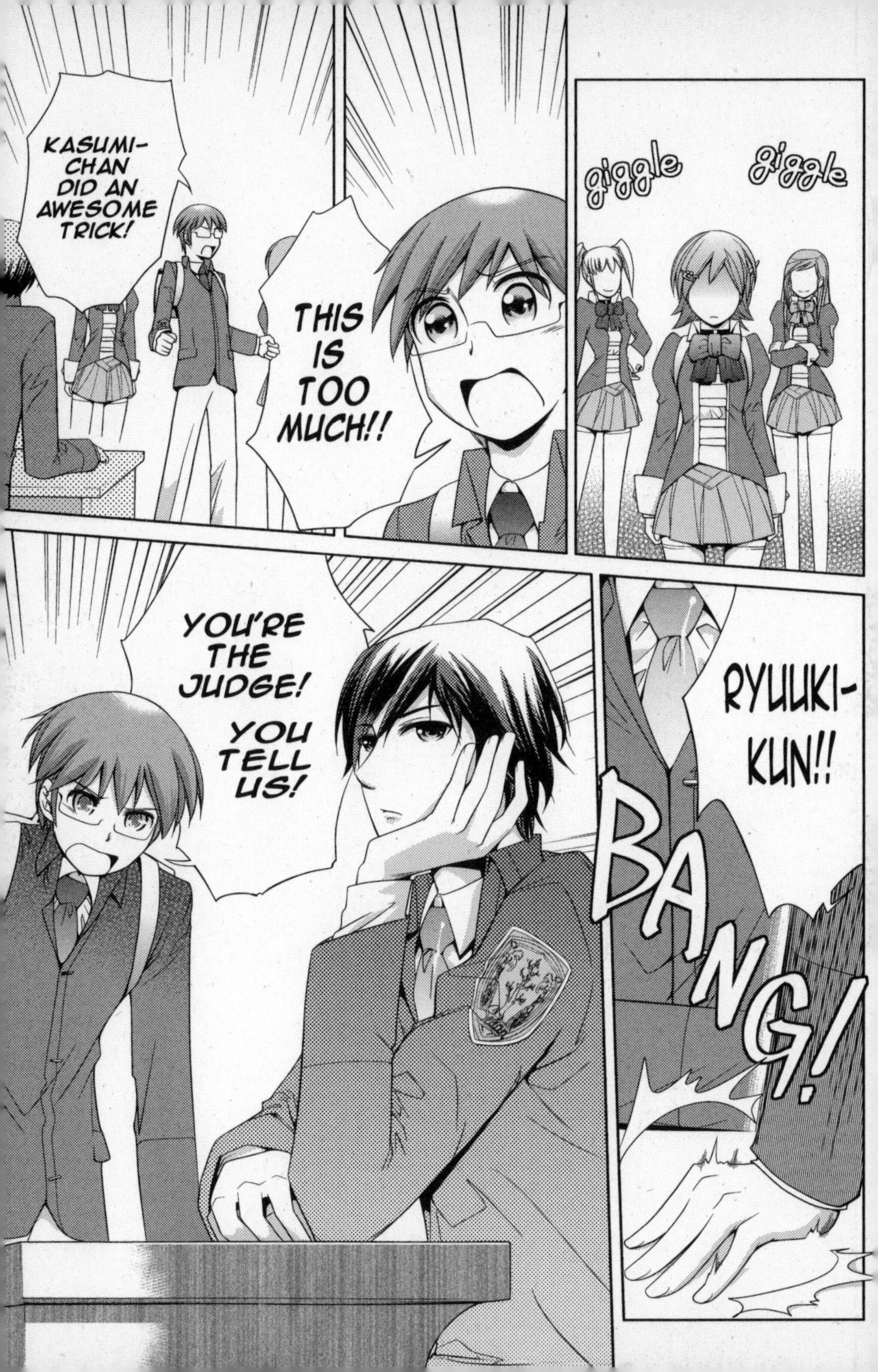
giggle giggle
THIS IS TOO MUCH!!
KASUMI-CHAN DID AN AWESOME TRICK!
RYUUKI-KUN!!
BANG!
YOU'RE THE JUDGE!
YOU TELL US!

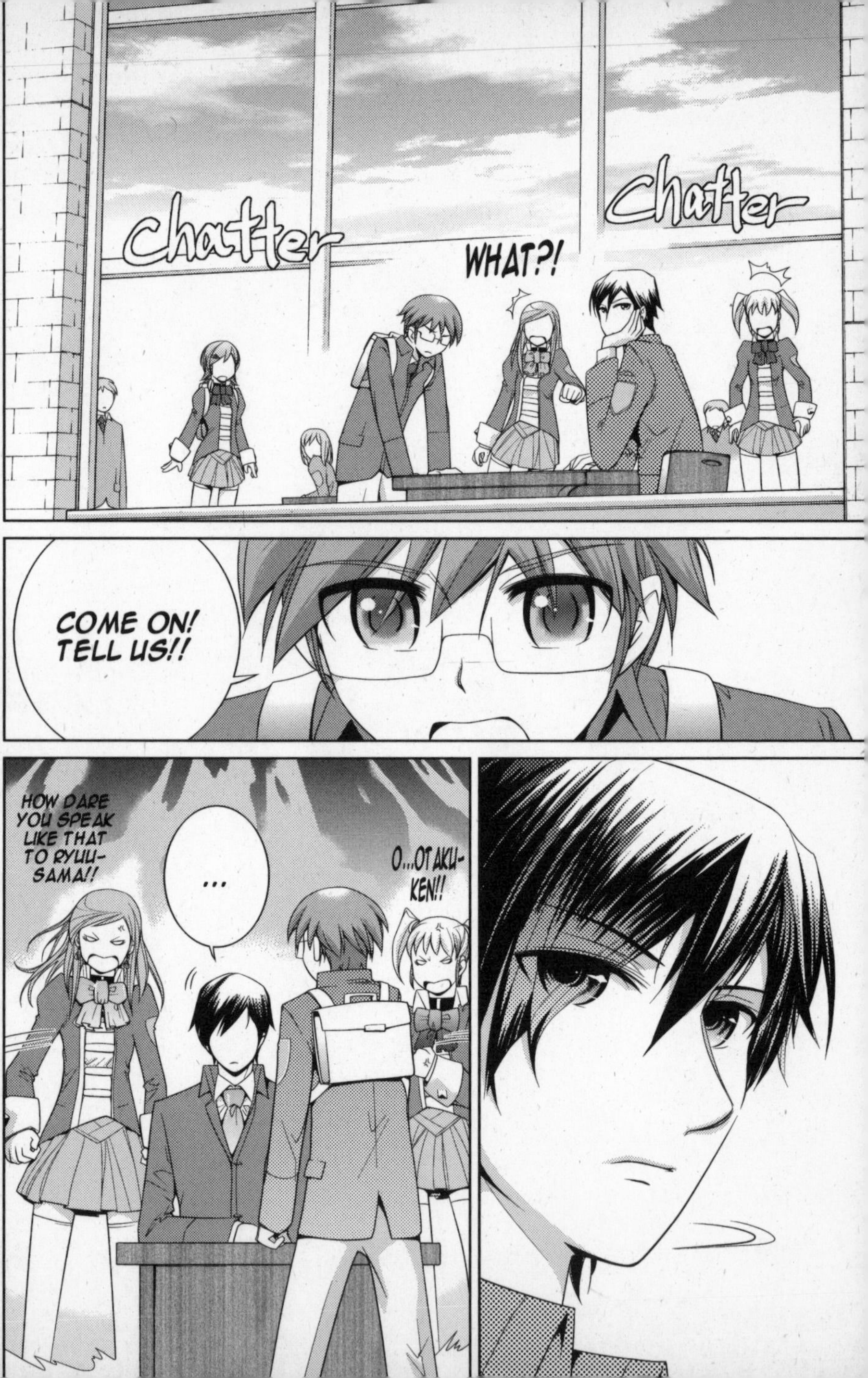
Chatter
WHAT?!
Chatter
COME ON! TELL US!!
O...OTAKU-KEN!!
...
HOW DARE YOU SPEAK LIKE THAT TO RYUU-SAMA!!

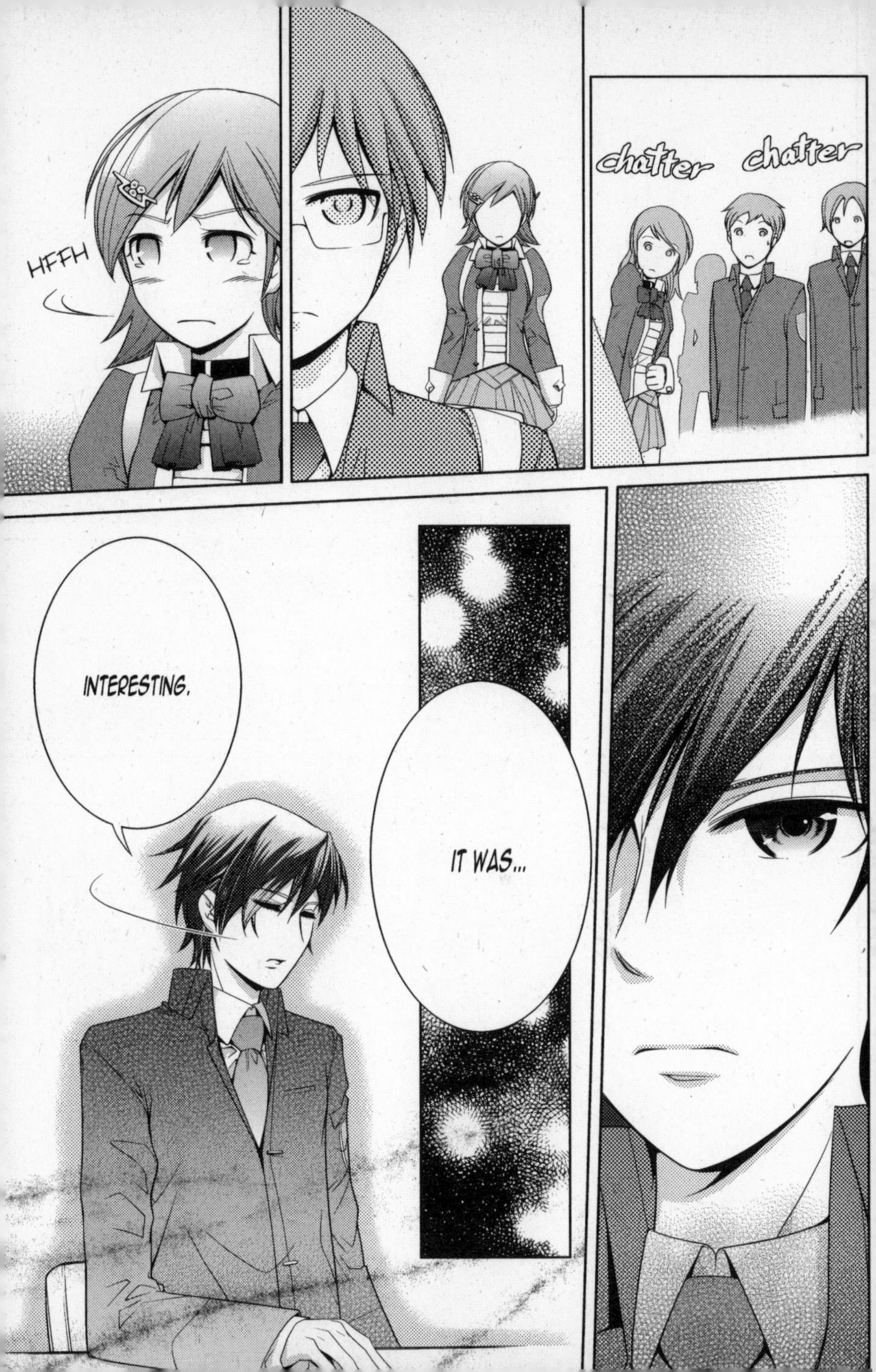
chatter chatter
HFFH
IT WAS...
INTERESTING.

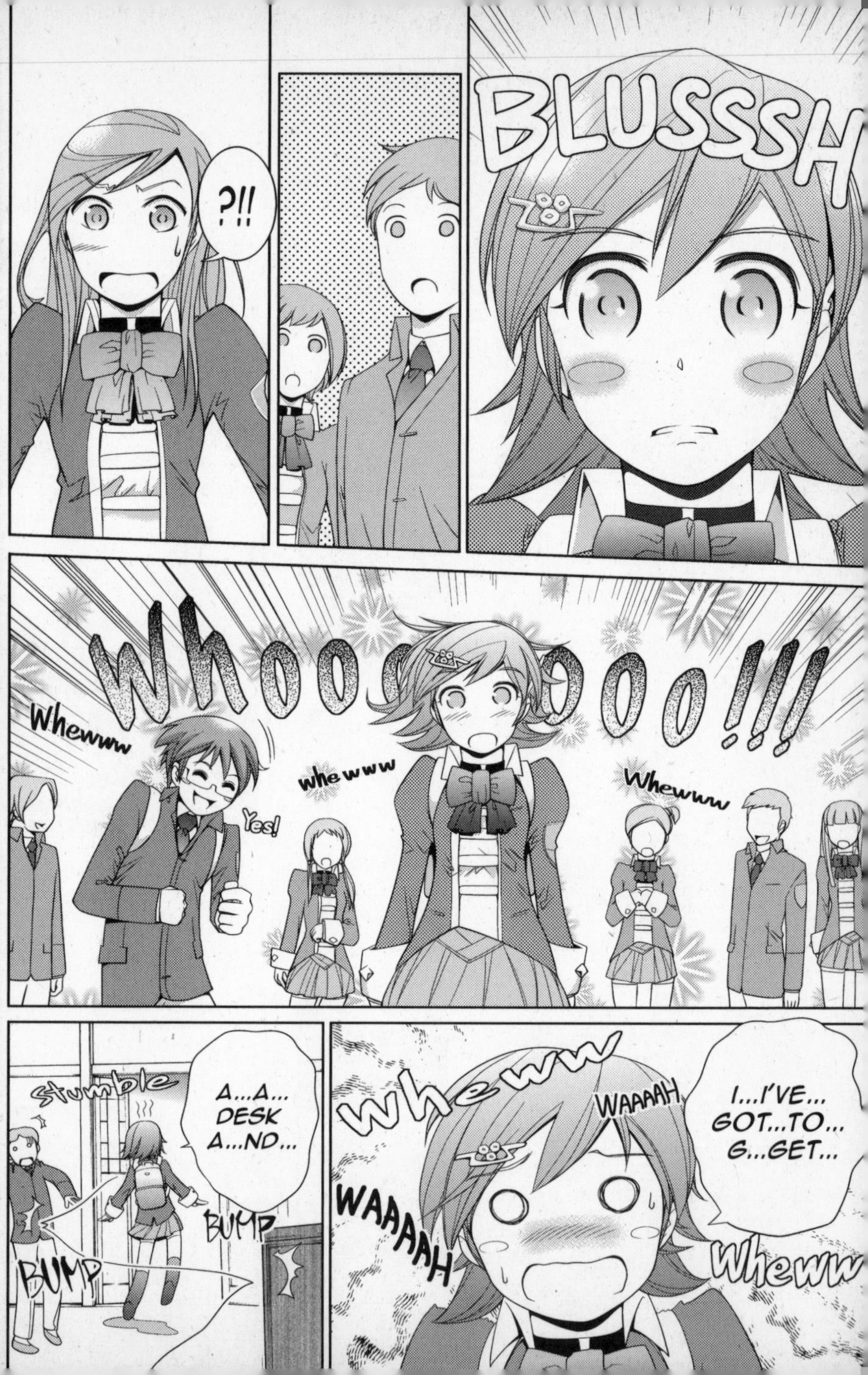
BLUSSSH
?!!
Whoooooooo!!!
Whewww
Wheww
whewww
Yes!
Whewww
WAAAAH
I...I'VE... GOT...TO... G...GET...
WAAAAAH
Wheww
A...A... DESK A...ND...
stumble
BUMP
BUMP

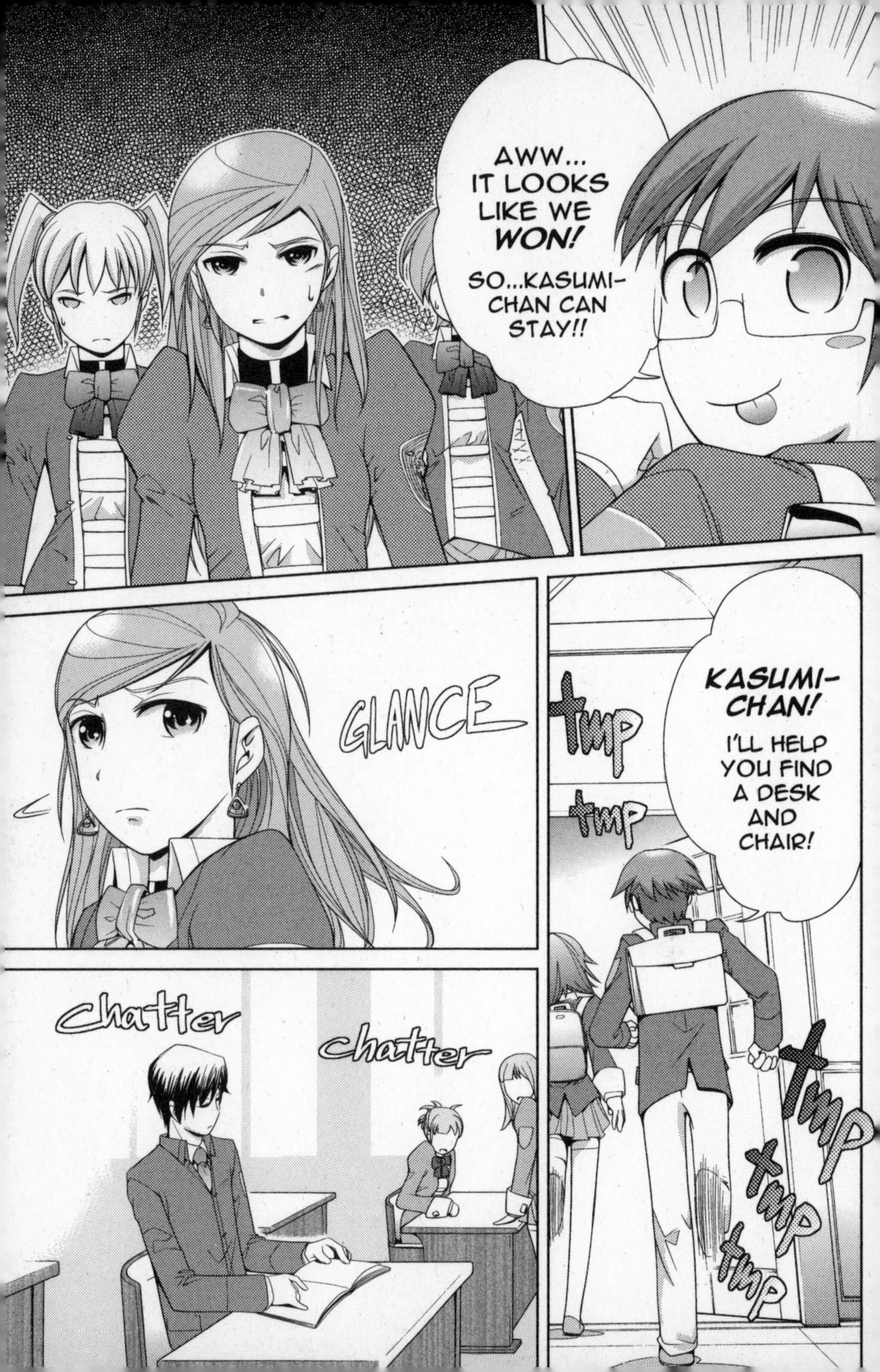
AWW... IT LOOKS LIKE WE WON!
SO...KASUMI-CHAN CAN STAY!!
KASUMI-CHAN!
I'LL HELP YOU FIND A DESK AND CHAIR!
tmp
tmp
tmp
tmp
tmp
GLANCE
Chatter
chatter

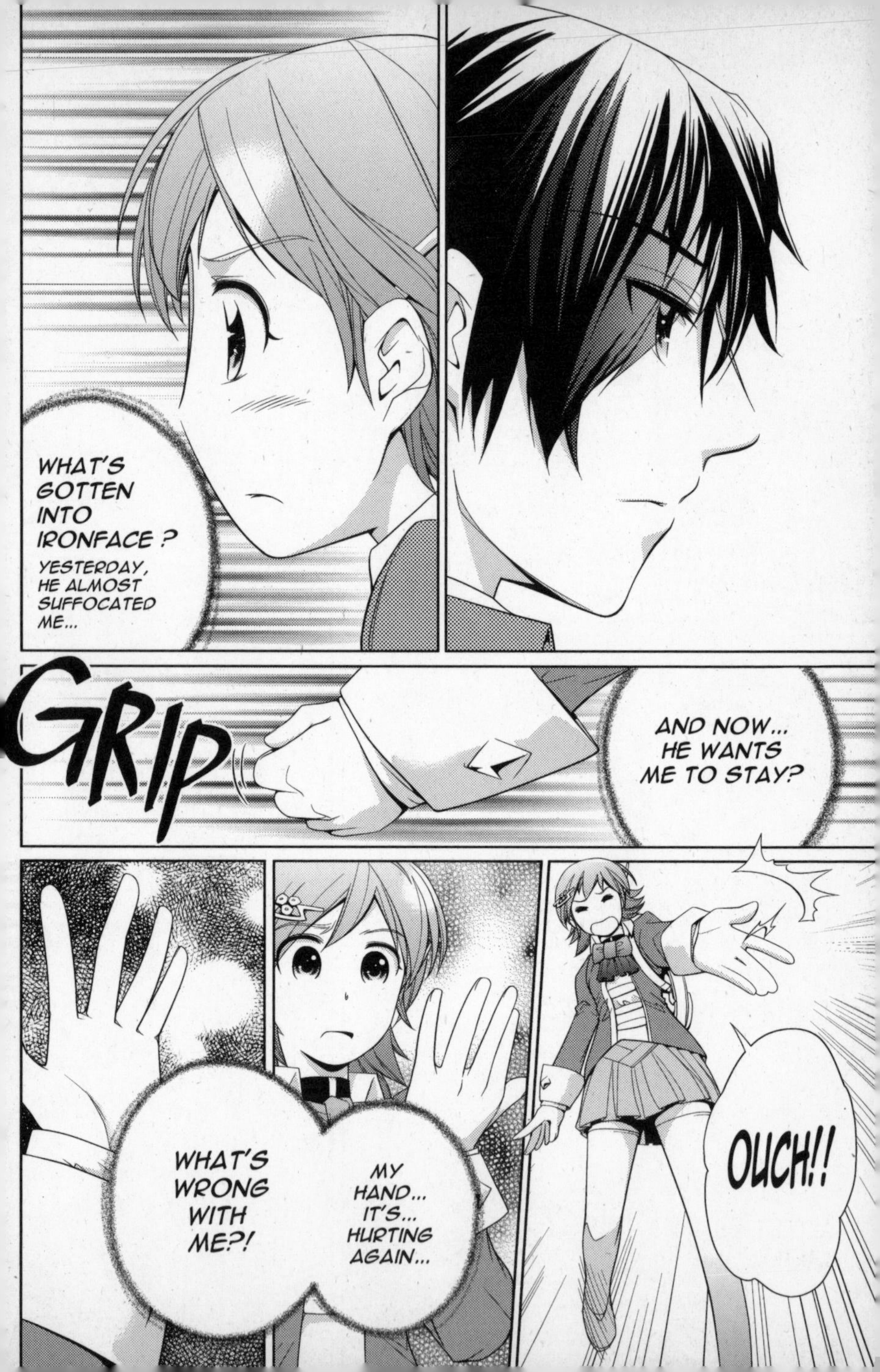
WHAT'S GOTTEN INTO IRONFACE ?
YESTERDAY, HE ALMOST SUFFOCATED ME...
AND NOW... HE WANTS ME TO STAY?
GRIP
OUCH!!
MY HAND... IT'S... HURTING AGAIN...
WHAT'S WRONG WITH ME?!

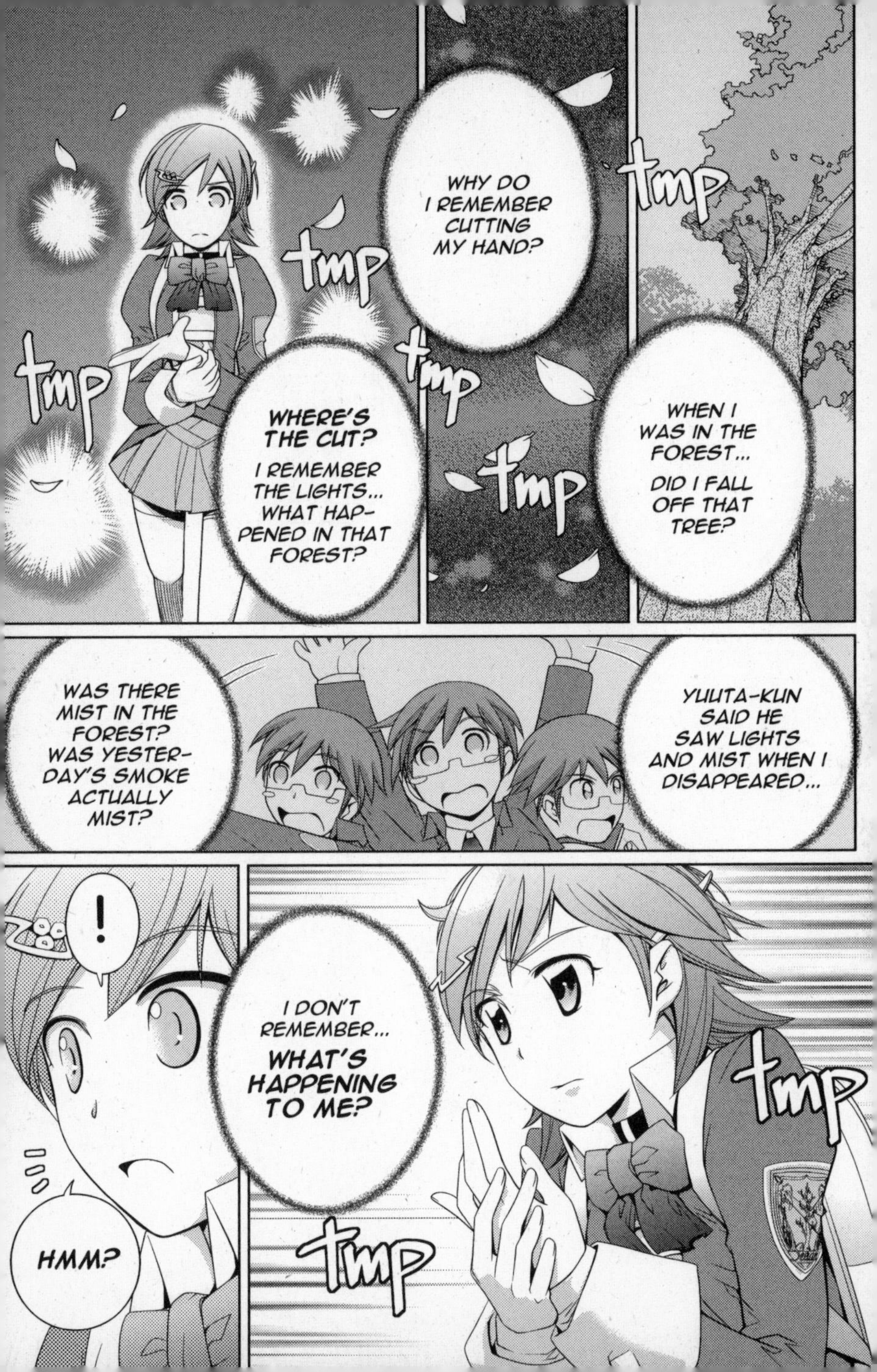
tmp
WHY DO I REMEMBER CUTTING MY HAND?
WHEN I WAS IN THE FOREST... DID I FALL OFF THAT TREE?
tmp
tmp
tmp
WHERE'S THE CUT? I REMEMBER THE LIGHTS... WHAT HAPPENED IN THAT FOREST?
tmp
YUUTA-KUN SAID HE SAW LIGHTS AND MIST WHEN I DISAPPEARED...
WAS THERE MIST IN THE FOREST? WAS YESTERDAY'S SMOKE ACTUALLY MIST?
tmp
I DON'T REMEMBER... WHAT'S HAPPENING TO ME?
tmp
!
HMM?

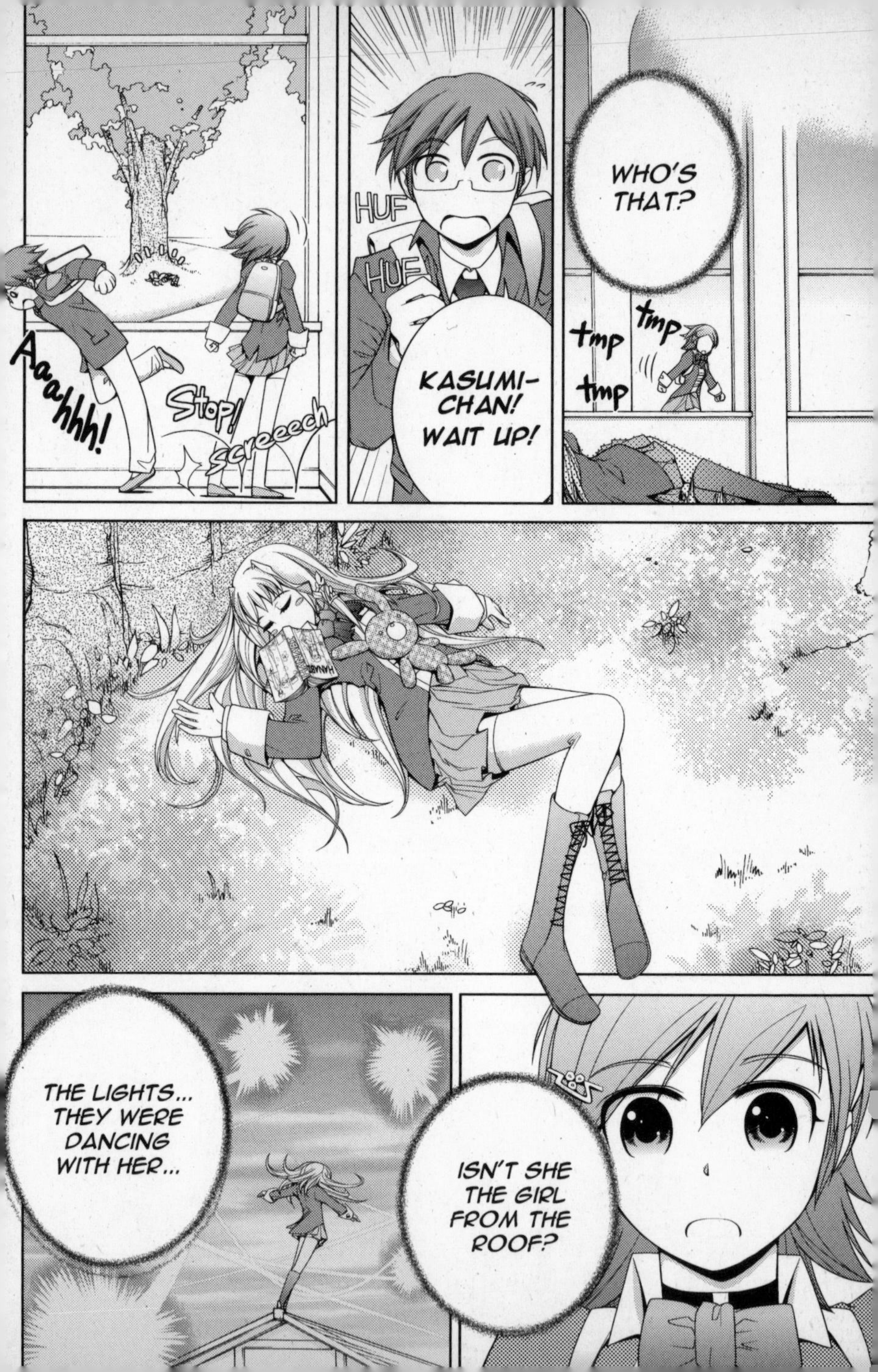
WHO'S THAT?
tmp
tmp
tmp
HUF
HUF
KASUMI-CHAN! WAIT UP!
Aaahhh!
Stop!
screeeech
ISN'T SHE THE GIRL FROM THE ROOF?
THE LIGHTS... THEY WERE DANCING WITH HER...

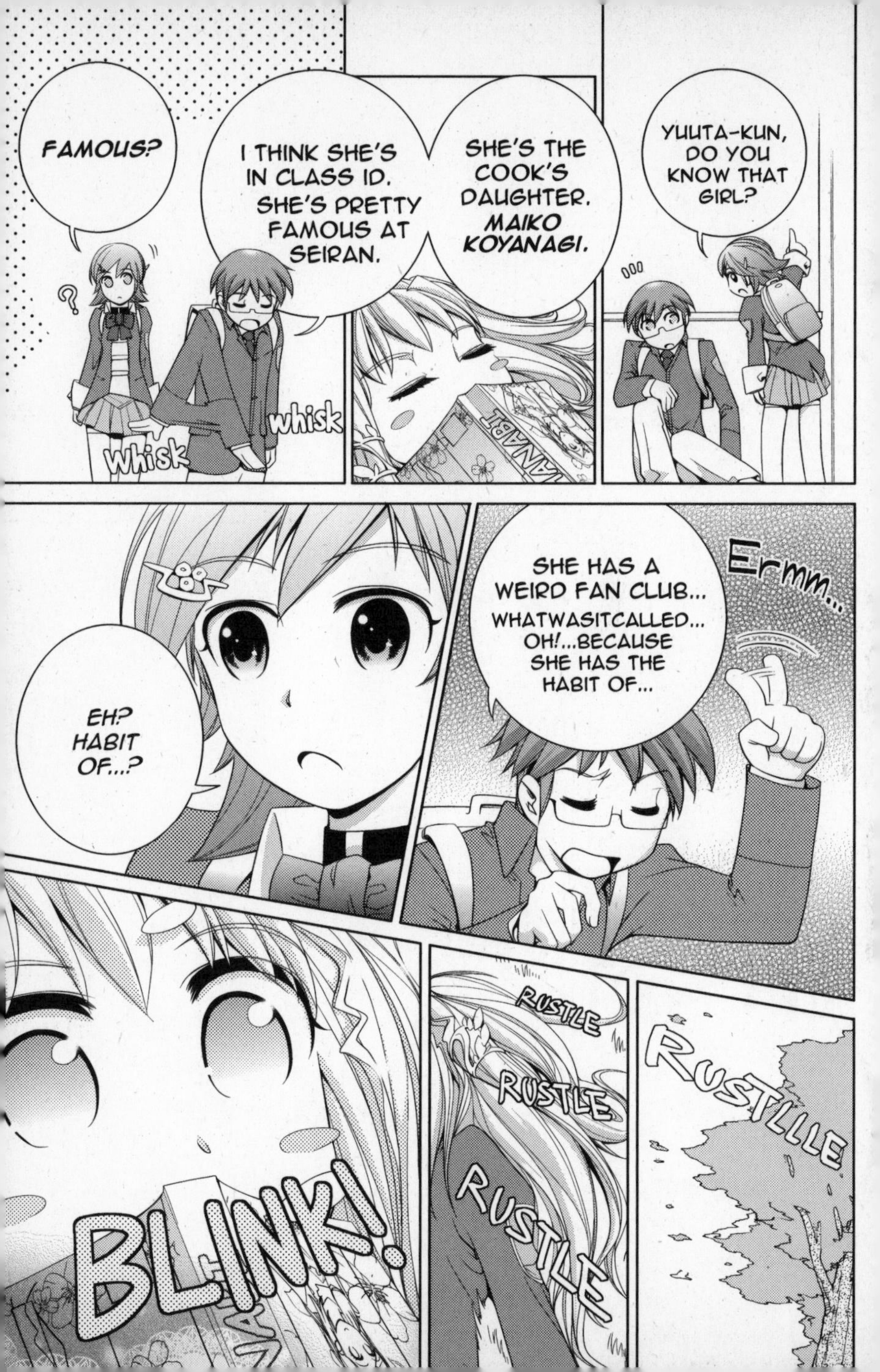
YUUTA-KUN, DO YOU KNOW THAT GIRL?
SHE'S THE COOK'S DAUGHTER. MAIKO KOYANAGI.
I THINK SHE'S IN CLASS 1D. SHE'S PRETTY FAMOUS AT SEIRAN.
FAMOUS?
whisk
whisk
Ermm...
SHE HAS A WEIRD FAN CLUB... WHATWASITCALLED... OH!...BECAUSE SHE HAS THE HABIT OF...
EH? HABIT OF...?
RUSTLLLE
RUSTLE
RUSTLE
RUSTLE
BLINK!

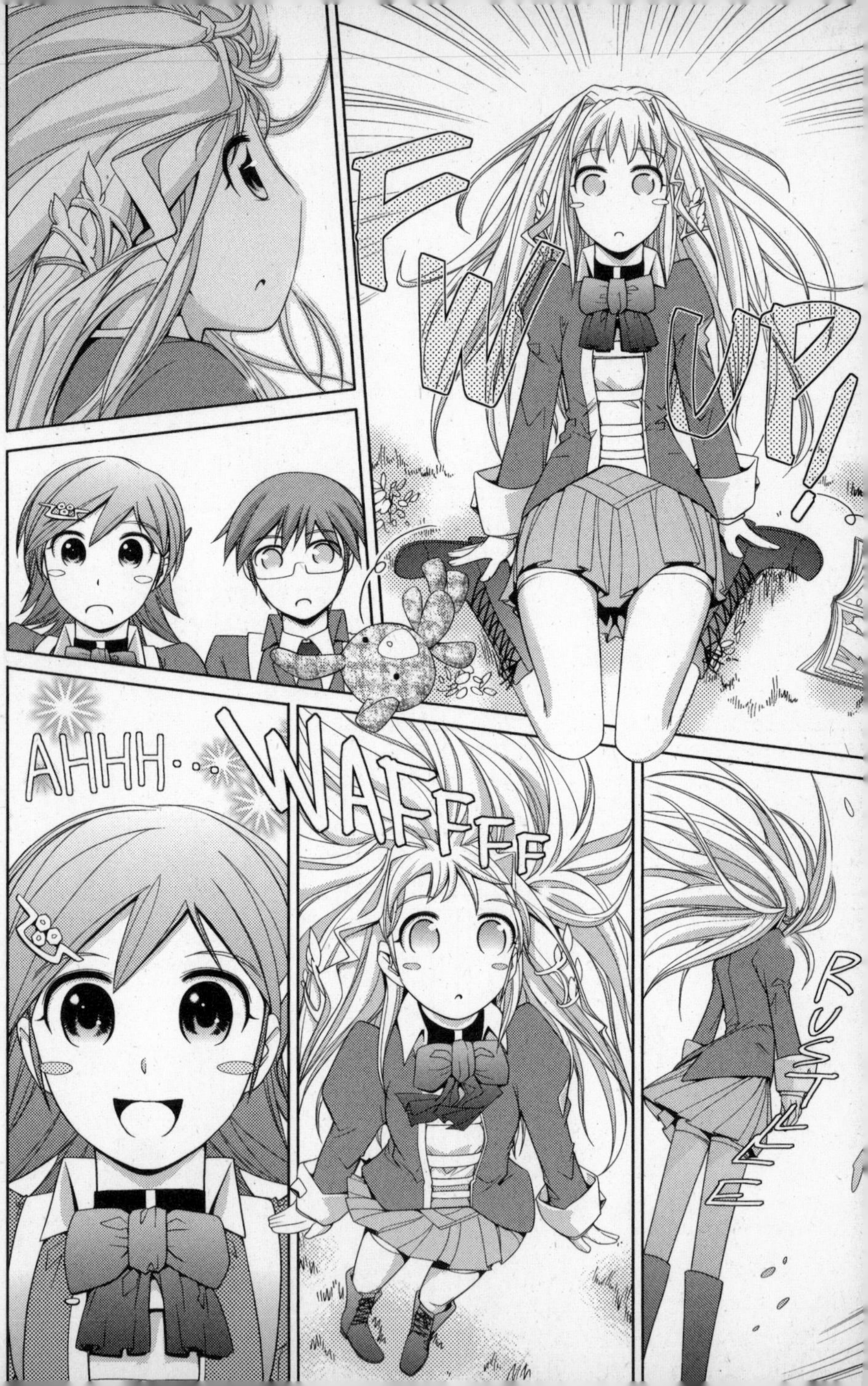
FWUP!
RUSTLLLE
WAFFFF
AHHH...

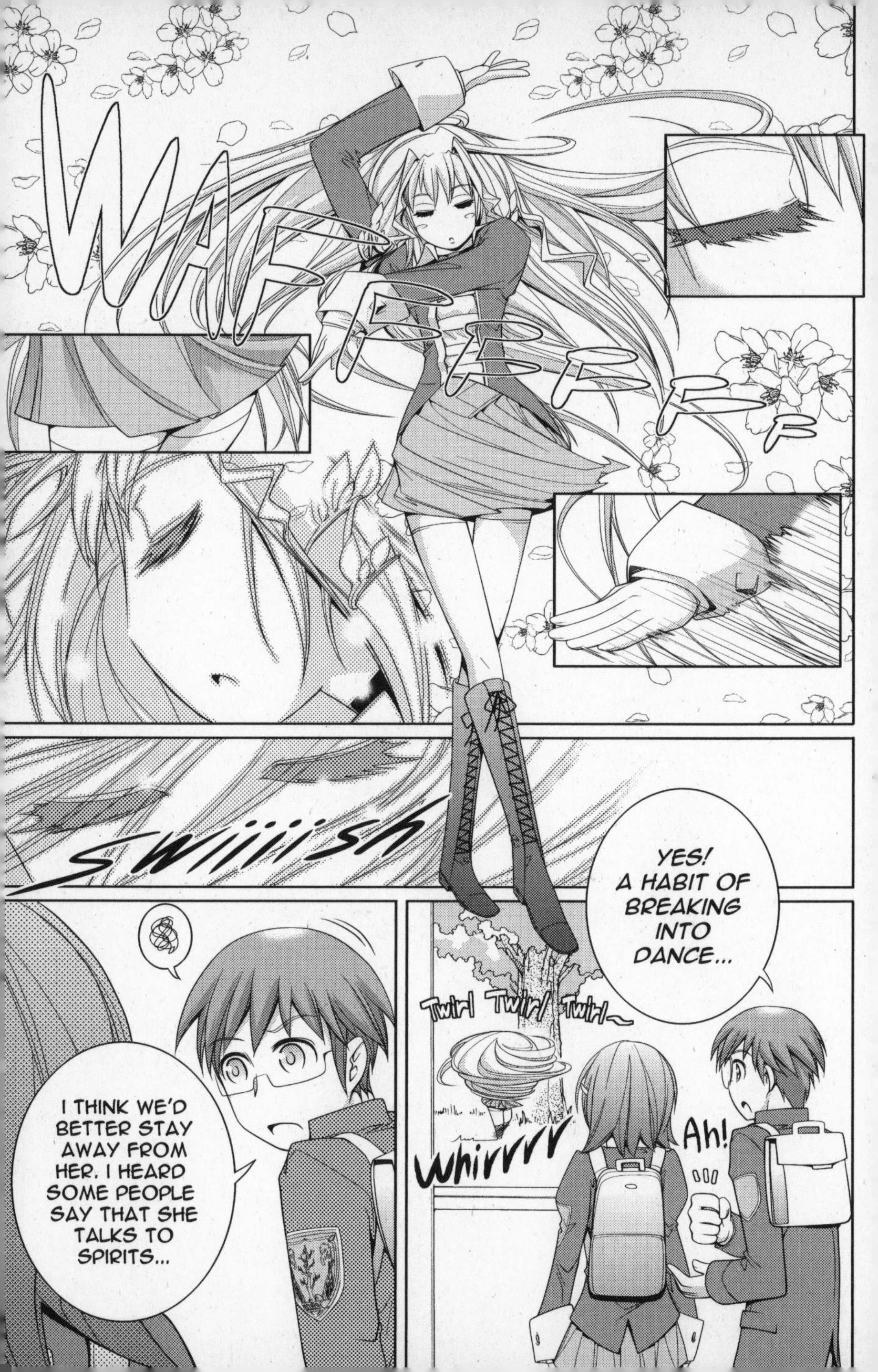
WAFFFFFF
SWIIIIISH
YES! A HABIT OF BREAKING INTO DANCE...
Twirl Twirl Twirl~
Whirrrrr
Ah!
I THINK WE'D BETTER STAY AWAY FROM HER. I HEARD SOME PEOPLE SAY THAT SHE TALKS TO SPIRITS...

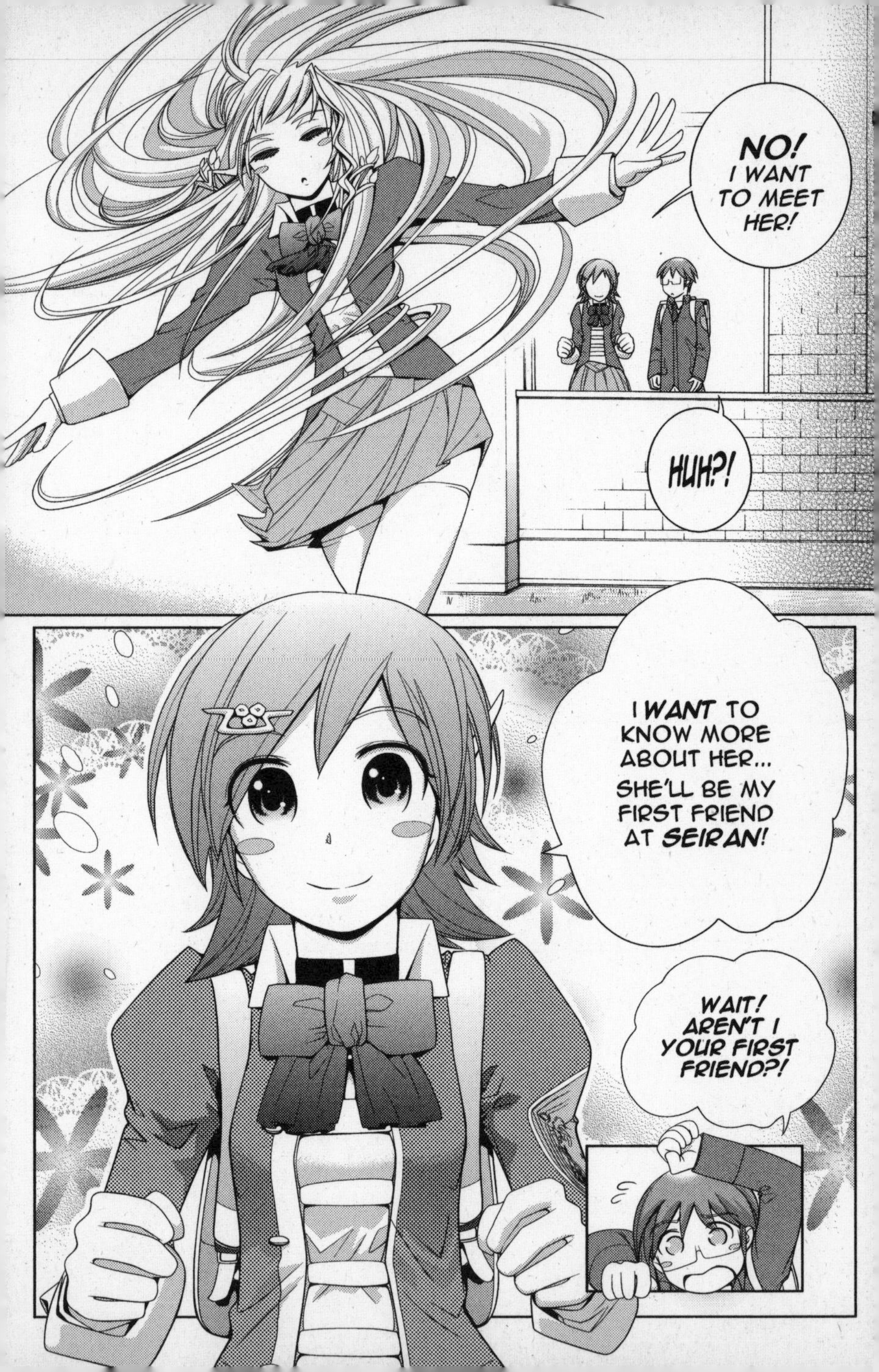
NO! I WANT TO MEET HER!
HUH?!
I WANT TO KNOW MORE ABOUT HER... SHE'LL BE MY FIRST FRIEND AT SEIRAN!
WAIT! AREN'T I YOUR FIRST FRIEND?!

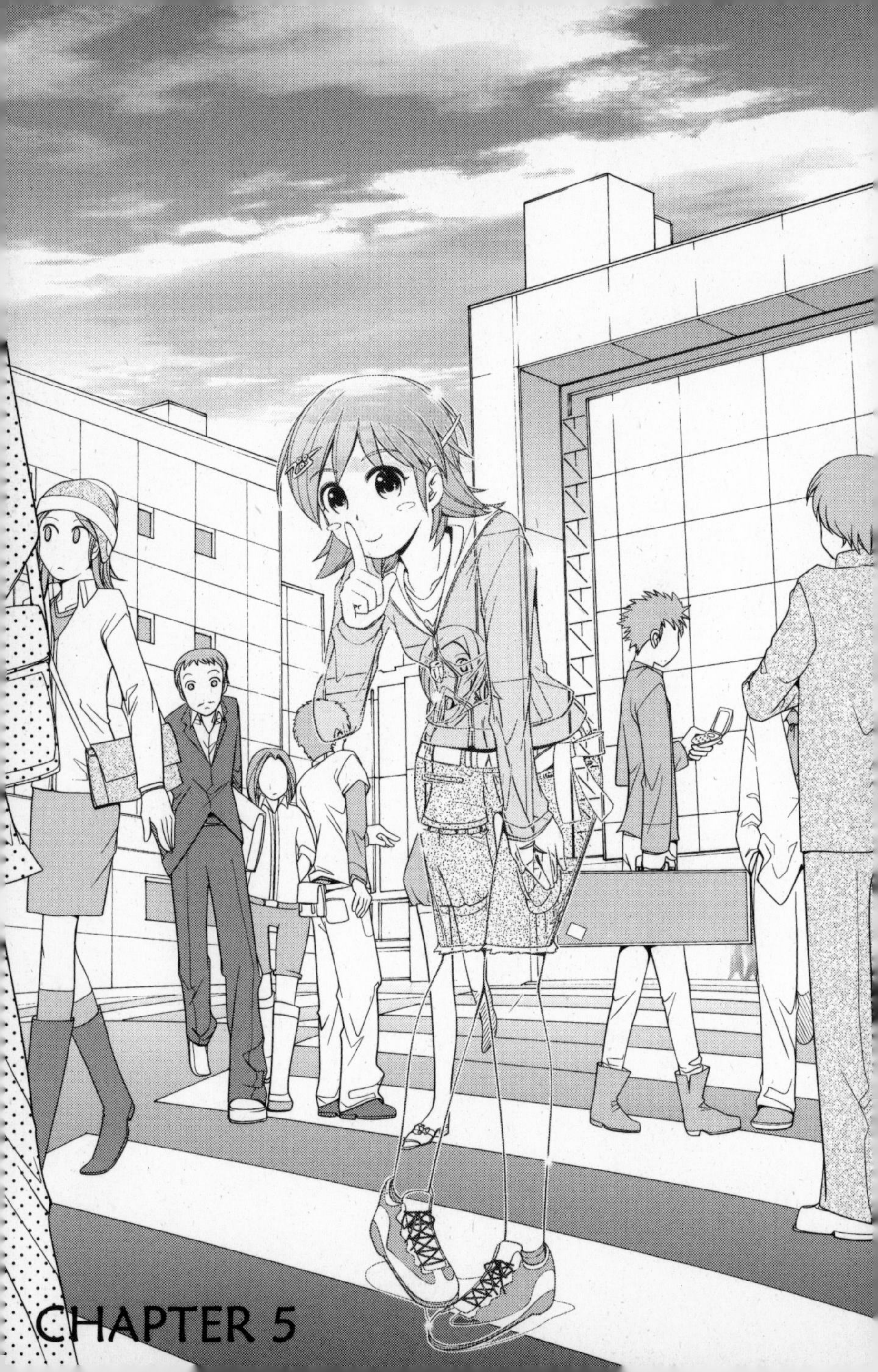

CHAPTER 5

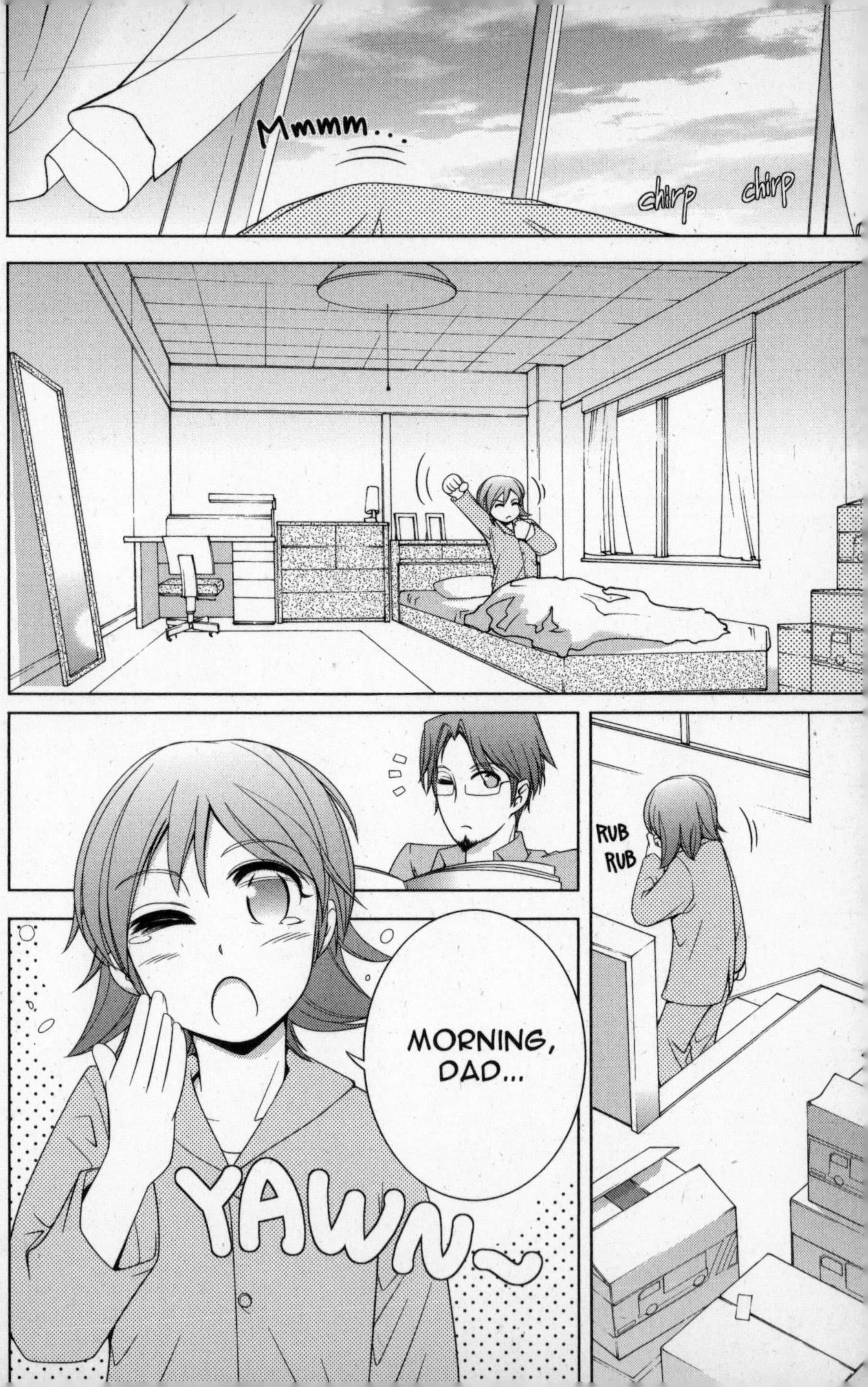
chirp chirp
Mmmm...
RUB
RUB
MORNING, DAD...
YAWN~

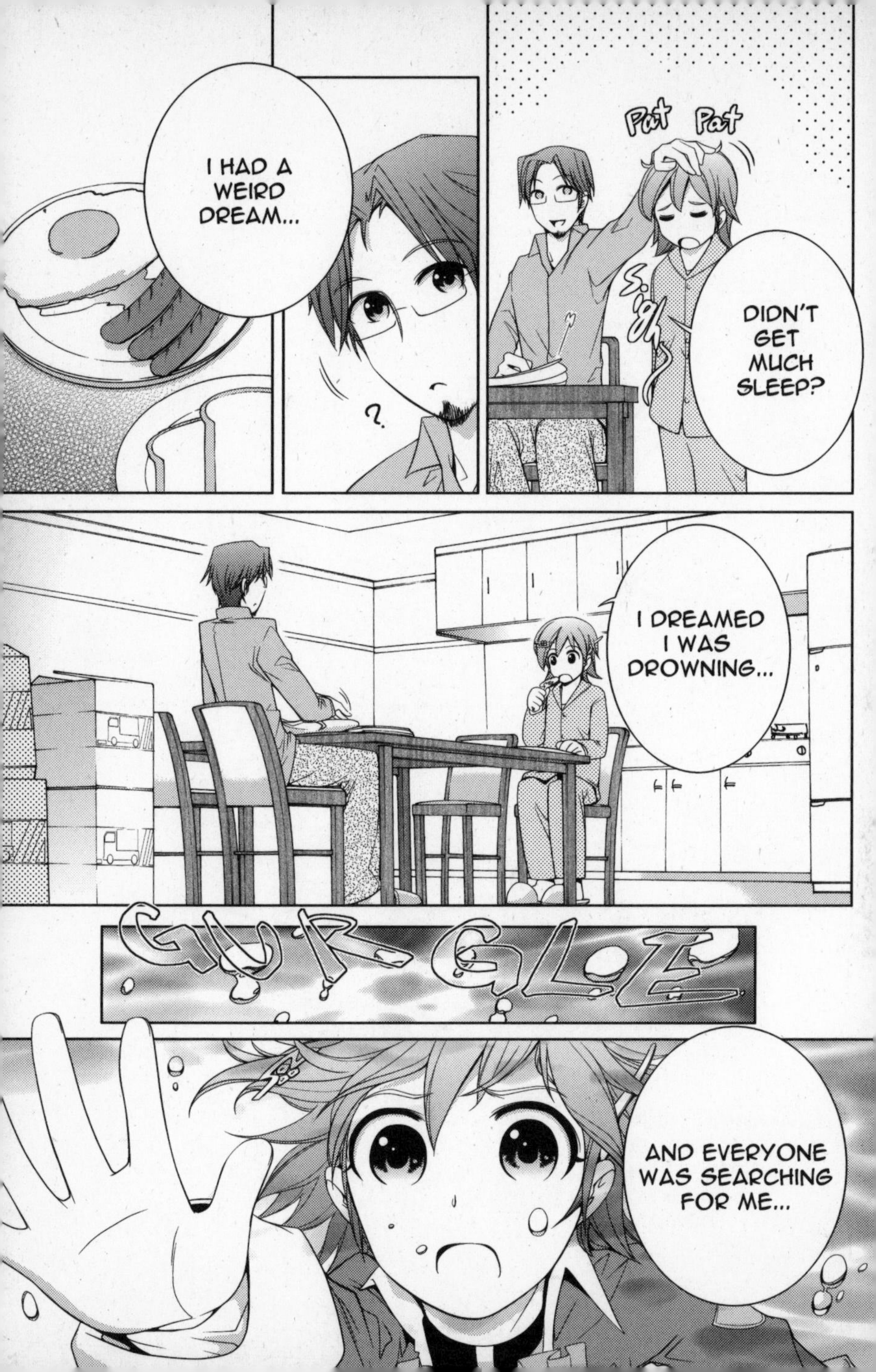
Pat Pat
Sigh
DIDN'T GET MUCH SLEEP?
?
I HAD A WEIRD DREAM...
I DREAMED I WAS DROWNING...
GURGLE
AND EVERYONE WAS SEARCHING FOR ME...

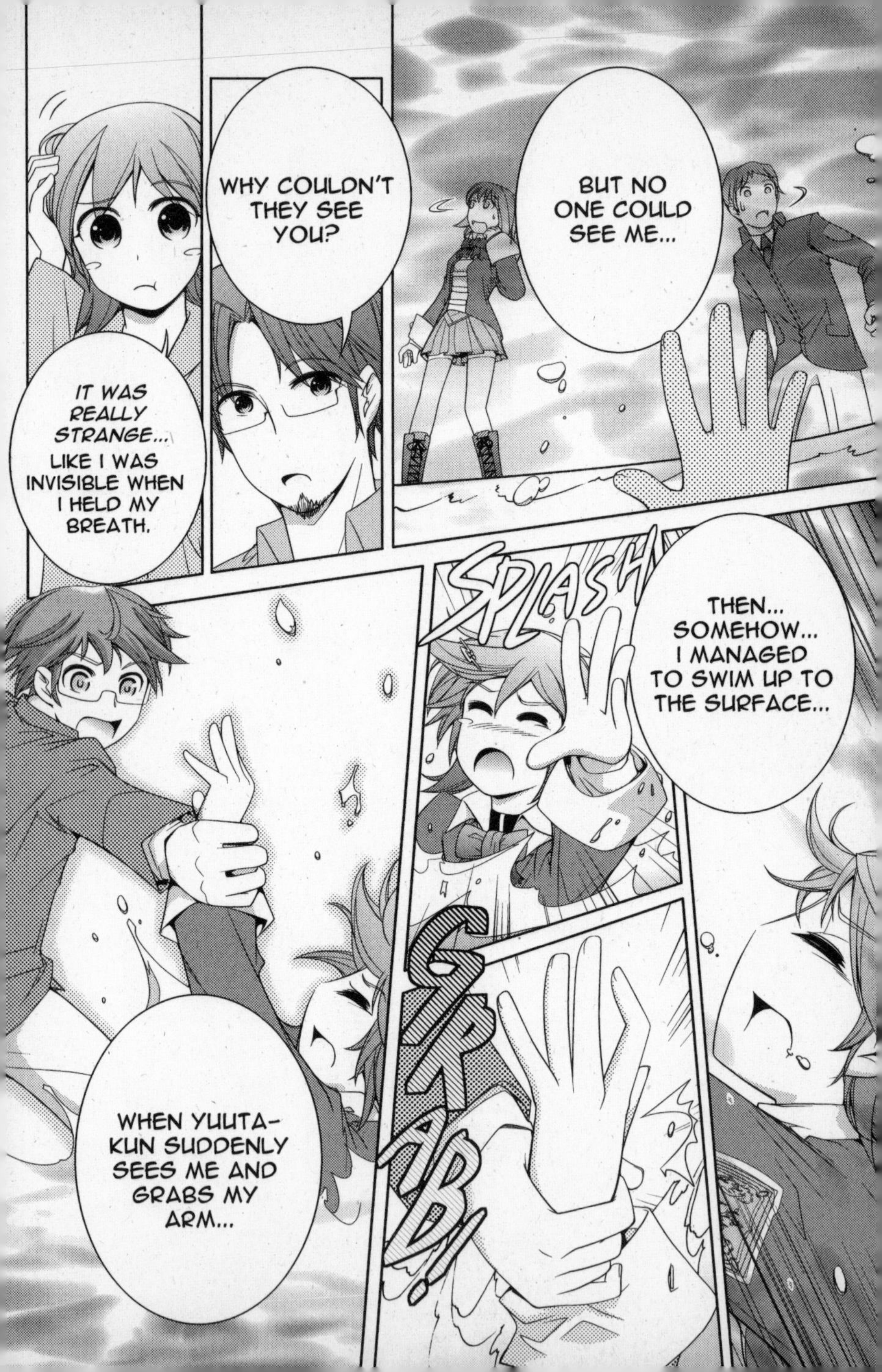
BUT NO ONE COULD SEE ME...
WHY COULDN'T THEY SEE YOU?
IT WAS REALLY STRANGE...
LIKE I WAS INVISIBLE WHEN I HELD MY BREATH.
SPLASH
THEN... SOMEHOW... I MANAGED TO SWIM UP TO THE SURFACE...
GRAB!
WHEN YUUTA-KUN SUDDENLY SEES ME AND GRABS MY ARM...

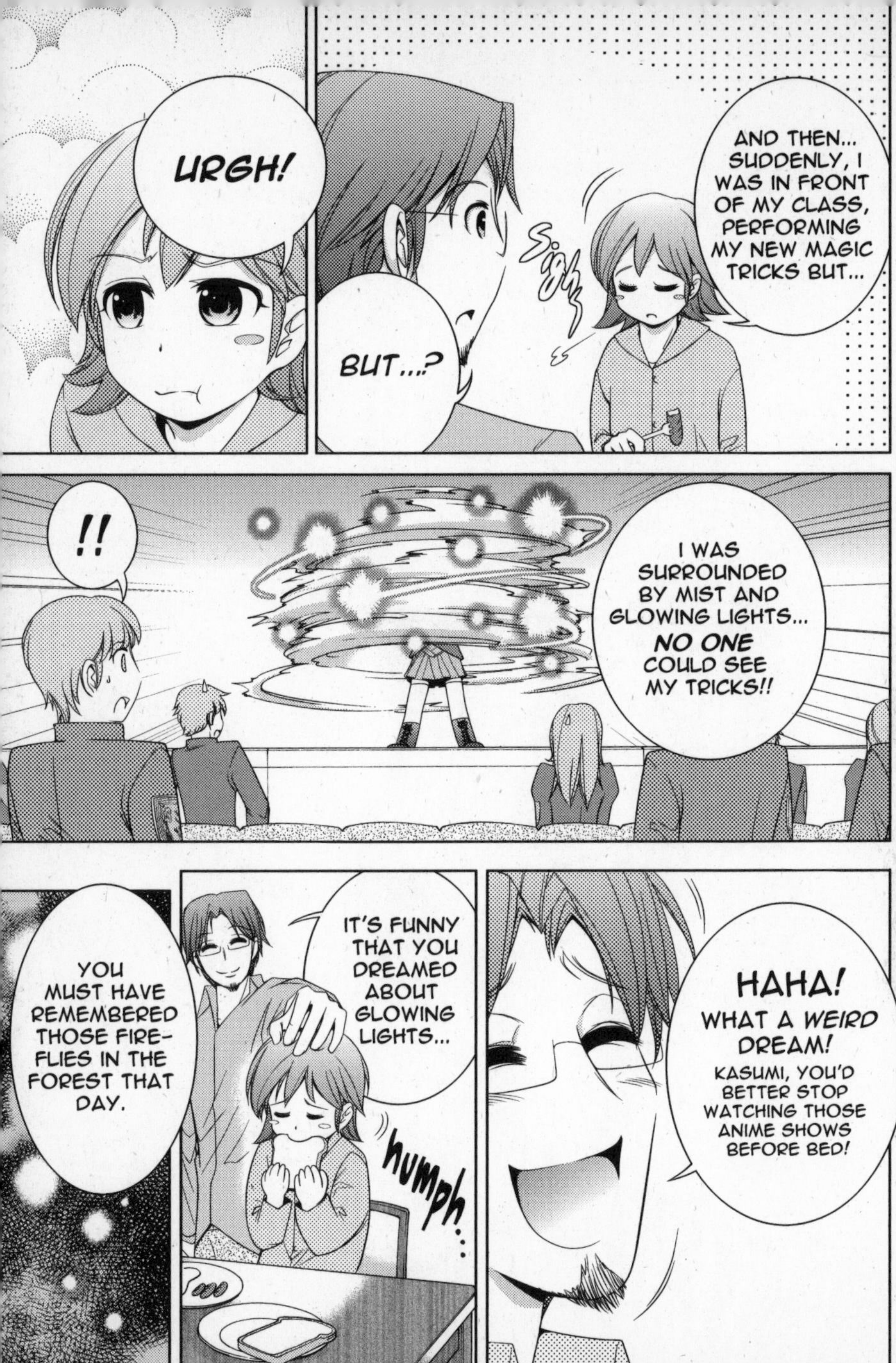
AND THEN... SUDDENLY, I WAS IN FRONT OF MY CLASS, PERFORMING MY NEW MAGIC TRICKS BUT...
sigh
BUT...?
URGH!
I WAS SURROUNDED BY MIST AND GLOWING LIGHTS... *NO ONE* COULD SEE MY TRICKS!!
!!
HAHA! WHAT A *WEIRD* DREAM!
KASUMI, YOU'D BETTER STOP WATCHING THOSE ANIME SHOWS BEFORE BED!
IT'S FUNNY THAT YOU DREAMED ABOUT GLOWING LIGHTS...
YOU MUST HAVE REMEMBERED THOSE FIRE-FLIES IN THE FOREST THAT DAY.
humph...

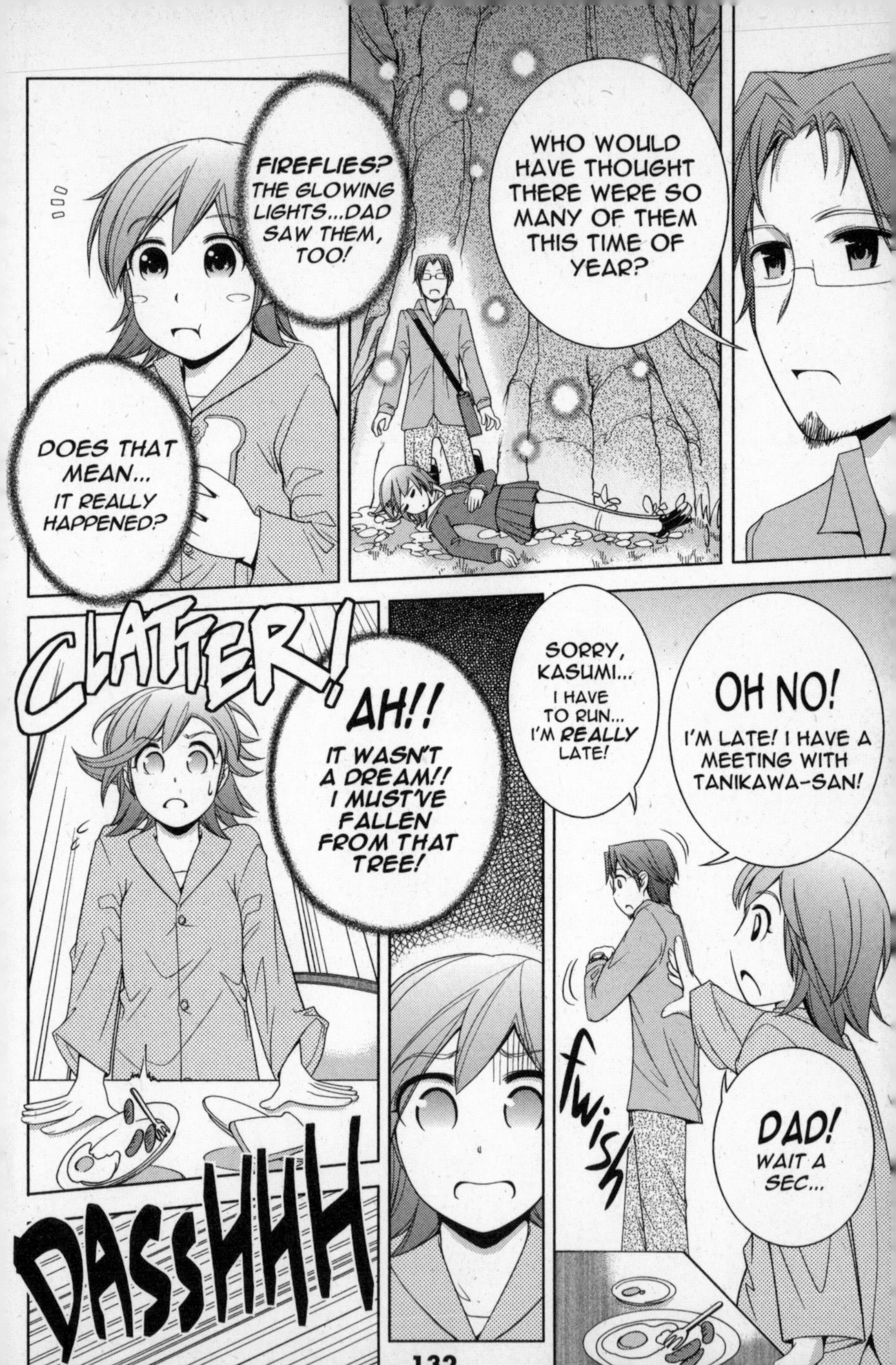
WHO WOULD HAVE THOUGHT THERE WERE SO MANY OF THEM THIS TIME OF YEAR?
FIREFLIES? THE GLOWING LIGHTS...DAD SAW THEM, TOO!
DOES THAT MEAN... IT REALLY HAPPENED?
OH NO! I'M LATE! I HAVE A MEETING WITH TANIKAWA-SAN!
SORRY, KASUMI... I HAVE TO RUN... I'M REALLY LATE!
fwish
DAD! WAIT A SEC...
CLATTER!
AH!! IT WASN'T A DREAM!! I MUST'VE FALLEN FROM THAT TREE!
DASSHHH

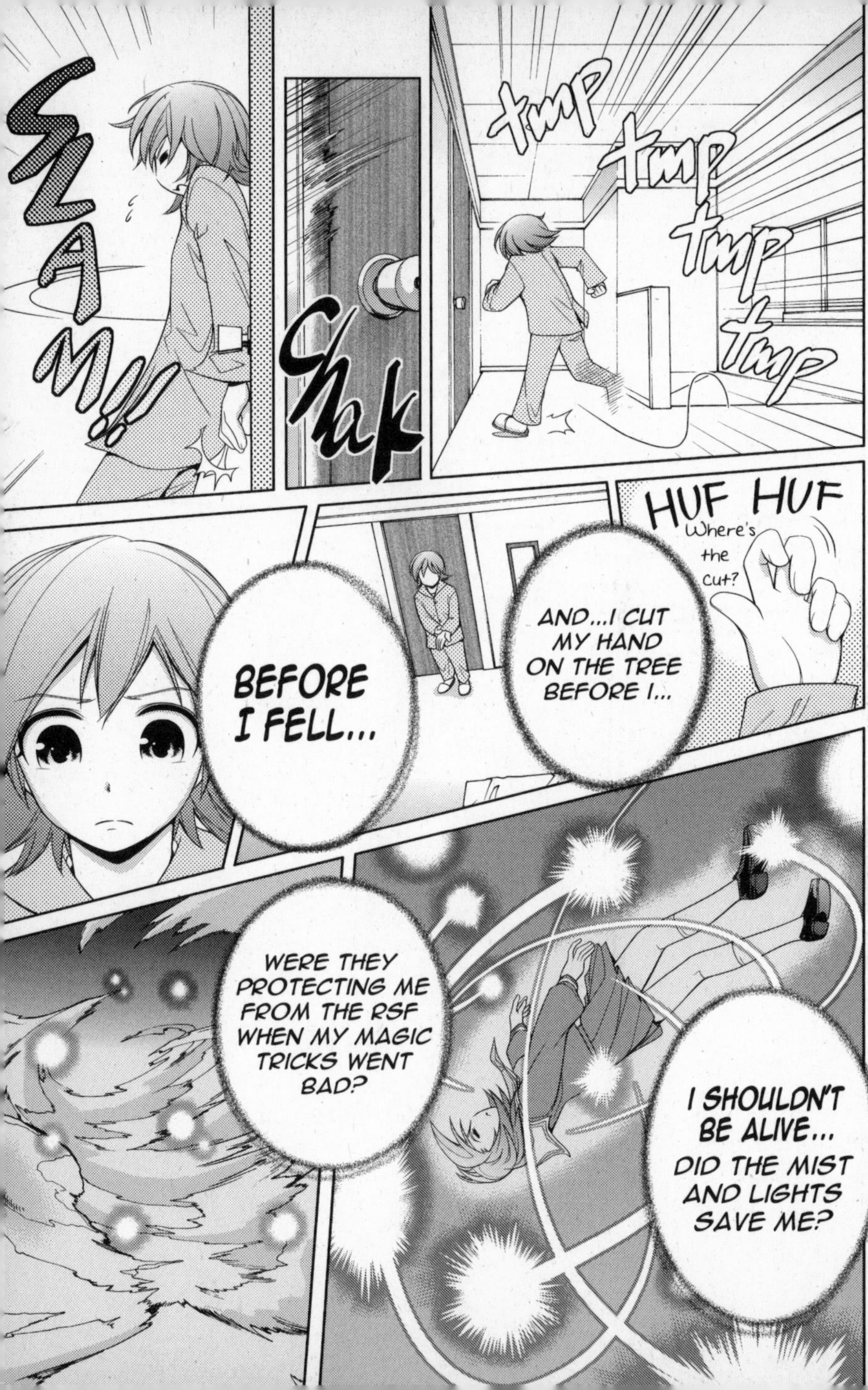
tmp tmp tmp tmp
Chak
SLAM!!
HUF HUF
Where's the cut?
AND...I CUT MY HAND ON THE TREE BEFORE I...
BEFORE I FELL...
I SHOULDN'T BE ALIVE... DID THE MIST AND LIGHTS SAVE ME?
WERE THEY PROTECTING ME FROM THE RSF WHEN MY MAGIC TRICKS WENT BAD?

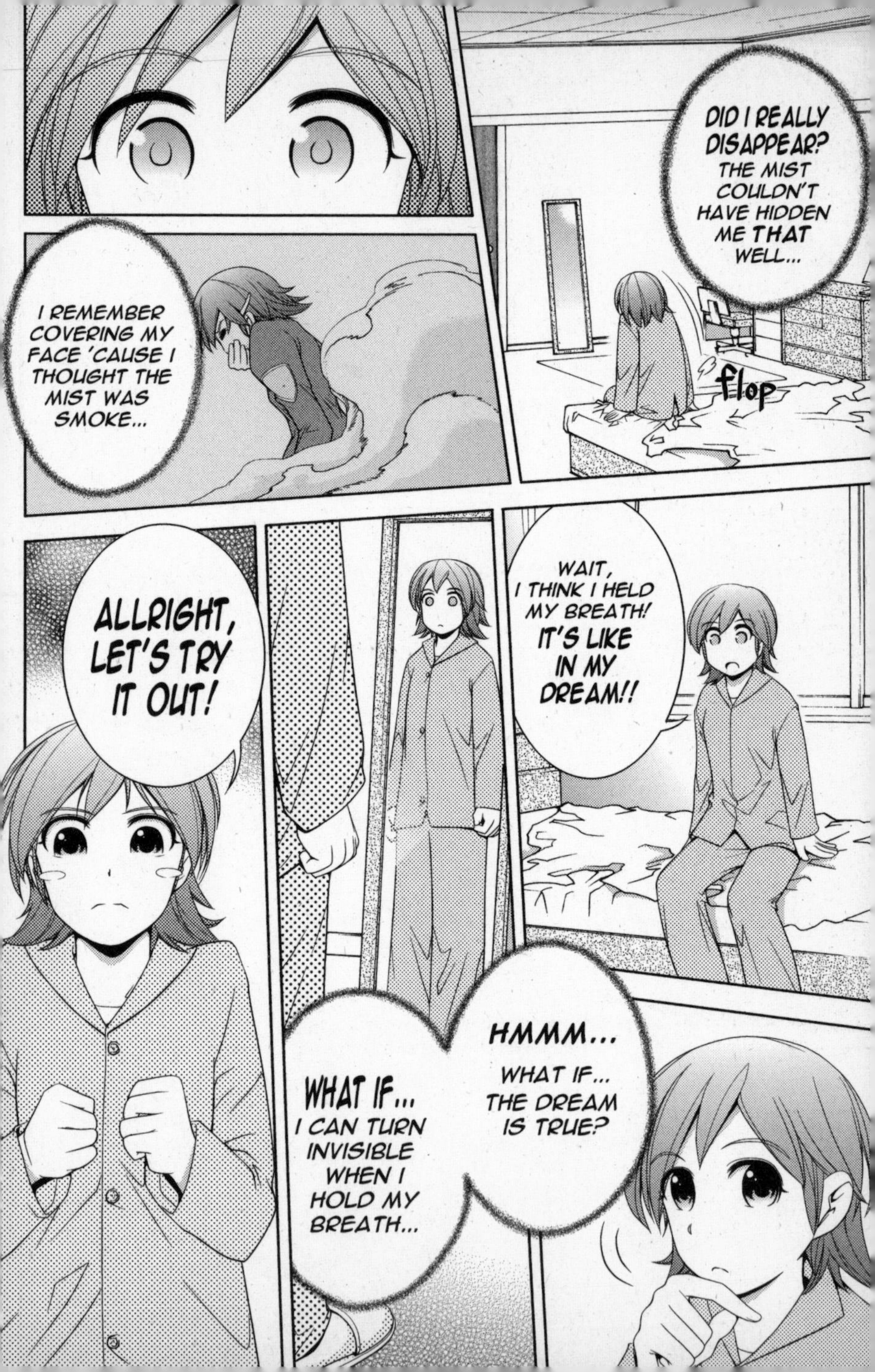
DID I REALLY DISAPPEAR? THE MIST COULDN'T HAVE HIDDEN ME THAT WELL...
flop
I REMEMBER COVERING MY FACE 'CAUSE I THOUGHT THE MIST WAS SMOKE...
WAIT, I THINK I HELD MY BREATH! IT'S LIKE IN MY DREAM!!
HMMM... WHAT IF... THE DREAM IS TRUE?
WHAT IF... I CAN TURN INVISIBLE WHEN I HOLD MY BREATH...
ALLRIGHT, LET'S TRY IT OUT!

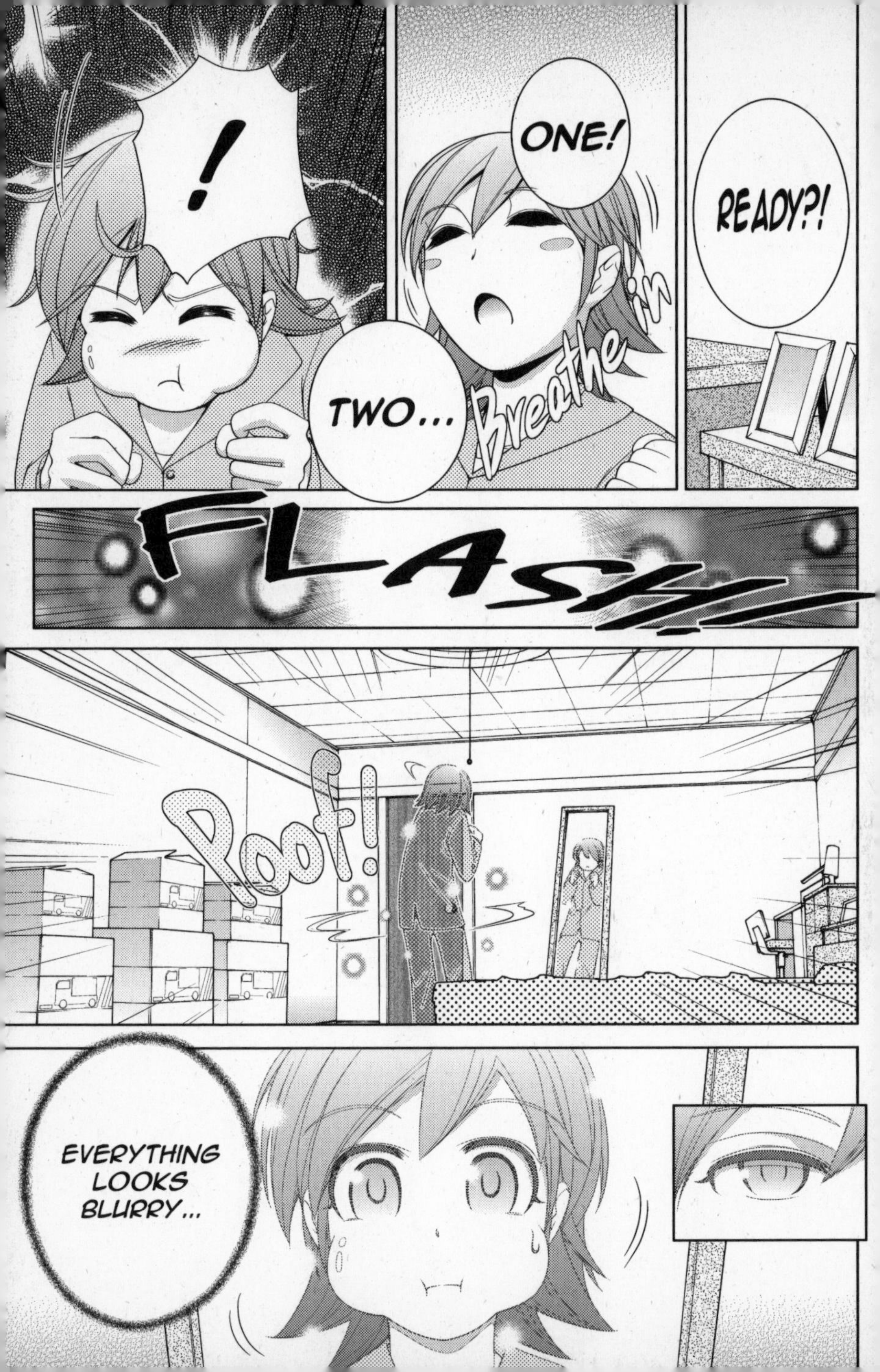
READY?!
ONE!
Breathe in
TWO...
!
FLASH
Poof!
EVERYTHING LOOKS BLURRY...

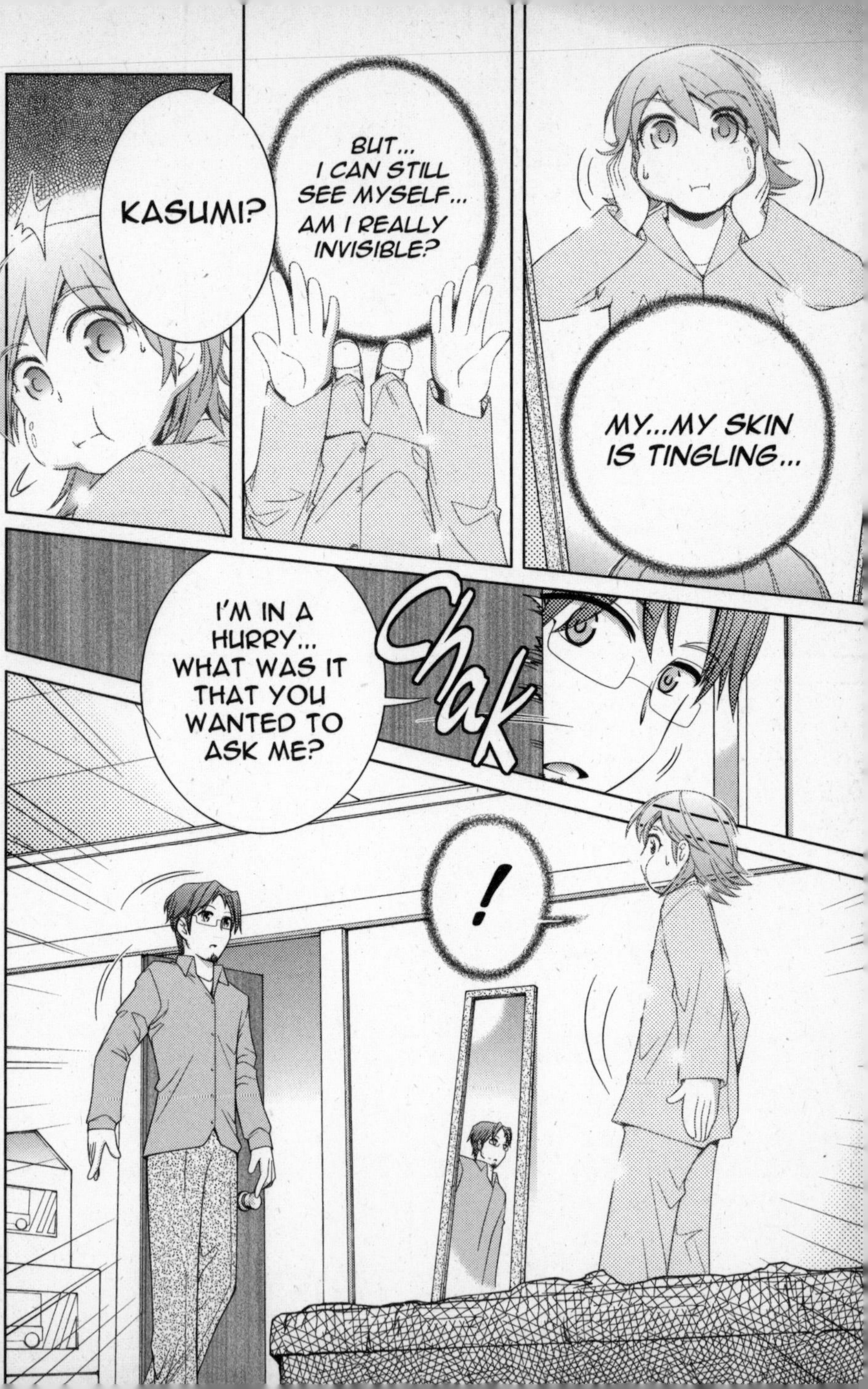
MY...MY SKIN IS TINGLING...
BUT... I CAN STILL SEE MYSELF... AM I REALLY INVISIBLE?
KASUMI?
Chak
I'M IN A HURRY... WHAT WAS IT THAT YOU WANTED TO ASK ME?
!

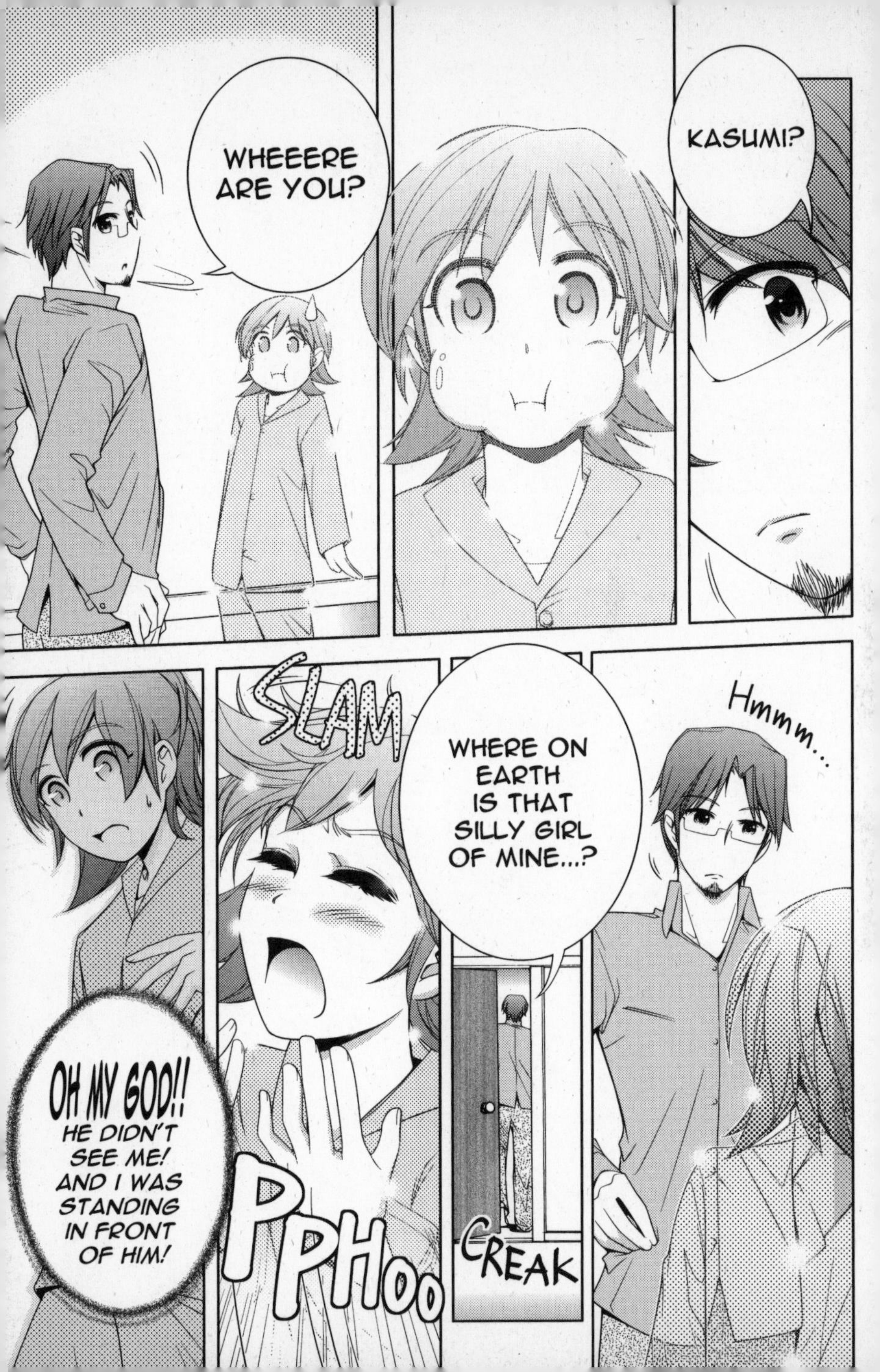
KASUMI?
WHEEERE ARE YOU?
Hmmm...
WHERE ON EARTH IS THAT SILLY GIRL OF MINE...?
CREAK
SLAM
PPHOO
OH MY GOD!! HE DIDN'T SEE ME! AND I WAS STANDING IN FRONT OF HIM!

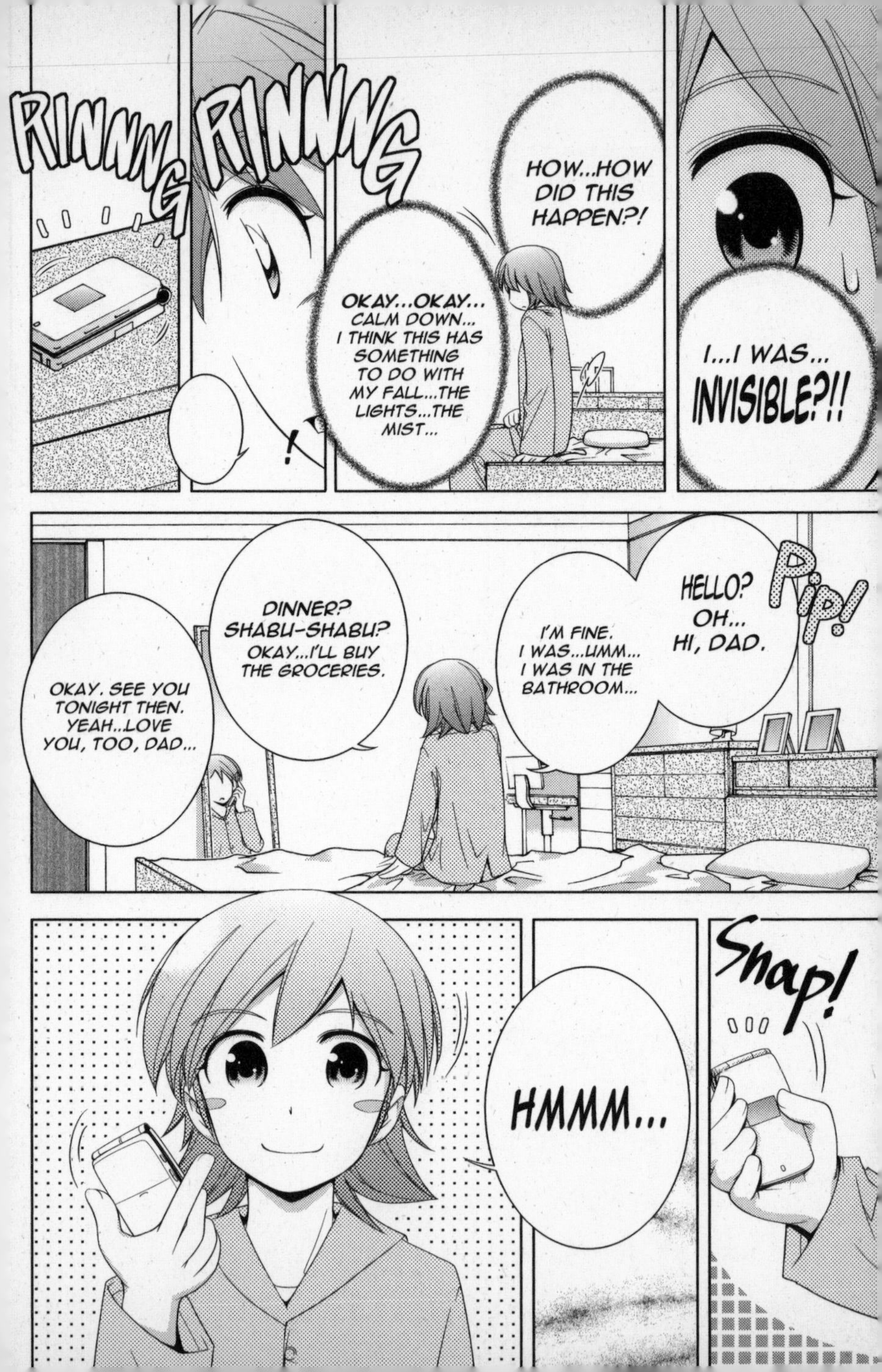
I...I WAS... INVISIBLE?!!
HOW...HOW DID THIS HAPPEN?!
OKAY...OKAY... CALM DOWN... I THINK THIS HAS SOMETHING TO DO WITH MY FALL...THE LIGHTS...THE MIST...
RINNNG RINNNG
!
Pip!
HELLO? OH... HI, DAD.
I'M FINE. I WAS...UMM... I WAS IN THE BATHROOM...
DINNER? SHABU-SHABU? OKAY...I'LL BUY THE GROCERIES.
OKAY. SEE YOU TONIGHT THEN. YEAH...LOVE YOU, TOO, DAD...
Snap!
HMMM...

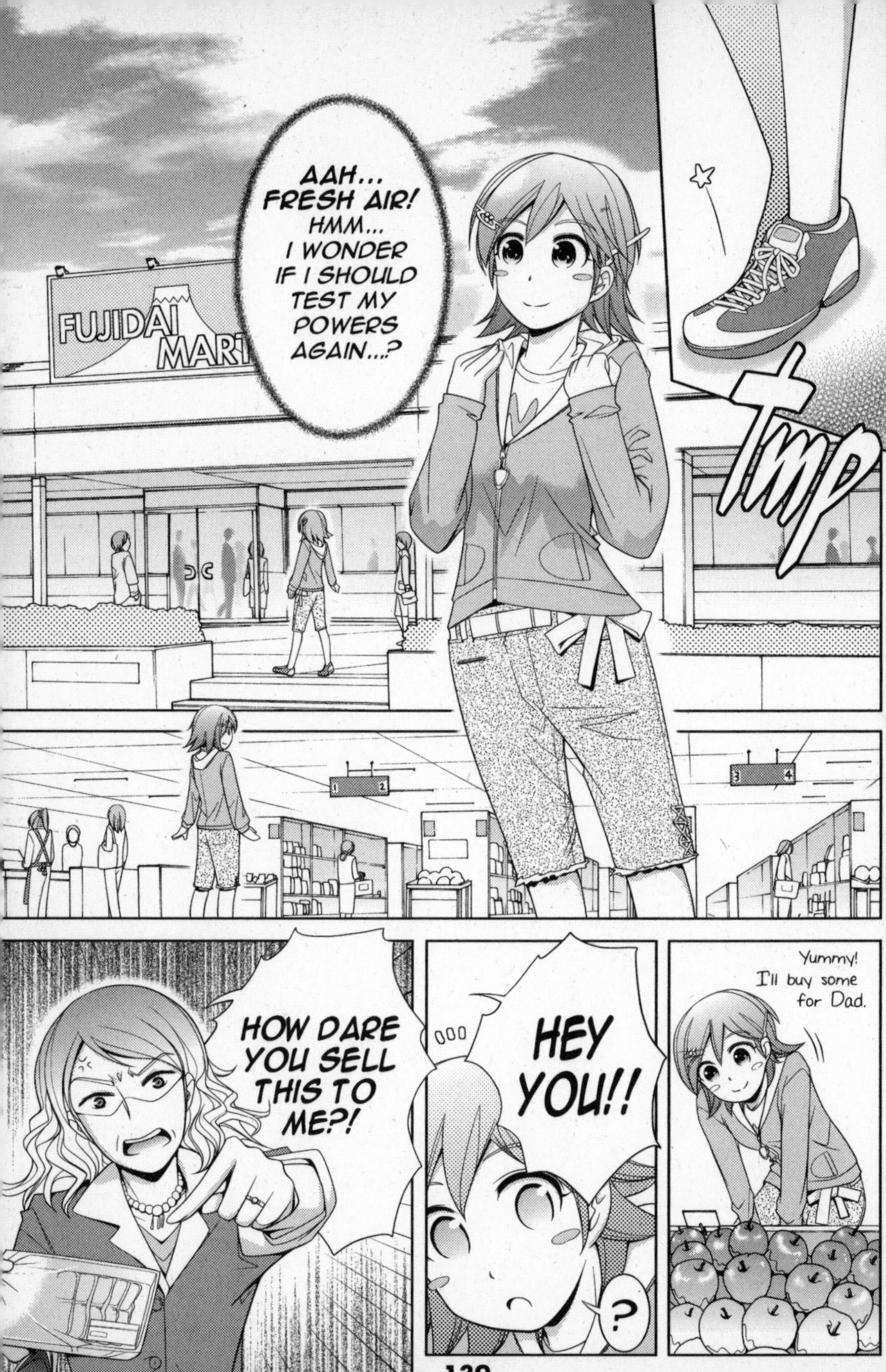
tmp
FUJIDAI MAR
AAH... FRESH AIR! HMM... I WONDER IF I SHOULD TEST MY POWERS AGAIN...?
Yummy! I'll buy some for Dad.
HEY YOU!!
?
HOW DARE YOU SELL THIS TO ME?!

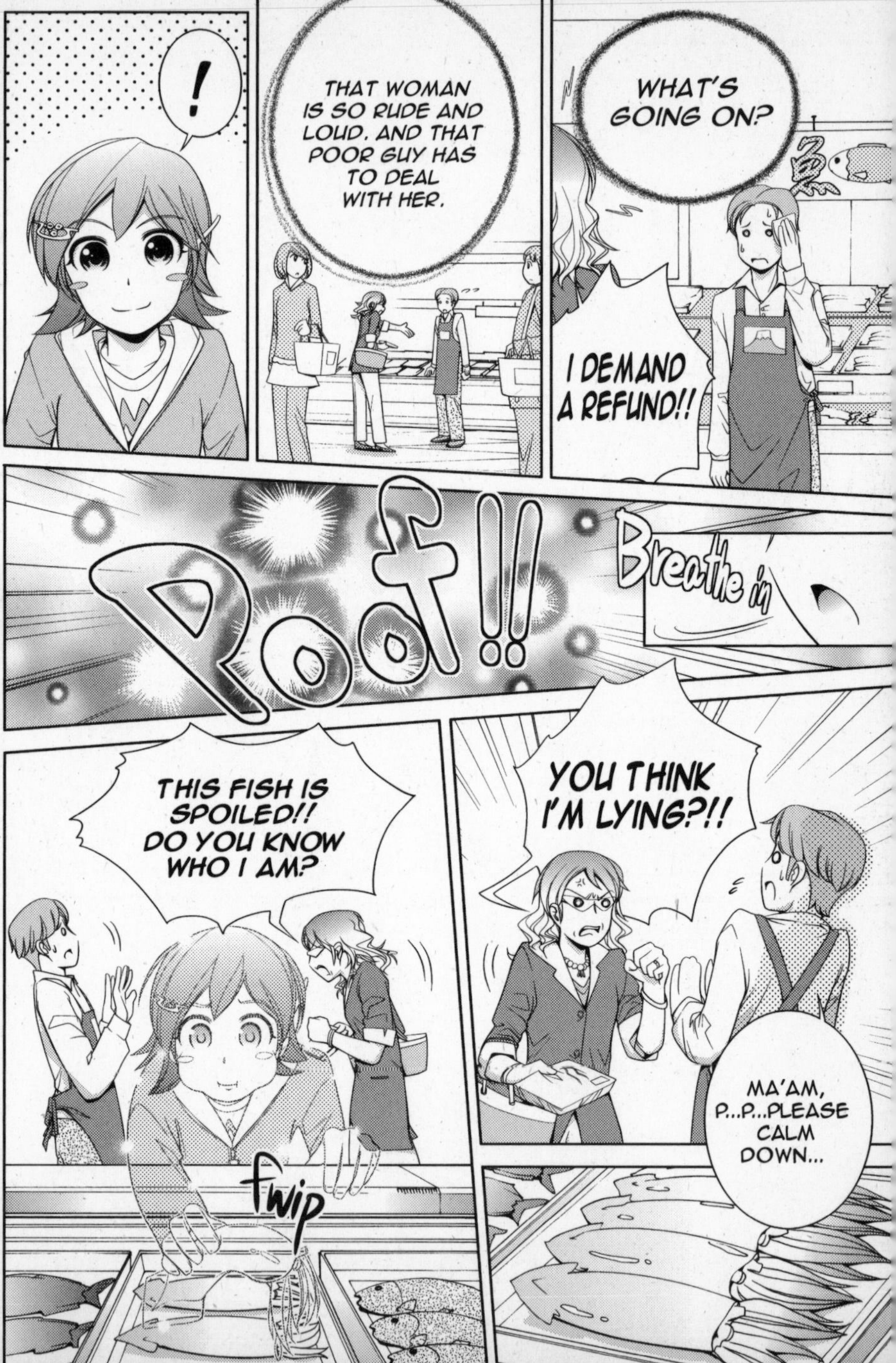
WHAT'S GOING ON?
I DEMAND A REFUND!!
THAT WOMAN IS SO RUDE AND LOUD. AND THAT POOR GUY HAS TO DEAL WITH HER.
!
Breathe in
Poof!!
YOU THINK I'M LYING?!!
MA'AM, P...P...PLEASE CALM DOWN...
THIS FISH IS SPOILED!! DO YOU KNOW WHO I AM?
fwip

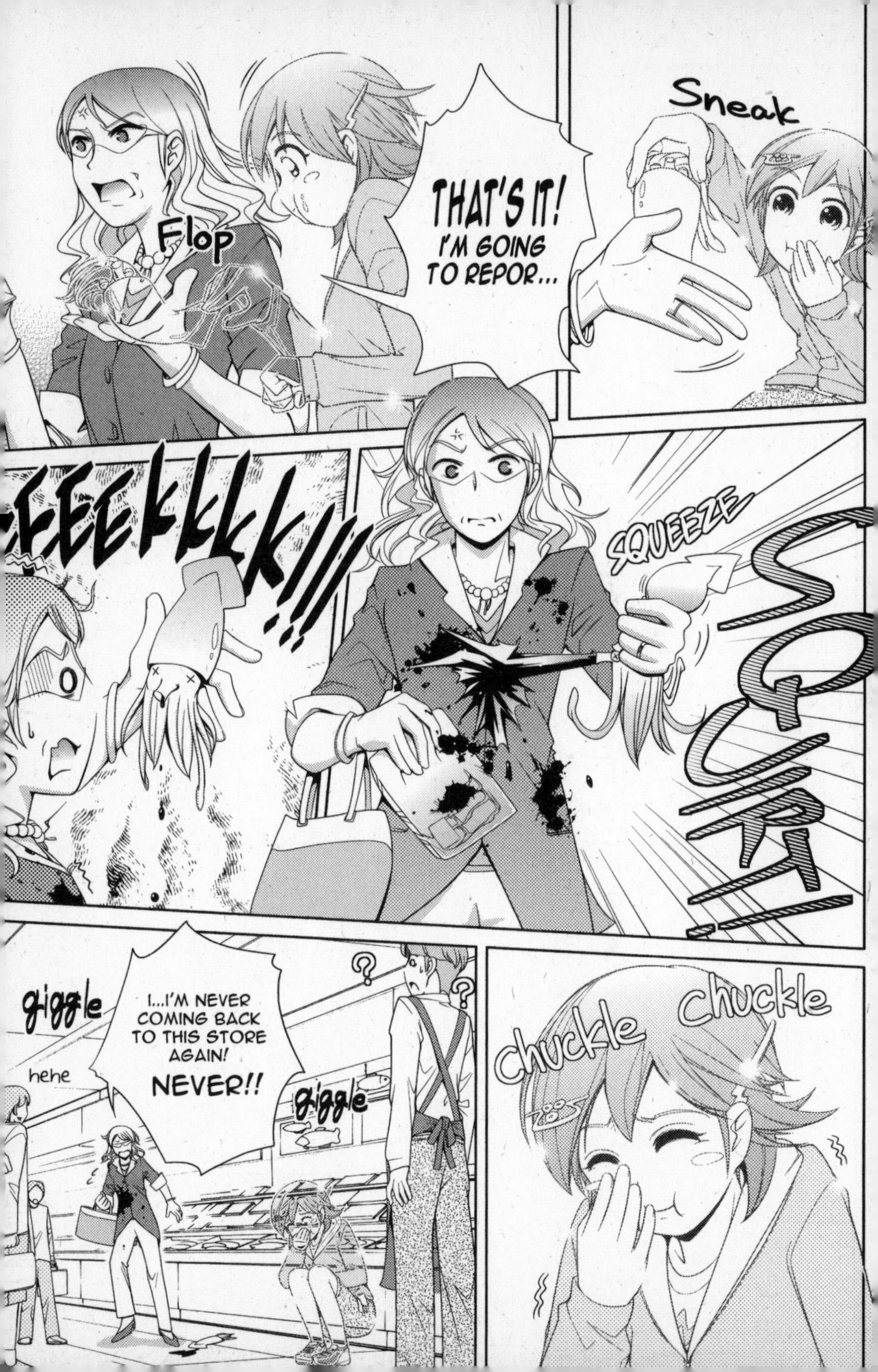
Sneak
THAT'S IT! I'M GOING TO REPOR...
Flop
SQUIRT!!
SQUEEZE
EEEKKKKK!!!
Chuckle
Chuckle
?
?
I...I'M NEVER COMING BACK TO THIS STORE AGAIN! NEVER!!
giggle
hehe
giggle

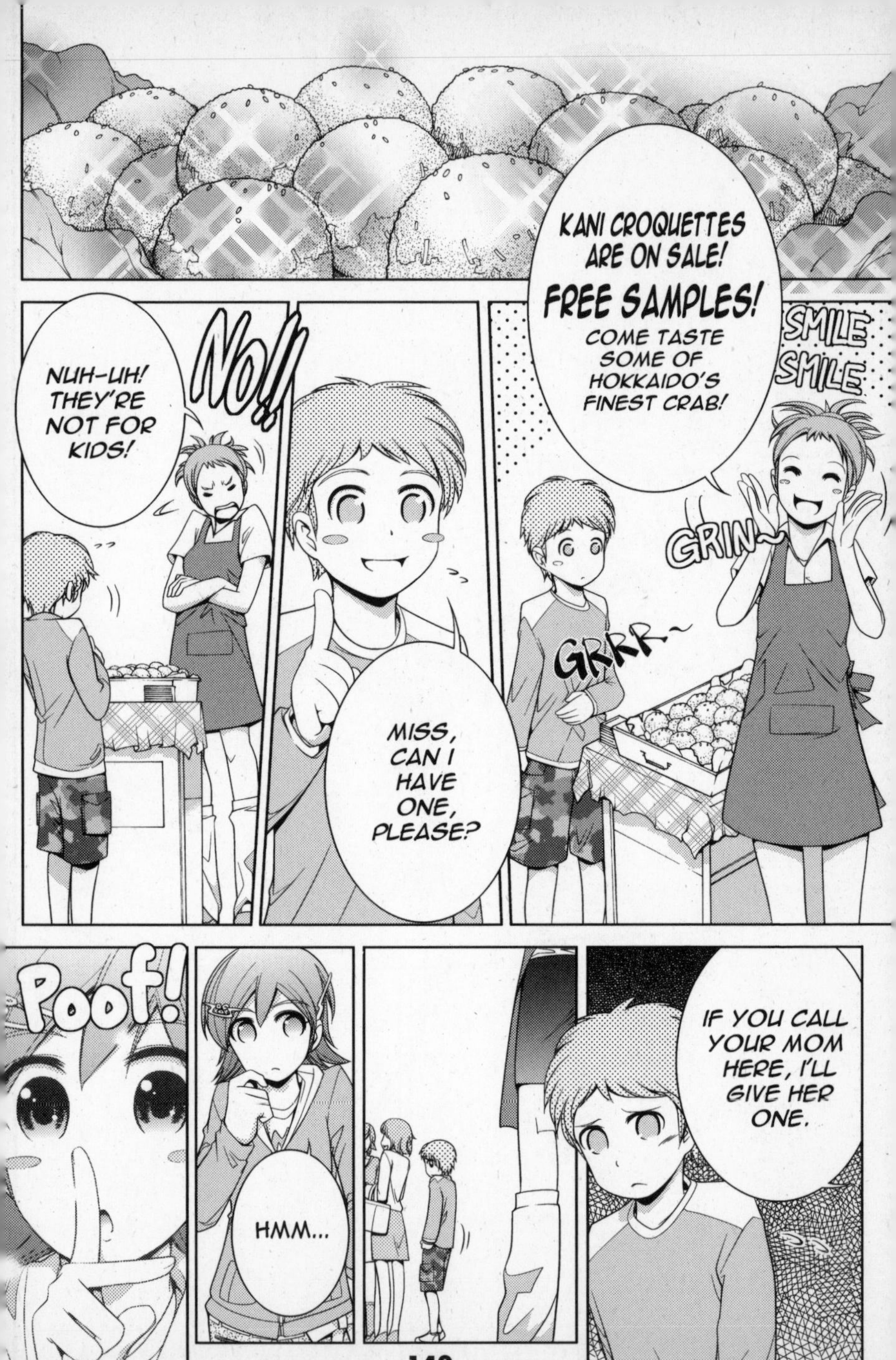
KANI CROQUETTES ARE ON SALE!
FREE SAMPLES!
COME TASTE SOME OF HOKKAIDO'S FINEST CRAB!
SMILE
SMILE
GRIN~
GRRR~
MISS, CAN I HAVE ONE, PLEASE?
NO!!
NUH-UH! THEY'RE NOT FOR KIDS!
IF YOU CALL YOUR MOM HERE, I'LL GIVE HER ONE.
HMM...
Poof!

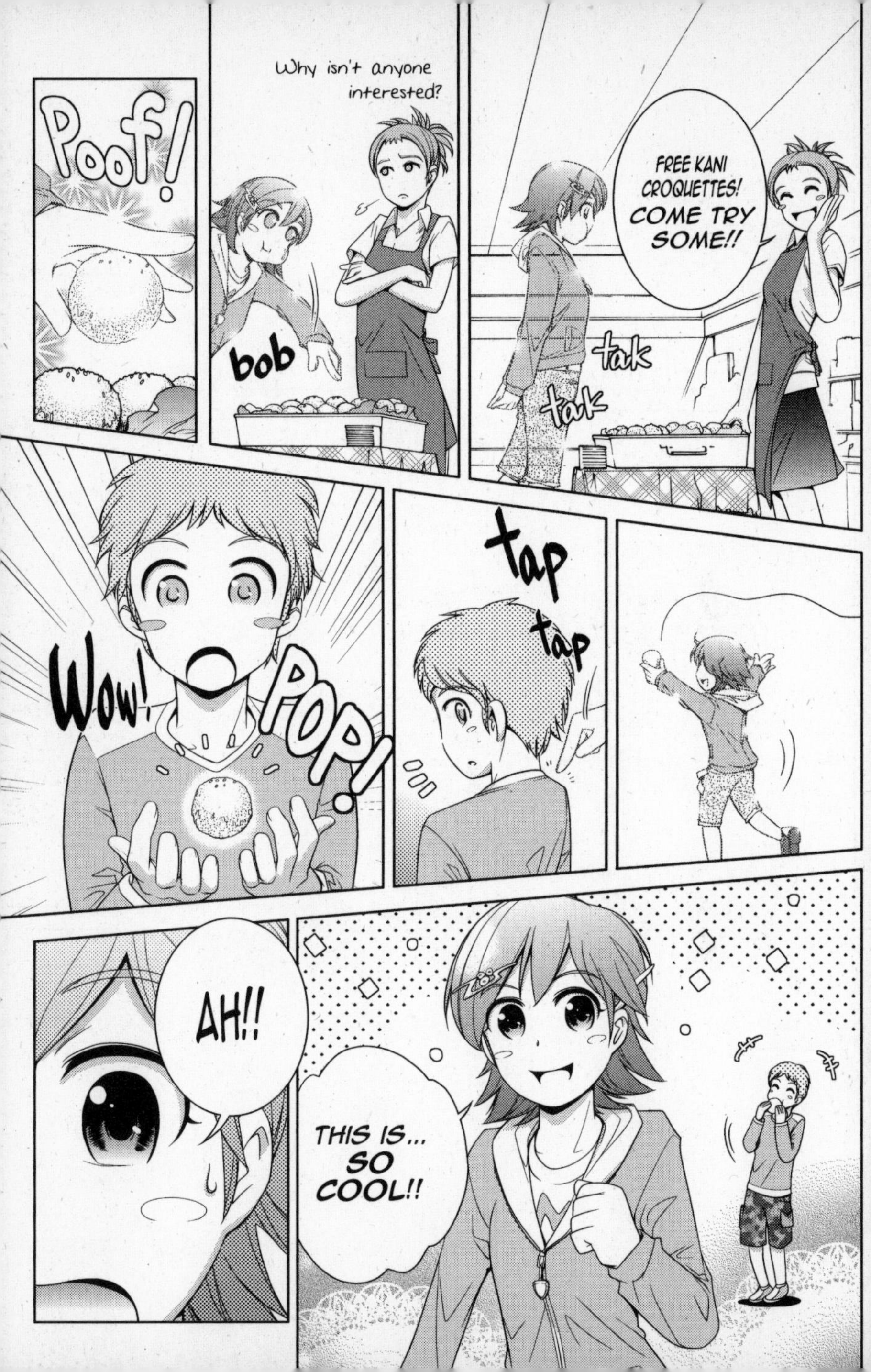
FREE KANI CROQUETTES! COME TRY SOME!!
tak
tak
Why isn't anyone interested?
bob
Poof!
tap
tap
Wow!
POP!
THIS IS... SO COOL!!
AH!!

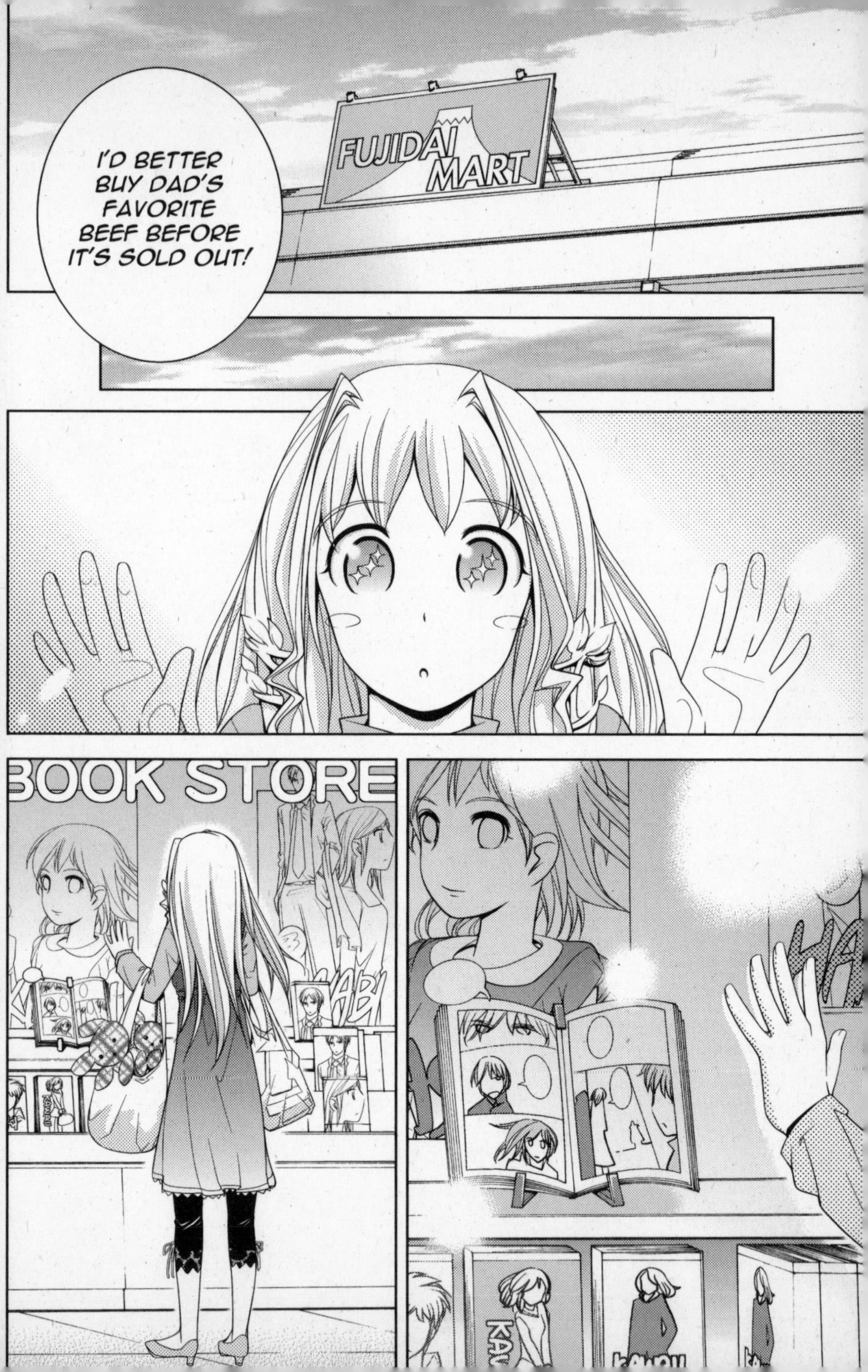
FUJIDAI MART
I'D BETTER BUY DAD'S FAVORITE BEEF BEFORE IT'S SOLD OUT!
BOOK STORE

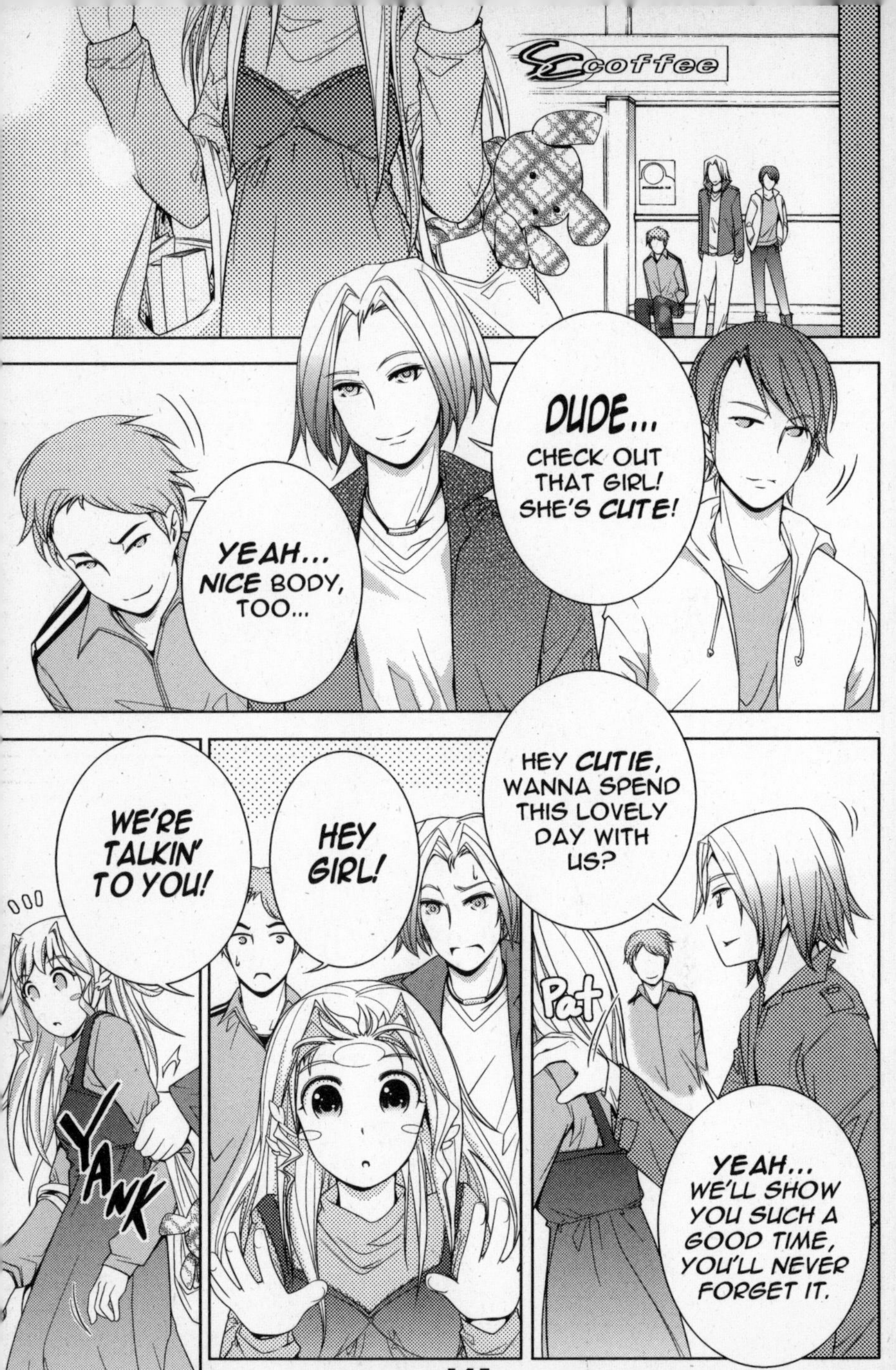
coffee
DUDE... CHECK OUT THAT GIRL! SHE'S CUTE!
YEAH... NICE BODY, TOO...
HEY CUTIE, WANNA SPEND THIS LOVELY DAY WITH US?
Pat
YEAH... WE'LL SHOW YOU SUCH A GOOD TIME, YOU'LL NEVER FORGET IT.
HEY GIRL!
WE'RE TALKIN' TO YOU!
YANK

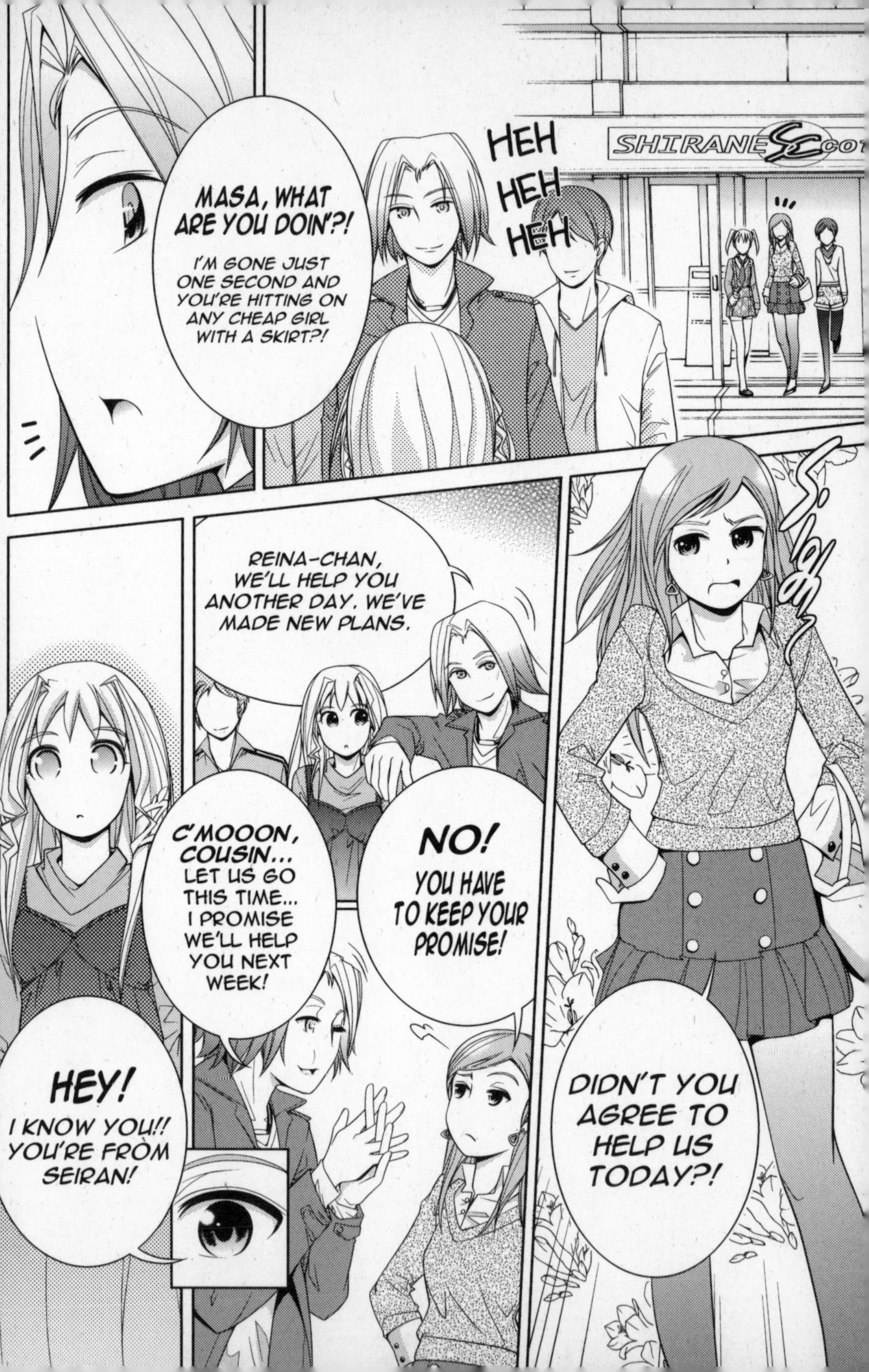
HEH HEH HEH
SHIRANE
MASA, WHAT ARE YOU DOIN'?!
I'M GONE JUST ONE SECOND AND YOU'RE HITTING ON ANY CHEAP GIRL WITH A SKIRT?!
Sigh
DIDN'T YOU AGREE TO HELP US TODAY?!
REINA-CHAN, WE'LL HELP YOU ANOTHER DAY. WE'VE MADE NEW PLANS.
C'MOOON, COUSIN... LET US GO THIS TIME... I PROMISE WE'LL HELP YOU NEXT WEEK!
NO! YOU HAVE TO KEEP YOUR PROMISE!
HEY! I KNOW YOU!! YOU'RE FROM SEIRAN!

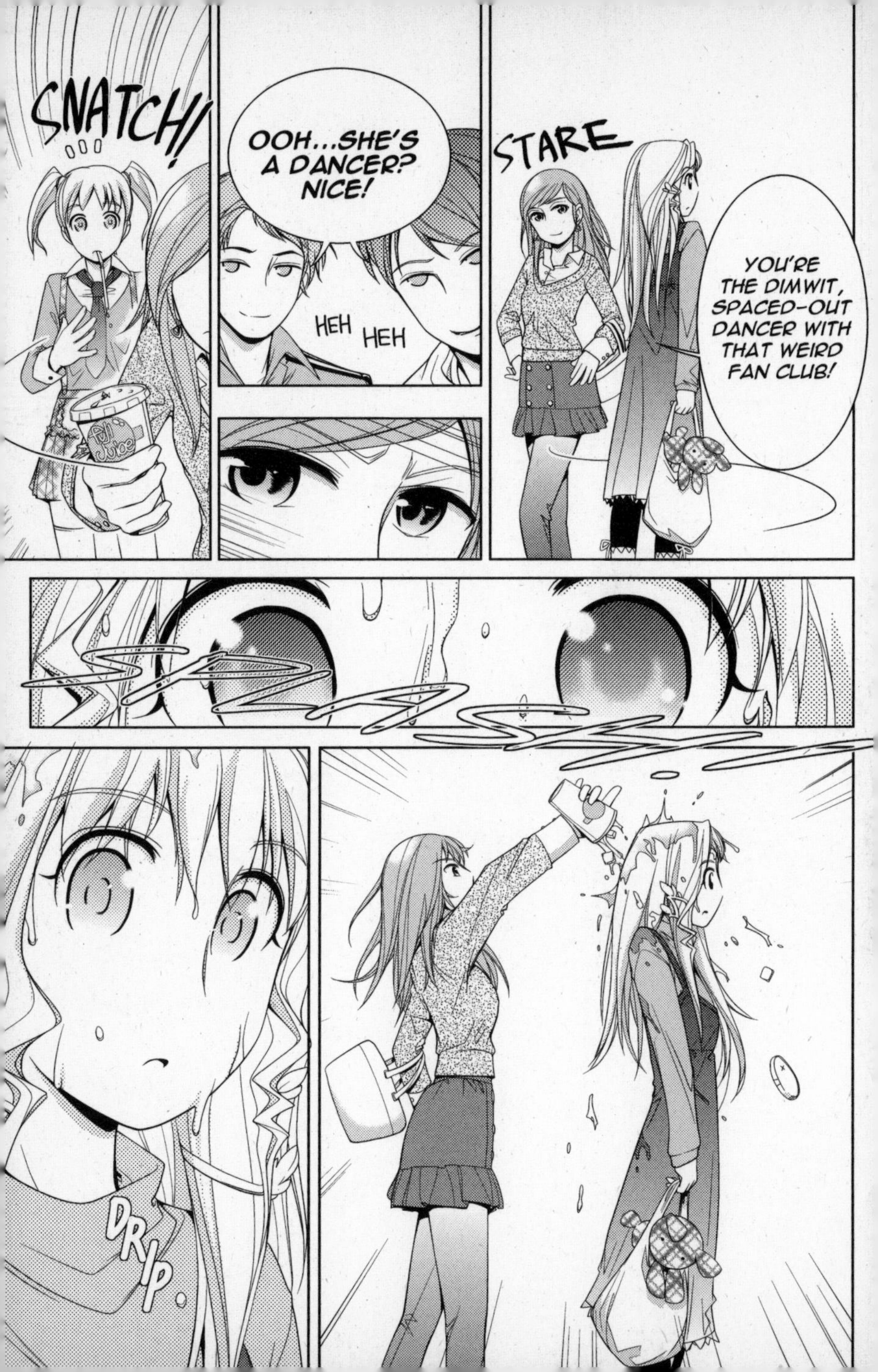
STARE
YOU'RE THE DIMWIT, SPACED-OUT DANCER WITH THAT WEIRD FAN CLUB!
OOH...SHE'S A DANCER? NICE!
HEH HEH
SNATCH!
SPLASH
DRIP

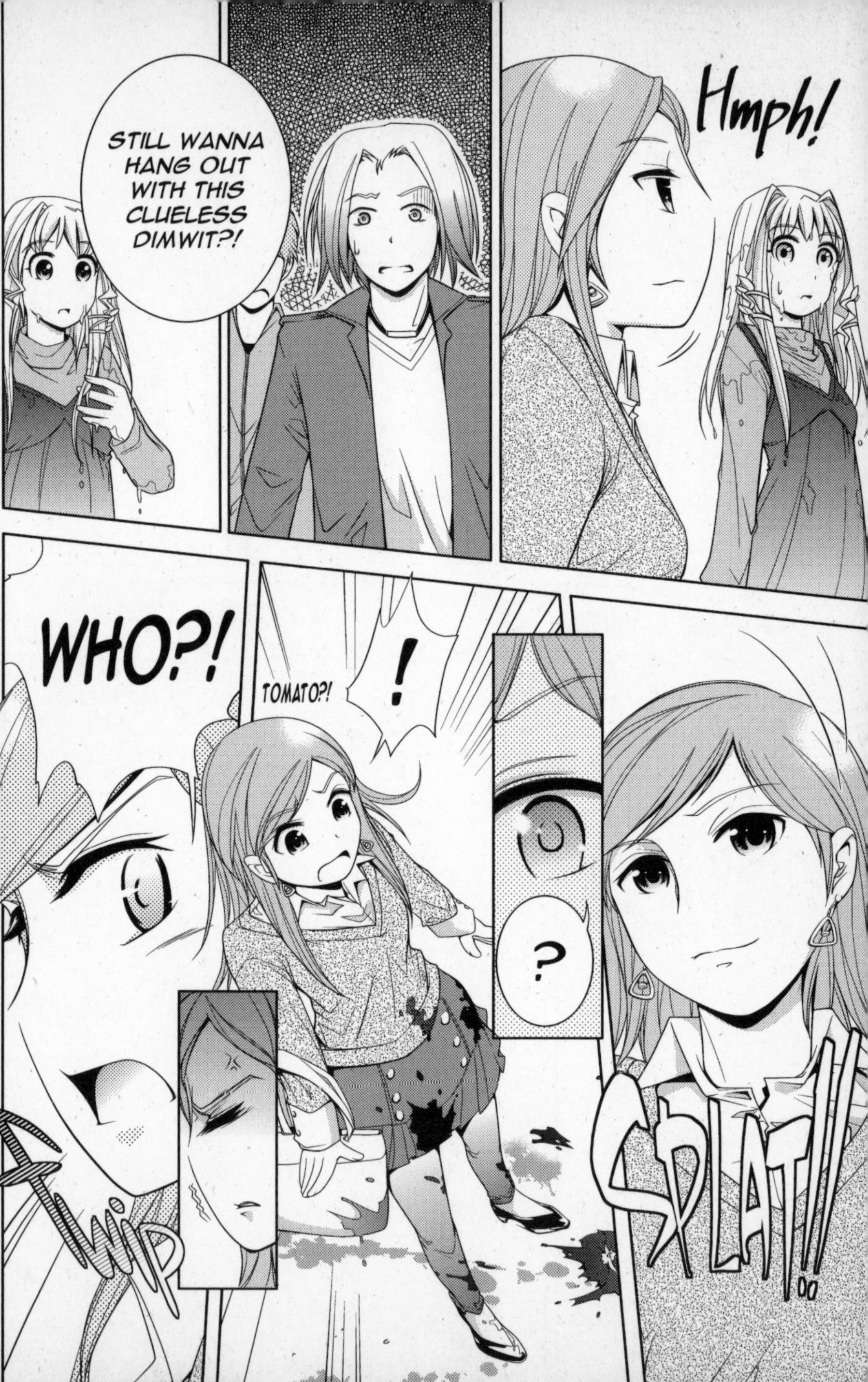
Hmph!
STILL WANNA HANG OUT WITH THIS CLUELESS DIMWIT?!
SPLAT!!
?
!
TOMATO?!
WHO?!
Fwip

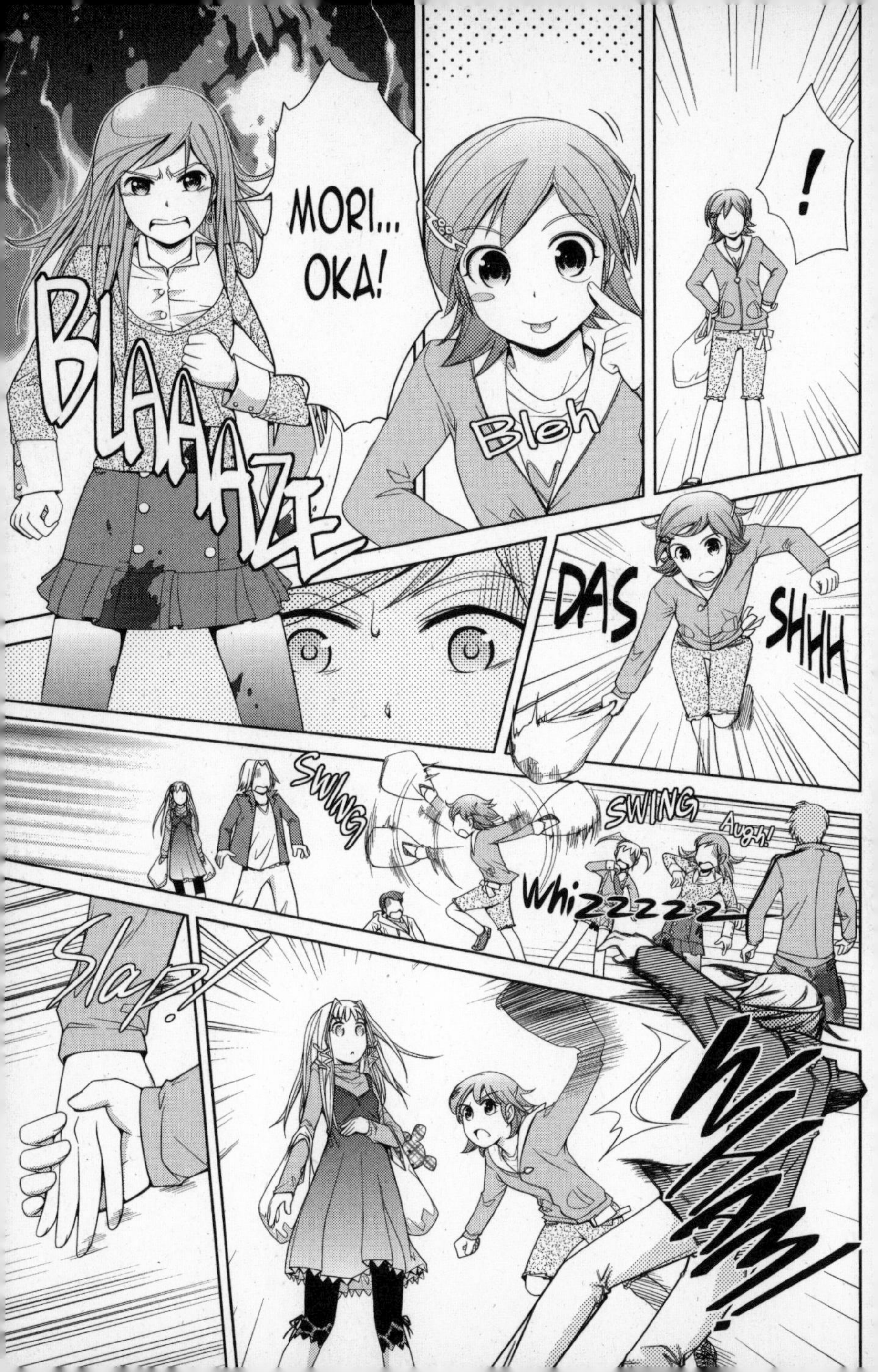
!
Bleh
DAS
SHHH
MORI... OKA!
BLAAAAZE
SWING
Augh!
Whizzzzzz
SWING
WHAM!!
Slap!

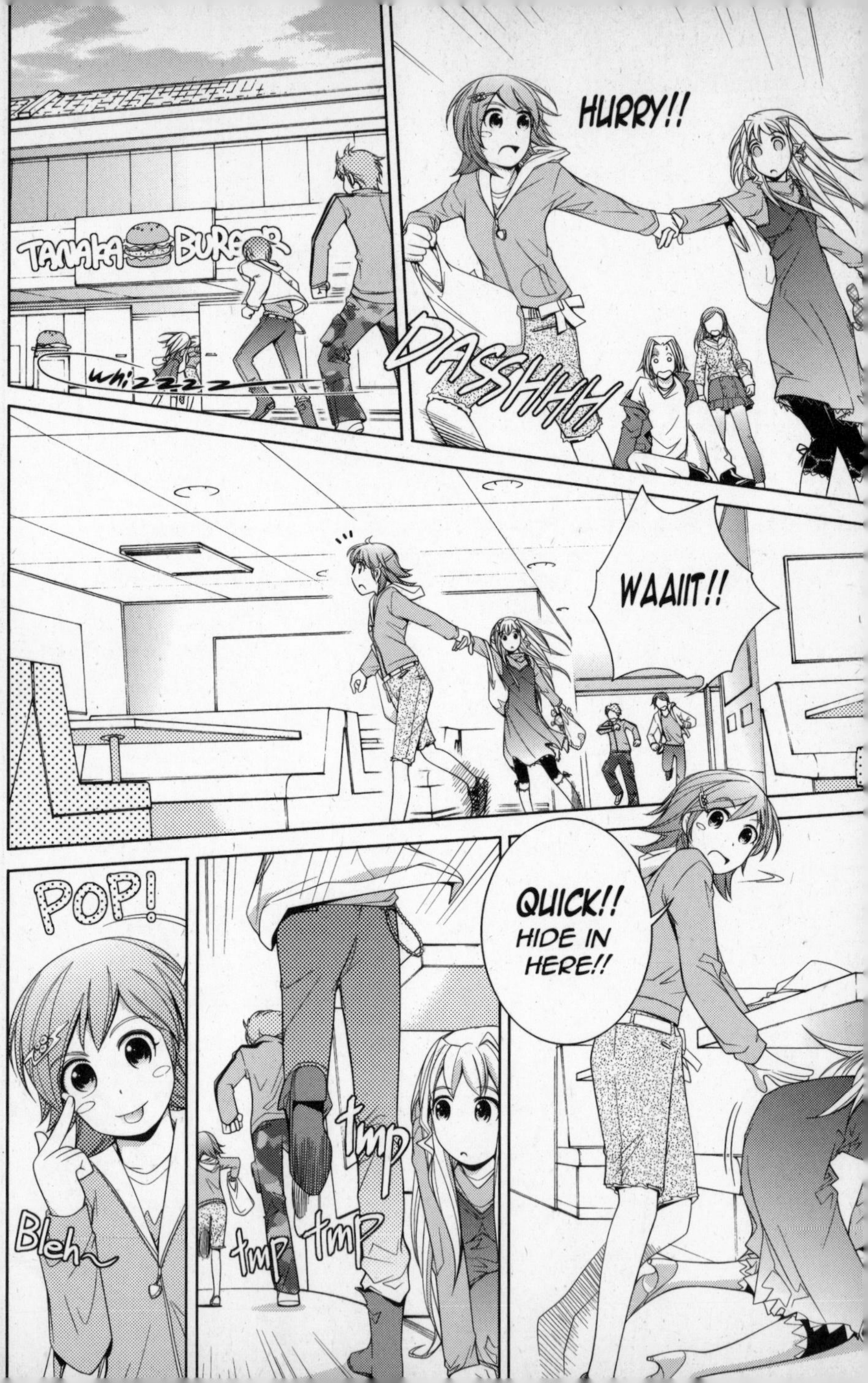
HURRY!!
DASHHH
TANAKA
whizzzz
WAAIIT!!
QUICK!! HIDE IN HERE!!
tmp
tmp tmp
POP!
Bleh~

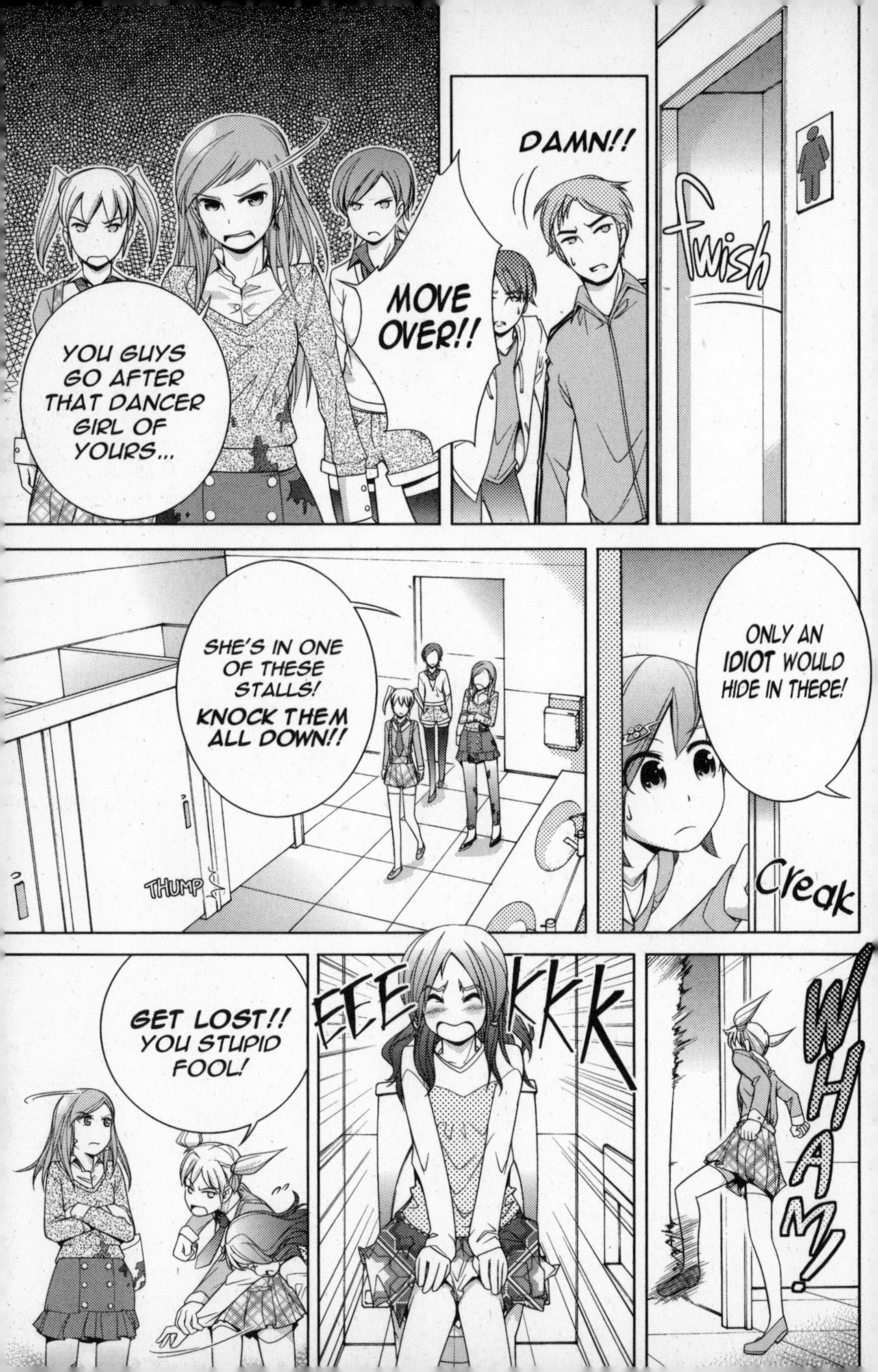
fwish
DAMN!!
MOVE OVER!!
YOU GUYS GO AFTER THAT DANCER GIRL OF YOURS...
ONLY AN IDIOT WOULD HIDE IN THERE!
Creak
SHE'S IN ONE OF THESE STALLS! KNOCK THEM ALL DOWN!!
THUMP
WHAM!
EEEKKK
GET LOST!! YOU STUPID FOOL!

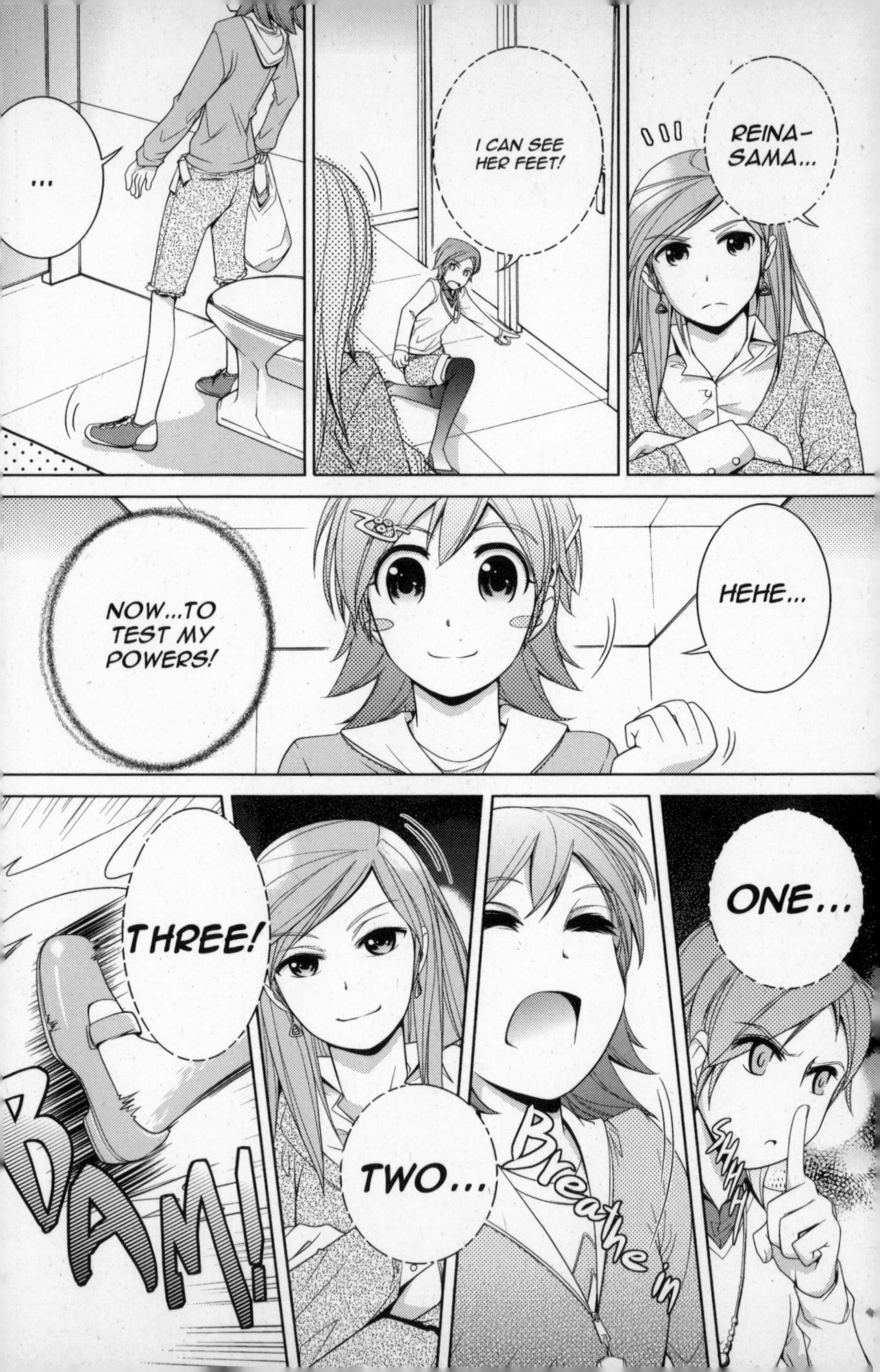
REINA-SAMA...
I CAN SEE HER FEET!
...
HEHE...
NOW...TO TEST MY POWERS!
ONE...
SHHH
Breathe in
TWO...
THREE!
BAM!!

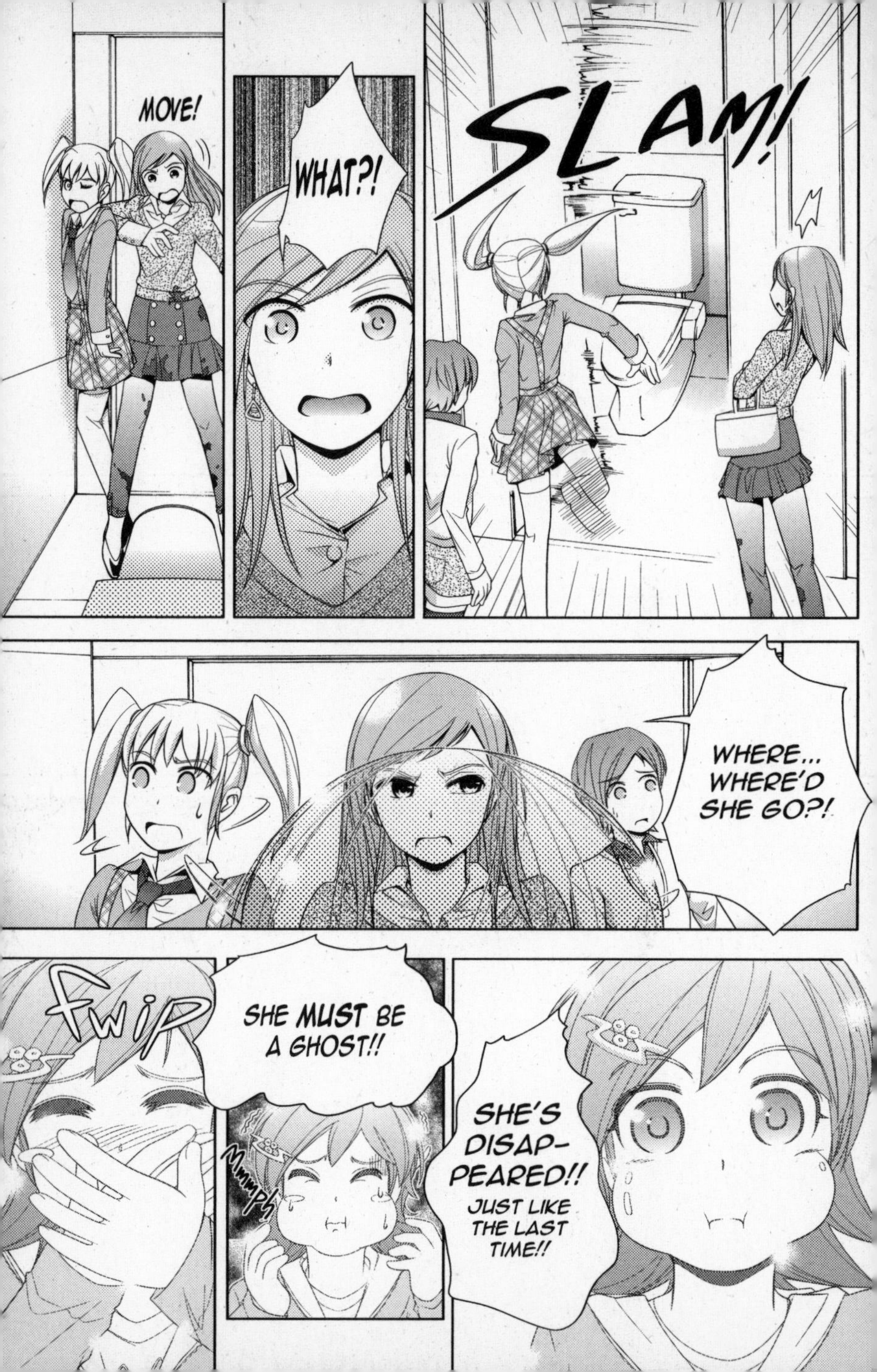
SLAM!
WHAT?!
MOVE!
WHERE... WHERE'D SHE GO?!
SHE'S DISAP-PEARED!!
JUST LIKE THE LAST TIME!!
SHE MUST BE A GHOST!!
Mmmph
fwip

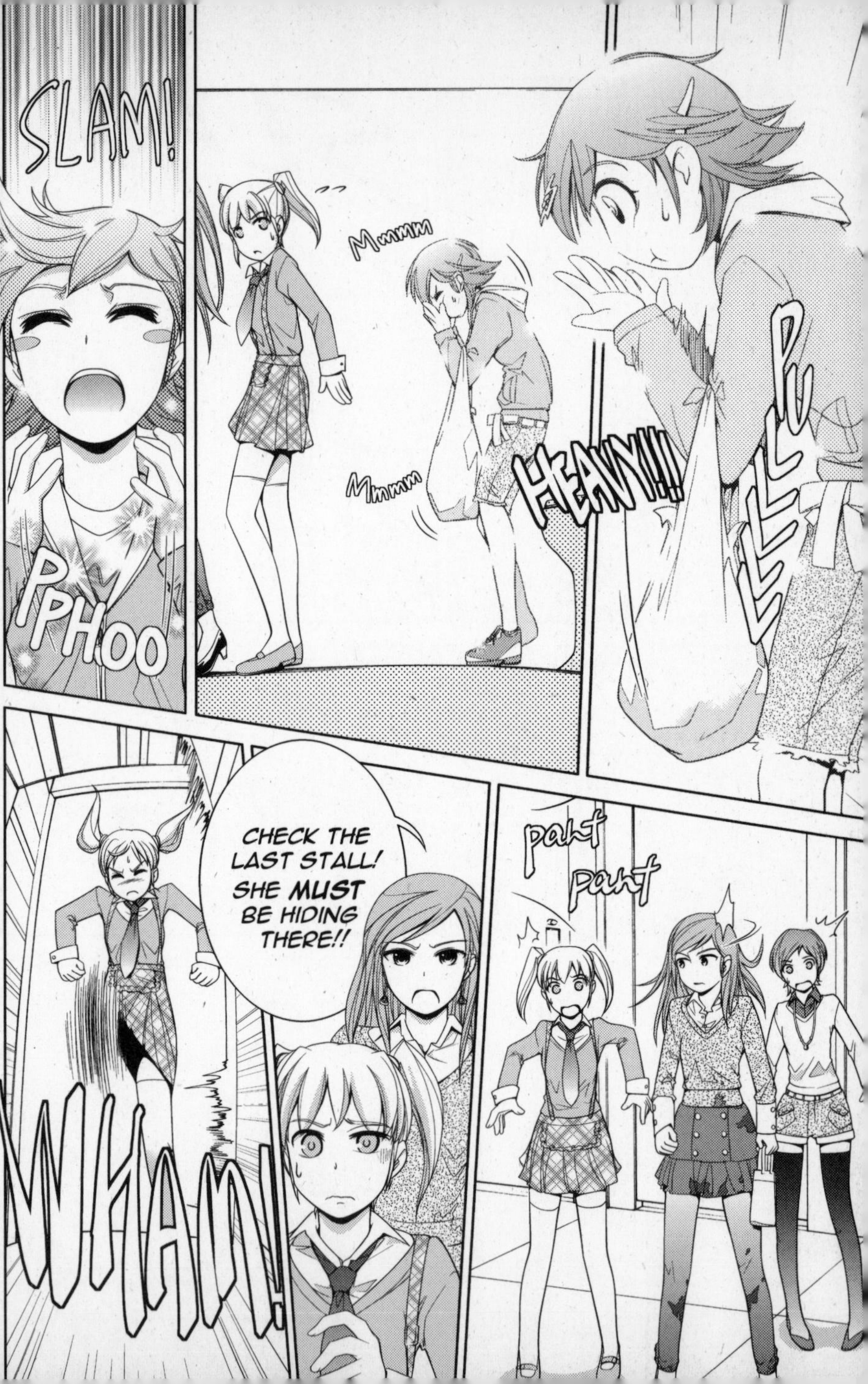
PULLLLL
HEAVY!!!
Mmmm
Mmmm
SLAM!
PPHOO
pant
pant
CHECK THE LAST STALL! SHE MUST BE HIDING THERE!!
WHAM!

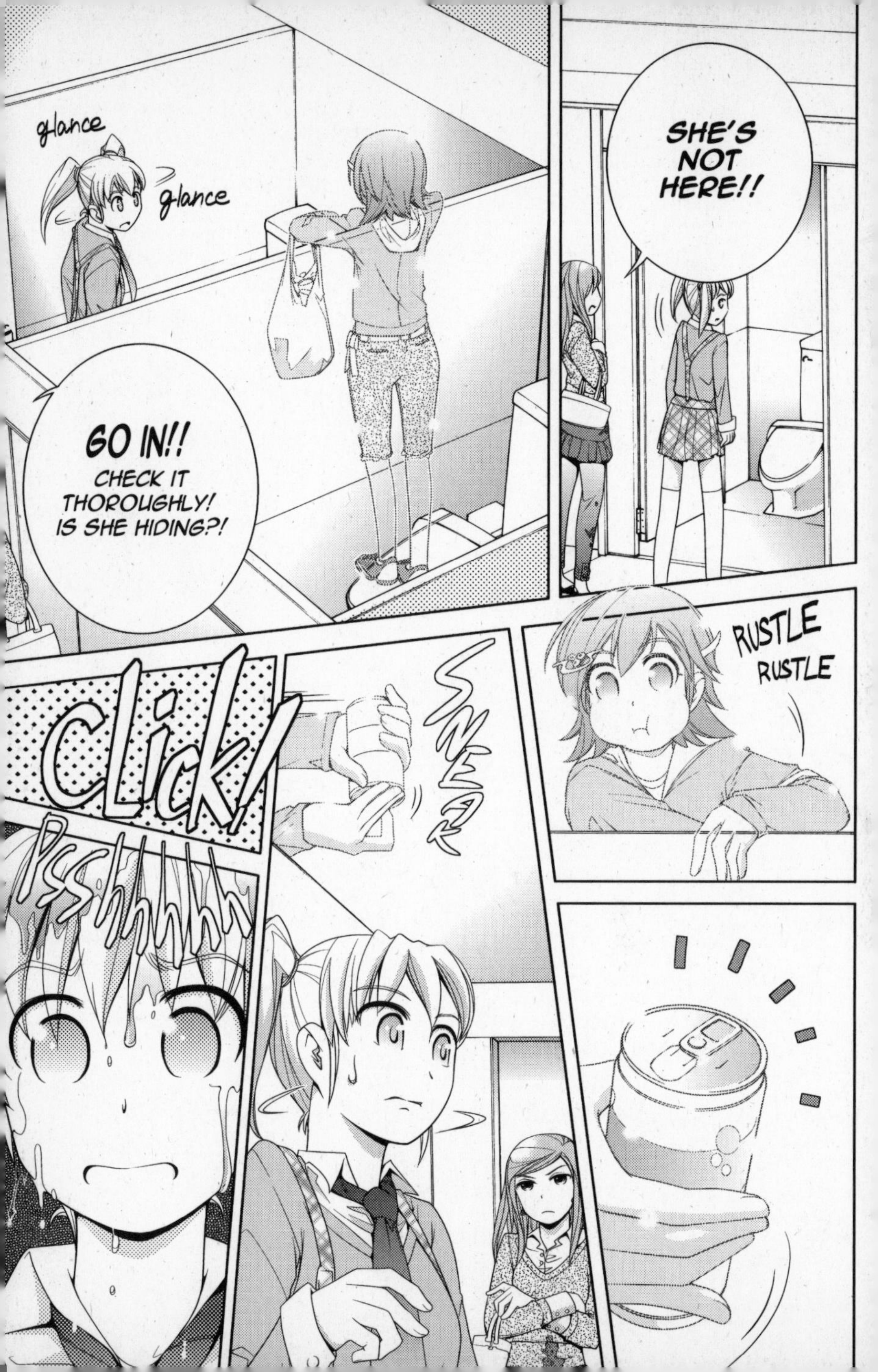
SHE'S NOT HERE!!
glance
glance
GO IN!! CHECK IT THOROUGHLY! IS SHE HIDING?!
RUSTLE
RUSTLE
SNEAK
Click!
Psshhhhh

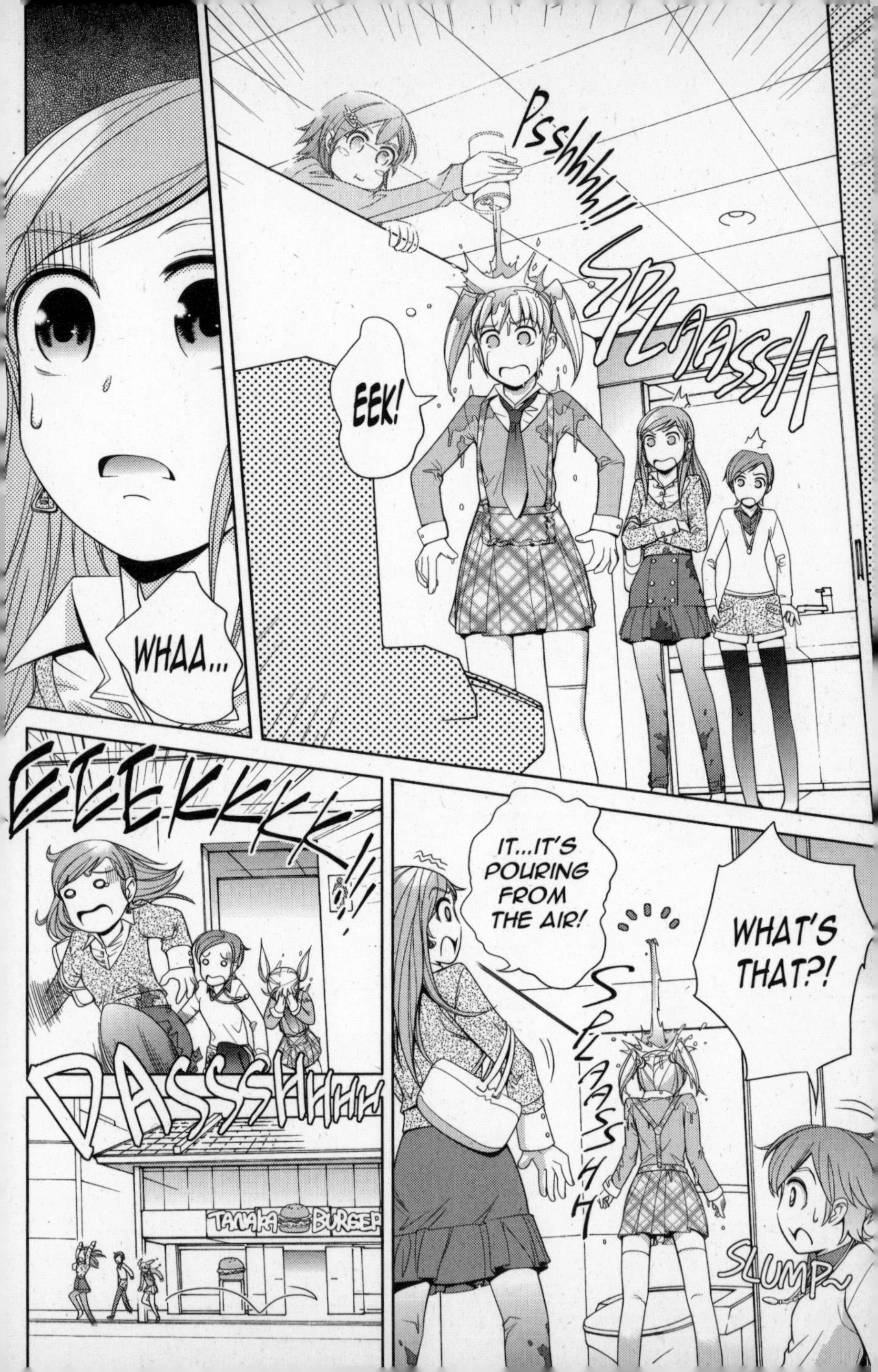
Psshhh!!
SPLAASSH
EEK!
WHAA...
WHAT'S THAT?!
IT...IT'S POURING FROM THE AIR!
SPLAASSHH
SLUMP~
EEEKKKK!!!
DASSSHHHH
TANAKA BURGER

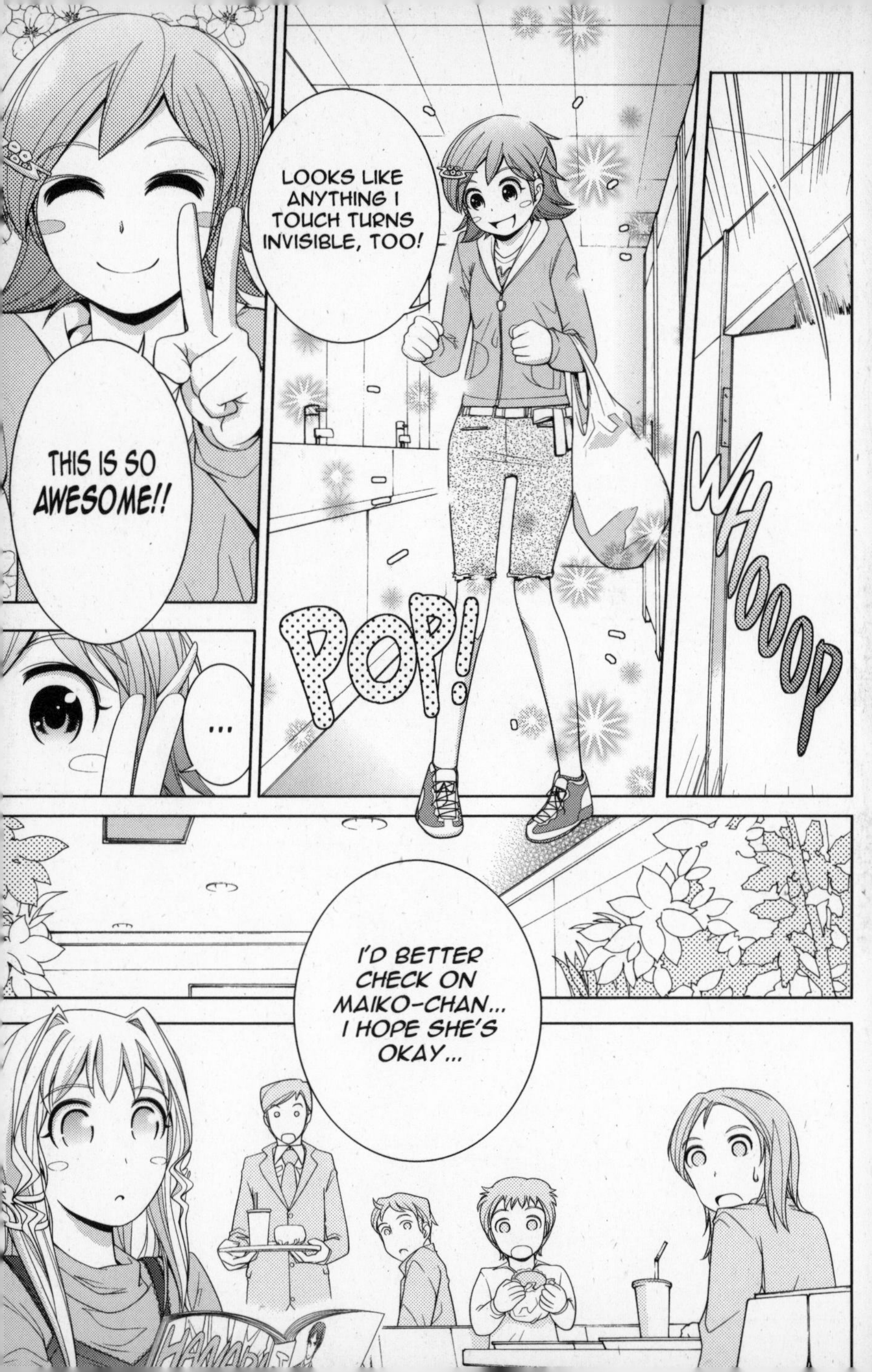
WHOOOOP
LOOKS LIKE ANYTHING I TOUCH TURNS INVISIBLE, TOO!
POP!
THIS IS SO AWESOME!!
...
I'D BETTER CHECK ON MAIKO-CHAN... I HOPE SHE'S OKAY...

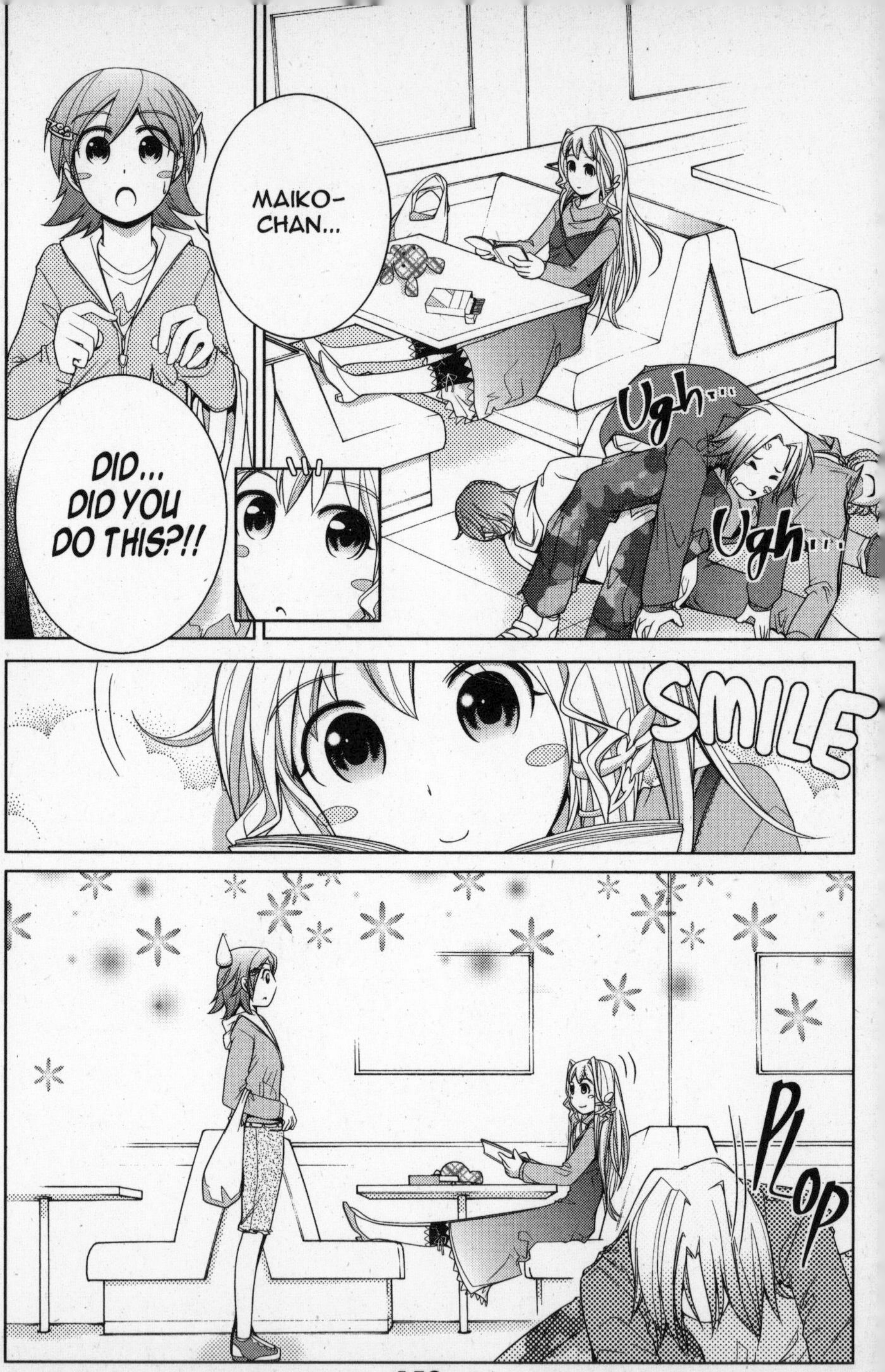
Ugh...
Ugh...
MAIKO-CHAN...
DID... DID YOU DO THIS?!!
SMILE
PLOP

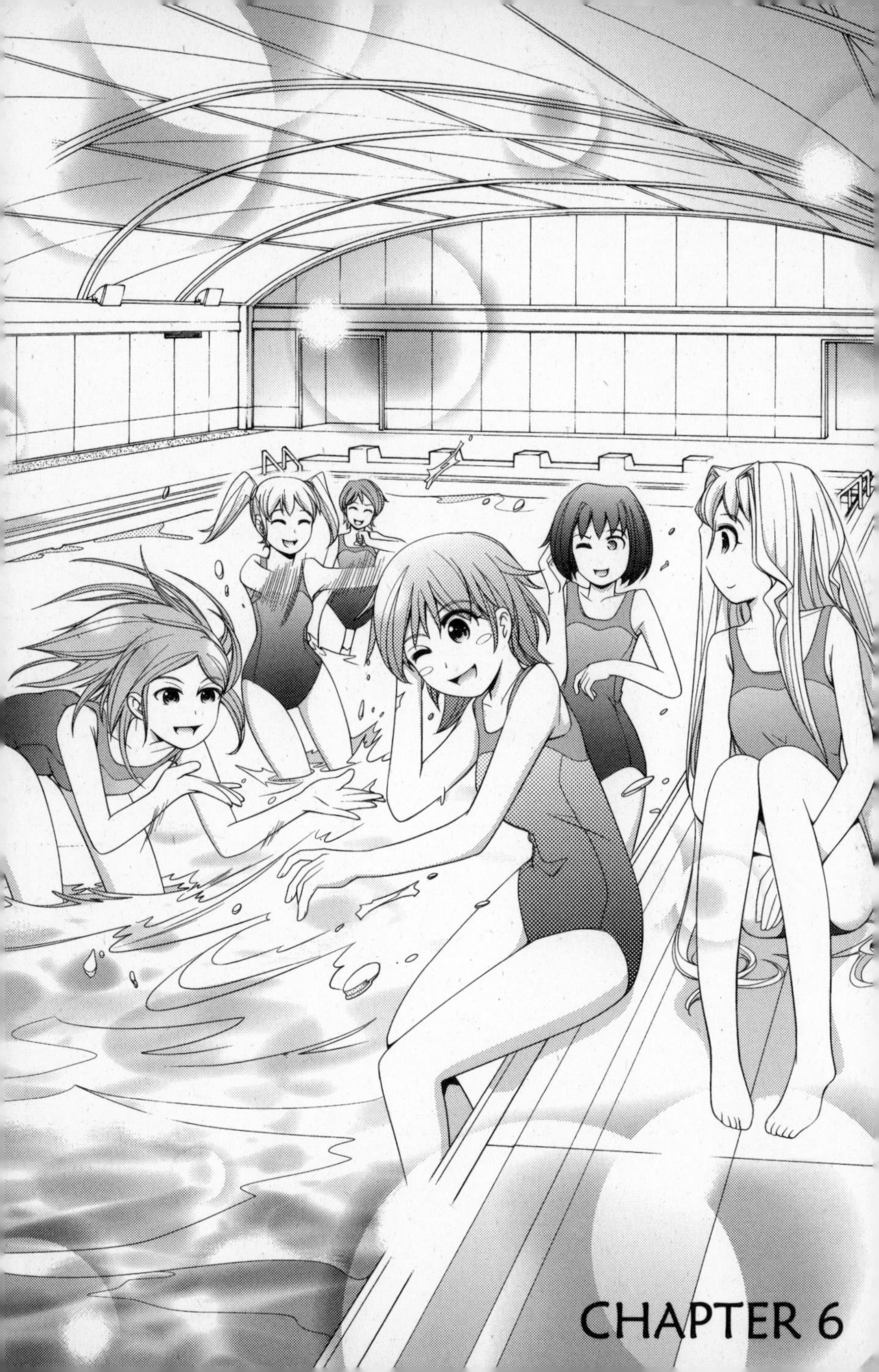

CHAPTER 6

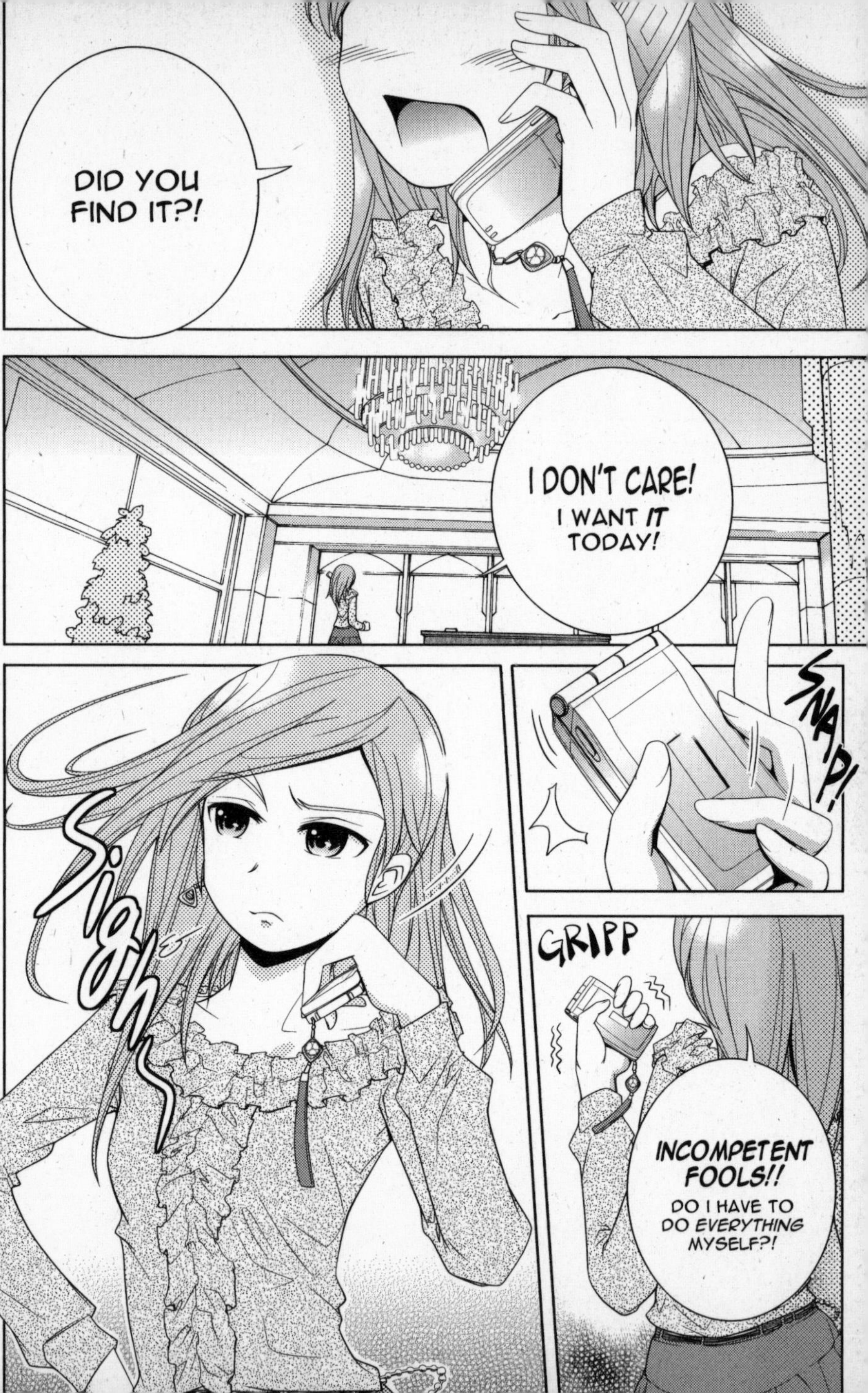
DID YOU FIND IT?!
I DON'T CARE! I WANT *IT* TODAY!
SNAP!
GRIPP
INCOMPETENT FOOLS!! DO I HAVE TO DO *EVERYTHING* MYSELF?!
Sigh

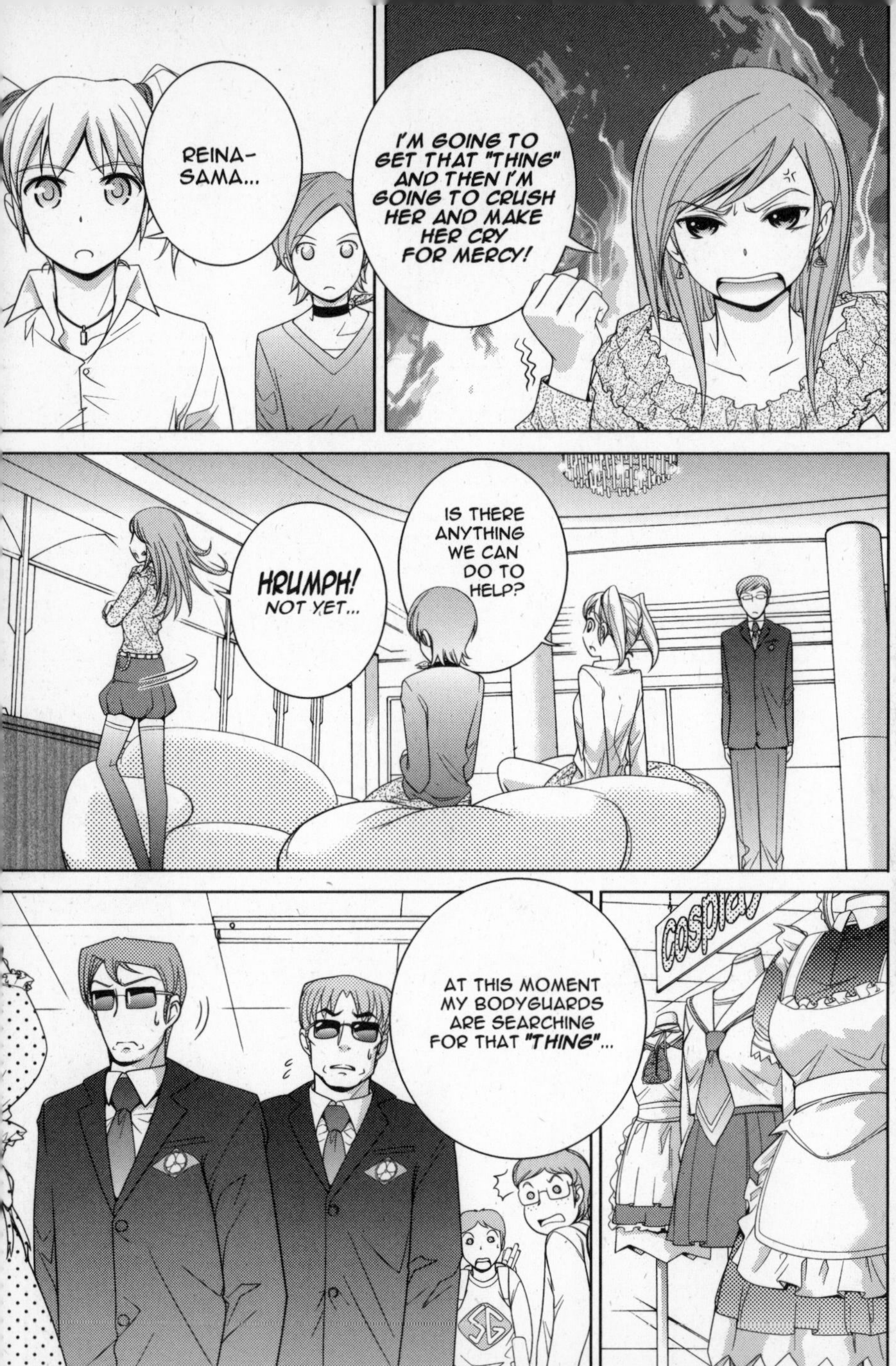
I'M GOING TO GET THAT "THING" AND THEN I'M GOING TO CRUSH HER AND MAKE HER CRY FOR MERCY!
REINA-SAMA...
IS THERE ANYTHING WE CAN DO TO HELP?
HRUMPH! NOT YET...
cosplay
AT THIS MOMENT MY BODYGUARDS ARE SEARCHING FOR THAT "THING"...

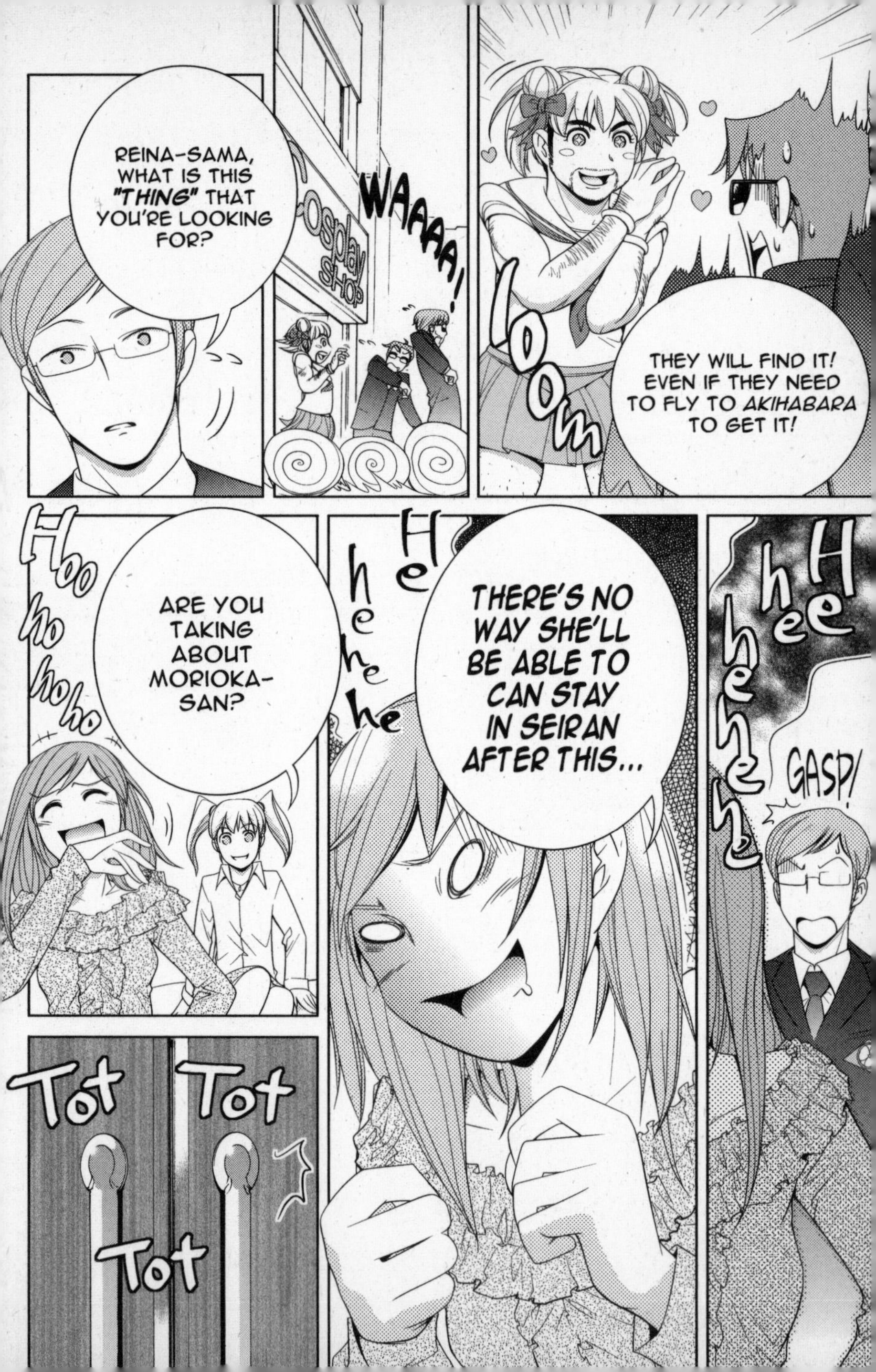
loom
THEY WILL FIND IT! EVEN IF THEY NEED TO FLY TO AKIHABARA TO GET IT!
Cosplay SHOP
WAAAAA!
REINA-SAMA, WHAT IS THIS "THING" THAT YOU'RE LOOKING FOR?
Hhee hehehe
GASP!
He he he he
THERE'S NO WAY SHE'LL BE ABLE TO CAN STAY IN SEIRAN AFTER THIS...
Hoo ho hoho
ARE YOU TAKING ABOUT MORIOKA-SAN?
Tot Tot
Tot

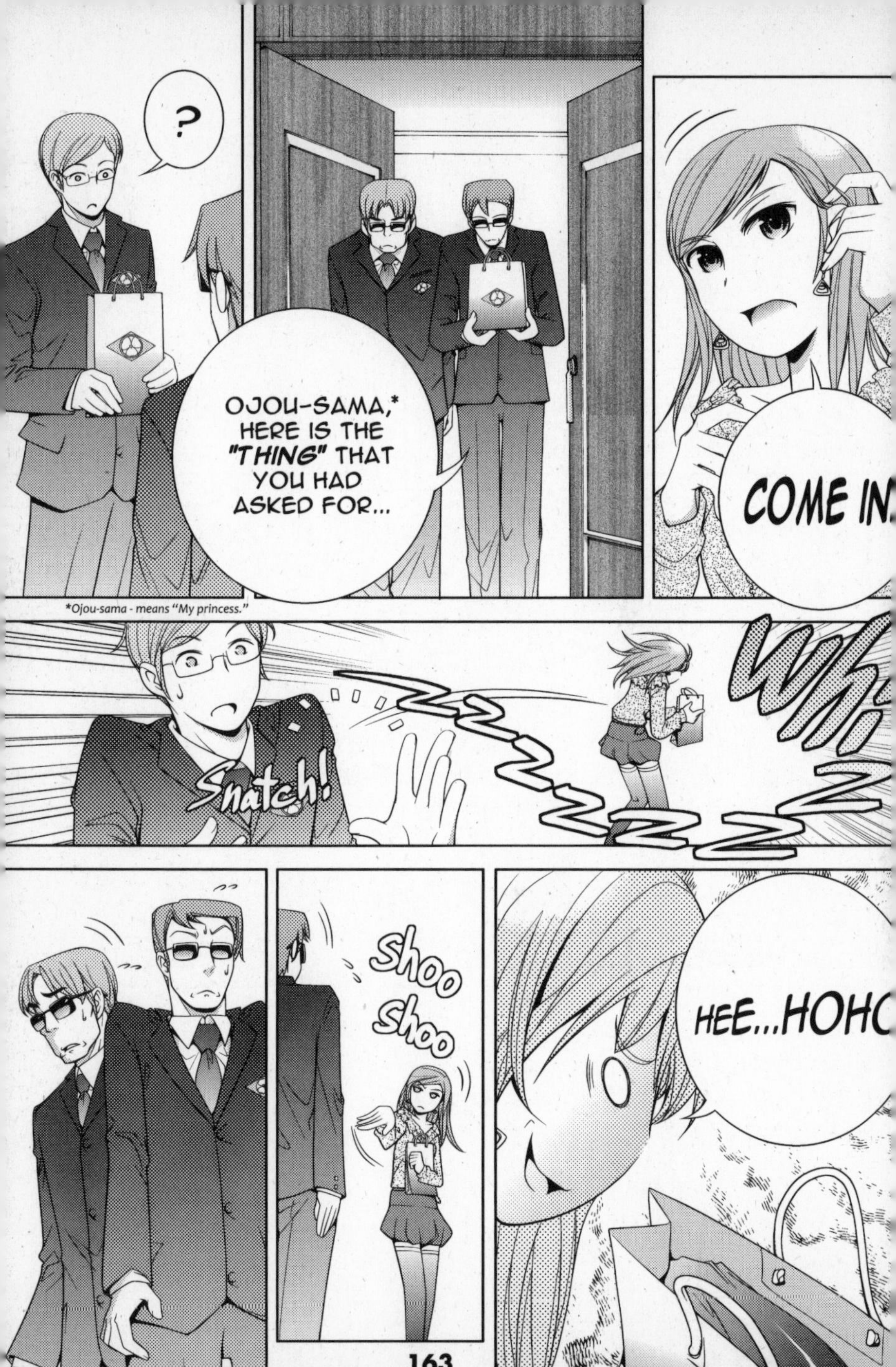
COME IN
OJOU-SAMA,* HERE IS THE "THING" THAT YOU HAD ASKED FOR...
?
Whi
Snatch!
HEE...HOH
Shoo Shoo
*Ojou-sama - means "My princess."

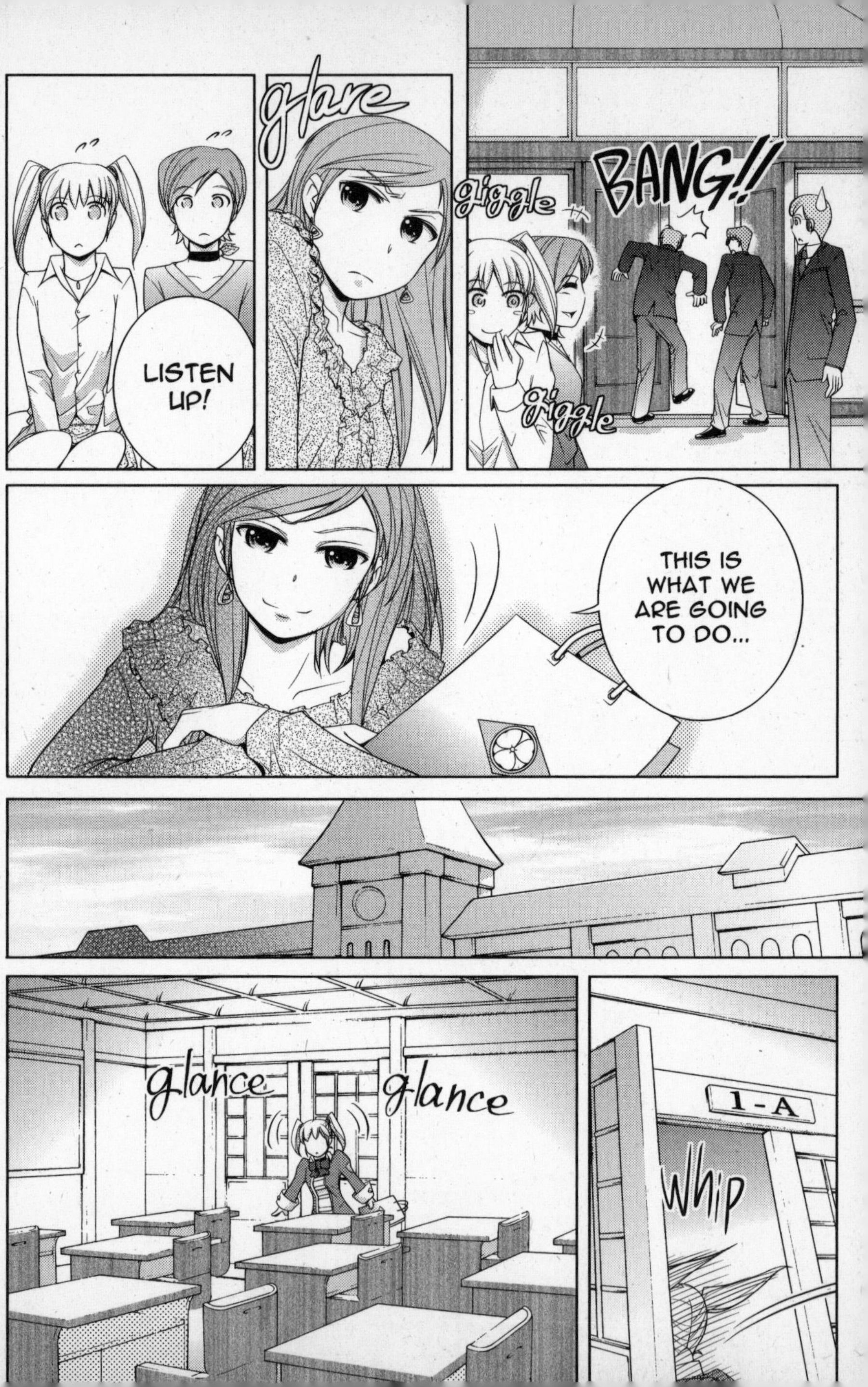
BANG!!
giggle
giggle
glare
LISTEN UP!
THIS IS WHAT WE ARE GOING TO DO...
1-A
Whip
glance
glance

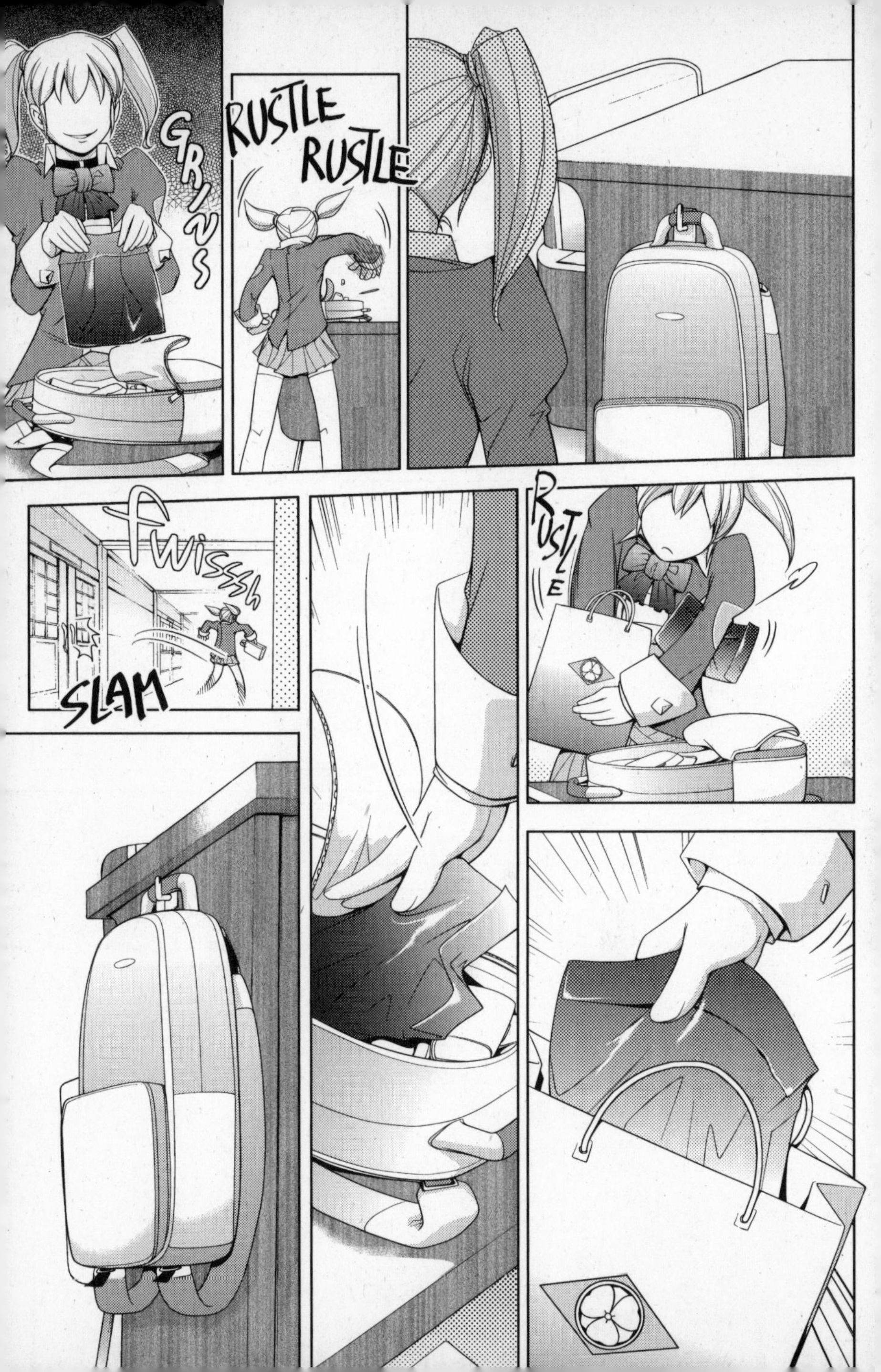
RUSTLE RUSTLE
GRINS
RUSTLE
FWISSSH
SLAM

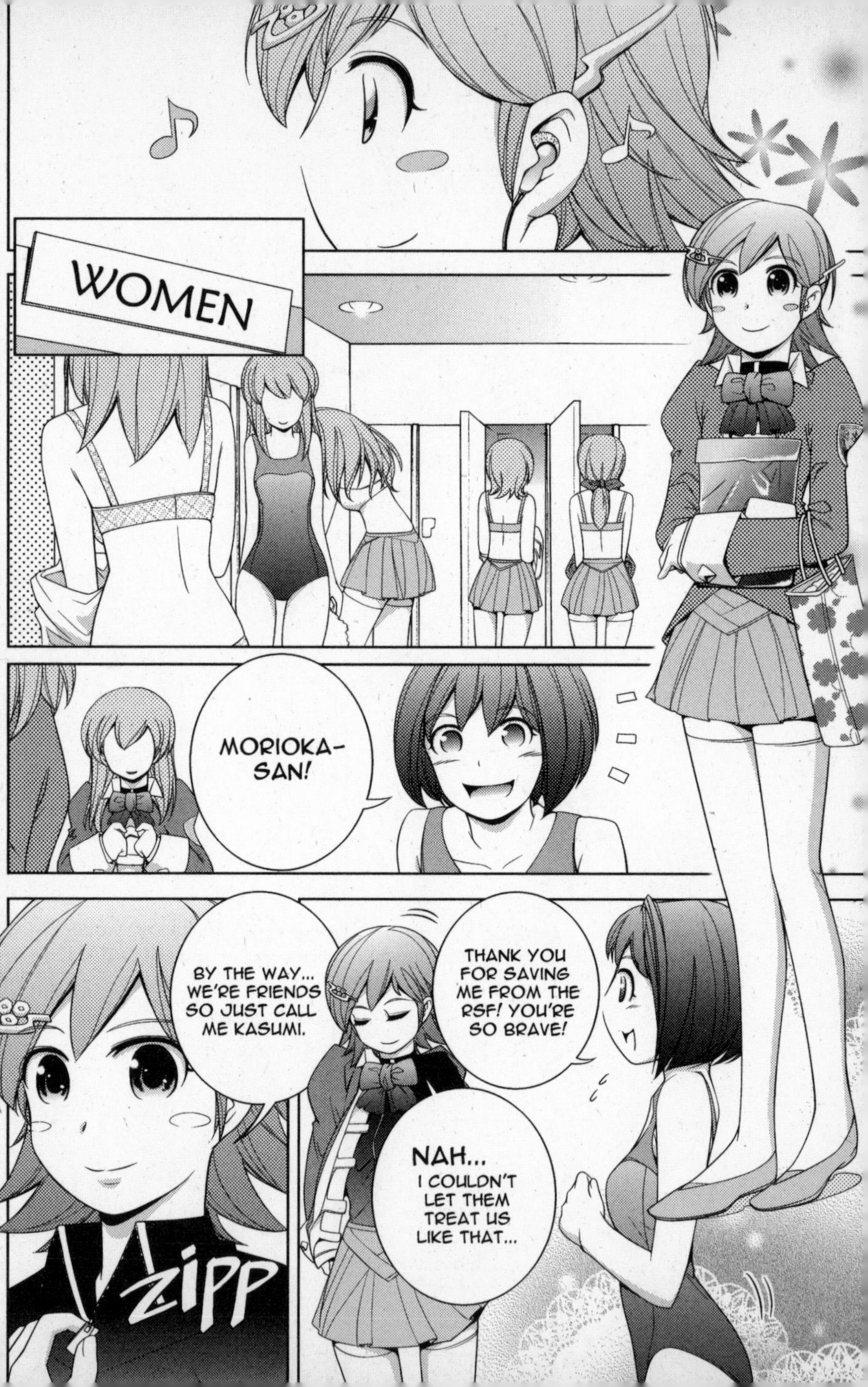
WOMEN
MORIOKA-SAN!
THANK YOU FOR SAVING ME FROM THE RSF! YOU'RE SO BRAVE!
NAH... I COULDN'T LET THEM TREAT US LIKE THAT...
BY THE WAY... WE'RE FRIENDS SO JUST CALL ME KASUMI.
ZIPP

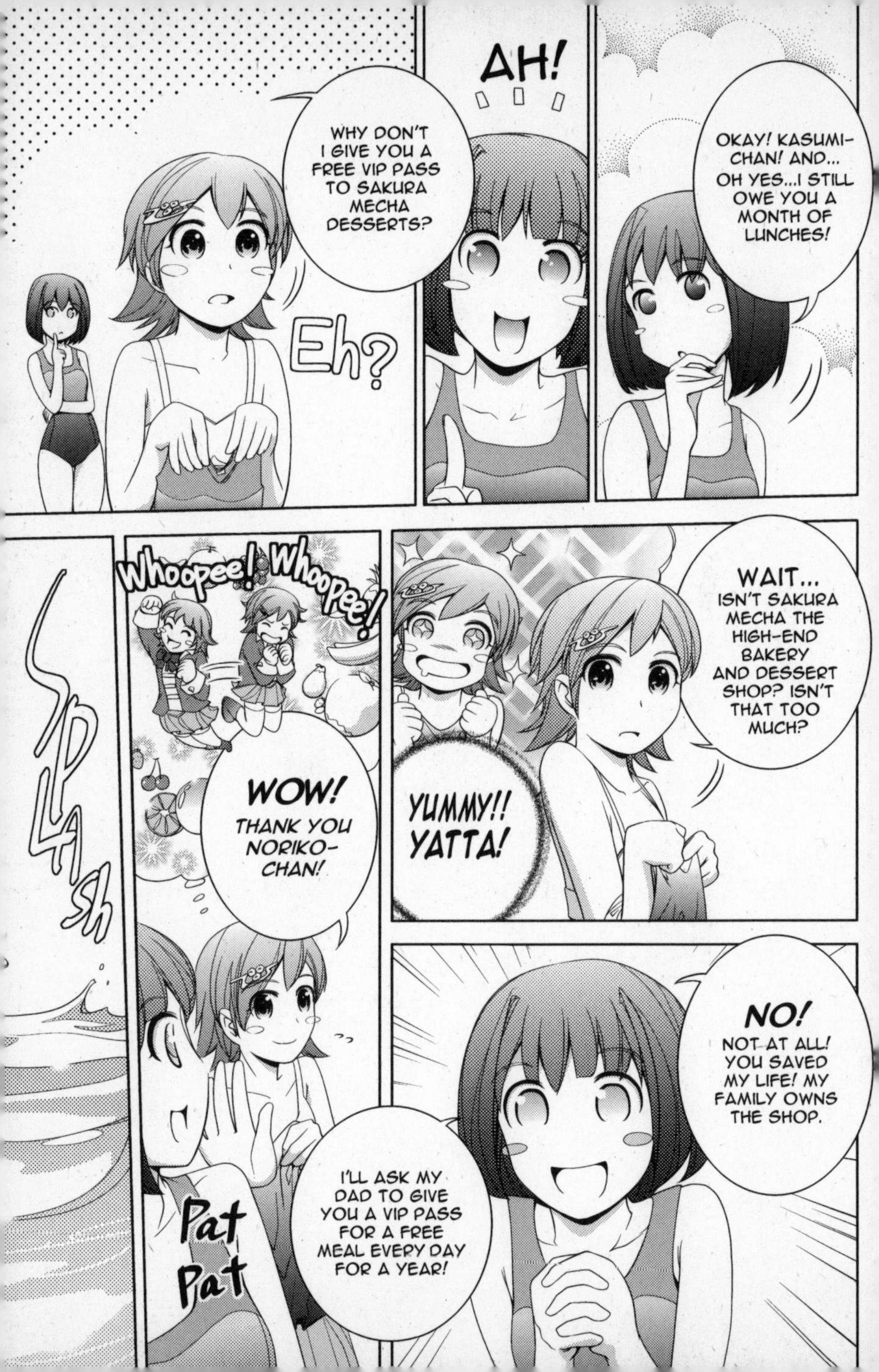
OKAY! KASUMI-CHAN! AND... OH YES...I STILL OWE YOU A MONTH OF LUNCHES!
AH!
WHY DON'T I GIVE YOU A FREE VIP PASS TO SAKURA MECHA DESSERTS?
Eh?
WAIT... ISN'T SAKURA MECHA THE HIGH-END BAKERY AND DESSERT SHOP? ISN'T THAT TOO MUCH?
YUMMY!! YATTA!
Whoopee! Whoopee!
WOW! THANK YOU NORIKO-CHAN!
NO! NOT AT ALL! YOU SAVED MY LIFE! MY FAMILY OWNS THE SHOP.
I'LL ASK MY DAD TO GIVE YOU A VIP PASS FOR A FREE MEAL EVERY DAY FOR A YEAR!
Pat Pat
SPLASH

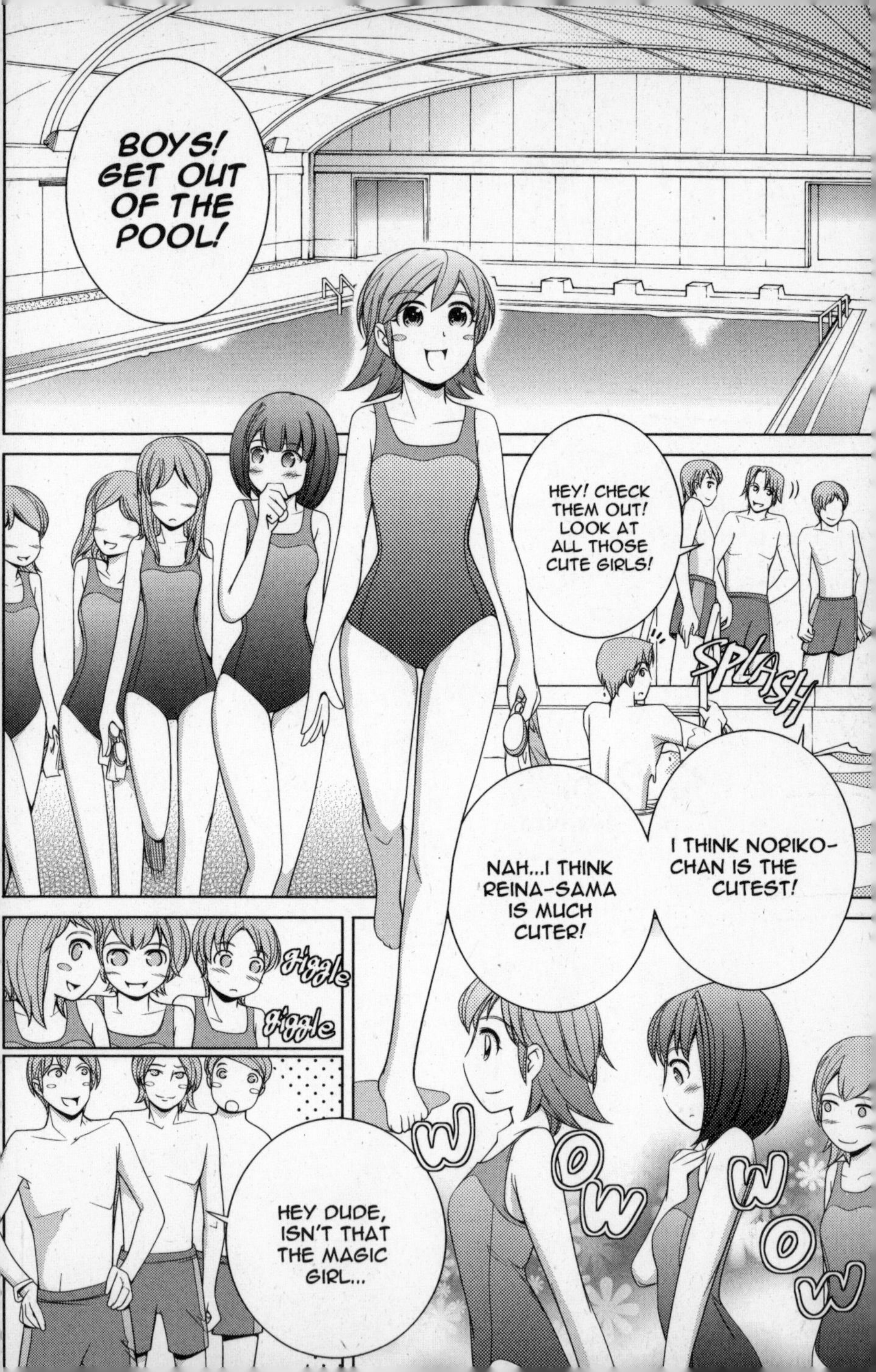
BOYS! GET OUT OF THE POOL!
HEY! CHECK THEM OUT! LOOK AT ALL THOSE CUTE GIRLS!
SPLASH
I THINK NORIKO-CHAN IS THE CUTEST!
NAH...I THINK REINA-SAMA IS MUCH CUTER!
giggle
giggle
WOW
WOW
WOW
HEY DUDE, ISN'T THAT THE MAGIC GIRL...

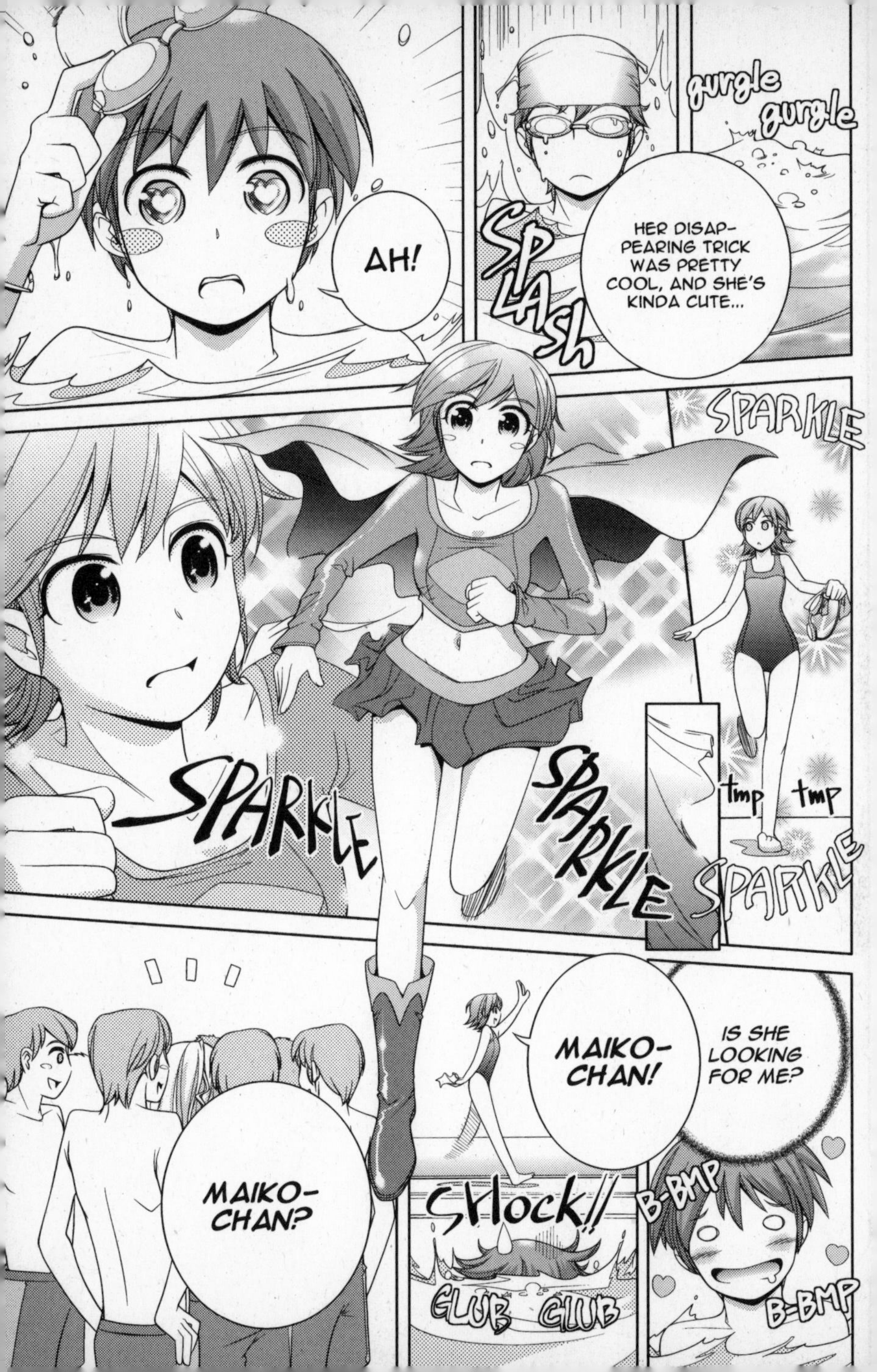
gurgle gurgle
SPLASH
HER DISAP-PEARING TRICK WAS PRETTY COOL, AND SHE'S KINDA CUTE...
AH!
SPARKLE
tmp tmp
SPARKLE
SPARKLE
SPARKLE
IS SHE LOOKING FOR ME?
B-BMP
B-BMP
MAIKO-CHAN!
SHLOCK!!
GLUB GLUB
...
MAIKO-CHAN?

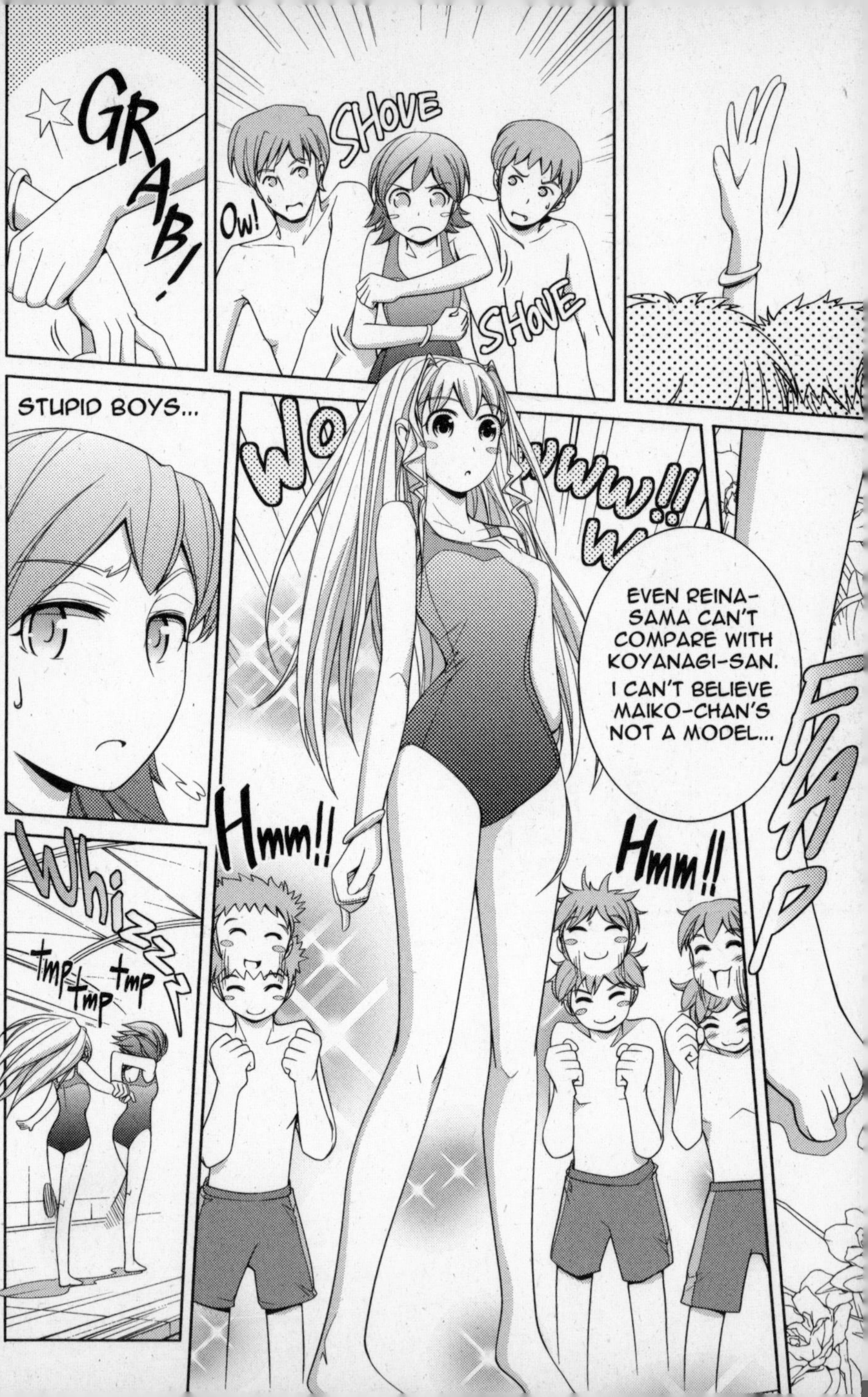
SHOVE
Ow!
SHOVE
GRAB!
FLAP
EVEN REINA-SAMA CAN'T COMPARE WITH KOYANAGI-SAN. I CAN'T BELIEVE MAIKO-CHAN'S NOT A MODEL...
Hmm!!
Hmm!!
STUPID BOYS...
Whizzz
tmp tmp tmp

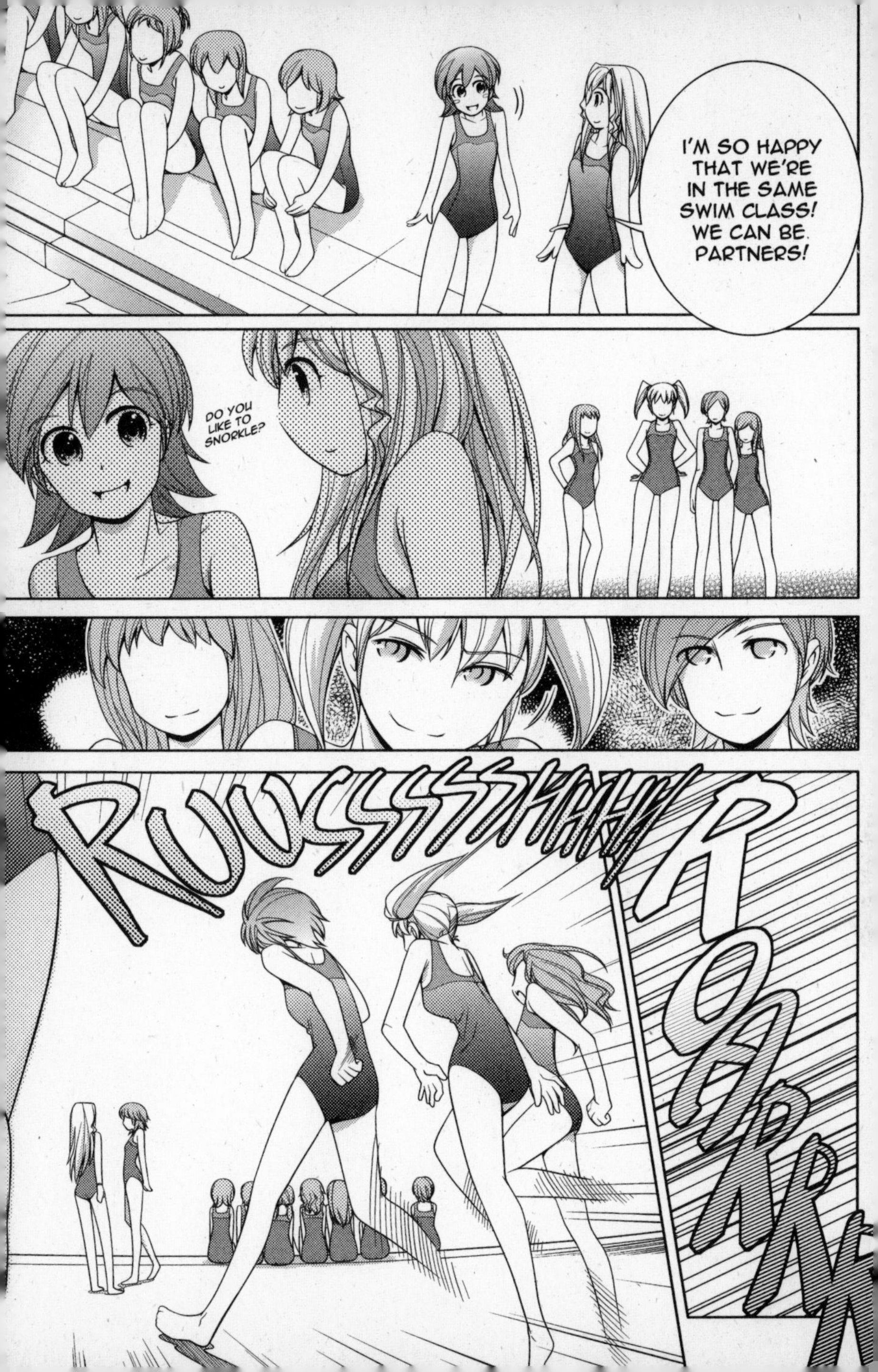
I'M SO HAPPY THAT WE'RE IN THE SAME SWIM CLASS! WE CAN BE PARTNERS!
DO YOU LIKE TO SNORKLE?

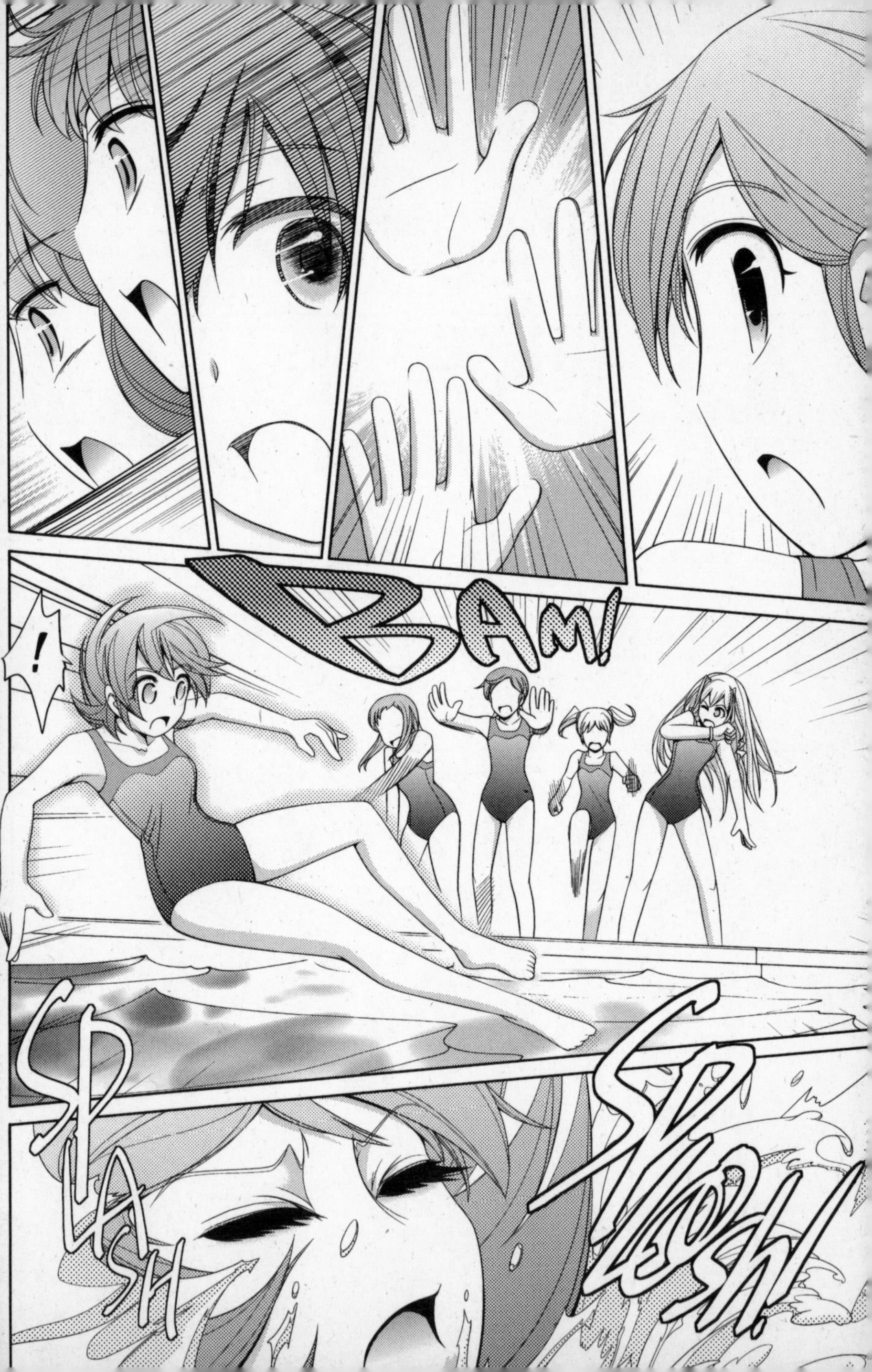
BAM!
!
SPLASH!
SPLASH

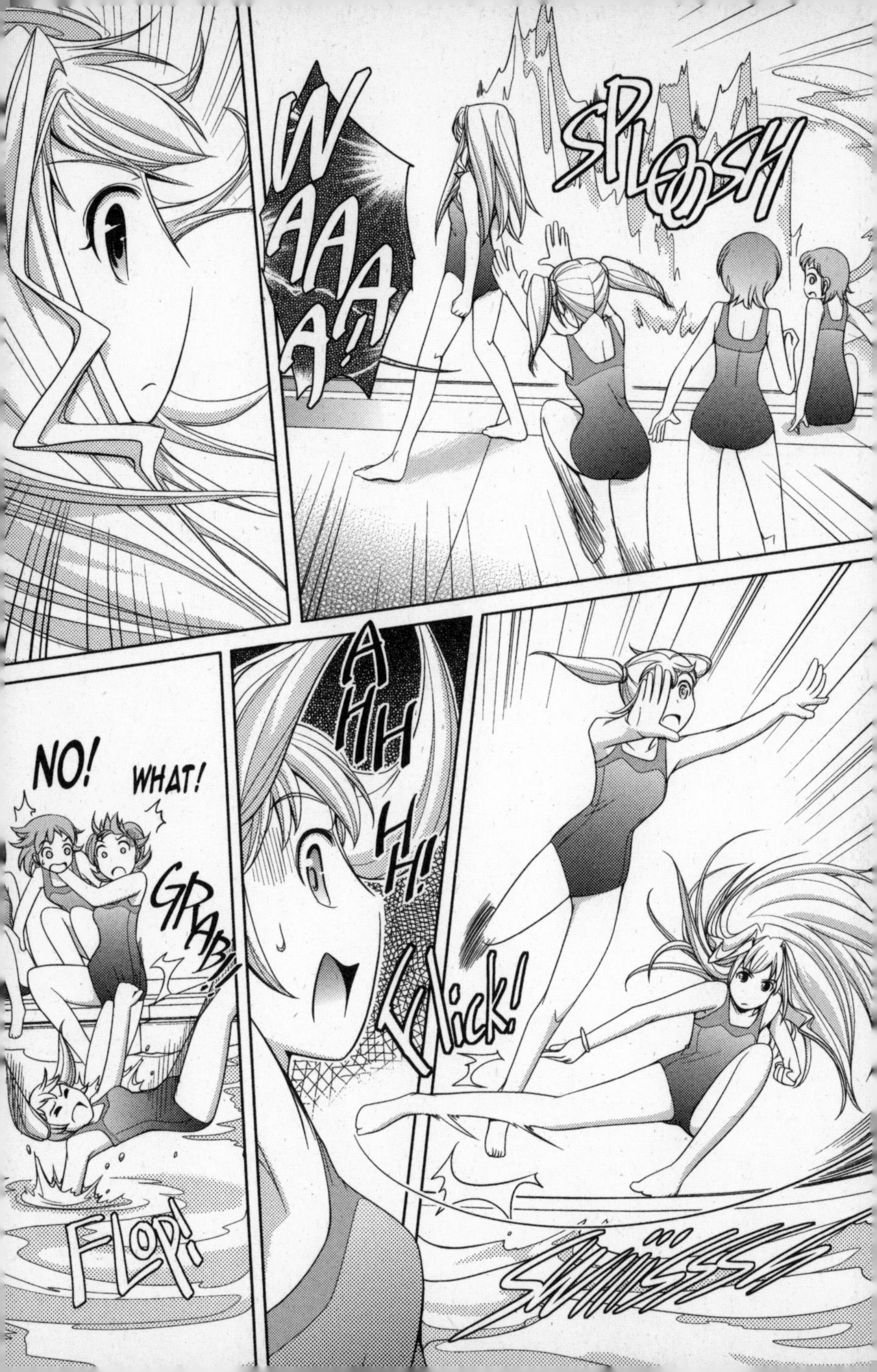
SPLOOSH
WAAAAA!
AHHHH!
Kick!
SWISSH
NO!
WHAT!
GRAB!!
FLOP!

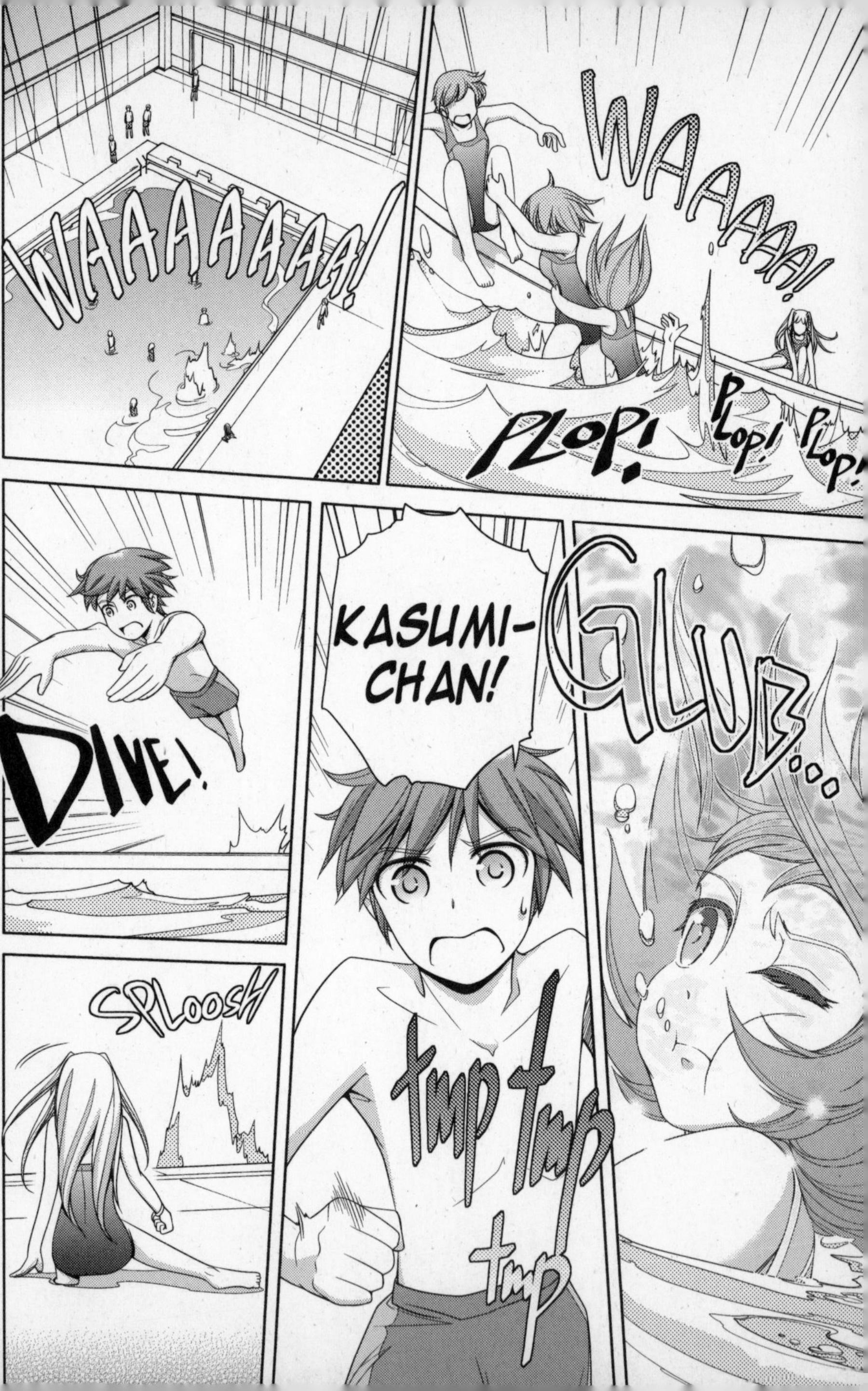
WAAAAAA!
PLOP!
PLOP!
PLOP!
WAAAAAAAA!
GLUB...
KASUMI-CHAN!
tmp tmp
tmp
tmp
DIVE!
SPLOOSH

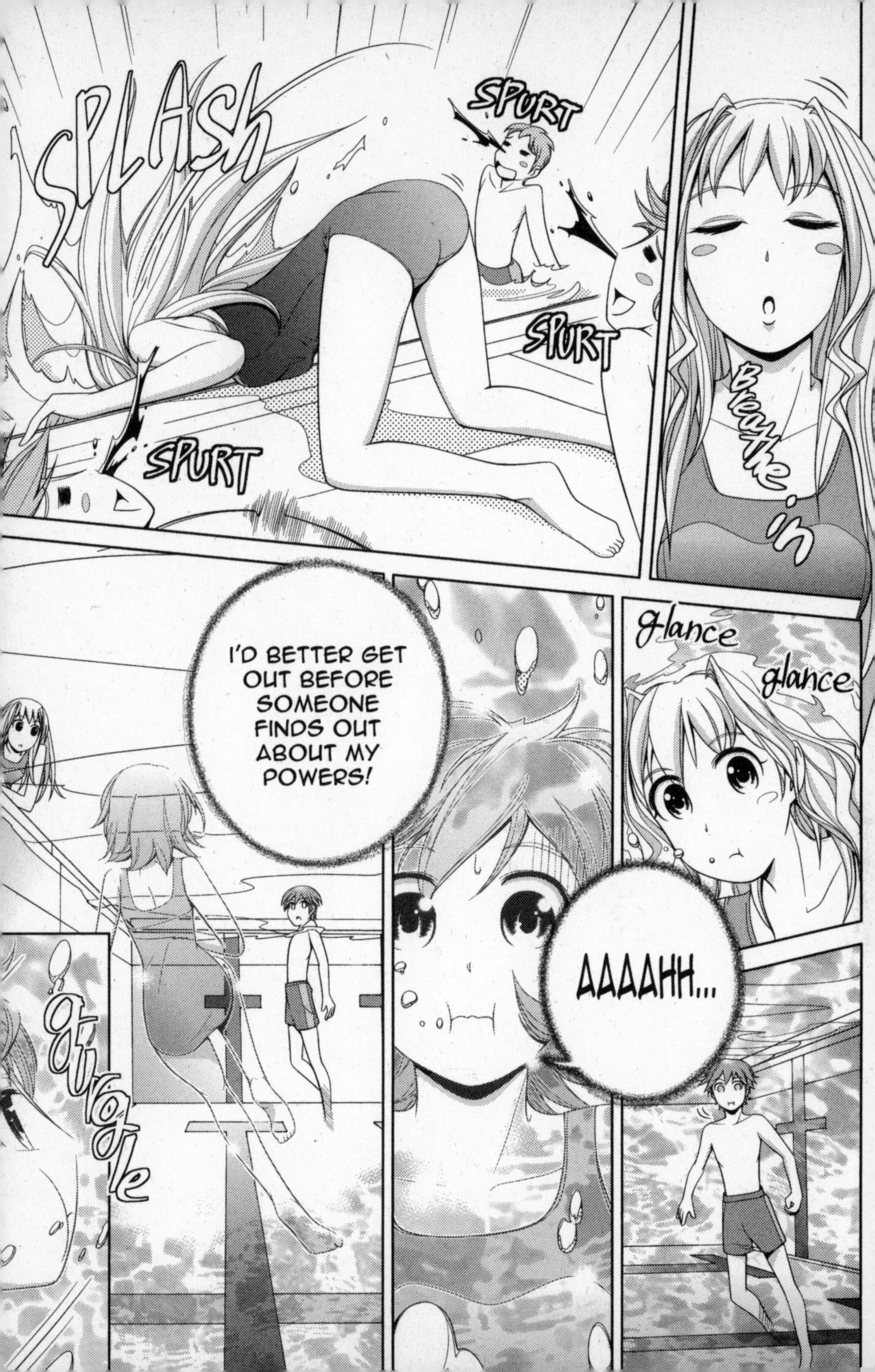
Breathe in
SPURT
SPURT
SPLASH
SPURT
glance
glance
I'D BETTER GET OUT BEFORE SOMEONE FINDS OUT ABOUT MY POWERS!
AAAAHH...
gurgle

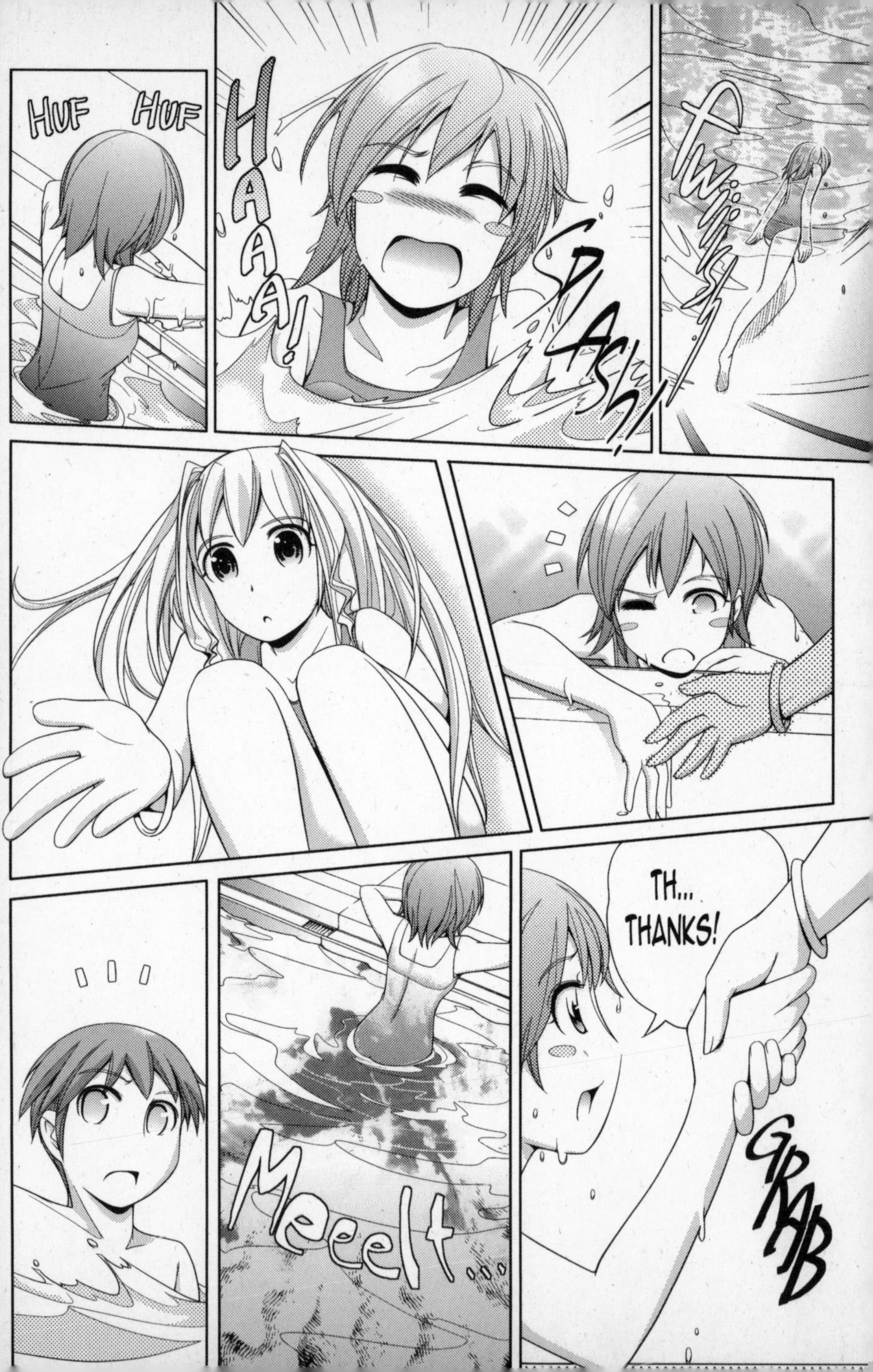
Fwiiish
HAAA!
SPLASH!
HUF HUF
TH... THANKS!
GRAB
Meeelt...

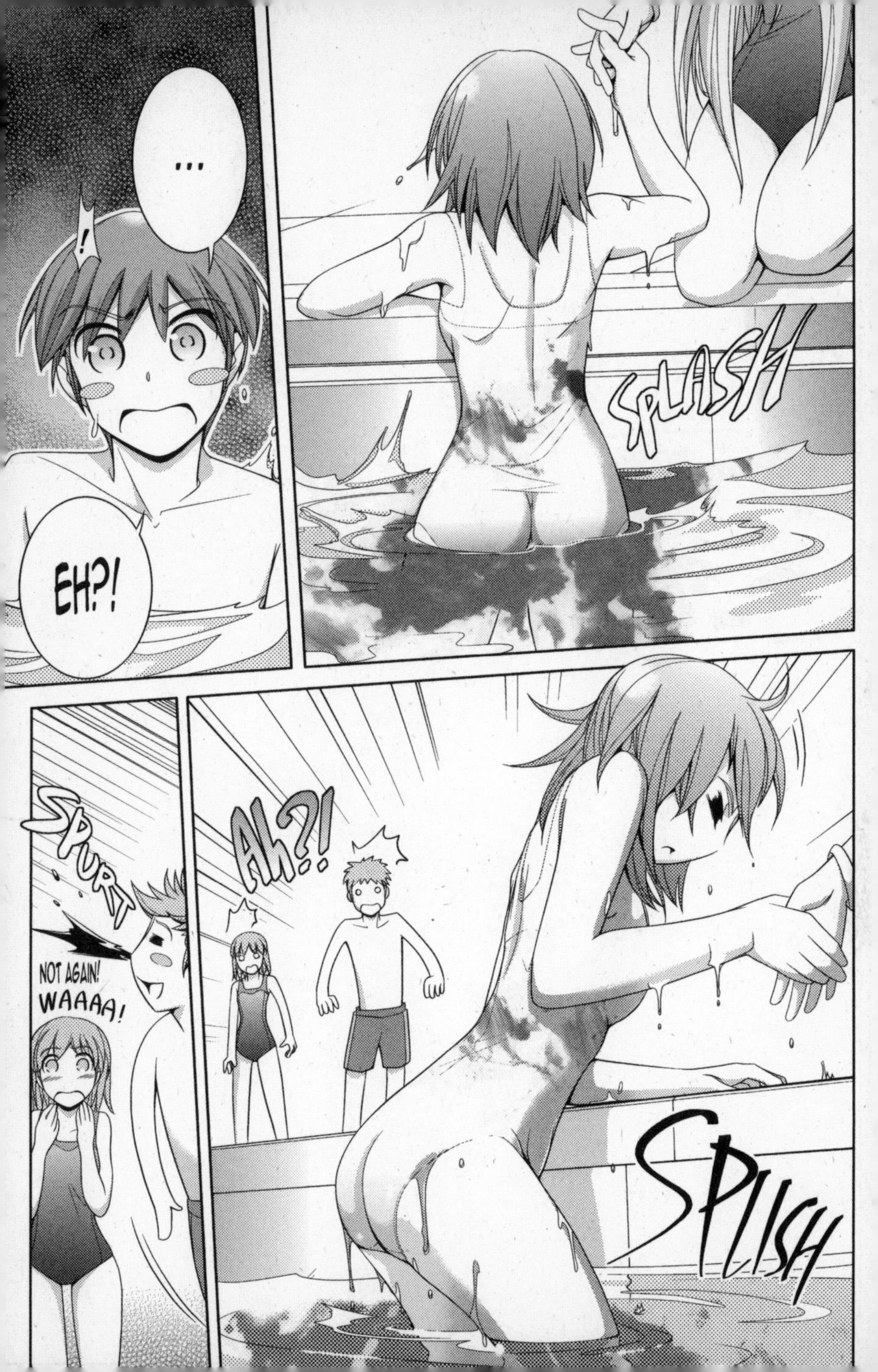
SPLASH
...
!
EH?!
Ah?!
SPLISH
SPURT
NOT AGAIN!
WAAAA!

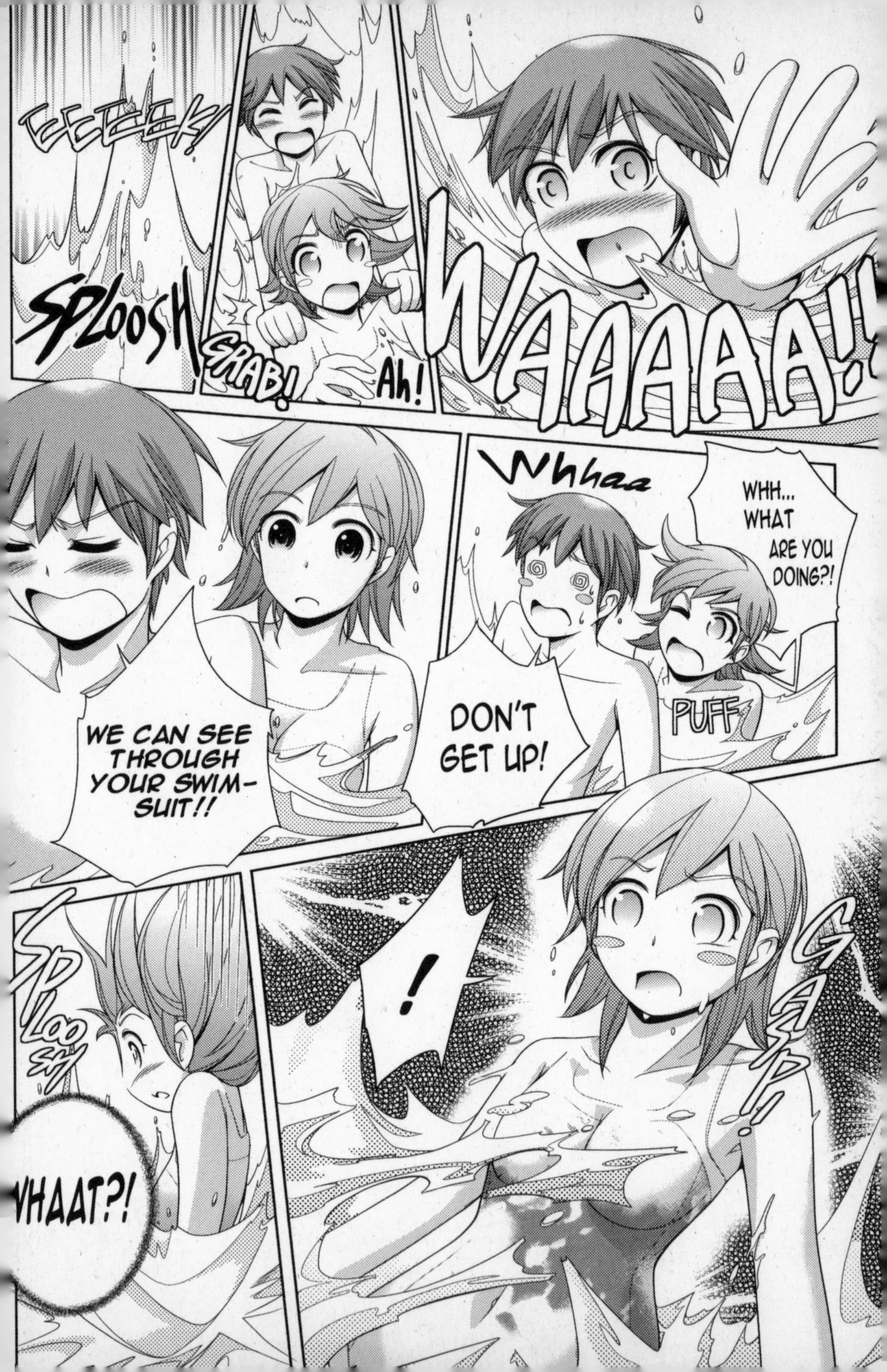
WAAAAA!!
Ah!
GRAB!
EEEEEEK!
SPLOOSH
WHH... WHAT ARE YOU DOING?!
Whhaa
PUFF
DON'T GET UP!
WE CAN SEE THROUGH YOUR SWIM-SUIT!!
GASP!
!
SPLOOSH
WHAAT?!

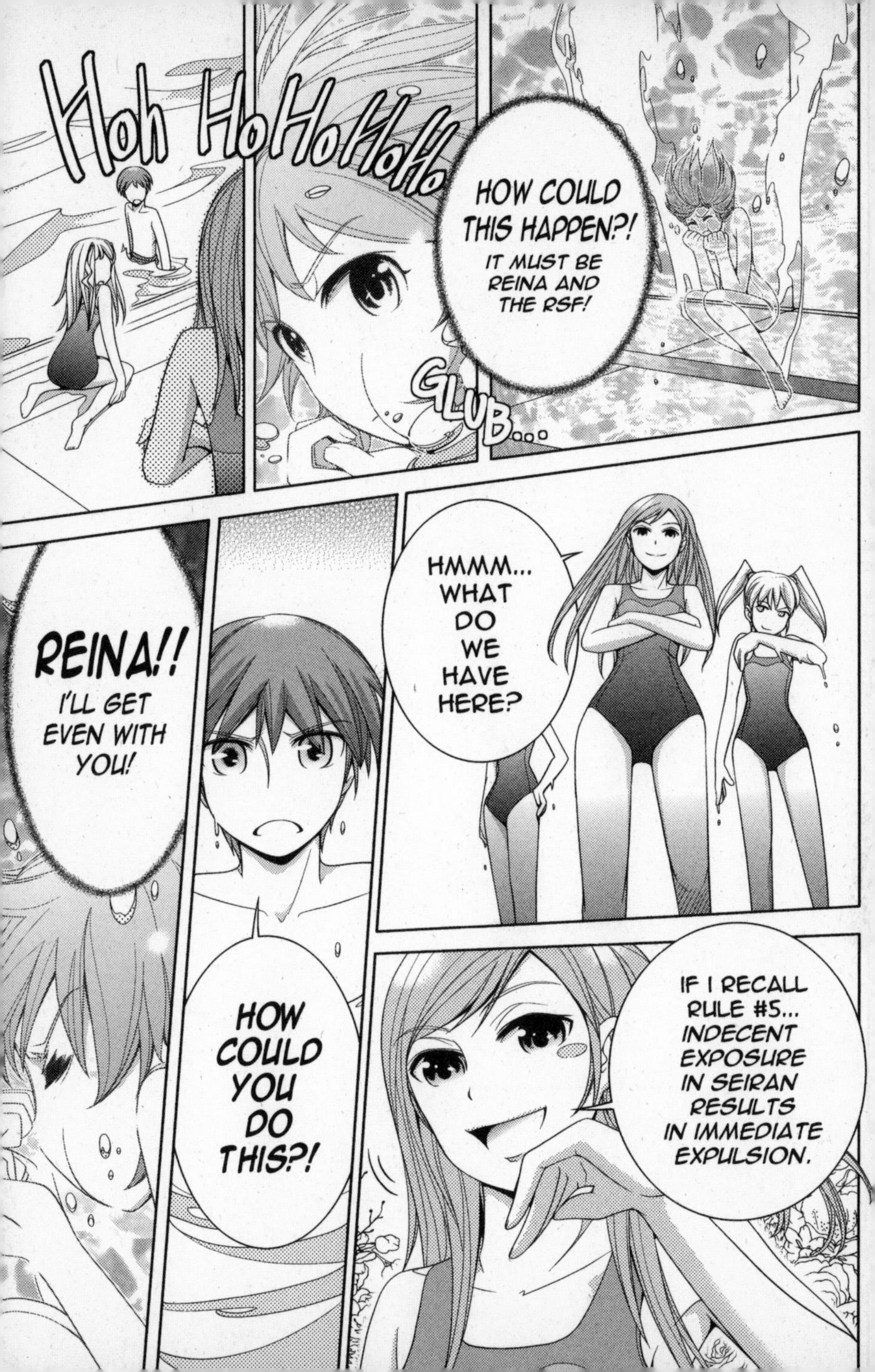
HOW COULD THIS HAPPEN?!
IT MUST BE REINA AND THE RSF!
GLUB...
Hoh HoHoHoHoHo
HMMM... WHAT DO WE HAVE HERE?
IF I RECALL RULE #5... INDECENT EXPOSURE IN SEIRAN RESULTS IN IMMEDIATE EXPULSION.
HOW COULD YOU DO THIS?!
REINA!!
I'LL GET EVEN WITH YOU!

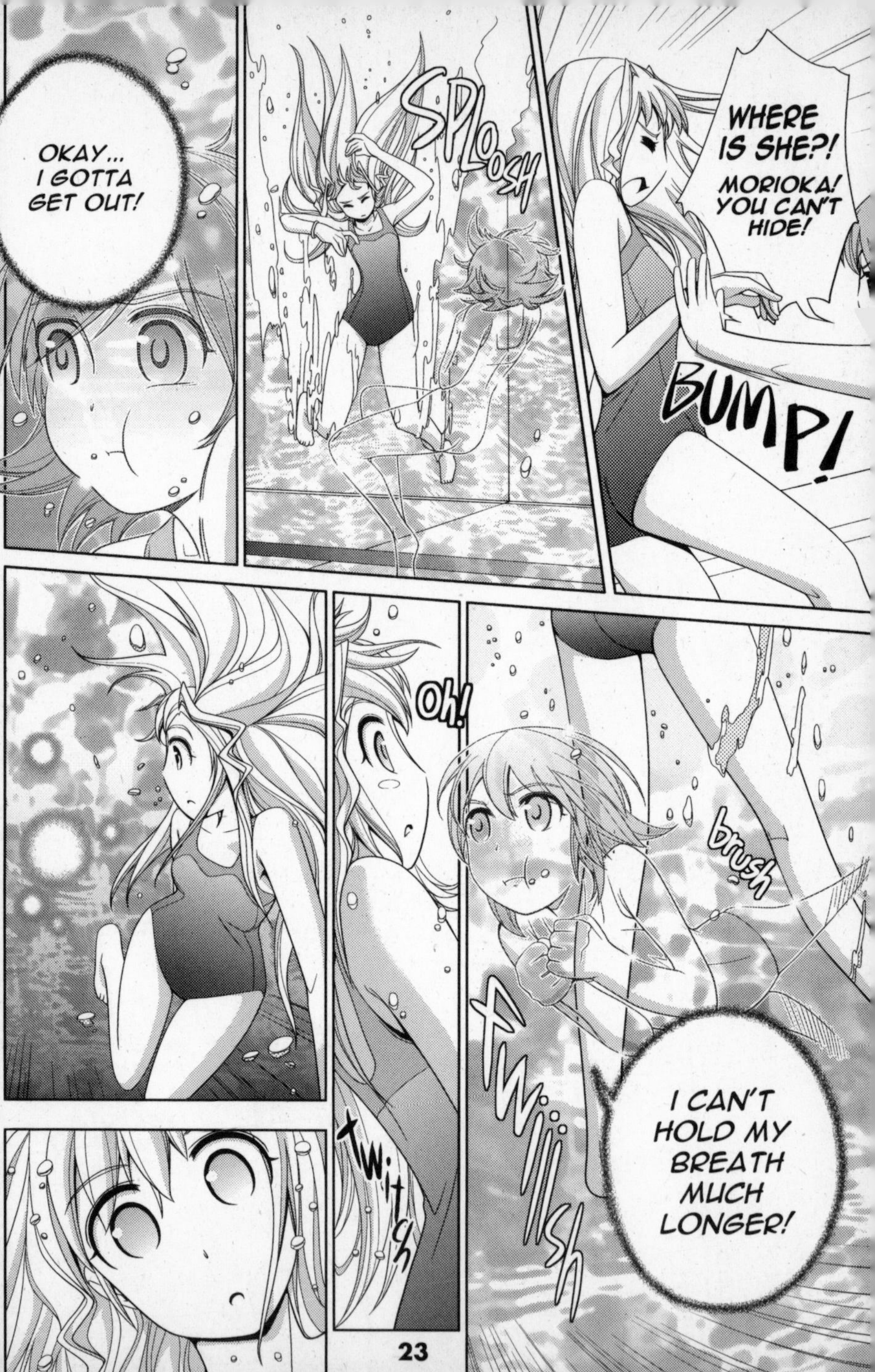
WHERE IS SHE?!
MORIOKA! YOU CAN'T HIDE!
BUMP!
SPLOOSH
OKAY... I GOTTA GET OUT!
brush
FWiiiSh
I CAN'T HOLD MY BREATH MUCH LONGER!
oh!
twitch

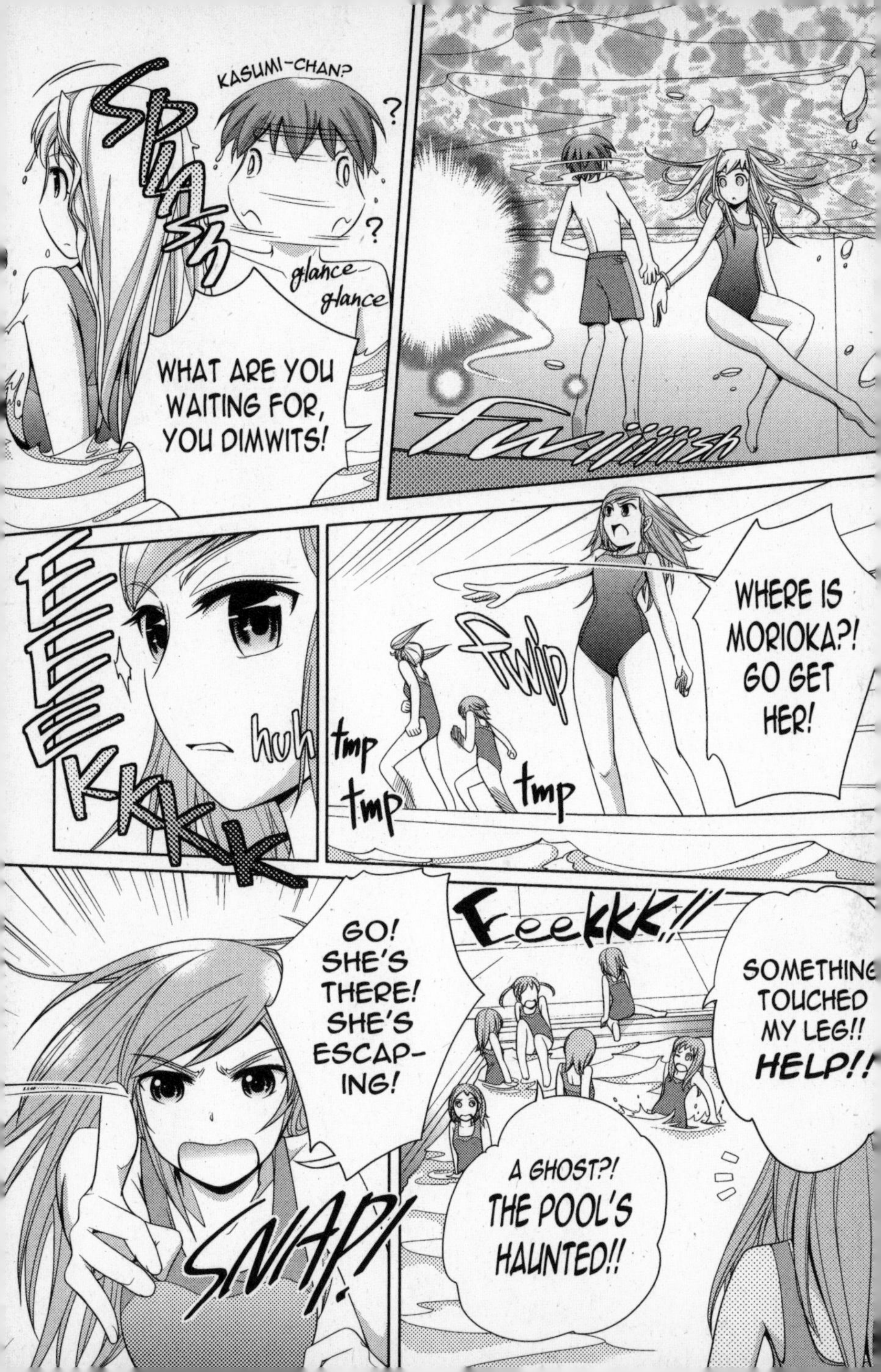
Fwiiiiish
KASUMI-CHAN?
?
?
SPLASH
glance glance
WHAT ARE YOU WAITING FOR, YOU DIMWITS!
WHERE IS MORIOKA?! GO GET HER!
fwip
tmp tmp tmp
huh
EEEEKKKK
SOMETHING TOUCHED MY LEG!! HELP!!
Eeekkk!!
A GHOST?! THE POOL'S HAUNTED!!
GO! SHE'S THERE! SHE'S ESCAP-ING!
SNAP!

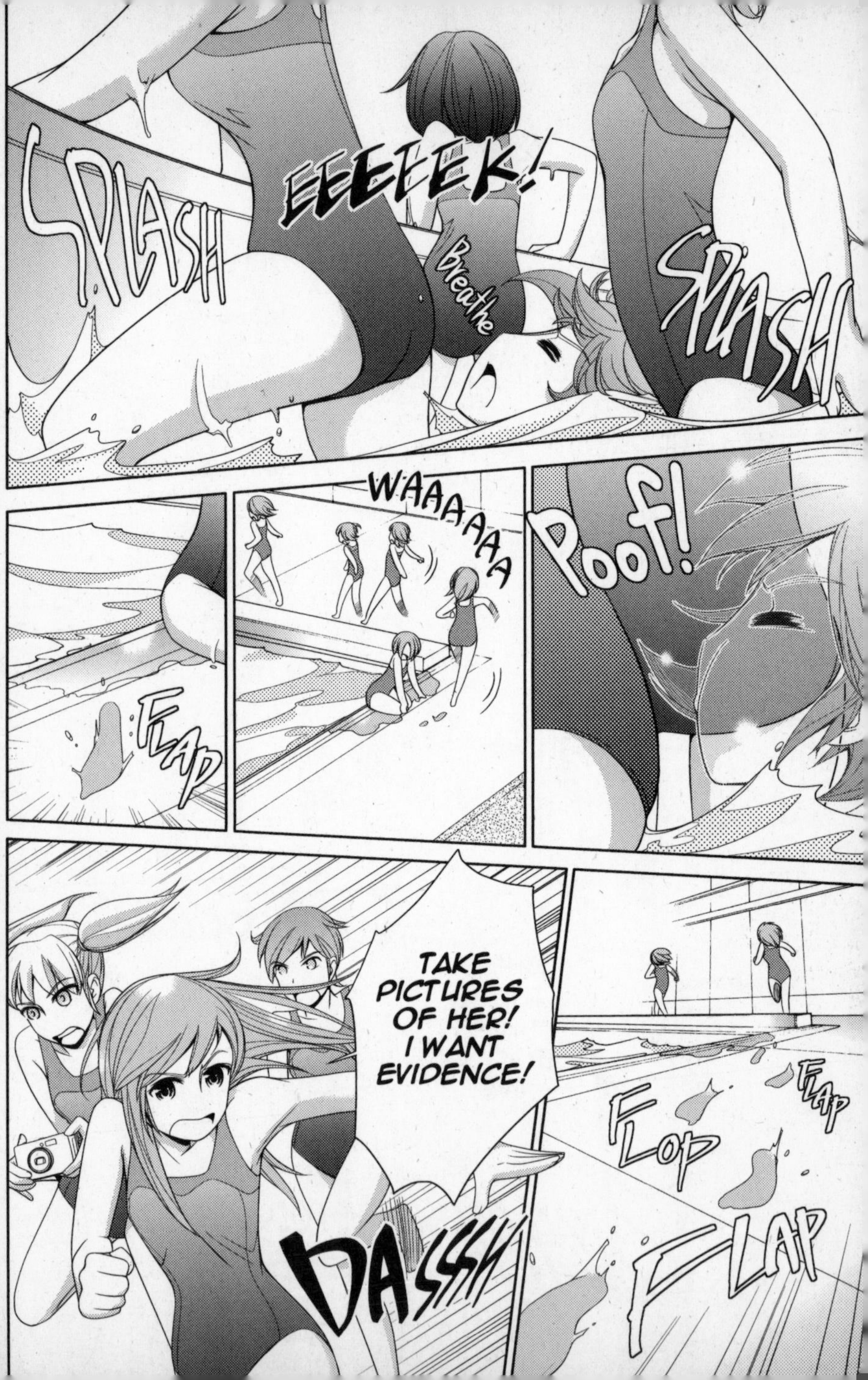
EEEEEK!
SPLASH
Breathe
SPLASH
Poof!
WAAAAAAA
FLAP
FLAP
FLop
FLAP
TAKE PICTURES OF HER! I WANT EVIDENCE!
DASSSH

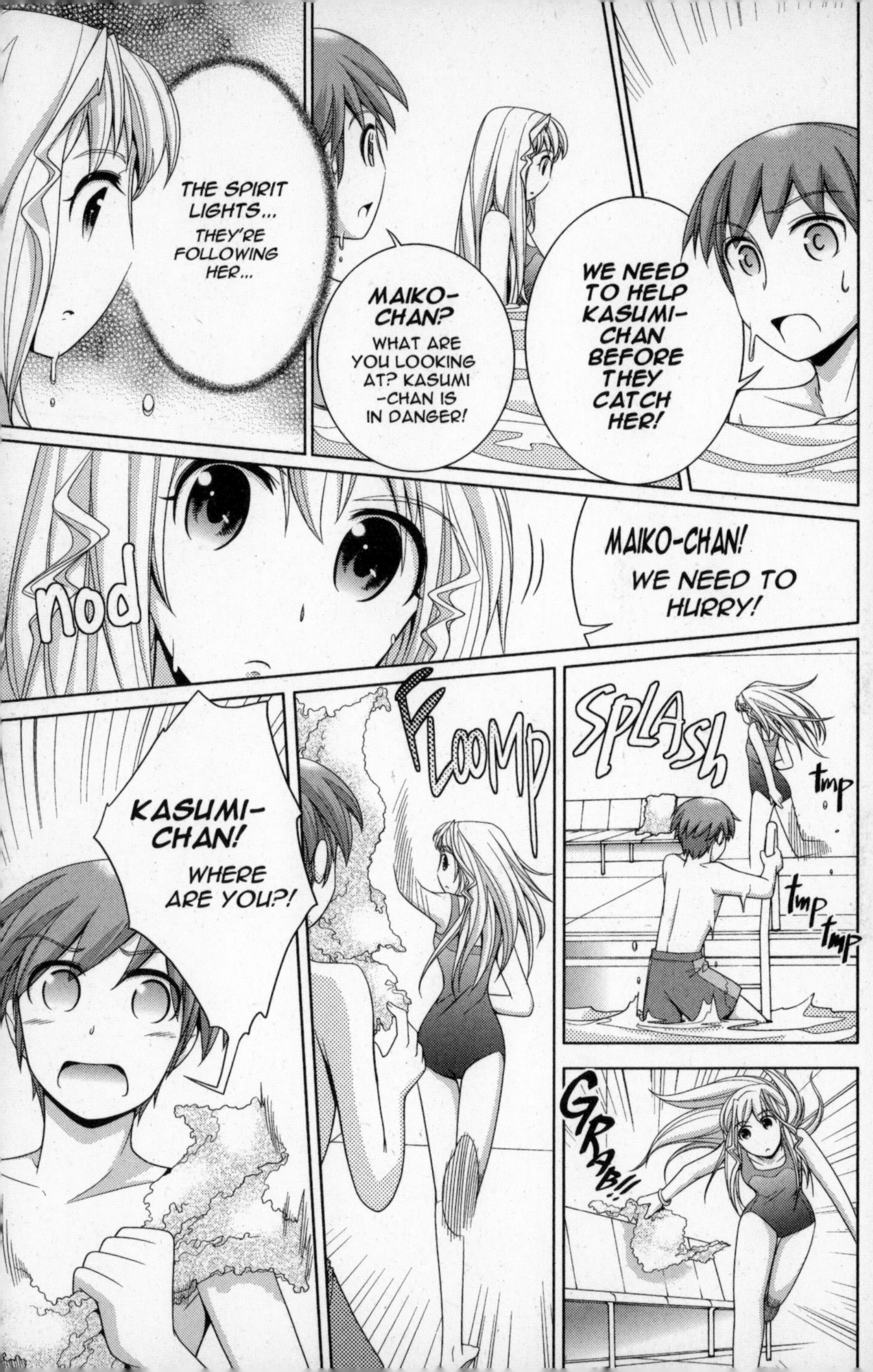
WE NEED TO HELP KASUMI-CHAN BEFORE THEY CATCH HER!
MAIKO-CHAN? WHAT ARE YOU LOOKING AT? KASUMI-CHAN IS IN DANGER!
THE SPIRIT LIGHTS... THEY'RE FOLLOWING HER...
MAIKO-CHAN! WE NEED TO HURRY!
nod
SPLASH
tmp
tmp tmp
GRAB!!
FLOOMP
KASUMI-CHAN! WHERE ARE YOU?!

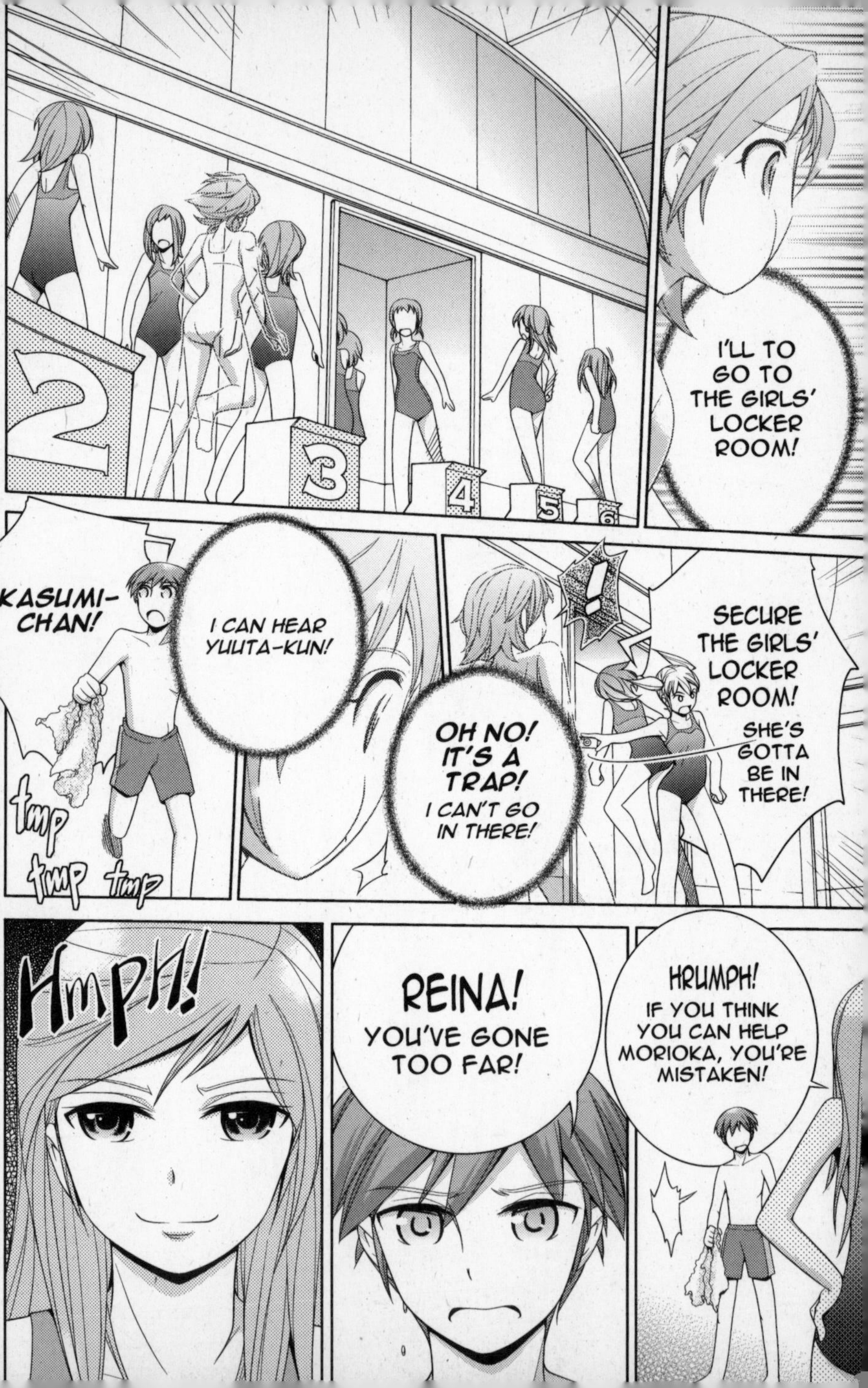
I'LL TO GO TO THE GIRLS' LOCKER ROOM!
SECURE THE GIRLS' LOCKER ROOM!
SHE'S GOTTA BE IN THERE!
!
OH NO! IT'S A TRAP! I CAN'T GO IN THERE!
I CAN HEAR YUUTA-KUN!
KASUMI-CHAN!
tmp tmp tmp
HRUMPH! IF YOU THINK YOU CAN HELP MORIOKA, YOU'RE MISTAKEN!
REINA! YOU'VE GONE TOO FAR!
Hmph!

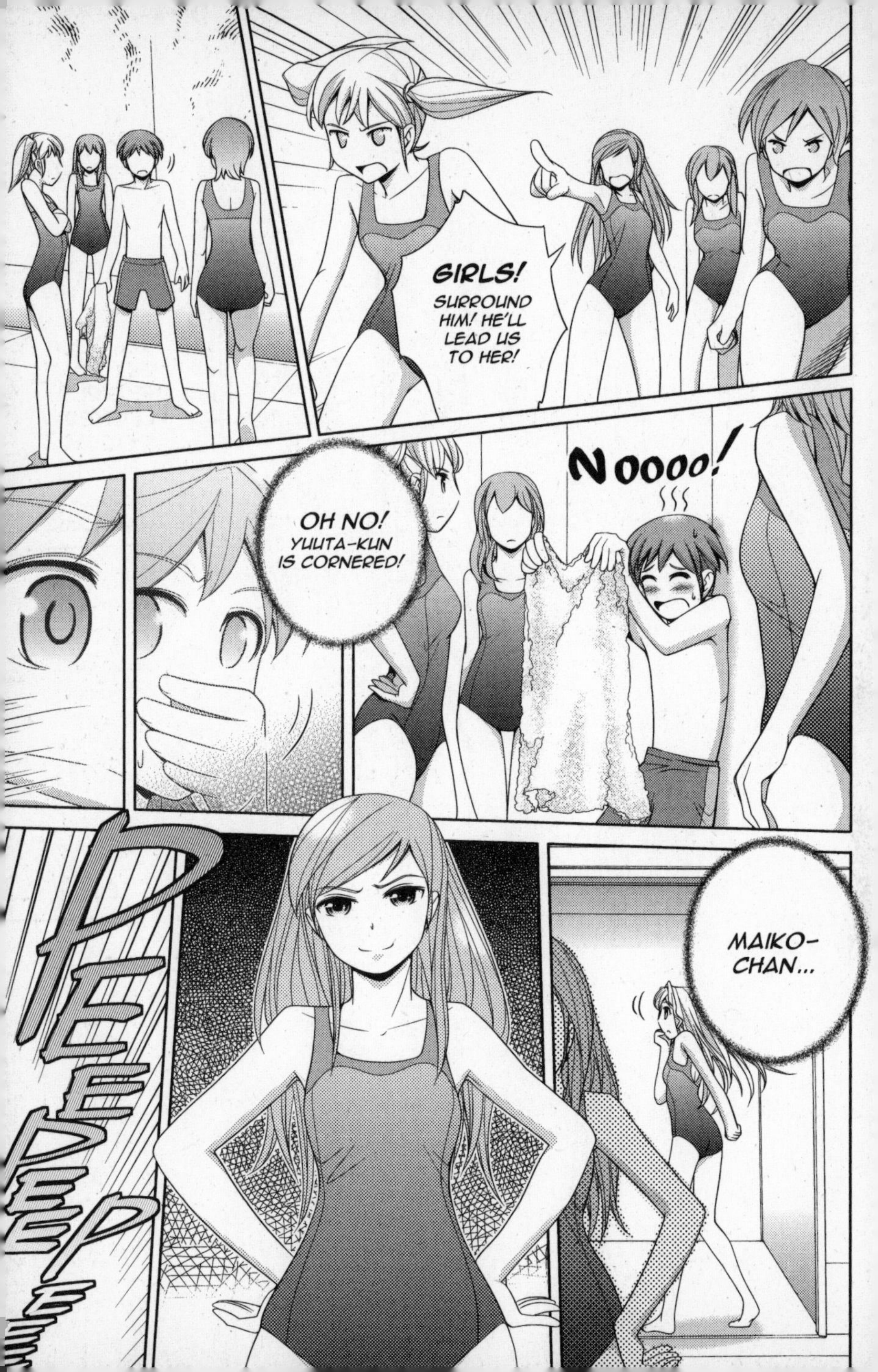
GIRLS!
SURROUND HIM! HE'LL LEAD US TO HER!
Noooo!
OH NO! YUUTA-KUN IS CORNERED!
MAIKO-CHAN...
PEEDEEP

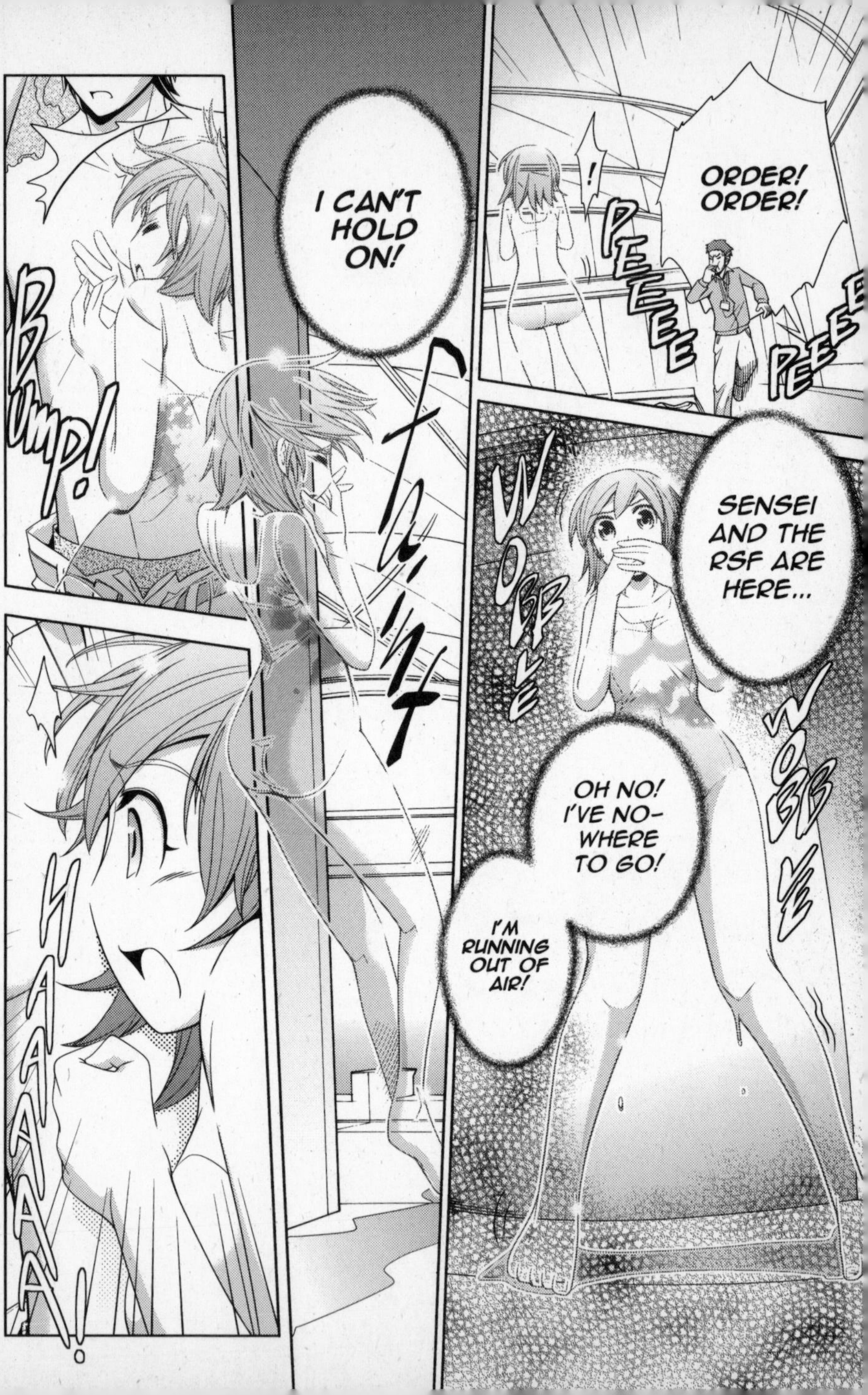
ORDER! ORDER!
PEEEE
PEEEE
!
SENSEI AND THE RSF ARE HERE...
WOBBLE
OH NO! I'VE NO-WHERE TO GO!
I'M RUNNING OUT OF AIR!
WOBBLE
I CAN'T HOLD ON!
BUMP!
HAAAAAAAA!

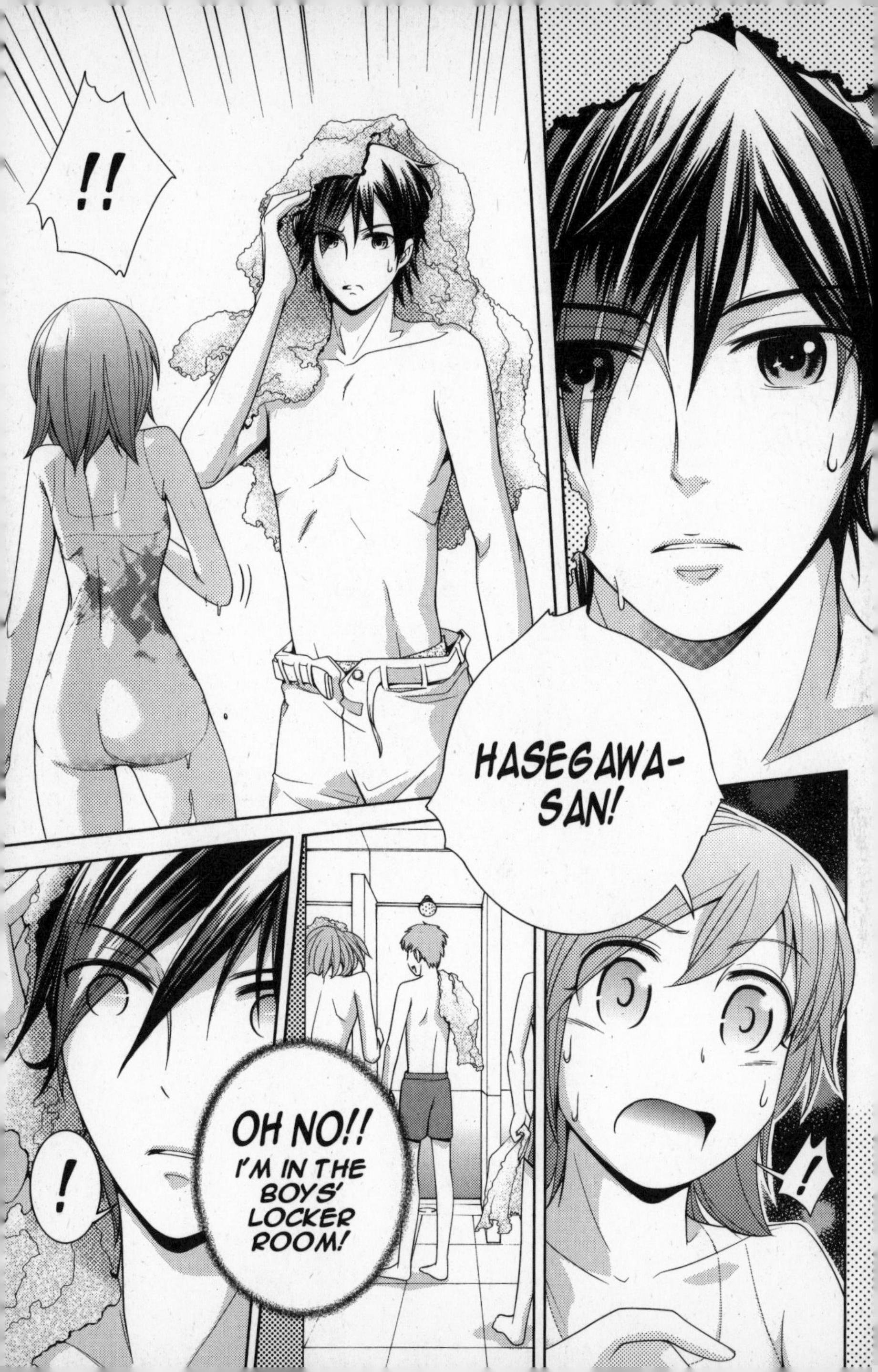
!!
HASEGAWA-SAN!
!
OH NO!! I'M IN THE BOYS' LOCKER ROOM!
!

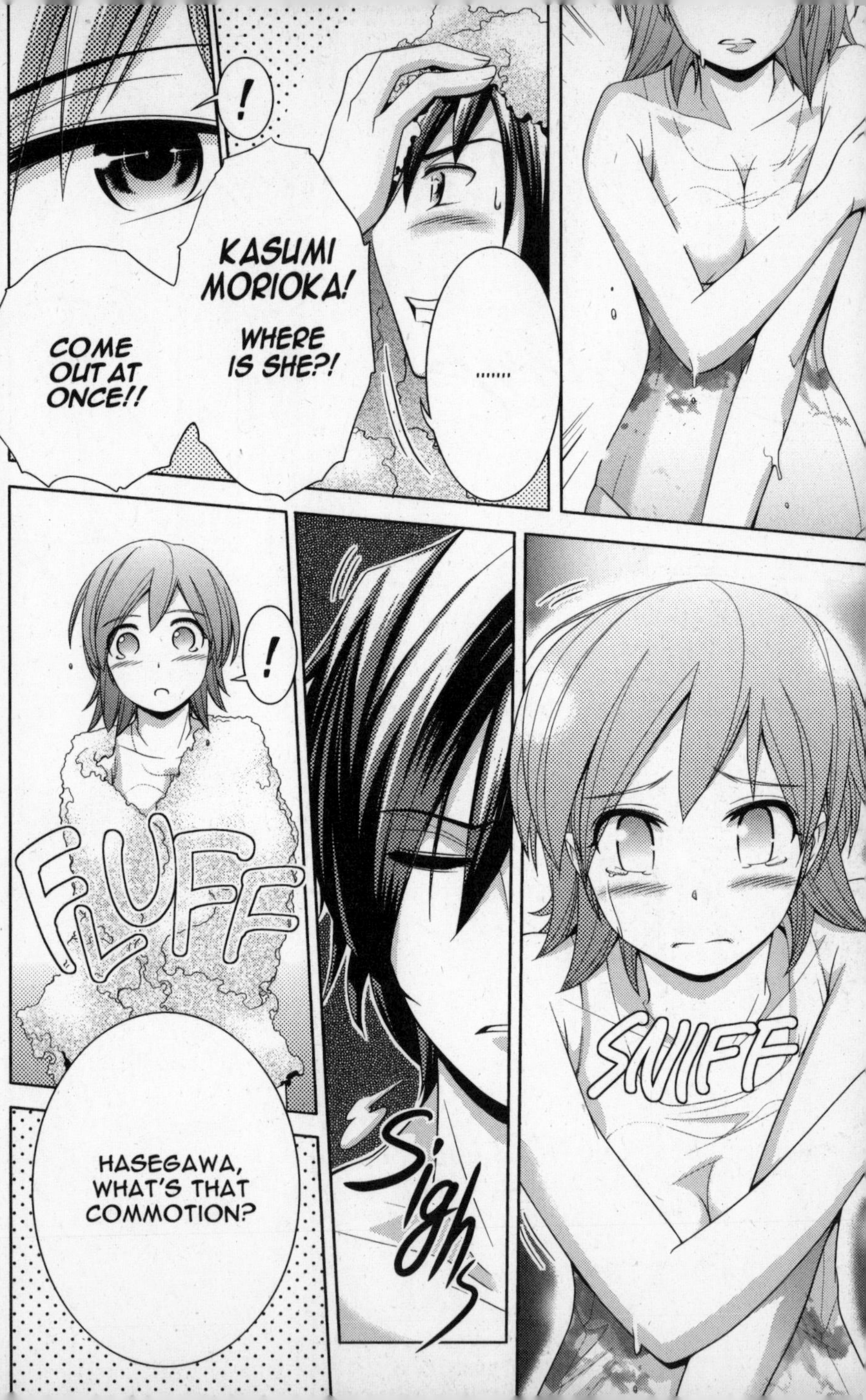

......
!
KASUMI MORIOKA!
WHERE IS SHE?!
COME OUT AT ONCE!!
SNIFF
Sigh
!
FLUFF
HASEGAWA, WHAT'S THAT COMMOTION?

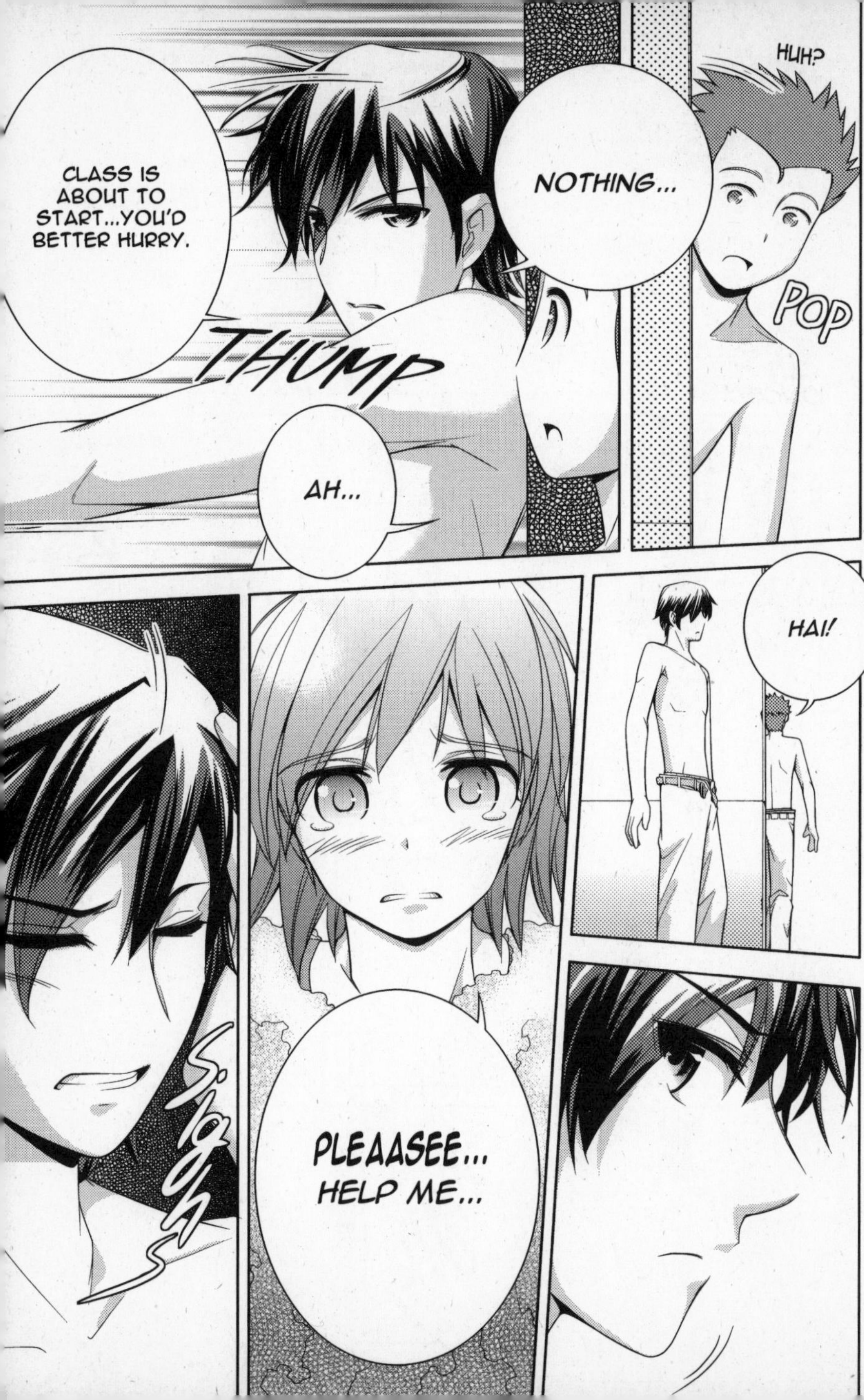
HUH?
POP
NOTHING...
CLASS IS ABOUT TO START...YOU'D BETTER HURRY.
THUMP
AH...
HAI!
PLEAASEE... HELP ME...
SIGH

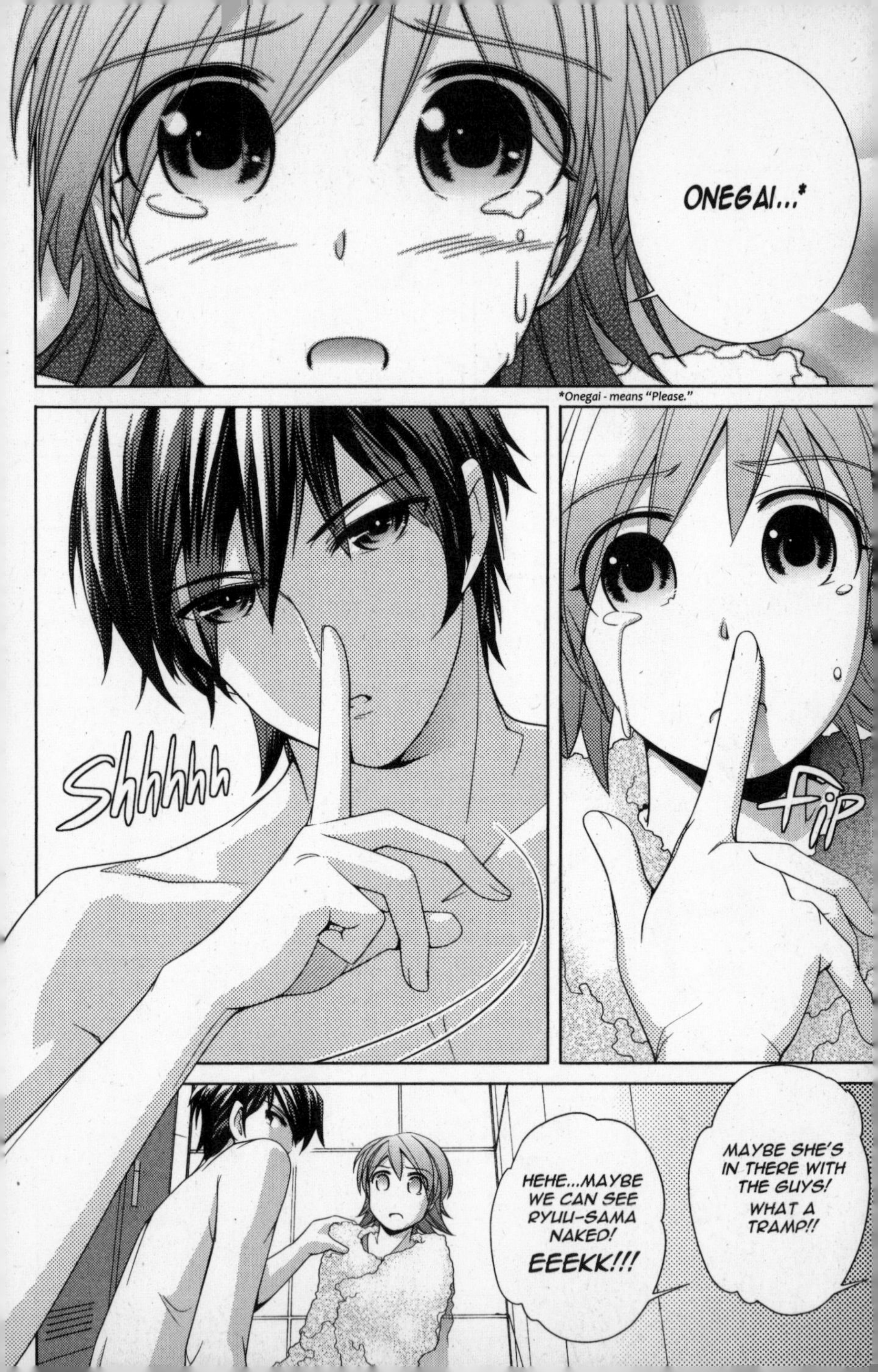
ONEGAI...*
Fip
Shhhhh
MAYBE SHE'S IN THERE WITH THE GUYS! WHAT A TRAMP!!
HEHE...MAYBE WE CAN SEE RYUU-SAMA NAKED! EEEKK!!!
*Onegai - means "Please."

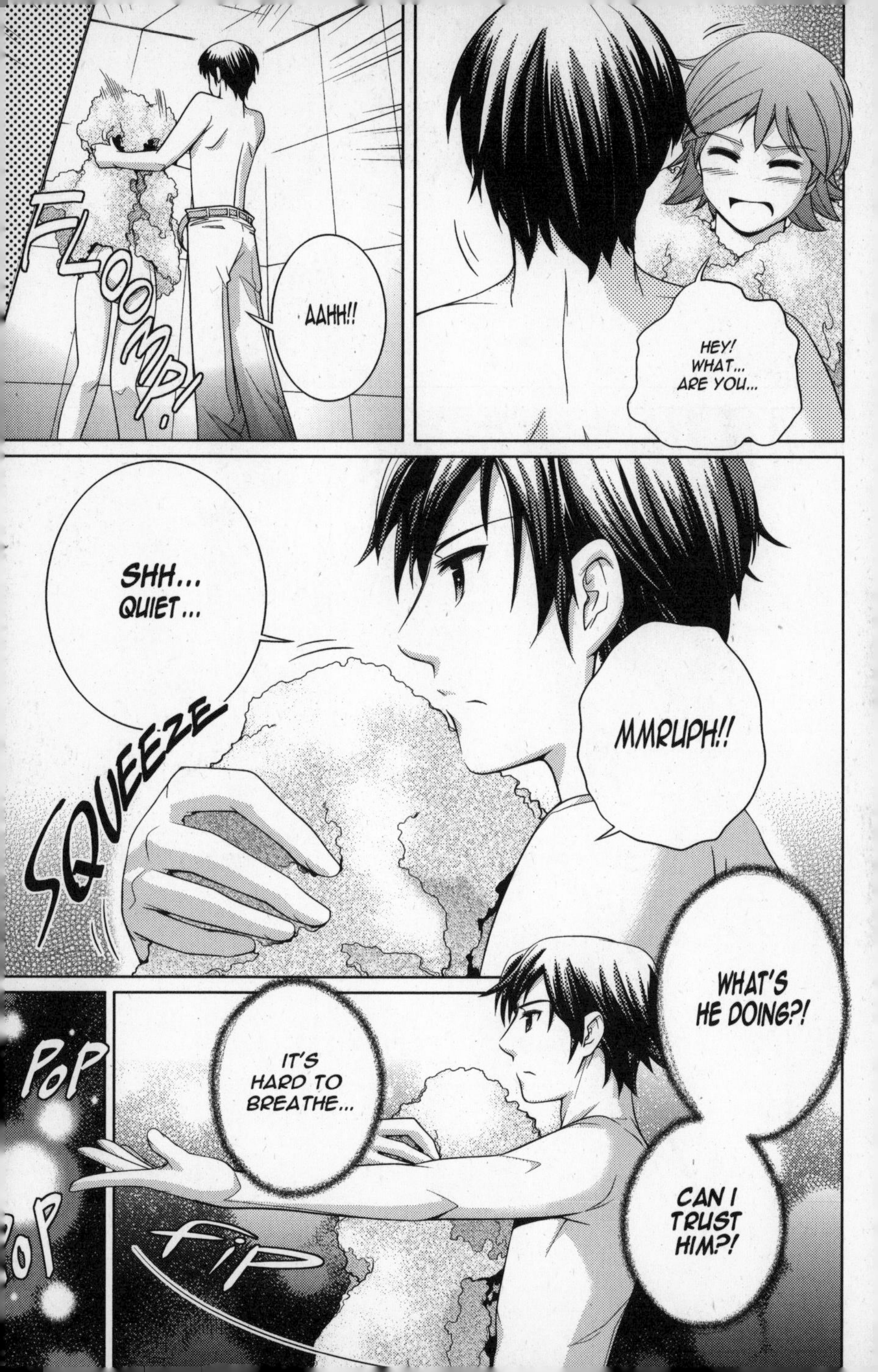
HEY! WHAT... ARE YOU...
FLOOMP!
AAHH!!
SHH... QUIET...
MMRUPH!!
SQUEEZE
WHAT'S HE DOING?!
CAN I TRUST HIM?!
IT'S HARD TO BREATHE...
FIP
POP
POP

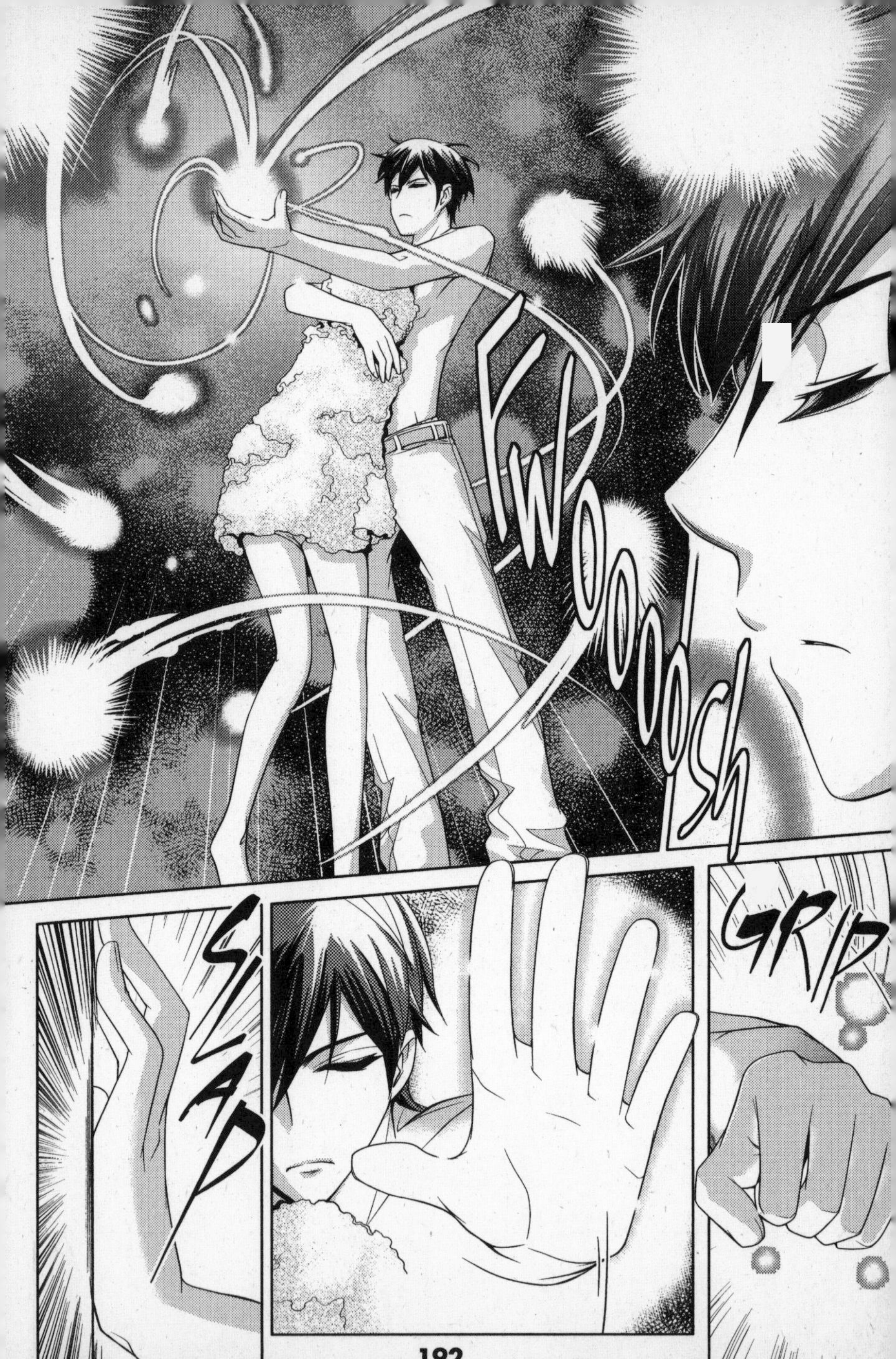
FWOOOOOSH
GRIP
SLAP

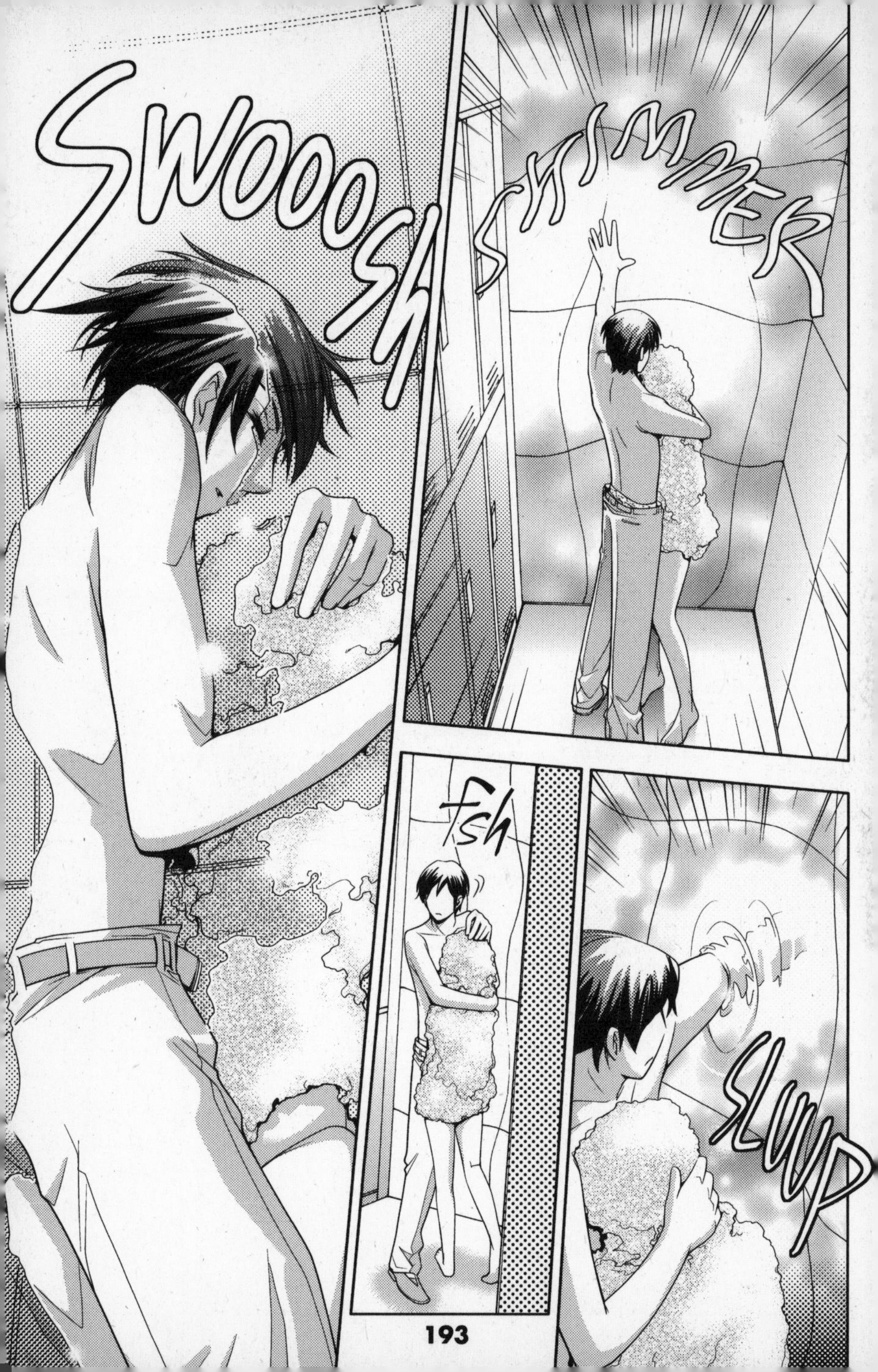
SHIMMER
SLUUP
fsh
SWOOOSH

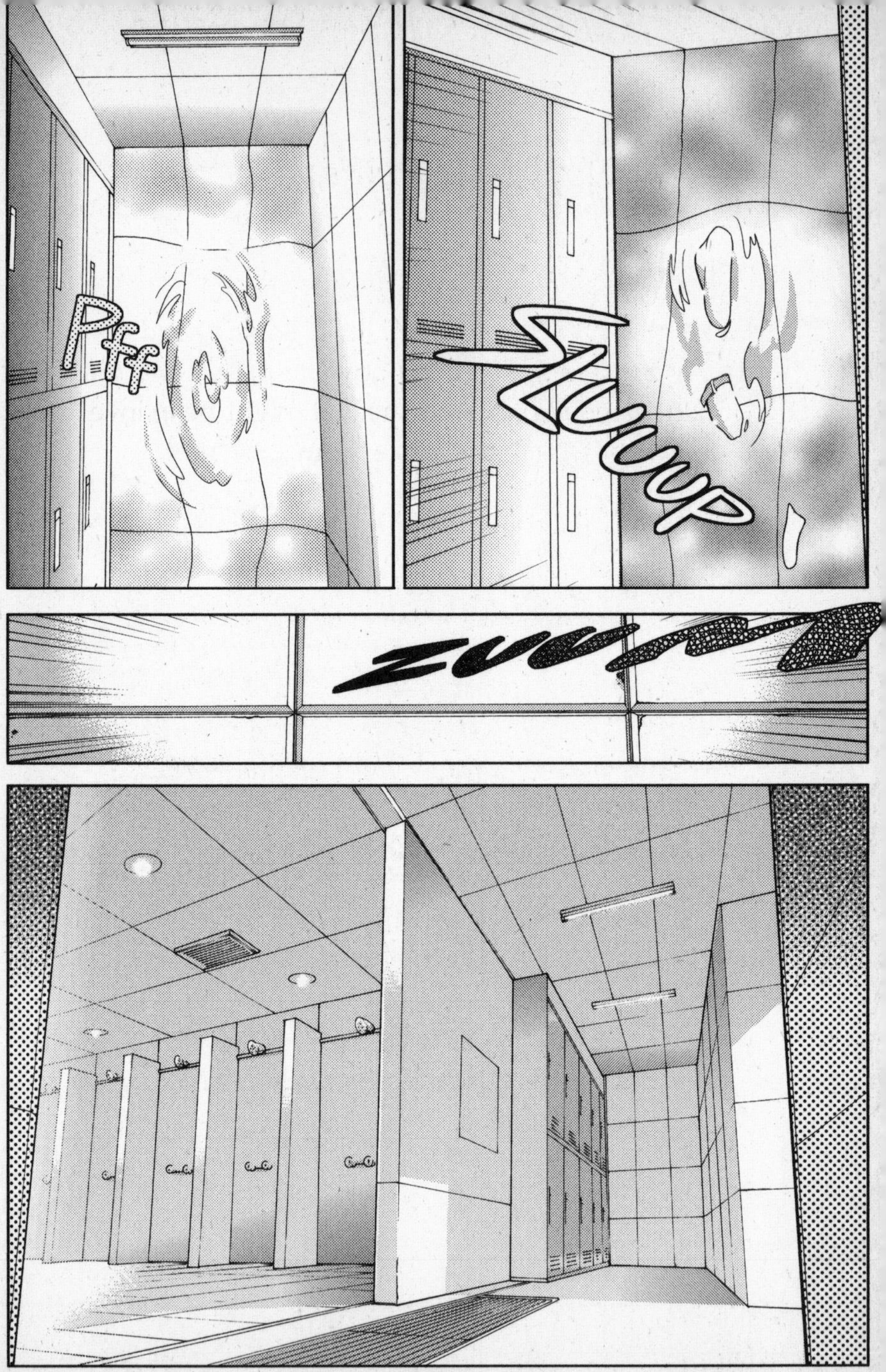
Zuuup
Pfff
Zuuum

In Volume 2...

Kasumi has a simple plan for high school:
Make new friends and fall in love. She's already got
the friends, her faithful fanboy Otaku Ken and the
kindhearted Maiko. And she just might be in love
with Ryuuki, the hottest guy in school.

But fate has something a little more *magical*
in store for Kasumi. Ryuuki seems to know her
secret—and hints that he has a few secrets of his
own. And she unexpectedly becomes the object
of another boy's affections when the alluring
"Feather Prince" declares his love for her. And
then she discovers the secret behind her magical
powers from the mysterious being who holds the
key to Kasumi's amazing destiny!

Can't wait for Volume 2?
Check out www.kasumimanga.com for the latest
sneak peeks and info about the *Kasumi* series!

Bonus Feature:
Maiko The Manga-ka

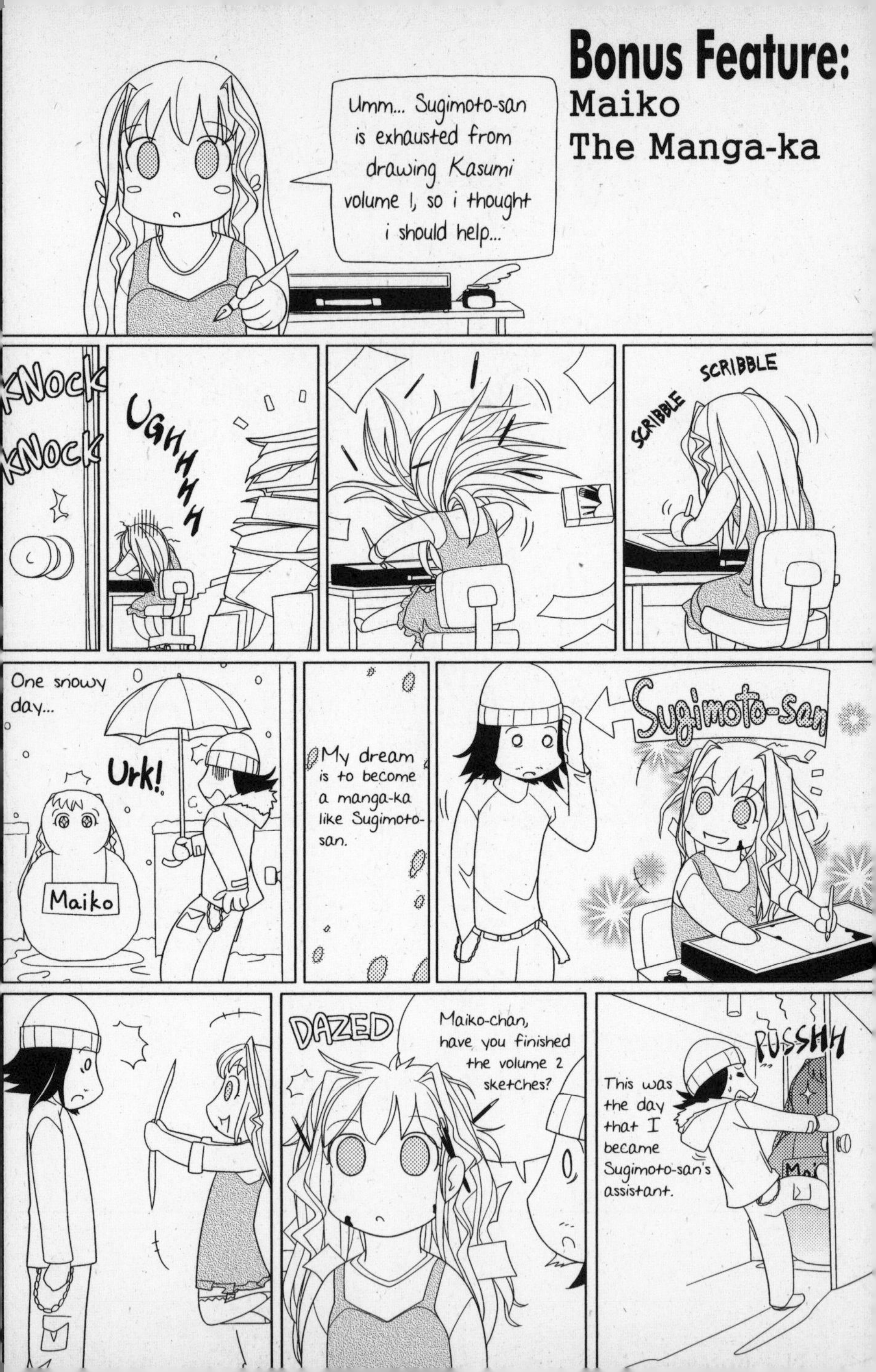
Umm... Sugimoto-san is exhausted from drawing Kasumi volume 1, so i thought i should help...
SCRIBBLE
SCRIBBLE
UGHHHHH
KNOCK
KNOCK
Sugimoto-san
My dream is to become a manga-ka like Sugimoto-san.
One snowy day...
Urk!
Maiko
PUSSHH
This was the day that I became Sugimoto-san's assistant.
Maiko-chan, have you finished the volume 2 sketches?
DAZED

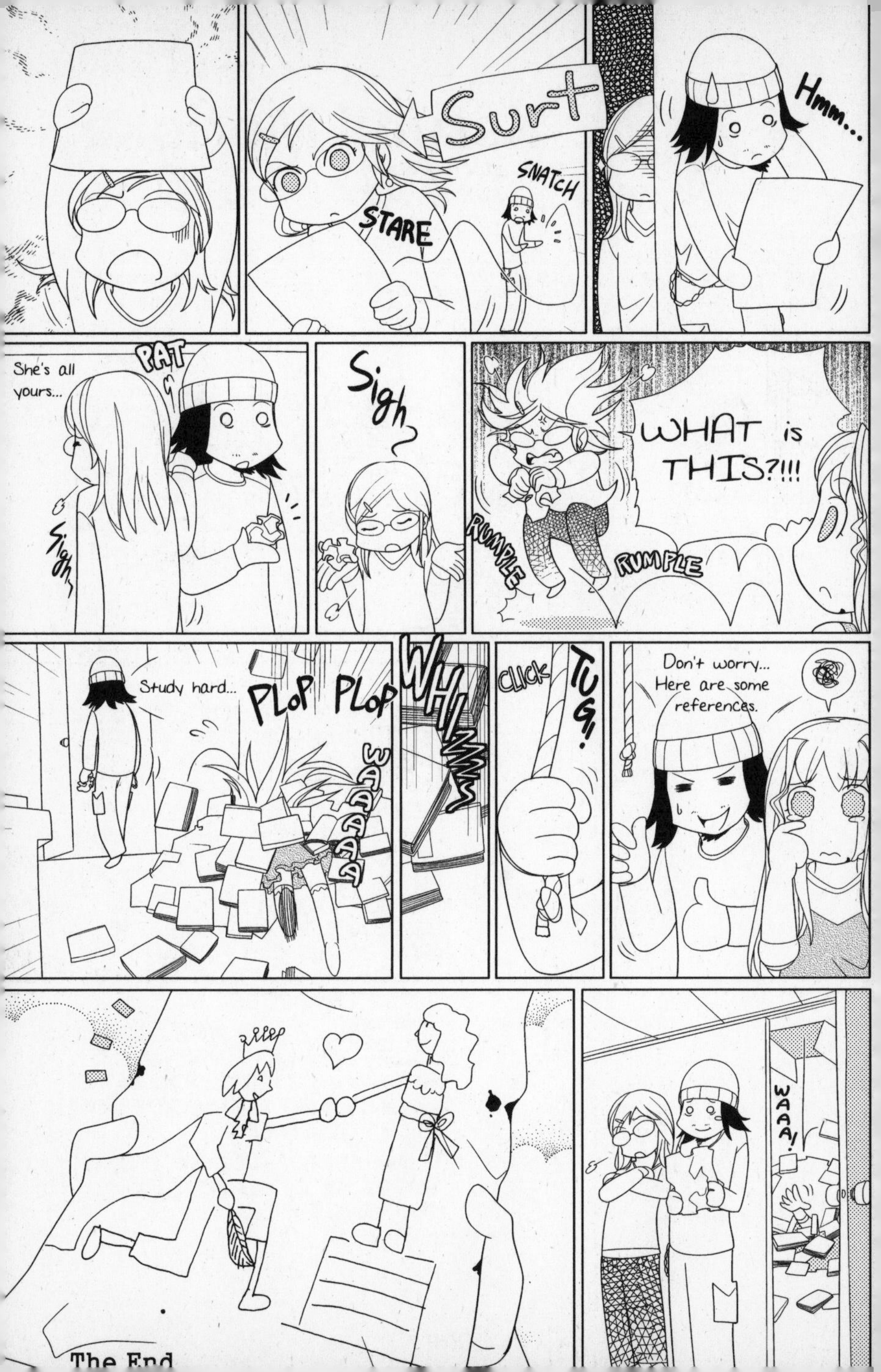
Hmm...
Surt
SNATCH
STARE
WHAT is THIS?!!!
RUMPLE
RUMPLE
Sigh
PAT
She's all yours...
Sigh
Don't worry... Here are some references.
TUG!!
CLICK
WHIZZZ
WAAAAAA
PLOP PLOP
Study hard...
WAAA!
The End

Kasumi Morioka
かすみ　森岡

SPECIAL POWERS:
SHE TURNS INVISIBLE WHEN SHE HOLDS HER BREATH.

5' 2" INCHES
BLOOD TYPE: O+
AGE: 16
ARIES

HOBBIES:
- PRACTICING HER MAGIC TRICKS
- LISTENING TO J-POP
-SHOPPING

FAVORITE PHRASE:
"CHECK THIS OUT!"

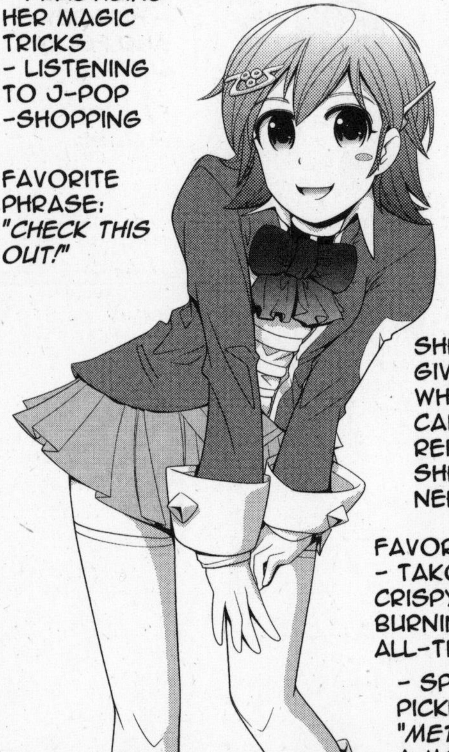

PERSONALITY:
SHE'S A HAPPY, CHEERFUL GIRL. SHE DOESN'T LIKE TO BE ALONE AND TAKES HER FRIENDSHIPS SERIOUSLY. SHE'S A LOYAL FRIEND AND WILL DO ANYTHING TO HELP THOSE SHE CARES FOR.

KASUMI LIKES ADVENTURE AND SOMETIMES CAN BE IMPULSIVE AND FOOLHARDY.

SHE'S NOT THE SORT TO GIVE UP AND STANDS UP FOR WHAT SHE BELIEVES IN, WHICH CAUSES HER PROBLEMS WITH REINA AND THE RSF. IN A WAY, SHE'S THE "HERO" THAT SEIRAN NEEDED.

FAVORITE FOODS:
- TAKOYAKI! ALL FLAVORS. THE CRISPY, SAUCY OUTSIDE AND THE BURNING HOT OCTOPUS ARE HER ALL-TIME FAVORITES!

- SPICY KARE RICE WITH LOTS OF PICKLES. KASUMI TOOK UP THE "*METEOR HOT KARE CHALLENGE*" A MONTH AGO AND LOST HER VOICE FOR A WEEK!

- DESSERTS! PUDDING, STRAW-BERRY ICE CREAM, CUSTARD PUFFS...OSHI-SO!

Ryuuki Hasegawa

竜樹　長谷川

SPECIAL POWERS:
HE CAN WALK THROUGH WALLS AND OTHER SOLID OBJECTS WHEN HE CLOSES HIS EYES.

PERSONALITY:
HE'S A QUIET, MYSTERIOUS GUY WHO DOESN'T SAY MUCH OR REVEAL HIS EMOTIONS. HE DOESN'T LIKE TO BE BOTHERED BY PEOPLE AND PREFERS TO BE LEFT ALONE TO HIS BOOKS.

RYUUKI WAS VOTED TO BE THE PRESIDENT OF THE STUDENT COUNCIL BECAUSE OF HIS CONNECTIONS AND HIS MYSTERIOUS CHARISMA. HE ACCEPTED THE POSITION SIMPLY BECAUSE IT WOULD BE MORE TROUBLE TO DEAL WITH EVERYONE IF HE REJECTED IT.

HE'S KIND OF AN ABSENTEE PRESIDENT WHO'S NEVER AROUND AND LEAVES THE COUNCIL TO REINA TO RUN. HOWEVER, AT TIMES OF NEED AND HE CAN BE A POWERFUL AND INFLUENTIAL LEADER.

HIS COLD EXTERIOR BEGINS TO CRACK WHEN HE HAS TO DEAL WITH KASUMI'S AMAZING POWERS. ONE WONDERS WHY THE ELUSIVE RYUUKI IS HELPING KASUMI...

5′ 11″
BLOOD TYPE: AB
AGE: 16
SCORPIO

HOBBIES:
- READING
- HISTORY AND FOLK-LORE

FAVORITE PHRASE:
"..."

FAVORITE FOODS:
- SUSHI
- COFFEE
- ITALIAN

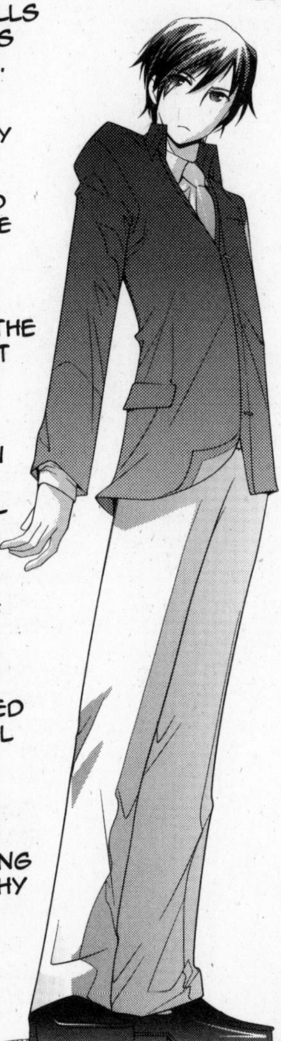

Yuuta Goodwin
祐太　グッドウィン

5′ 6″
BLOOD TYPE: B
AGE: 16
SAGITTARIUS

SPECIAL POWERS:
HE DOESN'T HAVE SPECIAL POWERS BUT IF HE KNEW KASUMI AND RYUUKI HAD THEM... HE WOULD BE SOOO ENVIOUS!

HOBBIES:
- READING SUPERHERO COMICS
- WATCHING SUPERHERO MOVIES
- COLLECTING SUPERHERO MEMORABILIA
- MEETING SUPERHERO ACTORS AND CELEBRITIES AND ANYTHING SUPER-HERO!!

FAVORITE PHRASE:
"THAT'S SO AWESOME!"

FAVORITE FOODS:
- CHEESEBURGERS
- OMU-RICE
- SHAVED ICE

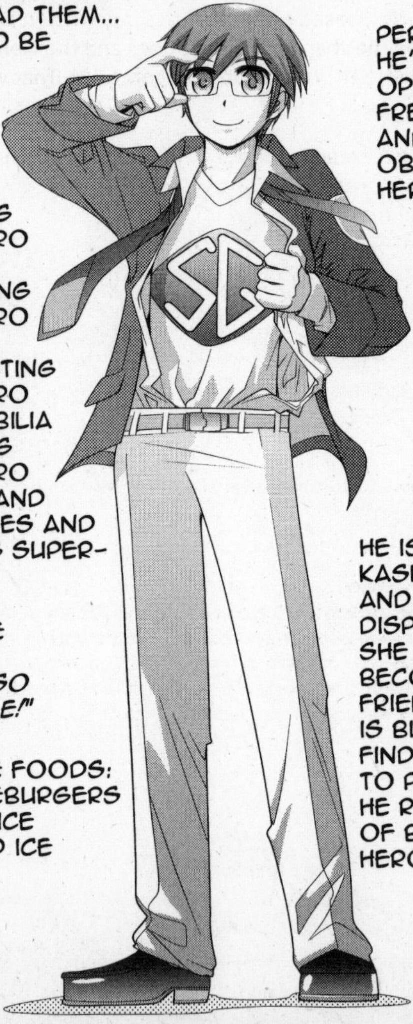

PERSONALITY:
HE'S AN EXTREMELY OPTIMISTIC AND CARE-FREE GUY. HE'S FRIENDLY AND HAS A HUGE OBSESSION WITH SUPER-HEROS.

HE DOESN'T THINK BADLY OF OTHERS. EVEN THOUGH HIS CLASSMATES MOCK HIM AND CALL HIM OTAKU-KEN, AFTER CHUCK KEN, HIS FAVORITE SUPERHERO. HE ACCEPTS IT AS A NICKNAME AND DOESN'T FRET ABOUT WHAT OTHERS THINK OF HIM.

HE IS ENAMORED OF KASUMI'S MAGIC TRICKS AND HER CHEERFUL, SPUNKY DISPOSITION. HE THINKS SHE IS SOO COOL! HE BECOMES KASUMI'S FIRST FRIEND. WHEN KASUMI IS BULLIED, OTAKU-KEN FINDS HIMSELF FIGHTING TO PROTECT KASUMI. WILL HE RISE TO THE CHALLENGE OF BECOMING KASUMI'S HERO?

Sugimoto's Thoughts...

...Thank you for reading *Kasumi*, volume 1. I'd like to thank the Kasumi team, Surt-san, Stanley-san, and Harumi-san, who are true professionals and give their best at all time. Also, I appreciate the support that the staff at Del Rey Manga have given me. I'm honored to be able to work with all of you.

...One day, an email came to me from overseas. It was an invitation from Surt-san to work together on a manga project, based on an original story written by her. I was a bit wary at first, but when I read the character descriptions and the vibrant story, the characters came alive in my head, and were anxious to come out. That was the mome I joined the manga team.

Manga...The first manga that I ever read was the story about a blue, robotic cat who came from the future. The story gave me many dreams. I was so crazy about this mar that I remember memorizing all the dialogues.

Ever since then, manga has given me many dreams and aspirations. Time passed by, a after some twists and turns, I became a manga artist myself. Now, through Surt-san's story, *Kasumi*, I have the joy of sharing my dreams with all of you.

Hirofumi Sugimoto

* And thanks to Natuki-san, Komamiya BON-san, and Tanaka Yoshihiro-san, who helped me create the artwork!

Hirofumi Sugimoto (www.h-sugimoto.com)
He graduated from the Illustrator Department of Chiyoda Institute of Art and Technology, and aft some bumps and detours, joined the world of manga creation. While pursuing his manga career, he also designed landscapes, buildings, and mechanics for the full CG animation for "*Run=DIM*" ((C)IDEA FACTORY/Digital Dream Studios). He worked as chief of staff at Wrench Studio, and late became a freelancer. He is currently working on the art for *Kasumi*.

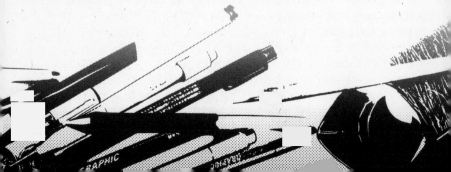

You're going the wrong way!

Manga is a completely different type of reading experience.

To start at the *beginning*, go to the *end!*

That's right! Authentic manga is read the tradi-tional Japanese way—from right to left. Exactly the opposite of how American books are read. It's easy to follow: Just go to the other end of the book, and read each page—and each panel—from right side to left side, starting at the top right. Now you're experiencing manga as it was meant to be!